Into The Crucible

Into the Crucible

People and events that shaped the Town of Widnes

Into The Crucible

© Jean M. Morris 2018

All rights reserved

This book is copyright. Subject to statutory exception and to provisions of relevant collective licensing agreements, no part of this publication may be reproduced, stored in a retrieval system, or transmitted in any form or by any means, without the prior written permission of the author.

Typeset in Palatino 10/14

This book is sold subject to the conditions that it shall not, by way of trade or otherwise, be lent, re-sold, hired out, or otherwise circulated without the publisher's prior consent in any form of binding or cover other than that which it is published and without a similar condition including this condition being imposed on the subsequent purchaser.

SPRINGFIELD-FARRIHY PUBLISHING

*Dedicated to my father, the late Michael Lucas,
who nurtured my love of history*

Into The Crucible

Cover Illustration **"Widnes Alkali Workers"**
from Pearson's Magazine (1896)

CONTENTS

Postscript 2018	9
Foreword	15
1845 Map of Widnes	18
Beginnings	19
Industry	41
The Irish	89
The Lithuanians and Poles	135
The Welsh	193
What they left behind	207
Everyday Life	223
Education	331
Crime	359
Culture	375
The War Years	381
Epilogue	397
Appendix	402
Bibliography	407

Postscript 2018

This book was originally published in 2005 by Countyvise. The second edition was published in 2008 by Arima Publishing. This third edition differs slightly from the previous versions as it includes additional information that the earlier publishers, Countyvise and Arima, did not incorporate.

Sadly, since the first edition of this book was published in 2005 some of the people who appear in my acknowledgements have passed away. The Irish historian, Dr. Patrick C. Power, who wrote the foreword to this book, died in 2008 and Lord Ashley of Stoke, who composed the back page endorsement, died in 2012. They were both exceptional human beings and each, in their own fields, were giant personalities of their era. Patrick Power was an Emeritus Professor of History and Ancient Languages and a renowned historian, writer and broadcaster in Irish Studies, whilst Jack Ashley, Lord Ashley of Stoke, was an exceptional parliamentarian who served with distinction in both The House of Commons and The House of Lords. He was also the acknowledged champion of disabled and underprivileged members of society and was, without doubt, the greatest Widnesian of our age. Both were very dear and valued friends who, through their own experience and talent, guided me through the minefield of research and writing and encouraged me along the way. I dedicate this new edition of *"Into the Crucible"* to their memories.

Jean M. Morris

Acknowledgements

Widnes is home to many of us but our own links with the town may not stretch back as far as we imagine. A large percentage of today's population are only able to trace their roots in this town back to less than 150 years ago. In most cases their ancestors arrived here as part of an immigrant workforce who were attracted by the employment opportunities brought about by the needs of a new and growing chemical industry.

Over the years there have been a number of excellent books on the history of Widnes and its outlying districts. Charles Poole's *"Old Widnes and its Neighbourhood"* and George E. Diggle's *"History of Widnes"* gave valuable insights into the development of the town from its earliest beginnings right up until the 1960s. In more recent times *"Widnes through the Ages"* by local author Arthur Whimperley provided a further superb contribution to our written history. In my own sphere of nineteenth century social interest, *"The History of the Chemical Industry in Widnes"*, by D. W. F. Hardie, provided a picture of rapid industrial growth over a relatively short period of time. It also gave a fascinating insight into the backgrounds and personalities of the industrialists who were responsible for the town's commercial development. Furthermore the information regarding our early industrial expansion enabled me to observe the collective social effect of the chemical trade on our area.

Apart from local history books, the story of the industrial development and urbanisation of our town has been well documented in a variety of historical records. Each has provided a picture of brisk industrial innovation and growth over a comparatively short period of time. We know that this growth, and the swelling population, provided profit and dividends for factory owners but it also created serious social and environmental problems. These problems, which were inherent in all developing industrial areas at that time, included atmospheric pollution, poor housing, overcrowding, disease and a certain amount of lawlessness.

Although any historical study can obviously only be drawn from previously recorded evidence to which all historians must refer, this book is not intended to be a repetition of too many facts already covered in earlier local books. Whilst these other books have, in the main, concentrated on the general history of the area or on the lives of well-known personalities, the primary purpose of *this* work is to survey and record our history from a different perspective. The diverse elements and motivations which contributed to the building up of a new social order in Widnes have never been examined in detail in previous local books. Therefore, this contribution is intended to be a history of people and community as well as a general overview of historical urban and industrial progression.

The development of our first industrial society is both interesting and important in the history of Widnes. The origins of local communities and the contribution they made in creating our local identity is worthy of investigation for several reasons. Not least of these reasons is the fact that our first industrial society formed an entirely new type of multi-faceted populace made up of different religions, ethnicities and traditions. The incomers were different in many respects to the indigenous inhabitants and their arrival, and the inception of heavy industry, was to drastically change the social structure and physical landscape of the town forever. In this book I have endeavoured to show the intricate composition of the local population during the early years of our industrialisation. We will see that the workers who came to Widnes were from numerous parts of this island. They also came from Ireland, Poland, Lithuania and several other countries. Unfortunately, the reader may feel that the information in this book does not provide a balanced picture. It is unavoidably weighted more heavily with information on the Irish population. The reasons for this are: that there is more recorded information available on this particular ethnic group and of course they represented the largest immigrant group in this town.

While writing this book I received assistance from so many people that it would be impossible to mention all by name. However, the following people deserve special credit. An enormous debt of gratitude is owed to my friend Dr. Patrick C. Power, the eminent and highly respected Irish historian, who has encouraged and helped me in this project and many others. I especially thank him for writing the foreword for this book. I greatly appreciate the help, friendship and support he has given over the years.

I would like to acknowledge the assistance given to me by the staff of St. Helens, Warrington and Liverpool Central Libraries and the staff at the National Library of Ireland, Dublin. I especially thank the staff of Widnes Library and Rosie Parker and Nikki Lamb in particular. I also thank the staff of The National Archives at Kew, the Liverpool, Cheshire and Lancashire Record Offices and the Public Record Office and National Archives of Ireland for their help. The assistance of the staff of the Lithuanian Embassy and the British Embassy in Vilkavisk is also gratefully acknowledged. I also thank Vida Gasperas, of *The Lithuanian Society*, for valuable help and translations and also for permission to include quotes from material in their archives.

My good friend Maureen Tilsley, of Stoke Technical College, kindly shared much of her own research with me and I would like to thank her for her generosity and encouragement. I was fortunate also to have been able to call on my old friend Dr. William Petrie who enabled me to gain access to significant records and, as usual, was enormously liberal with his help, support and expert advice. John Miller, the Scottish historian, gave me information on the Lithuanians in Lanarkshire and gave permission for me to include that in this book. He also made numerous journeys to his local archives where he painstakingly copied relevant information for me. I am extremely grateful for his help, especially as sometimes this assistance was completely unsolicited. Councillor Tony McDermott, the Leader of Halton Borough Council, offered help and support as did the staff of The Catalyst, particularly Paul Meara, who gave me unlimited access to archive files and sourced photographs for me. Robert Martindale and Peter Jackson provided photographs and I thank them both for their help. I would also like to express my gratitude to Tom Fleet who gave me a copy of his *History of Widnes Rugby Club* and kindly allowed me to use extracts.

I would especially like to thank my cousin, Kevin Lucas, who read the manuscript for egregious errors, any that remain will be entirely my own. Kevin generously undertook this task when demands on his time were exceptional, so I am most appreciative of his help and useful suggestions. A special thank you also goes to the individual members of the Karalius, Myler and Kaloski families for allowing me to include some of their history in these pages. My thanks also go to the numerous people who shared and copied documents for me. I would

Into The Crucible

also like to record my grateful appreciation to the many people who were willing to share memories as well as written and oral family history with me. Most of these people wish to remain anonymous but they know who they are, and I thank them most sincerely for their valuable contributions to this book.

And finally, but certainly not least, I would like to express my sincere gratitude to my dear friend The Rt. Hon. Lord Ashley of Stoke for writing such a wonderful endorsement for the back cover of this book. As a native of this town he has been a remarkable example to all of us and we are justly proud of his many great achievements. I consider it a personal privilege to have his name appear on the cover of this book.

Foreword

"God made the country and man made the town"
(William Cowper 1731-1800)

This book on Widnes examines the situation in a Lancashire industrial town that drew its workforce from far and wide and accepted immigrants from deprived areas in Europe as well as from Wales, Scotland and Ireland. They were the life force of the factories but also faced difficulties in being accepted by the indigenous workers.

Widnes became part of the extension of the Industrial Revolution to the countryside in the mid-19th century. From being a small rural hamlet, it became the site of significant industrial effort where chemical factories were the most important providers of labour. At first it had two of the necessary three "R`s" for this purpose, which were river and road, later it had the third one, the railway. In this book, we are introduced to the industrialisation of this little corner of the United Kingdom. This was one of the hundreds of important crucibles where the industrial might of the United Kingdom was forged, a nation that was for over a century and a half the industrial centre of the world.

In the early years of the Industrial Revolution there was a very large reservoir of rural people to draw on for factory work. The excess population of the countryside began to gravitate towards these factories, where there was a fixed weekly wage available and the working hours, though long, were known and determined already. This attracted the rural labourer and the smallholder, who had been at the mercy of wind and weather for their incomes, who never had any certain fixed wages and whose work was usually seasonal.

This source of labour had been drawn on for some generations and was nearing exhaustion in the 19th century when a serious shortage of workers was felt. It was especially serious for the new industrial complexes, as in Widnes, which was built on what were green field sites and were in an area that had been bled white of all available labour for the great giant of Liverpool and its many satellites. There was only one way to satisfy the need for workers and this was with large waves of immigrants. Since nobody usually wishes to leave country and native place to search for work, the immigrants had to come from lands where the economies were collapsing and a large reservoir of labour was available from what was an overpopulated countryside.

Ireland after 1825 was highly suited to supply labour. By 1831 the results of the *Act of Union* between Great Britain and Ireland had brought about the collapse of the nationwide woollen trade. People were hungry due to an Act that had been trumpeted as a benefit for all but which bound Ireland to its chief trade competitor, so that much of its limping industries were crushed out of existence. In some cases, boats were hired to bring whole families to England, this new El Dorado.

Hitherto, the only Irish workers who came to England were the migrant workers who came each year. They worked on farms from May and departed home in September. The large numbers of migrants who came to England in the early and later 19th century stayed permanently and eventually they and their descendants became absorbed into the population of their new homeland.

Among the other migrants who came to work in the chemical factories of Widnes were those who were in effect fleeing from oppression by the Russian Empire in the conquered lands of Lithuania and Poland. These were as much asylum seekers as they were migrant workers. Asylum seekers in those days were also as much resented as they were welcomed and yet they were necessary to the economy and welfare of the town, which could not function as a social unit without them.

The poor migrant has always been greeted at the best with neutral feeling and at the worst with resentment in every society throughout the world. It was thus in Widnes also. The differences, which divided the immigrants from the local people, included language, customs, appearance and sometimes above all, religion; these were enough to

Foreword

arouse resentment among the native inhabitants. In turn they found shelter in their ghettos among their fellow migrants until the years had blurred the differences and their descendants were absorbed into the English population.

Life had very rough edges in industrial towns of the 19th century and Widnes was no exception to this. Excessive drinking was often the only recreation available for the men, while the women slaved to rear families, which were often depleted by high infant mortality and the children grew up in squalid surroundings. It was in this crucible that peoples of different nations were welded into the citizenry of another country.

**Patrick C. Power
2005**

Into The Crucible

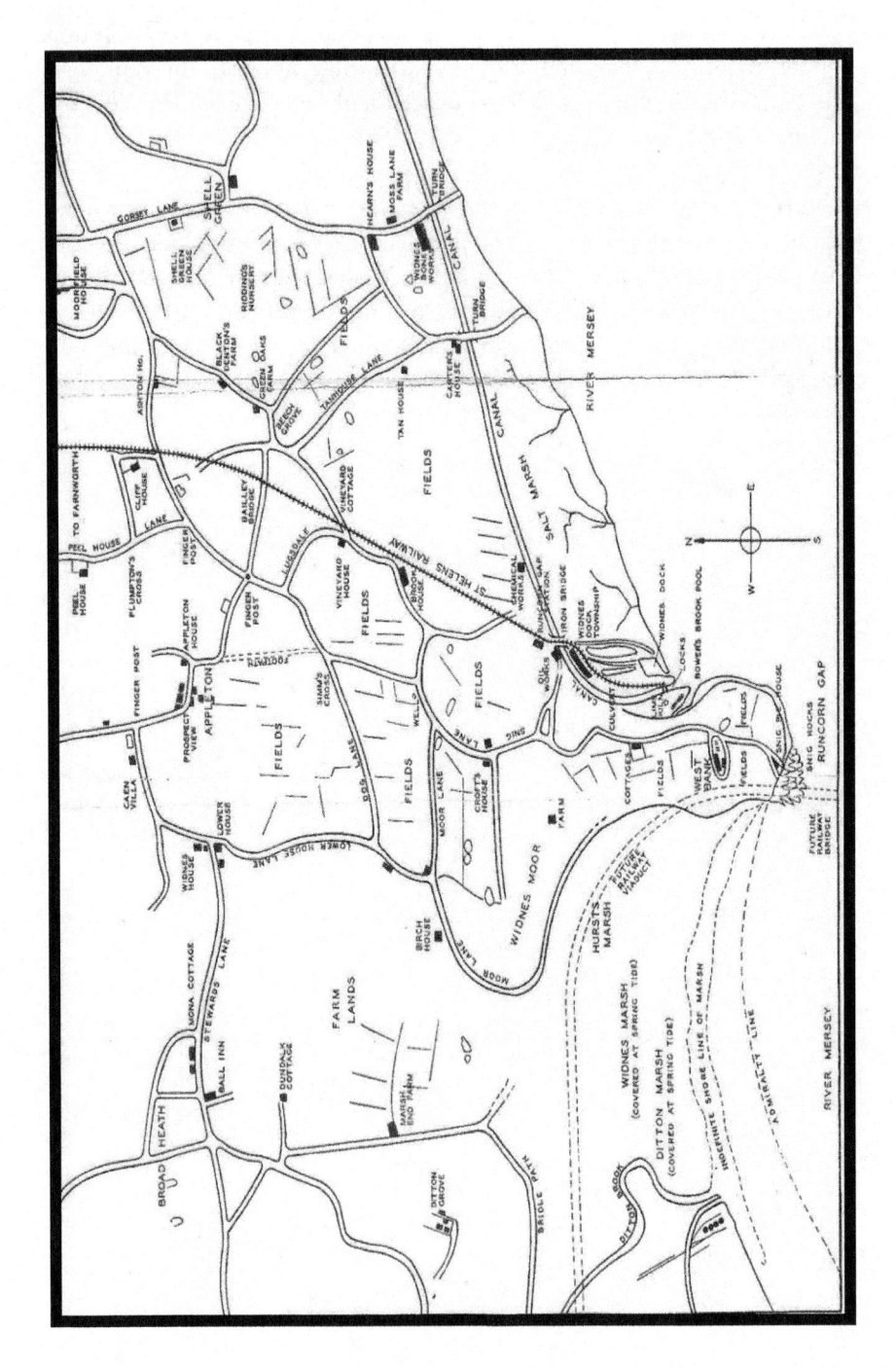

1845 Map of Widnes

Beginnings

The census returns for Widnes with Appleton in 1811 give the population figure of 1204 and tell us that there were 611 males and 593 females. There were 247 families occupying 246 houses. Their employment statistics at that time were particularly interesting. The returns inform us that there were 100 families employed in agriculture, 126 in trade, manufacturing or handicrafts and 21 unspecified.[1]

The Industrial Revolution, the term used to describe the processes of industrialisation and change which occurred in Britain during the 18th and 19th centuries, had a dramatic effect in many parts of Lancashire as rural areas were transformed into dense industrial locations. In coalmining districts there was an increase in production due to the heavy demand for coal to provide steam power for these new industries, as well as for the traditional domestic use. In other parts of the county the cotton industry expanded and chemical manufacture developed. By 1801 population changes had begun as people moved from the countryside into towns where this industrialisation had occurred. This new process of industrial development had radical consequences both socially and economically on all levels of society. Obviously these effects were most acute in small rural areas like Widnes where there was a small indigenous population with an established way of life.

When we examine the 19th century development of Widnes as an industrial centre we can see that the chemical industry flourished in Widnes not least because of its favourable location. Nearby, St. Helens already had a number of recognized industrial activities. Coal mining was well established and had been a source of employment in the area for centuries and, as a result, a strong connection had been formed between the St. Helens coalfield and the Cheshire saltfields. By the mid-18th century glass production was also a firmly established

---

1 *Census Returns 1811* – Lancashire Record Office

industry in the town and by the end of that century breweries, a copper works and a foundry also existed. Chemical industries made an appearance in St. Helens in the first decades of the 19th century and by the late 1830s there were four alkali works in the town. The presence of glassworks in St. Helens obviously made it appealing to alkali manufacturers because synthetic soda was an important raw material in the glassmaking industry. Later, in the late 1830s, saltcake replaced soda in this manufacture.

All of these industries relied heavily on the canal system of transport. The St. Helens mine owners were dependant on the canals to carry their coal and local manufacturers needed the canals for the import of some raw materials, such as salt from Northwich, limestone from North Wales and oils and pyrites from Ireland and Spain. Some of these materials were imported into the port of Liverpool and then transported by canal to St. Helens. Therefore the canals provided a vital transportation network for all local industry. As these inland waterways had previously been the main method of moving goods, the arrival of the railways provided a welcome and effective alternative for the manufacturers. The railway route known as the *"St. Helens to Runcorn Gap Railway"* commenced in St. Helens and was officially opened in 1833. The alkali industrialist James Muspratt was among the original subscribers to this railway company. He purchased 15 shares at £100 per share. Peter Greenall, who had brewing, coal and glass manufacturing interests in the area, was also a shareholder as was Thomas Hazelhurst, the Runcorn soap boiler, who purchased 5 shares. As the new system of transport developed it also gave Widnes an important rail link. In addition to this *The Sankey Navigational Canal*, which had just been extended beyond Fidler's Ferry to Spike Island, and which offered the more established form of transport, was close by.

Initially, the new rail transportation costs compared quite favourably with the old canal system. However, a merger in 1845 of *The Sankey Navigational Canal Company* and *The Runcorn Gap Railway Company* resulted in *The St. Helens Canal and Railway Company* being formed. The new company, which now formed a local transport monopoly, immediately set about planning extensions to their system. In order to raise revenue for this expansion they announced an increase in freight charges on almost everything except coal. Interestingly, the transportation costs for coal did not increase because the majority of

Beginnings

shareholders in the new Canal and Railway Company were owners of local coalmines. Obviously transport costs were of vital importance to alkali manufacturers as around ten to twelve tons of raw materials were needed to produce just one ton of alkali by the Leblanc process. Therefore, the price rise meant that the St. Helens alkali producers were faced with hugely increased production costs.

Despite being more costly for St. Helens manufacturers, the increased rail and waterway transportations were instrumental in highlighting the advantages derived from creating a manufacturing base in Widnes. It was clear that transportation to and from Widnes would be more economical because it was nearer to the source of raw materials, being the meeting point of the routes of communication with the coalfields of southwest Lancashire and the Cheshire saltfields. Widnes also enjoyed the geographical benefit of its natural position on the river, providing the opportunity for shipment of goods for import and export. However, it should be pointed out that the transport facilities that eventually brought manufacturers to Widnes over a decade later were already in place in Widnes as early as the 1830s. For that reason, I think it is safe to assume that the increase in freight charges was one of the major factors that emphasised the competitive advantages of Widnes as a location for alkali manufacture. Furthermore the fact that there was plenty of cheap land available, in a scantily populated area, also meant that Widnes was an excellent place to have a manufacturing base.

Surprisingly, Widnes was something of a late-starter and had managed to remain virtually free of industrial development or significant large scale commercial enterprise until this time. Across the river, the opening of The Bridgewater Canal in 1761[3] had made Runcorn an important canal port. In addition, the opening of the Bridgewater Canal's Runcorn Docks in 1776 further enhanced Runcorn's status and subsequently stimulated trade between Liverpool, Manchester and other northern towns such as Warrington, which was connected to Runcorn in 1804 by the opening of the Runcorn-Latchford Canal. Apart from its first-rate water communications, industrially, Runcorn had been a going concern as early as 1803 when John Johnson, a Weston farmer, built a "soap works" on the Bridgewater Canal near Greenway Road. In 1816 a "soap and rosin works" was opened on the opposite

---

[3] Bridgewater Canal opened in 1761 but was not fully completed until 1772.

side of the Bridgewater Canal by Thomas Hazelhurst. This factory, known as *The Camden Works*, developed into a large and profitable company. A further soap factory, owned by two Irishmen called Dennis Kennedy and Thomas Maguire, opened at Rocksavage in 1833. In fact, soap manufacture reached such proportion that in 1835 Runcorn was the fifth largest soap producing town in England. In addition to these soap manufactories, there was an acid works and a tannery in the town. Besides these lucrative endeavours stone quarrying and shipbuilding were also well established and important local industries.

Although Runcorn was obviously a thriving centre for the manufacture of soap, its neighbour across the river was a more tranquil place. Even though there were several small cottage type enterprises it would appear that prior to 1830 Widnes had been comparatively untouched by any form of heavy industry. Employment statistics tell us that in 1801 the population of Widnes was 1063 and of this figure 662 were workers. 38% of the workforce was involved in the old crafts of canvas making, watchmaking and file-making, while 60% of the workers were in agricultural occupations. By 1841 the population figure was 2209. In 1851 this figure had risen to 3211 but by 1871 this number had grown to 14,359.[4] This rapid increase in population is inexorably linked with the growth of industry. The 1851 census is especially interesting as it shows how the occupational structure was beginning to change. The census ten years later, in 1861, is even more enlightening as it clearly shows the decline of watchmaking and the gradual waning employment in the weaving trade.

John Hutchinson, known as the *"Father of Widnes"*, first moved to Widnes around 1847. By 1849 he had established his No. 1 Works on a strip of land between the canal and the dock at Spike Island. Before coming to Widnes Hutchinson had managed the Chemical Factory owned by Andreas Kurtz in Sutton, St. Helens. Being an astute young man he obviously recognised that the increased freight charges would have a detrimental effect on the St. Helens industries. So within a few weeks of the first increase in transport costs he applied for a lease of land at Widnes. This land was the property of the newly merged *St. Helens Canal and Railway Company* and had originally been set aside for improving their dock facilities and storage space. On 20th November 1848 Hutchinson was given a 42-year lease, with the Canal and Railway

---

[4] *Population Survey – Archives & Local Studies Service*, Cheshire CC.

Beginnings

Company having the option to reclaim it at any time within 21 years, with a twelve months' notice. On 20th May 1850 the lease was extended from 42 to 75 years and in August 1853 an adjoining plot of land was leased on the same terms. In July 1856 it was agreed to accept 20 years' purchase[5].

While we know that Hutchinson initially leased land from the Canal & Railway Company, historical documentations also reveal that as John Hutchinson's chemical venture at Widnes began to thrive, he started to acquire additional land in the neighbourhood. The manner in which Hutchinson became the owner of land at Widnes Marsh and the surrounding area has not been written about in great detail elsewhere. However, one of his contemporaries, writing in private correspondence in 1910, gave an interesting account. It appears that John Hutchinson, having perceived the enormous potential advantages Widnes had to offer, invited the Conservator of the upper Mersey, Admiral Evans, to dine with him. During dinner Hutchinson suggested to Admiral Evans that the Government might do well to sell the great portion of marshland that stretched along the edge of the Mersey towards Ditton. This land was sometimes flooded by the tide and when free from water was used as salt leys for cattle. The rental received by the Government for this stretch of land was very small. Hutchinson managed to persuade Admiral Evans to recommend to the Government that the land should be sold to him, freehold, for a capital sum of £12,500. The transaction was completed and the large expanse of marshland duly became the sole property of John Hutchinson.

It is generally believed that John McClellan arrived in Widnes around the same time as Hutchinson but some evidence suggests that he was here slightly earlier. Within a relatively short space of time other manufacturers began to appear. In 1850 William Gossage opened his works on the opposite side of the canal to Hutchinson. In 1852 Frederic Muspratt arrived. Shortly afterwards, in 1853, after a brief period working for Hutchinson, Henry Deacon opened his own works in Widnes. Therefore this small but brilliant group of enterprising men should be regarded as the founding fathers of the Widnes chemical trade. By 1855 the area around Spike Island was well populated by

---

[5] *A Mersey Town in the Industrial Revolution* - T.C. Barker & J.R. Harris

numerous alkali factories. These factories were mainly wooden structures that were erected quickly and cheaply.

In later years, as the area developed, John Hutchinson's wealth increased considerably. Not only did he enjoy the profits from his own alkali company, there were also ground rents from the land on which various other works had been built and from the use of the dock. Another income was derived from the continually increasing payments for the large amount of alkali waste which other manufacturers were allowed to tip on his land. It was estimated that the rents and dues he received each year brought in as much as the entire purchase price he had paid to the Government for this land. Furthermore, Hutchinson's enterprising disposition was seemingly boundless for, in addition to the healthy revenue he acquired from his land rentals, he also had brickworks which supplied bricks for local projects including the viaducts associated with the railway bridge.

As I have mentioned, the names of some of our early manufacturers are irrevocably linked with the development of Widnes. Several of them played a role not only in the industrial activities of the town but also in public service. Indeed, some manufacturers were seemingly involved in the management of all aspects of local life. However, it is interesting to note that nearly all these men originally came from outside the area. James Muspratt was Irish, William Gossage was from Lincolnshire and Hutchinson, although born in Liverpool, was a member of a family who originally came from Durham. All of these men contributed hugely to the expansion of Widnes as a centre of chemical manufacture. Some were scientific innovators, some masters of commercial entrepreneurship and some endowed with both vision and aptitude. However, whatever their talent or ability, there is no doubt that each was a brilliant man in his own right.

Henry Deacon, who was a student of Faraday, had previously been involved in the glassmaking industry in St. Helens where he invented improvements to apparatus used for grinding and smoothing plate glass. Born in London in 1822, he was educated in a Quaker School and seems to have excelled in mechanical and scientific subjects. Michael Faraday, a family friend who was connected through their shared

Beginnings

religious beliefs,[6] encouraged him in his studies of chemical and physical science and Deacon flourished under this guidance. His family apprenticed him to an engineering firm called Galloway & Sons in London, but this business went bankrupt. In order to complete his apprenticeship young Henry was subsequently sent to the firm of Nasmyth & Gaskell[7] which was located in Patricroft near Manchester. When he was still in his twenties he obtained a position as "chemist and engineer" with Pilkington Brothers at their glassworks in St. Helens. He appears to have made good progress with Pilkington's and in 1847 he was the highest paid employee with that firm. Nevertheless, despite his apparent success, shortly afterwards he left that Company and began working as manager for John Hutchinson in Widnes. However, Deacon's association with Hutchinson was relatively short-lived as it seems he had ambitions to open his own works. In 1853 in partnership with his previous employer, William Pilkington, of the St. Helens glassworks, Henry Deacon opened a chemical works in Widnes. Unfortunately the partnership did not last long and was terminated in what appeared to be quite acrimonious circumstances. Two years later, in 1855, when William Pilkington withdrew from the venture,[8] he described Henry Deacon as *"an unsociable, selfish and arrogant fellow"*[9].

William Gossage had a long and interesting career as an inventor with no less than 50 patents in his name which related to nearly every aspect of the chemical industry[10]. Sadly, locally, he is only remembered today as a soap manufacturer. Born in Lincolnshire in 1799 he was the youngest of 13 children. At twelve years of age he was apprenticed to his uncle who was a chemist in Chesterfield. He seems to have had a real aptitude for invention and lodged his first patent in 1823, which was for a portable alarum for clocks and watches. After leaving Chesterfield he moved to Leamington where he became a manufacturer of Leamington salts. From Leamington he moved on to Stoke Prior in Worcestershire where, in partnership with a Mr. Fardon, he started a

---

[6] Both belonged to a religious sect called *Glassites* or *Sandemanians* which practised a simple and literal form of Christianity based on the scriptures. The sect ceased to exist around 1890.
[7] The partner in this concern, Holbrook Gaskell, later joined forces with Henry Deacon to form the firm of Gaskell, Deacon & Co. in Widnes.
[8] For further reading see *Across The Gap* – Jean M. Morris (2017)
[9] *A Mersey Town in the Industrial Revolution* – T.C. Barker & J.R. Harris
[10] *A History of Widnes* - G.E. Diggle (Corporation of Widnes, 1961)

salt and alkali works known as The British Alkali Works. During this time he patented his *"Gossage Condensing Tower"* which was designed to reduce the nuisances caused by the manufacture of alkali. From 1844 to 1848 he was copper smelting in South Wales before returning briefly to Stoke Prior in 1848. In December 1849 Gossage and Fardon sold their interests in The British Alkali Works and finally parted company. In 1850, when he opened his Widnes factory, he was initially engaged in copper smelting and it was not until around 1855 that he turned his attention to the manufacture of soap. Despite the demands of running his successful soap manufacturing business he still found time to invent further improvements in connection with the manufacture of silicate of soda, iron, steel and gas. Over the following years Gossage took out a large number of patents including a patent for the famous "mottled soap" which rapidly gained in popularity. William Gossage, an extraordinary man, died at his home in Bowdon, Cheshire, in 1877.

Frederic Muspratt opened the Wood End Works in Widnes in 1852. His knowledge and experience in the chemical industry was acquired under the supervision of his father, James Muspratt. James Muspratt was born in Dublin on 12th August 1793. At the age of fourteen he was apprenticed to a druggist named John Micheltree in Dublin. In those days there were few facilities for learning science so it was the knowledge of drugs and chemicals, acquired in the laboratories of druggists and apothecaries that gave valuable practical training to many who were later to become eminent chemists. Young James Muspratt devoted himself to the study of theoretical and practical chemistry, but after the premature death of his parents he decided to seek a career in the services. By the age of nineteen he was in Spain taking part in the Peninsular War and served in both the army and the navy. After his return to Dublin in 1814 he began the manufacture of chemical products such as hydrochloric and acetic acids. He planned to expand into the manufacture of alkali by the Leblanc process; possibly hoping to seize the opportunities afforded by the repeal of the salt tax, but unfortunately he could not raise the capital to fund this venture. He also realised that perhaps Dublin was not an ideal base for this enterprise so he crossed The Irish Sea to Liverpool.

When Muspratt arrived in Liverpool there was already a number of people manufacturing soda by the Leblanc method. Thomas Lutwyche and William Hill pioneered this process in Lancashire and were

Beginnings

manufacturing in the Vauxhall area of Liverpool as early as 1814, however, it is thought that, subsequently, Muspratt's site at Vauxhall Road was the first *important* alkali works in Britain[11].

James Muspratt went to Liverpool in 1822 and leased land in Vauxhall Road beside the canal bank. The site was an abandoned glass works and the area around was at that time undeveloped. Over a period he enlarged his Liverpool works. When there was no further room for expansion he went into partnership with fellow Irishman, Josias Christopher Gamble, and together they opened a works in St. Helens. The partnership was dissolved after two years and Muspratt subsequently opened another factory, in Newton, where his son Frederic spent some time before moving to Widnes in 1852. His youngest son, Edmund Knowles Muspratt, took control of the Liverpool and Widnes factories in 1855 and in 1867 he formed the Widnes Metal Company. Another son, Richard Muspratt, was put in charge of the Muspratt works in Flint, North Wales. We can see that the Muspratt business expanded considerably over the years and, although James Muspratt seems have been financially involved in all these factories, they each appear to have been run by his sons as autonomous companies. In 1857 James Muspratt officially retired from business handing over complete control of the business to his sons.

Although we know little of the social lives of our early chemical entrepreneurs, we do know that James Muspratt senior was an extremely cultured man. From his earliest days in Ireland he had sought out the company of those in artistic, theatrical and literary circles in Dublin. During his time as an industrialist in this country he entertained many of the great actors, poets and writers of the day, including his friend Charles Dickens. Indeed, some of the most famous artistic or intellectual personalities of the era were guests at Muspratt's Seaforth Hall home. This imposing mansion, which was designed in classical Greek style by the Liverpool architect, Sir James Picton, was built on a tract of land he had purchased from the Earl of Sefton. The site, on the shore at Seaforth, with Gladstone Dock to the rear, was in later years occupied by a large mill belonging to *"Kellogg's"*.

---

[11] *Gore's Liverpool Directory* – listed Muspratt's works for the first time in 1823 as *"Muspratt & Abbott"*. In 1825 it appeared under Muspratt's name alone.

The Muspratt family made an enormous contribution to chemistry and chemical manufacture. The eldest son, James Sheridan Muspratt, founded the Liverpool College of Chemistry, an institute for training chemists. In 1890 Edmund Knowles Muspratt became a director of the newly formed United Alkali Company. Edmund was also involved in the establishment of the University of Liverpool and was Pro-Chancellor in 1907. The family's association with the chemical trade continued through to the next generation when Edmund's son, Max Muspratt, was elected onto the Board of the Imperial Chemical Industries in 1926.

When we read about the origins of the chemical trade in Widnes it is usually assumed that John McClellan's arrival in Widnes coincided with that of John Hutchinson so he shares the credit, along with Hutchinson, of having been in at the founding of the Widnes chemical industry. However an article in *The Chemical Trade Journal* (1923), written to celebrate the centenary of the establishment of the alkali industry, claims that McClellan's Widnes Works were fully operational more than two years before John Hutchinson arrived here. Like Hutchinson, John McClellan was from Liverpool. He was born in the city in 1810. His father, who was a Scottish linen merchant, owned a small business in Shaw Street. In 1839 John McClellan also had premises in the city, at 20 King Street, where he operated as a "drysalter". However in the period immediately before his arrival in Widnes he was trading as a borax manufacturer in Parliament Street in partnership with a man called Holden. This partnership was dissolved in July 1846 and it is assumed that he came to Widnes shortly afterwards. McClellan's first works in Widnes were thought to have been at Widnes Dock where he manufactured borax and tartar salts. Later his operation, known as The North British Chemical Company, moved to Lugsdale on a site east of the Widnes-St. Helens Railway line, where he produced alkali as well as borax. From 1865 onwards he played an active part in the municipal life of the town and was a member of the Local Board, becoming Chairman in 1869. In the mid-1870s McClellan's business was in difficulty and by 1879 it had gone bankrupt. John McClellan died at his home in Highfield Road (later to become the Widnes Maternity Home) in 1881. His estate amounted to very little, the net value being just £81.

Beginnings

Of course by far the most dominant figure during the inception of the chemical industry in Widnes was John Hutchinson, who is rightly credited with bringing the first *significant* chemical production to the town. Hutchinson came to Widnes from St. Helens where he had worked as a manager and chemist at the Kurtz factory in Sutton. He was just 22 years of age when he set up his first works in Widnes around 1847. By 1851 he was employing 100 men. In early directories he is described as a "lime burner". Sometime in 1853 Hutchinson took on a partner in his chemical venture. This business associate was Oswald Earle, who was married to Georgina Kinsey the younger sister of Hutchinson's wife, Elizabeth. The first official record of the Hutchinson and Earle partnership appears in local trade directories of 1853.[12] In the beginning, in addition to the alkali business, Oswald Earle operated a small lime works on the banks of the Widnes-St. Helens Canal. It is thought that Hutchinson and Earle ran these two enterprises as one company. By 1864 the main commercial side of the Hutchinson & Earle business was being conducted from offices they had leased at Lancaster Buildings in Tithebarn Street, Liverpool. The partnership with Earle ended some ten years later and was officially dissolved in 1864. The reasons for severing their business relationship are not known but, from letters which passed between the two men, it would appear that the parting was somewhat acrimonious. This discord was rather unfortunate in view of the fact that they were brothers-in-law. After 1864, following the departure of Earle, the business became known as John Hutchinson & Company.

John Hutchinson married Mary Elizabeth Kinsey in 1850 and shortly after the wedding the newlyweds leased Appleton Lodge (overlooking Appleton Delph) from John Smith. The marriage produced five children, two boys and three girls. Unfortunately John Hutchinson did not enjoy a long life as he died of consumption on 24th March 1865 aged just 40 years. Even though, in essence, John Hutchinson was a lifelong member of the Anglican Church in reality he was not a regular attendant at any church of any denomination. Nevertheless, in spite of this outward lack of religious expression, in his *"Last Will and Testament"* he expressed a specific desire that his sons would continue to follow the Anglican faith. Interestingly, despite this apparent loyalty to the established church, the religious arrangements in the Hutchinson

---

[12] *General Chemical Division News* – Centenary Edition 1950

Into The Crucible

home were slightly unusual. Although John Hutchinson, the head of the household, was Anglican there was also a huge Roman Catholic influence as Mrs. Hutchinson and their daughters were devout Catholics. The children were of mixed religions with the boys having been baptised in the Anglican faith while the girls were Roman Catholic. One would assume that John and Elizabeth Hutchinson had come to some amicable agreement regarding the religious education and affiliation of their children.

**Appleton Lodge – the home of John Hutchinson
(Now the site of St. Bede`s Car Park)**

Beginnings

It should be said that the Roman Catholic influence in the Hutchinson household was not due solely to Elizabeth Hutchinson. The Rev. Father Fisher, the Parish Priest from nearby St. Bede's Church, had a significant impact on the lives of the whole Hutchinson family. As well as being Father Confessor to Mrs. Hutchinson and the girls, Father Fisher acted as unofficial tutor to all the Hutchinson children at Appleton Lodge. More importantly, due to his closeness to the family, he was constantly on hand to offer help or advice on a variety of subjects. He and John Hutchinson, having both come to Widnes around the same time, found that they had a lot in common. They enjoyed many evenings of intellectually stimulating conversation and as a result a close and valued friendship developed between the two men. At the beginning of March 1865, when Hutchinson recognised that his illness was terminal, he made known his desire to be buried at a spot near the church where his friend would pass daily on his way to celebrate Mass. This request was unusual, particularly as he was not a member of the congregation nor was he a Roman Catholic. One wonders why St. Bede's Graveyard, which was conveniently close to his home and the church, was not deemed acceptable. However, his unusual request was granted by the Diocese and his mortal remains were laid to rest in the grounds of St. Bede's, immediately adjacent to the church and, as requested, at a spot where his friend would pass by each day.

There is no doubt that even though John Hutchinson's life was short he left an indelible mark on the face of Widnes. He achieved an enormous amount during his brief lifetime, including the creation of a hugely successful business which, at the time of his death, gave employment to almost 600 men. As well as possessing great vision he also had grand ambitions for the future development of his company, some of which he managed to accomplish before his death. The land he owned included an area of about 40 acres over which the Runcorn viaduct passed. On this land he had formed the West Bank Dock and projected an important system of private railways to run in connection with the dock and the land adjoining, as well as the railway system then in existence. His estate, as detailed in his Will, included not only his Widnes works and extensive land holdings in the town but also interests in copper mines in Spain.

John Hutchinson has been described as a man of remarkable temperament and no less than remarkable business ability. Had he lived longer there is no doubt that he would have achieved even greater wealth and distinction. One of his early workers, writing in 1910, spoke of Hutchinson's unusual collection of staff. In his Liverpool office, at Lancaster Buildings, the bookkeeper was a black immigrant from the southern states of America. In those days this was a most unusual appointment in a city still tarnished by the shameful echo of the slave trade. That writer was of the opinion that no other such appointment could have been found in Liverpool in that era. In Widnes, Hutchinson placed the management of his works into the hands of a Hungarian exile named Stephen Szabo, who with his brother, Count Szabo, had been prominent players in the Hungarian Revolution. Before coming to England Count Szabo had held a high position as a Minister under the Kossuth regime. Unfortunately, Stephen Szabo did not enjoy good health and found it necessary to leave the unhealthy atmosphere of Widnes. Sadly, he died not long afterwards. It was around this time that Henry Brunner became chief chemist and assistant manager at the Widnes works.

Naturally the progress of the chemical industry attracted other industries into the town. Service industries such as engineering, transport and building, together with the provision of food, drink, clothing etc. were essential to urban growth. Recognising the prospect of further industrial and urban expansion Thomas Robinson, a St. Helens ironfounder, set up a foundry in Widnes in 1861. If we are to describe John Hutchinson as the father of the chemical industry in Widnes then we must acknowledge that Thomas Robinson was the father of the foundry and engineering industry in the town. Thomas Robinson's career as an ironmaster began in unusual circumstances. Born in St. Helens in May 1814, as an orphaned child he was adopted by an uncle, John Cook. When he was old enough to work he was sent to Northwich where he was employed as an apprentice to a druggist. A blacksmith owned the neighbouring premises and very soon Thomas was finding the anvil far more interesting than the chemist's shop. He started to assist in the smithy whenever he could. Another uncle, Mathew Johnson, recognised his genuine enthusiasm for this work and decided to take him on as his apprentice at Wheelock Forge near Crewe. On completion of his apprenticeship he returned to St. Helens where he found work at The Vulcan Foundry near Newton-le-Willows. At the age of 26 he became a journeyman blacksmith in Liverpool, walking over 10 miles a day, six days a week, from his home in St. Helens.

Beginnings

In May 1841 Thomas Robinson, in partnership with his uncle, John Cook, opened a small workshop in Bridge Street, St. Helens. The firm of Robinson & Cook, engineers and iron founders, prospered. Within six years they had outgrown the premises in Bridge Street and had moved into larger premises at Pocket Nook, which became known as *"The Atlas Foundry & Engineering Works"*. The numerous chemical works in St. Helens provided the company with a large volume of engineering work. However, because of the amazing rapidity with which the chemical industry was developing in Widnes, it soon became clear to Robinson that the establishment of a works in that town would be advantageous. In 1861 Robinson came to Widnes and built a foundry in Lugsdale near to the railway line. As the industries in Widnes grew, he built another larger foundry on a site near an old farmhouse called Brook House, close by Bowers Brook on the east side of the L & N.W. Railway. He brought some of the workmen with him from St. Helens. John Cook's son, 26-year-old Joseph Cook, was charged with the management of the Widnes works. A few years later Joseph Cook left this position and became involved with *The Liver Alkali Works*. In 1874 when *The Atlas Chemical Company* was formed Joseph Cook became one of its first directors. After the departure of Joseph Cook in 1866 Thomas Robinson engaged the services of Benjamin Brown, an engineer of outstanding energy and ability. In 1884, two years before Robinson's retirement, he made Benjamin Brown a partner in the Company.

With the creation of these industries in Widnes there was a huge influx of people into the town. The increased population mainly comprised of unskilled immigrant labour, a large percentage being Irish. Later there were Lithuanians, Poles, Belgians and Swedes as well as large numbers of people from Scotland, Wales and other parts of this island. Obviously the indigenous workforce was none too happy about these new arrivals and their impact on local society. Later local newspapers reported meetings and letters of complaint to the Council and, indeed, even to Parliament, stating: *"The working people of Widnes were concerned that their jobs were being taken by pauper immigrants"*. It was feared that immigrant labour was undercutting the local labour market by working for less wages. Investigations by members of the Government established that this was certainly not the case. In retrospect one wonders if this claim was prompted simply by fear of the changes that had been brought about in local society. The rapid development of industry in the town had prompted a massive surge in population and had irrevocably transformed the social composition and destroyed an established way of life.

Widnes Dock was opened in 1831 and the first Dock Master was Mr. John Palin. After the opening of the St. Helens to Runcorn Gap Railway people began to move into the dock area. By 1841 Widnes had a population of 2209 with 42 families (about 200 people) living in the dock region. This area also appears to have housed the earliest industrial workforce in the south end of the town, as well as boatmen, railway workers and dockworkers. Contemporary portrayals of the dock locality and its residents do not provide a very wholesome image. In 1841 the district was described thus: *"Widnes Dock, where families of "flatmen", a very low class, unsettled in their behaviour, pass much of the time on the "flats" or "barges"."*[13] An Ordnance Survey map produced in 1847 shows a small settlement at Widnes Dock. However, by 1851 there was quite a sizeable community. The census of that year shows that this residential area was home to canal workers, watermen, flatmen, dock labourers, railway labourers and alkali workers.

Whilst the Dock area provided housing for the first wave of alkali workers, the rapid industrial expansion brought a further increase in population and a need for additional accommodation to house it. Because public transport was virtually non-existent, it was deemed sensible and advantageous to house people close to their place of work. Plots of land near to the chemical works were quickly developed. The earliest of these residential developments were around Waterloo and Newtown. As streets and commercial premises quickly sprung up, the town itself began to take shape. Obviously the lack of any municipal institution meant that the town was being built almost entirely by speculative building contractors. This meant that there was no planning control or serious restrictions regarding layout or density to adhere to. The only concern being to build quickly and cheaply.

Many of the early chemical workers came to Widnes from St. Helens and Liverpool where they had gained a little previous experience in industry. William Gossage also brought workers with him from Stoke Prior in Worcestershire and Muspratt brought some workers from Flint. However some of the later arrivals, which included Eastern Europeans

---

[13] *H.S.L.C. Vol.134.* - F.J. Williams

Beginnings

as well as large numbers of Irish, came directly from disembarkation at the Port of Liverpool. Most of these immigrants had hopes of travelling onwards to America and it has been said that some of the later Polish and Lithuanian immigrants, unable to read the tickets, had assumed that Liverpool was New York because of the splendour of its waterfront architecture.[14]

It is difficult to imagine today that over nine million people passed through the Port of Liverpool. The Irish and Eastern Europeans were heading for America, while the English were usually on course for Australia, New Zealand or South Africa. The Scottish emigrants mainly favoured Canada. For the very many immigrants who had insufficient funds to cross the Atlantic, Liverpool unavoidably became the end of the line. These newly arrived immigrants joined multicultural throngs on the Liverpool quays. There were huge masses of people, some leaving, some staying and others merely passing through. The hustle and bustle of the port in those days can only be imagined. Apart from the emigrant trade, Liverpool was the gateway to the Empire and traded all over the world. Many of the Irish arriving in the city found work on the docks and they were housed along Scotland Road which was a densely populated immigrant area. Most of those who decided to move on from the port, in search of work, made their way inland to the industrial and textile towns of Lancashire and Yorkshire.

The immigrants arriving in Widnes would probably have been struck initially by its grey bleakness. They would have been greeted by the sight of grey-black smoke belching out from the huge factory stacks into dark grey skies or curling up from chimneys on grey roofed buildings. They'd have seen row upon row of smoke streaked houses; long terraces in drab narrow streets, separated only by narrow squalid passages (entries) giving access to the backyards of dismal congested dwellings. The houses, crowded into the smallest available space, were sited unbelievably near to the factories. These factories sent out fetid odours, gases, and perilous dust that invaded both the lungs and homes of those who lived in such close proximity. Another thing that would have been immediately obvious to the immigrant was the absence of green spaces. There was a conspicuous lack of grass or any form of fertile plant life in the living and working areas in the industrial part of

---

[14] *"The Guardian Newspaper – G2"* Linda Grant (2003)

town. This would have been strange to them as most of the immigrants had rural origins and came from agricultural backgrounds. They were used to clean fresh air, trees and green fields. Their introduction to the chemical industry and its environment must certainly have been a shock to their systems. However, the immigrant soon learned to live amid this pall of smoke and the noxious odours that had earned Widnes the unenviable reputation of being one of the dirtiest and smelliest places in England.

Local newspapers of the time report high levels of fighting and drunkenness among the population. In George Diggle`s *"History of Widnes"* he draws attention to this but says that Widnes was no worse than any other industrial town of that period. However, if one were to read the back-issues of local newspapers you would notice that particular and unfair prominence was given to offences committed by the newcomers, notably the Irish and the "Poles". In actual fact this problem was by no means confined to the Irish, Poles or Lithuanians but was widespread among *all* the working-class population of this town and other towns where concentrated industrialisation had occurred. It was certainly not an ethnic problem but a social one which was extensive among all nationalities at that time. If one were to study local newspapers of that era, from any town where industry had developed, you would read similar stories.

While there is certainly no denying that there was a high degree of drink-related crime among the Widnes working class population, perhaps one should analyse the possible reasons for this. Robert H. Sherard`s famous *"White Slaves of England"* articles, which he wrote for *Pearson's Magazine* in 1896, give us an insight into the background of those crimes.
I quote from one article…………..

> *"Widnes is a populous town and one admires in its squalid courts and alleys the swarms of healthy children. "They are a fine race of men and women," said an informant "and their children are beautiful". One sees numerous and fine children, but never any old people. The touching contrast between May and December will be looked for in vain in Widnes, for here, as in St. Helens, as the leading Doctor in the latter town remarked to me "the men go off quickly". "It is a very unhealthy trade" he said "and if published statistics show but a small death-rate in the chemical trade, it is*

because the chemical yard only kills a man three parts out of four, leaving the workhouse to do the rest. The men are dismissed before they are actually dying. As a general rule, the men go from forty-five to fifty-five years of age. The tubes become blocked up and asthmatical; the gases destroy all elasticity of the tubes. The lime-men get soft stone. All get more or less anaemic. Asthma, kidney disease, chronic cystitis are the prerequisites of all."

"In answer to your question" the Doctor said; "It would not be wise to pass a chemical yard man at the ordinary rate for life insurance. The work certainly shortens life. For one thing the men cannot do their work unless they are half drunk. They drink and drink. I have one patient who drinks a half cask (eighteen gallons) of beer a week. They drink because they cannot eat. I know men who have brought their breakfasts, dinners, and teas back home because they could not touch them. A man cannot be healthy under these conditions".

This passage gives an image of the conditions and drinking habits of the chemical worker. It is particularly troubling to read that the Doctor was of the opinion that *"the men cannot do their work unless they are half drunk"*. This leads us to believe that working conditions in the alkali trade contributed to the high level of alcohol abuse in the town. Gruelling labour in sweltering conditions made workers extremely thirsty and therefore they became accustomed to drinking large amounts of liquid to replace the fluids they had lost through perspiration. As beer was more palatable to them than water, and in those days it was sometimes safer to drink, they consumed large quantities of alcohol. As a consequence, excessive drinking became an accepted part of daily life for most working men and drunkenness was common, even amongst children. To cater for the constant demand for alcohol, beersellers plied their wares from carts outside the factories and a proliferation of pubs were conveniently sited alongside works and housing.[15]

Not surprisingly the pubs were a great draw for working men after a gruelling day in the unpleasant and unhealthy atmosphere of an alkali factory. For the rural migrants especially it must have seemed that their new working environment was almost like being thrown into the jaws

---

[15] *"Across The Gap"* Jean M. Morris (Springfield-Farrihy 2016)

of hell. No doubt the pub was seen as a merciful release at the end of the day.   Perhaps we should also bear in mind that a large number of workers were young single men with no home base to return to after their day's work. They lived in lodging houses and probably found the ambience of the Public House more welcoming at the end of a long and arduous shift.   Many were economic migrants in a strange country, some only able to speak in their native tongue. The local pub created a warm social setting where they could meet and converse with their compatriots in an easy relaxed environment.   Although most of the early pubs were small and rough places, later on an increasing number of well-fitted pubs were opened and these provided a more comfortable and pleasant alternative to the cramped miserable hovels some of them called home.   Interestingly, several surveys relating to the consumption of alcohol show that the deeper the poverty of a district the higher the proportion of public houses to population.

The new residents of Widnes soon found themselves to be separated both physically and culturally from the more advantaged members of the native population.   In G. Sjoberg's model of the geographical structure of pre-industrial towns, the elite are set at the centre of the town and the poorer groups are clustered around the periphery[16]. As a town increases in size and population its society becomes fragmented. This usually involves the higher wealth or status groups separating from the commoner, or poorer, elements of society.   This certainly happened in Widnes but, unlike Sjoberg's geographical configuration, in our case the more affluent moved to the periphery while the poorer groups occupied the centre of the town.   The inner congested and factory dominated areas became home to the poorer groups while the more affluent and successful members of society moved outwards to airier and more pleasant environs.

It is interesting to read contemporaneous early accounts and opinions of the new manufacturing towns of Lancashire.   These give us an insight otherwise unimaginable to our modern minds and experience. William Cooke Taylor's letters, published in 1842, paint a vivid picture. His observations offer us a glimpse of what life may have been like in Widnes as industrialisation took hold. His letters also provide an image of the labouring classes in Lancashire at that time.   He says:

---

[16] *The Pre-Industrial City* – G. Sjoberg (1960)

"The population, like the system to which it belongs is new; but it is hourly increasing in breadth and strength. It is an aggregate of masses, our conceptions of which clothe themselves in terms that express something portentous and fearful.

The most striking phenomenon of the Factory System is the amount of population which it has suddenly accumulated: there has been long a continuous influx of operatives into the manufacturing districts from other parts of Britain; these men have very speedily laid aside all their old habits and associations, to assume those of the mass in which they are mingled. The manufacturing population is not new in its formation alone; it is new in its habits of thought and action, which have been formed by the circumstances of its condition, with little instruction, and less guidance from external sources." [17]

I think that this passage provides an important indication of how industrialisation changed the behaviour and attitudes of society in general. It reveals the fascinating concept that our first industrial society was *"new in habits of thought and action, which have been formed by the circumstances of its condition, with little instruction, and less guidance, from external sources"*. This extract would strongly suggest that the subsequent behaviour of the incomer, whether he was a native or an immigrant, was a result of his new environment rather than his previous way of life. Although a large degree of anti-social conduct was evident amongst the new population in Widnes our town was certainly not unique in this respect. Nor was this behaviour confined to individual ethnic groups. It was actually widespread amongst all sections of working society whatever their nationality or creed. Despite this being a fact, there was still a tendency to single out specific ethnic groups for particular criticism.

At the opening of the Liverpool Assizes Court sessions in 1884, Justice Butt made a controversial comment regarding what he considered to be an exceptionally large number of "Irish names" appearing before him. He said this proved an obvious criminal streak in the Irish character. An outraged local journalist, John Denvir, made much of this comment and issued an angry rebuttal. He pointed out

---

[17] *"Notes of a tour in the manufacturing districts of Lancashire"* (W. Cooke Taylor 1842)

that many of those with "Irish names" had been born and raised in England and their behaviour was the result of an English environment rather than any perceived ethnic influences. Mr. Denvir wrote:

> *"While offenders bearing Irish names are not out of all relation to the number of people in Liverpool, they are chiefly of a class who have never even seen Ireland and who have become contaminated by their surroundings in this country".*

John Hutchinson

Industry

In 1889 a correspondent reflecting on the changing face of Widnes made the following observations:

> "One can hardly imagine that Widnes, seeing its present state, was once frequented by pleasure seekers and picnicers. Yet such was the fact. We need not now expect to see the gay devotees of pleasure come to Widnes and its shady pleasant walks by the Mersey. Yet time was when the gardens of Widnes were well known, and the Lovers' Walk, shaded and arched over by green branches, was a sweet reality. When Snig Pie House ministered to a luxury of the epicure who delighted in the taste of snigs angled for and caught in the river hard by. Times are changed since the days when there was no house between Appleton Church and the Railway Station, with the sole exception of Solomon's Temple, the glory of which has also departed. The memory of these things is now fast dying out and instead of the pleasant odour of woodland we have the disagreeable smell of chemicals. Still the change in Widnes is entirely for the better and we have no reason for regret, and Widnes has now a reputation worldwide in extent and among a class of people different from pleasure seekers. Neither is Widnes an unhealthy place, as is shown by its death rate. For although pulmonary diseases may be fairly frequent, as I hear they are, yet there is a wonderful absence of fevers. In spite then of pleasant old memories of things gone for ever, Widnes has every reason to congratulate itself".

This passage, written around forty years after John Hutchinson opened his alkali factory in the town, tells of the changes brought about by four decades of industry. Before the dense acidic smoke from the alkali factories had blackened the countryside the area had been a rural idyll of fields and pastures, trees and hedges, and a collection of small villages comprising Farnworth, Appleton, Cronton, Upton and Widnes Dock. In 1841 the small population of just 2209 was concentrated in these areas.

At that time there were wide expanses of farmland, interrupted only by a scattering of houses and the barren areas that are signified on our

Into The Crucible

local maps by place names embodying elements such as Marsh, Moor, Heath and Moss. Lovely watercourses such as Bowers Brook and Stewards Brook, streams once renowned for their clear waters and leaping trout, flowed freely into the Mersey. Later, these pleasant streams were to become choked and polluted from the refuse of numerous factories.

In West Bank, the riverside and sandy beach had once attracted day-trippers, while close by the ancient ferry and its lone boatman transported passengers across the river. The river at this spot was a paradise for local fishermen and along its banks flora and fauna found a natural habitat in wide open spaces. Nearby, the landlord of the Boat House Inn, known locally as *"Snig Pie House"*, offered food and refreshment to travellers. Apparently the Inn's famous "eel (snig) pie" provided a unique culinary delight for its patrons. Beyond the Inn, on a site later occupied by the Hartland Methodist Church, stood West Bank House, the home of William Hurst who owned most of West Bank. From all accounts the south end of the town was a tranquil and charming place where wildlife was abundant and stags and does roamed freely around the common land known as Widnes Marsh. This idyllic landscape was only interrupted now and again by a few scattered dwellings.

We are fortunate to have several written examples to draw upon to visualise the area before the chemical industry irrevocably blighted the landscape. J. Fenwick Allen, in his book about the founders of the chemical industry, tells us that in pre-industrial times residence in Widnes *"was not only bearable but even inviting, bathers frequented the shores of the Mersey round about Woodend, and some of the young men kept their yachts there. Woodend was bright and sweet and salubrious"*. The same author, when describing the area at the time of William Gossage's arrival in Widnes, says:

"....fields with green hedge-rows and healthy trees still extended down from his house along the river past the old "Snig Pie House". This noted hostelry was still a favourite place for picnic parties. The Widnes Marsh was used by the neighbouring farmers to graze their cattle on. A prettily situated estate was the property of Mr. Wright, whose house, with its parklands, overlooked the river from behind the ferry".

Industry

In 1852, as industry increased, William Hurst leased large tracts of his land to building contractors who hastily constructed houses for the new industrial workforce. Before long, the wide expanses of land had been filled with rows of utilitarian housing and the noxious vapours from the alkali process had killed all trees and hedgerows in the immediate vicinity. The beautiful tree-lined landscape of West Bank had been replaced by a forest of factory chimneys that darkened the skies with smoke and fumes. Very soon the once rural idyll had disappeared from all but memory and the former rustic scene was rapidly supplanted by a new industrial and urban backdrop. [18].

Prior to the arrival of the chemical industries the indigenous population of Widnes earned its living in a variety of ways. Agricultural occupations would naturally have been evident; but mention should be made of the sailcloth industry that thrived in the Farnworth and Lunt's Heath districts in the northern part of the town. Early canvas/sailcloth production in Widnes was predominantly a domestic concern with the work being performed in the homes. Census records show that, like most cottage crafts of that era, whole families including men, women and children were involved in this work. However by 1825 a series of inventions, including the introduction of power looms, gradually took weaving out of the homes and into factories. Although this meant that the repetitive clack of the loom became a thing of the past in the little cottages of Farnworth and Lunts Heath, nevertheless, it was still a family occupation. Even when this activity transferred to factories children were still being put to work as bobbin winders; although in later times it was illegal to employ children.

Sailcloth was produced commercially in a number of other districts in south-west Lancashire and had been the subject of a petition to the House of Commons in 1704. Some of our neighbouring towns also had significant colonies of weavers who originally worked in their own homes and then transferred their labour to the thriving sailcloth factories. In Warrington the Gaskell family had owned and operated a sailcloth factory in Latchford for generations and sometime around 1820

---

[18] In the late nineteenth century Henry Brunner described Bowers Brook in the following terms: *"the air of this culvert contains sulphuretted hydrogen in sufficient quantity at times to be dangerous to human life"*.

Thomas and William Kidd opened a factory in Tontine Street, St. Helens. By 1825 there were at least five commercial weaving sheds located around Farnworth and Lunts Heath. The most notable of these were owned by William Norland, Thomas Shaw, Thomas Smythe, Longton & Leather and the brothers Thomas and William Kidd, who also owned the sailcloth factory in St. Helens. It is worth drawing attention to the Kidd family and their lengthy commercial connection with the Farnworth area of Widnes. This family had a particularly long association with the canvas industry and had worked as sailcloth makers since the 18th century. In the early 1860s another member of the family, Robert Kidd, was in business as a canvas merchant in Farnworth. He was working in partnership with a man called John Woodhouse and their company, trading under the name of Kidd and Woodhouse, was listed as canvas manufacturers and brewers.

In the Cronton, Farnworth and Appleton districts the watchmaking industry, and the various trades allied to it, played a particularly important role. Like the early sailcloth industry, it was also a domestic trade which was widespread in the numerous small villages of south-west Lancashire. The components produced in these areas were made by skilled craftsmen who usually worked in small workshops in their own homes. It was generally the case that sons and other family members were also apprenticed to this trade. In consequence, we find a continuity of names in lists of local watchmakers during the 19th century. Particularly mention should be made of the Abbott family and William Garnett who were long established in the area. In Directories of 1825 the main watchmakers, or watch tool and movement manufacturers, in Farnworth were William Doward, John Roskel, James Abbott and Thomas Gee. In Cronton we find the names of George Plumpton, Brian Younge, Thomas Alcock, John Fazakerley, Samuel Davies and William Unsworth. In the Upton district J. Glover seems to have been the only person recorded in this occupation.[19]

Larger "master watchmakers" from Prescot employed most of our local home-based watchmakers. The outworkers were employed on a piecework basis. These local artisans usually concentrated on the manufacture of one or two specific parts. They were extremely skilled and worked to a high degree of precision. When the watch and clock parts, made in our local villages, were installed into the timepiece the

---

[19] *Baines`s History, Directory and Gazetteer of Lancashire* - 1825

man who performed the final operations of finishing and assembling put his own name and town on the dial.[20]

Wiredrawing was another trade carried out in the Appleton area. D.W.F. Hardie, in his *"History of the Chemical Industry in Widnes"*, quotes from James Nasmyth's autobiography of 1891 in which Nasmyth relates a conversation with Peter Stubs, a Warrington filemaker. Mr. Stubs was of the opinion that the wire-drawers, toolmakers and file-cutters of pre-industrial Widnes were the traditional descendants of the old armourers. These armourers had provided armour and heraldic devices for the local baronies. Stubs had said: *"In his opinion, the craftsmen were the direct descendants of a swarm of workmen from Hugo de Lupus's original Norman hive of refined metalworkers, dating from the time of the Conquest"*.

Although Runcorn was the principal provider of local stone and a leading employer in this industry, the sandstone quarries at Appleton, Cronton and Farnworth provided a source of employment for a small number of Widnes workers. Other local occupations included those relating to the river such as fishing and boat-building. There were also some small cottage industries which provided a service for the local inhabitants such as brewing, dressmaking and shoemaking. A small brewery had been established at Widnes House by James Cowley and there were numerous dressmakers and shoemakers throughout the district. Obviously dressmakers and shoemakers were ubiquitous in the mid-19th century. These were generally small domestic trades catering mostly for local needs. The introduction of the sewing machine in the 1860s brought noticeable changes to both these occupations but, in the case of shoemaking, this industry still required skilled men to cut out the leather for the shoes.

In neighbouring towns industry was also evident. Soap-making, stone quarrying and shipbuilding were to the fore in Runcorn, while in St. Helens coalmining, glassmaking and copper smelting were the main concerns. In addition, the Sutton area of St. Helens was also famous for pottery. In Sutton, the local clay was made into coarse earthenware items that were sent to Liverpool for the African and West Indian

---

[20] For further reading see *"Across The Gap"* – Jean M. Morris 2016

trade[21]. In Warrington, the Patten family opened the first copper works in Lancashire at Bank Quay in 1720. This firm appears to have done its main trade in supplying copper and brass goods to the African slave trade. Indeed, many of the local industrialists, such as Thomas Case who owned a colliery in St. Helens, were also the owners of African slave ships.

Among the numerous occupations mentioned in the 1851 census for Widnes were wheelwright; publican; beer retailer; blacksmith; joiner; wagoner; bobbin winder; groom; laundress; corn dealer; carter and cooper. We can see from this census that these activities and other types of work such as canvas weaving; watchmaking; toolmaking and wiredrawing, as well as the usual agricultural and river occupations, were generally carried out by indigenous residents. However, it is interesting to note the type of work that was generally *not* performed by members of the native population. In the census of 1851 the following named occupations, professions or *descriptions* mostly applied to people who originally came from outside the area (beyond a 15-mile radius). School Teachers; Clergymen; Land Proprietors; Annuitants; Police and Railway workers. However, perhaps it is also worth mentioning that in later years there was an inevitable change in the structure of some work and the origins of the people who performed it. F. J. William's study of occupational trends indicates that, at one time, the coopering trade became the only skilled trade over which the Irish had complete control. [22]

By the middle of the 19th century the face of Widnes was changing rapidly. This was largely aided by the social effect of the railways in that it made movement much easier. In earlier days people had been restricted to living and working in or near to the areas where they were born. Few people moved long distances as they usually walked, carrying their belongings with them, so they seldom ventured further than the next town or county. The coming of the railway was to change all that. Apart from transporting people into town the railway also provided employment. The census of 1851 lists a number of railway workers in Farnworth and other parts of the town. This census also allows us see a pattern of movement of Irish labourers from the St.

---

[21] *A Mersey Town in the Industrial Revolution* – T. C. Barker & J. R. Harris
[22] "*A case of occupational mobility in the Industrial Revolution*" [4] F.J. Williams –- H.S.L.C Vol.134

Industry

Helens and Manchester areas to our locality. This would be in line with the growing trade in alkali production in Widnes.

By 1851 there were a number of established oil works in Widnes. Local maps show that, prior to the arrival of the alkali industry in 1847, there were already two works located near to Runcorn Gap Railway Station and the canal bank respectively. One is thought to have been an oil works which produced vegetable oil. This company was run by three Irishmen, Michael Carroll (from Kilkenny), Edward Scilly (from Roscommon) and James Giloran (from Sligo). Patrick McBride, a cooper from Leitrim, was also associated with this business. There was another oil works in the same vicinity in the early 1840s. This was registered under the name of John Wilson and Company. The other men associated with this firm were Samuel Salmon Berend and Patrick Hayes. In later years this business was in the sole ownership of Patrick Hayes who was involved in oil production in this area for a considerable time. Unfortunately Mr. Hayes was declared bankrupt in 1852 and subsequently left Widnes to start a new life in Australia. As an additional point of interest, Mr. Hayes was the first owner of the large house in Highfield Road which later served as Widnes Maternity Hospital.

Although Widnes had attracted numerous new alkali factories, the alkali industry in St. Helens continued to expand during the middle decades of the century, although this expansion was within established firms and not from the formation of new ones.[23] As mentioned earlier, one of the main reasons for the appearance of Leblanc alkali production in Widnes was the 1848 increase of freight charges on canals and railways. Another very important reason was the continuing civil actions being brought against alkali manufacturers in other places. Atmospheric pollution and the dumping of offensive waste, both of which were unavoidable by-products of alkali production, had become a serious problem. As Widnes was a more sparsely occupied area it was expected that there was less likelihood of complaints.

Complaints about the damaging effects of the alkali industry were numerous in all the areas in which this trade had been established. In

---

[23] *Made in Lancashire* – Geoffrey Timmins - (Manchester University Press) 1998.

St. Helens, manufacturers had been involved in numerous expensive legal actions as a result of complaints from local property owners about the noxious effects of the alkali trade. Several wealthy landowners were prolific and influential objectors. They declared that the alkali industry was responsible for killing off trees and hedgerows on their estates. Some complained that their tenants' livestock was also at risk from eating poisoned grass and that the value of their land was being diminished. Even as early as 1827 James Muspratt's Everton factory had been cited as a public nuisance because of the smoke and fumes discharged from his Vauxhall Road premises. In October of that year *The Liverpool Mercury* published a letter that read:

> *"Regarding the chemical works, such volumes of sulphurous smoke as to darken the whole atmosphere in the neighbourhood, so much so that the church of St. Martin-in-the-Field cannot be seen from the houses at about one hundred yards distance, the stones of which are already turned a dark colour from the cause. The scent is almost insufferable, as well as injurious to the health of persons residing in the neighbourhood".*

Ten years later Muspratt was indicted before the Liverpool Spring Assizes for *"creating and maintaining a nuisance within the Borough of Everton to the annoyance and injury of the inhabitants thereof"*. During this period posters were pasted on walls around Liverpool attacking James Muspratt and his operation at Vauxhall Road. The complaints were also numerous in St. Helens. One of the most persistent plaintiffs was Sir John Gerard who owned an estate at Windle which was downwind of St. Helens and the majority of the factories. His and other similar court cases became a constant drain on manufacturers' resources, with some damages reaching up to £40,000. In fact, in September 1846 the Court heard two cases brought by Sir John Gerard in the space of two days. One was against Crosfield's which resulted in Sir John being awarded damages of £3000 and the following day he received damages of £4000 from a complaint against the Muspratt factory. Both these awards represented significant sums of money in 1846 and would have put a considerable dent in manufacturers' profits.

As Widnes was an area of low population at that time, incoming manufacturers presumed that they would be less likely to receive complaints about the unavoidable escape of hydrochloric acid gas. However, despite this optimism, after the establishment and rapid

Industry

development of the alkali industry Widnes manufacturers were faced with similar complaints. Landowners and farmers in the surrounding areas claimed that the alkali factories had adverse effects on vegetation and had caused a fall in land values. Sir Richard Brooke, who owned property at Cuerdley and an estate and land at Norton, was prominent among the complainants. These complaints, although valid, were remarkable for a number of reasons. One of the main reasons being that people like Sir Richard Brooke and other major landowners had sold large tracts of their land to manufacturers, specifically for industrial development. It would seem that most landowners had a hypocritical nimby-like approach to the subject of industrial growth. Although landowners profited greatly from the sale of land to developers they did not want industry on their own doorstep. They were quite happy to benefit from the proceeds of land sales but they did not want the unwholesome environment created by chemical manufacture to encroach upon their own estates. Unfortunately it seems they could not have one without the other[24].

After the arrival of Hutchinson and McLellan other manufacturers appeared in brisk succession. By 1855 there were seven alkali works operating near to the terminal of the St. Helens to Runcorn Gap Railway and the St. Helens Canal[25]. Factories, which were often little more than large sheds, appeared almost overnight. They were erected very quickly and cheaply, mainly built of wood and lit at night by means of small lamps, known as "duck lamps" which burned colza oil. D.W.F. Hardie tells us that the "saltcake house" was usually made of pitch pine, as this wood is particularly resistant to the action of muriatic acid[26].

Obviously, with the rapid expansion of the alkali industry, the complaints regarding atmospheric pollution and its damaging effect did not abate but rather escalated. There was continuing criticism and objections from landowners. Despite this, the industry expanded at an alarming rate and by the 1870s there were probably around 24 chemical factories in Widnes. In 1878 when Lord Derby brought a petition before

---

[24] *"Across The Gap"* – Jean M. Morris (Springfield-Farrihy 2016)
[25] *A Scientific Survey of Merseyside* - W.A.Smith (British Assoc. for the advancement of Science) Liverpool 1953
[26] *A History of the Chemical Industry in Widnes* - D.W.F. Hardie

Parliament, regarding the damaging effects of the alkali trade, Edward Sullivan, one of our prominent local manufacturers, wrote to *The Times* to give the manufacturers' viewpoint. He said:

"The alkali industry is a necessity in a manufacturing country. If it is an evil it is a necessary one. Sulphuric acid, the base of all alkali products, may be called the heart of all manufacturing industries. The consumption of it is the surest gauge of their condition. There is scarcely a manufactured article in daily use that is not more or less dependent upon it. To enhance the cost of its production by hasty or ill-judged legislation would enhance the cost of half the industrial products of the country. It is not the greed of the manufacturers that has increased the number of alkali works, but it is the increased trade of the country that has demanded an increased supply of an indispensable element of production." [27]

Whilst the alkali industry thrived in the southern region of the town, the old sailcloth trade in the north of the town had slowly diminished. By 1856 there were only two sailcloth/canvas manufacturers still in production, namely Kidd & Company and Thomas Shaw & Sons. On 14th October 1865 the business operated by Robert Kidd & John Woodhouse filed for bankruptcy. Trade had further reduced by 1870 and as a consequence there was only one factory in the area to maintain the last vestige of this old craft. The proprietors of that last remaining factory were Joseph Bushby & Co., who also had premises in Strand Street in Liverpool. Despite the fact that trade had reduced drastically, in 1872 there was a very slight improvement in this remaining business. *The Runcorn Guardian* reported that the mill owned by Bushby & Co., which had for some time been running on short time, was now working full time. The article stated that: *"As this was the only factory of the kind in the district it was hoped that the improvement would be permanent"*. Nevertheless it was obvious that despite any optimistic expectations this industry was in serious decline and it was only a matter of time. In fact the writing was on the wall as the demand for sailcloth waned mainly because of the introduction of steam shipping which meant that vessels no longer required canvas for sails.

After 1851 we also see the gradual deterioration in watch and file making in the area. Census returns show us that family members were no longer being apprenticed into these trades. The main reason for this

---

[27] Edward Sullivan – *The Times* (December 1878)

Industry

decline was due to increased international competition and tariffs. A 30% tariff in the USA had a detrimental effect on the trade which, sadly, heralded the eventual demise of this local craft after 1875. By the mid-1870s many of the traditional local artisans, who had previously worked in cottage industries, were being forced to seek alternative forms of employment. Around this time we can see a gradual movement of local men into the chemical trade. Interestingly, despite the chemical industry having been well established as the main source of employment in the area for almost thirty years, prior to the mid-1870s there seems to have been some reluctance on the part of the indigenous population to enter into the alkali industry.

Local directories of that time demonstrate the changes in importance of assorted occupations. They show how the new industrial climate had marked the gradual demise of some of the old trades, which were subsequently replaced by new products and occupations. Chemical works; oil and grease manufacturers; iron and brass founders; boilermakers; copper smelters; iron manufacturers; lead smelters; lime merchants; soap manufacturers; timber merchants etc. were all flourishing in this new "boom town". We also see the development and growth of the shopping and residential areas which were necessary to provide accommodation and services to an expanding population.

The establishment of alkali factories had brought great changes and pollution to the town. The Leblanc process of manufacturing alkali[28] involved a system whereby salt was decomposed with sulphuric acid with the formation of sodium sulphate (saltcake) and the consequent release of hydrochloric acid gas. In this operation the semi-liquid mass was heated in a reverberatory furnace and periodically raked to promote the escape of hydrochloric acid gas. This area of work was always marked by the presence of a tall chimney that drew the fire and helped to dissipate the acid fumes into the upper atmosphere. The Leblanc process was very wasteful as the chlorine went into the atmosphere and the sulphur onto the waste heaps. The later Solvay process, which was put into practice by the Brunner and Mond partnership at Winnington, meant that by the end of the 1880s the Leblanc process was almost obsolete.

---

[28] This process was first used in England in the first decades of the 19th century by William Losh at his Walker-on-Tyne Works.

Into The Crucible

In addition to alkali manufacture in the town, William Gossage's soap works expanded and prospered. Towards the end of the 19th century Gossage's was one of the largest soap works in the world, with a workforce numbering almost 800. Between the years 1862 and 1886 the Gossage Soapworks was estimated to have produced 200,000 tons of mottled soap. This mottled soap, which was then unique to Gossage's, contained coloured impurities (due to iron compounds) which spread through the soap and produced coloured veins to give it a distinctive appearance. A large proportion of this product was destined for export to Africa, India and China. In fact, the soap produced by William Gossage & Sons at their Widnes works represented about 50% of Britain's total soap exports. An additional point of interest, regarding the export of Gossage soap to Africa, occurred during the Boer War. During that conflict Widnes soldiers who were serving in Pretoria were astonished to see remnants of Gossage's wooden soapboxes made into garden fencing.

> **GOSSAGES SOAPS**
> PURE TALLOW
> MOTTLED & SCENTED
>
> WILLIAM GOSSAGE & SONS, Ltd., ARE SOLE MAKERS OF
> *Magical* and *The Right Sort*
> REGISTERED BRANDS.
>
> The following PRIZE MEDALS were obtained—
>
> | LONDON 1862. | GOLD MEDAL. | PARIS 1867. | DUBLIN, 1865. |
>
> Being the HIGHEST AWARDS for Excellence in Quality of SOAPS.
>
> The best proof of this excellence is the fact that the output from these Works, although only Established in 1855, has been for many years the LARGEST IN THE UNITED KINGDOM and, it is believed, in THE WORLD.
>
> WORKS WIDNES, LANCASHIRE.

Copper smelting also became an established local trade. This industry had started off as small-scale affairs in The Lake District and Cornwall, based on similar lines to the tin industry. However with the arrival of the Industrial Revolution copper was in demand as a component of brass, which was used for industrial machinery. With

Industry

this increased demand production moved from Cornwall to various other places including London, Bristol and the Midlands. Later, the development of the reverberatory furnace meant that coal could be used in metal smelting. Because of this, the industry further developed near to areas where this source of fuel was easily available, such as the coalfields of South Wales. During the mid-19th century the "wet-process" of production was developed which enabled copper manufacturers to extract copper from burnt pyrites. This may have encouraged copper manufacturers to move towards Widnes and other places where alkali was produced.[29]

The Copper smelting process was first attempted in Widnes by Charles Lambert and William Gossage. Charles Lambert was a South Wales copper smelter who set up his works in Widnes around 1850. His works was located by the canal on what was later to be the site of the Widnes Alkali Company factory. From 1844 to 1848 William Gossage was copper smelting in South Wales. When he came to Widnes in 1850 he carried on with methods he had devised of extracting sulphur from copper ores but he had limited success with this process. However, he then began experimenting on a method of obtaining copper from burnt pyrites, which was the waste material usually discarded after burning iron pyrites during the alkali production process. Alas, the owners of the pyrites mines soon became aware of Gossage`s process of copper recovery so they began to extract the copper themselves before selling the pyrites. As a consequence, in 1855 William Gossage turned his full attention to manufacturing the commodity that became synonymous with his name, soap.

Later, with the subsequent introduction of Henderson's "wet-process" the town became a major centre for the copper industry. The Glasgow based Tharsis Sulphur and Copper Company, founded by Charles Tennant, gained a foothold in Widnes by buying The Lancashire Metal Company and The Widnes Metal Company. In the mid-1880s Thomas Bolton & Sons and James Hawke Dennis arrived in the town from Staffordshire and Macclesfield respectively. Bolton's was first established in Staffordshire in 1783 when copper ores were mined on Ecton Hill. This company's manufactures were used in the earliest steam locomotives. In fact, Thomas Bolton's Birmingham works

---

[29] Pyrites was burned during the alkali manufacturing process.

Into The Crucible

had the distinction of providing the copper for the firebox of Stephenson's famous *"Rocket"*, which won the Rainhill Trials in 1829. In 1881 Thomas Bolton & Sons bought the Mersey Copper Works and set up their Widnes works, for smelting and rolling copper, on a site in Hutchinson Street. Among the later "copper" arrivals in Widnes were David and Alex McKechnie, the sons of Duncan McKechnie. Duncan McKechnie had originally operated from the Old Quay works in Runcorn but this company was taken over by The United Alkali Company in 1891. Following this, his sons decided to establish a new separate company in Widnes. In 1891 the McKechnie Brothers set up a copper and silver refining works in the town and moved on to copper sulphate production two years later in 1893.

The foundry industry was also expanding in Widnes as the demand for cast-iron vessels for use in the chemical industry increased. Thomas Robinson had originally set up The Widnes Foundry in Lugsdale near to the railway line. As demand for his work increased he opened a larger premises near a farm called Brook House, close to Bowers Brook, on the east side of the railway. Robinson's new foundry had the advantage of having the first steam-driven overhead travelling crane for handling the heavy ladles of molten metal. This foundry could also claim the distinction of having manufactured the first private locomotive used in Widnes, which was commissioned by John Hutchinson.

On Robinson's heels came The Ditton Brook Iron Company, which was formed in 1862, for the smelting and manufacture of iron *"in all or any of its various branches"*. This company, which traded under the brand name *"Ditton"*, was a manufacturer of plant for collieries and chemical works. The list of subscribers to the company is interesting, as it demonstrates how entrepreneurs of those times often branched out into other areas.

Samuel Stock, St. Helens (Colliery owner)
David Gamble, St. Helens (Manufacturing Chemist)
James Haddock, Ravenhead Colliery, St. Helens
William Thorburn, Ditton Brook (Iron Manufacturer)
Joseph Henry Robinson, Whitehaven (Iron Master)
Edward Pierpoint, Liverpool (Coal Agent)
William Blackmore, Liverpool (Solicitor)

Industry

Some of the people named are worth further mention. David Gamble, who later became Sir David Gamble when he was created Companion of the Order of the Bath in 1887, was born in Dublin in 1823. He was the first Mayor of St. Helens on its incorporation in 1868 and later donated land on which the Gamble Institute was built. He served 25 years as Colonel of the 2nd Volunteer movement of the Lancashire Regiment.

William Thorburn lived at Ditton Brook House. He had numerous interests in the iron trade in this country and abroad. He was also involved in the Spanish iron trade and was a director of the Bilbao Iron Company. His interests in Britain included works in Scotland, North Wales, Cumberland and Sunderland. He was involved in the Hematite Iron Works in Workington and Cleaton Moor; The Eskett Iron Ore Company in Cumberland; Iron mines near Abergele and a factory at Ruabon in North Wales. It would appear, from information in the 1871 and 1881 census returns for Ditton and Halebank, that he was instrumental in bringing workers to Widnes from many of those places.

James Haddock, of the Ravenhead Colliery in St. Helens, has the dubious distinction of being remembered mainly for one quote *"St. Helens is a place where they are licensed to make smells".* Perhaps it is also interesting to note, when looking at how businessmen of those times diversified, that by the early 1830s many of the colliery owners in and around St. Helens also owned or part-owned salt-works in Cheshire. In addition, many coal proprietors had financial interests in the St. Helens Railway and Canal Companies. Unfortunately, several of them also had some form of involvement with the African slave trade.

Among the numerous small firms that were set up to service the various trades in Widnes was one that survived in the town up until relatively recently. Handley & Beck is a name familiar to most of us of a certain age. I was quite astonished to discover that the firm was originally founded as far back as 1830 when Mr. W. Banton Gibson opened the first premises in Bridge Street, Runcorn. The Widnes, Waterloo Road premises, was bought from John Hutchinson in 1864 and another branch was opened later in Widnes Road. In 1872 the partnership of Mr. Handley and Mr. Beck was formed and continued up until 1896 when Mr. Francis Beck took sole control. He died at the turn of the century and the business passed to his two sons. The firm originally manufactured wrought iron nails for the assorted trades in the area. It survived in Widnes from the early days of the chemical industry right up to the 21st century!

The new alkali industries created serious environmental problems. Clouds of poisonous smoke belched out into the atmosphere and undiluted acid poured unchecked into local brooks. For every ton of soda produced, twelve tons of waste was dumped in toxic mounds in various locations around the town. There had been some attempt to address the problem of atmospheric pollution with legislation in the form of the 1863 *Alkali Works Act,* whereby manufacturers were required to condense at least 95% of the hydrochloric acid gas. The alkali manufacturers did their best to adhere to these regulations but often found it was nigh on impossible. As the acid could not be contained in the works, the next best thing was to disperse the gas over as wide an area as possible in order that its effect might be spread thinly instead of being concentrated. This called into being the tall chimneys that were such a necessary and pronounced feature of the alkali works.

The important subject of working conditions and the pay of alkali workers should also be mentioned here. The process was a dirty and laborious one that had serious detrimental effects on health. W. A. Campbell in his book *"The Chemical Industry"* gives the following description of the various processes in the alkali factory.

"The Saltcake men (known as pot-men) were the roughest men in the works, their job was to charge, rake and empty the saltcake furnaces, in the course of which they were exposed to gushes of hydrochloric acid gas. The saltcake was then trundled into barrows and taken to the black-ash section. R.H. Sherard in his "White Slaves of England" wrote that a saltcake man could be recognised by his toothless mouth and that the saltcake department (decomposing house or pot-house) was characterised by the heaps of bread crusts, which the men could not eat. [30]

The revolver men made the black-ash, and theirs was a responsible job; upon the senior men in this section rested the decision of when to pour the mass. The black-ash was run into bogies; square iron boxes on wheels, and then allowed to cool. Finishing men worked on the lixiviation and crystallization

---

[30] *The Chemical Industry* - W.A. Campbell (Longman) 1971

of soda and sometimes on the treatment with lime to yield caustic soda. It was not a particularly arduous job, but it carried the risk of falling into a vat. The elite of the works, however, were the bleaching powder men, the bleach packers and lime dressers. The lime dresser spread the lime on the floor or on the shelves, an operation which was not dangerous but merely unpleasant; his hands and arms were smeared with grease, his trouser-legs wrapped with sheets of brown paper and theoretically, his face protected by a mask and goggles. The bleach packer raked out the chlorinated lime into casks. He was similarly protected, for he had the additional hazard of chlorine gas to contend with. Bleaching powder men received far higher wages than the other men".

Incidentally, some works, especially the Widnes Alkali Works, used ponies for pulling the bogies. These bogies were full of scorching black-ash and, although conditions for workers was dire in every sense, we should remember that these poor animals were also put to work in appalling conditions of extreme heat and toxic fumes.

The early 1870s was a period of intense industrial activity and increasing population. The reason for this may be due in part to the recovery of the American market after the slump that had been caused by the American Civil War. A published description of Widnes in *Worrall`s Directory of 1876* paints a graphic picture of the town at that time.

"Here are some of the most extensive chemical works in the kingdom, copper smelting works, soap works, locomotive and wagon grease, oil and paint works, lead works, iron foundries, engineering establishments etc. Every facility is afforded for the transmission of the articles manufactured, and the conveyance of the raw material used in the different works both by water and rail. Additional railway accommodation is about to be afforded by the construction of a branch from the Cheshire Lines Committee's railway near Farnworth, connecting the town with the Midland, Great Northern, and Manchester, Sheffield and Lincolnshire systems".

In the 1880s a correspondent for a Manchester Journal wrote about life among the chemicals at Widnes. He started his account by saying that *"there are few people who have not heard of stinking Widnes and its melancholy surroundings, where trees and hedges, and grass alike have the look*

Into The Crucible

of being scorched up as if by fire". The article described the working conditions and general lifestyle of the chemical worker in this town:

> "The conditions under which the workman in the chemical works carries on his daily labour are most injurious, although the death rate is not nearly as high as might be expected. The main harm is done by the vapours which, when inhaled, set up certain and characteristic diseases. For instance, the vapour of sulphuretted hydrogen produces severe diarrhoea, rapid pulse, and symptoms of low or typhoid fever; chlorine produces suffocation, cough, and laboured breathing; vapour of nitric acid produces throat affections; the vapour of muriatic acid will produce disease of the membranes lining the mouth, nose and throat. The work is so detrimental to clothing that many of the men wear suits of paper – some of them having a new one every day.
>
> Taking a stroll through Widnes what most strikes the visitor as peculiar is the complexion of the workers amongst the chemicals. It is a kind of leaden paleness, and around the eyes the majority have a lack lustre appearance that betokens most unhealthy surroundings. Yet muscularly the men seem strong, and move along with anything but the lagging uncertain steps one would expect from their faces.
>
> Talking to one man, a worker among chloride of lime, I asked "is there much drunkenness here among your mates?" "Not so much as you would think", was the reply "considering the thirst our work produces. There are some men who drink a lot of stuff, but at the same time there are a larger number of abstainers. I've been one myself for thirty years, and am and always have been in perfect health. There are not many moderate drinkers in proportion to the number of men. It seems somehow as if when a man got a good start on ale, he went the whole hog and got reckless. In our work, none is the best motto".
>
> The workers of Widnes are like most other workers, the prey of jerry-builders. Some cottages I noticed were so wretchedly flimsy that if there had not been some dozen of them standing together they would inevitably have fallen down. Row after row, street after street, of four and six roomed cottages of one stereotyped pattern gives shelter to the weary workers. I wonder how it is no variety is introduced into workingmen's homes! They all seem to me to be on a dead level of uniformity that is enough to crush every vestige of individuality out of those unfortunate enough to have to dwell in them. I never remarked this more than at Widnes, where the

polluted heavy atmosphere serves to emphasise the evil. I can scarcely wonder at men seeking the warm, brilliant, cosy parlour of the public house".

This account is interesting as it gives an outsider's view of our town. The people who lived here had become acclimatized to this environment. They just got on with their lives however unpleasant their work and surroundings. A different writer tells us that *"in the 1870s and 1880s Farnworth and Appleton stood villages apart, above the smoke and the mist that drifted around the black stalagmites of the chimneys of industrial Widnes"*.

Another record informs us that:

"In 1887, chemical works in Widnes burned 960,000 tons of coal, releasing sulphur dioxide into the air. This combined with rain to form dilute sulphuric acid, which descended on the town. Rivers and streams became polluted with chemical waste. Bowers Brook, which ran under Hutchinson's No. 2. Works in a culvert, was a trout stream in pre-industrial times. With the growth of industry it became an obnoxious sewer".

Despite the previous booming industrial climate, a considerable blow was dealt to the town when The Ditton Brook Iron Works & Foundry suspended operations in 1885. The hardship was felt particularly in the Ditton and Halebank neighbourhoods. At a meeting of the Local Board, Mr. Carey, one of the members, took a gloomy view of the prospects for the town. He expressed a fear that the alkali trade was also in a poor condition and was likely to worsen. He said, *"That there was every probability that before many years were over that old industry of the town would be extinct"*. The following year there was a slight downturn in some local industries. Of course the peculiar position of manufacturing in Widnes meant that even in a minor pinch of bad times the effect was felt across the community. The nature of local industry meant that the Widnes workforce lacked the insulation that would have been provided by a more varied form of employment. At a meeting of *The Prescot Board of Guardians* in February 1886 attention was directed to the number of men who were out of work in Widnes. It was said that:

"The majority of the persons who are paupers, or who receive relief, either regularly or at intervals, are drawn from what we have termed the lower

Into The Crucible

ranks of the working classes, who find their employment, precarious enough it may be, in the chemicals yards and on the various works".

Fortunately, by 1889 the chemical industry had recovered and had expanded again at a considerable rate. Although the town was now offering plentiful employment, the working conditions and hours of work were still causes of great dissatisfaction among the workforce. In November 1889 a union organiser,[31] Mr. P. J. King, held a number of meetings in the town. The purpose of these meetings was to instigate the formation of a local branch of *The Chemical Labourers' Association*. Mr. King had no great difficulty in finding new members among the chemical workers of Widnes. *The Widnes Weekly News* made a full and interesting report of the meeting. I quote below selected extracts from the 7th December 1889 edition of that newspaper.

A PROPOSED CHEMICAL LABOURERS' ASSOCIATION - ANOTHER MEETING HELD AT WIDNES

Last Sunday afternoon a largely attended meeting was held in the old Theatre Royal, Wellington Street, to hear another address from Mr. P. J. King, of London, in favour of forming a Union of chemical labourers in Widnes. The meeting was of a most enthusiastic nature. Mr. King's proposals being received in a very cordial manner. In the course of his address, Mr. King said that at the meeting held in St. Paul's Chambers last week he told them why he had taken up the cause of the chemical labourers, and why he intended to stick to it until such time that he had made it, as he anticipated he would do, a great success. From a statement made to him he thought it was a matter that deserved consideration and that if they would give him some evidence of their sincerity, he would do what they desired. They had given him that evidence of their sincerity, and he was there advocating the chemical labourers' cause. What he had done in St. Helens he intended doing throughout the length and breadth of the land where chemical labour was found (applause). He was pleased to tell them the progress the Union had made since he took it up.

He continued by quoting the number of men joining each week. He said that because of the enthusiasm in Widnes and the number of people attending the meetings, he felt that the success of the union in Widnes was assured. Mr. King also told his audience that:

---

[31] P.J. King was from St. Helens but based in London

Industry

"There was evidence shown that such an institution to improve their unfortunate condition was desired (hear hear!). They meant to secure that no man should work more than eight hours a day, in an enervating and unhealthy atmosphere of the chemical works, and that additional remuneration be paid for any Sunday work they might do (a voice: "very good" and applause). He would give them a picture of a chemical labourer's life which came under his notice a few days ago at the Whiston Workhouse. The tales he listened to, and the sights he saw there would make any man with a heart within him espouse the cause of the chemical labourers, and never desist until he had accomplished all the objects for which that association had been formed. He visited every ward in the workhouse and found 90 per cent of the inmates were chemical labourers suffering from the same complaint, chronic bronchitis, brought on in the discharge of their duties in the chemical yard. They seemed to think it was their lot, from the fact that they never complained. One of the men whom he questioned and who was but 38 years of age, but had the appearance of a man nearer 60, was suffering from that dreadful disease brought on by reason of unhealthy employment in the chemical yards, and yet although so many occupied the pauper's place in the workhouse, there was no one who would lift a hand to better their condition. Another case, which came from Widnes, was a man named McGarry, who had lost both his legs whilst employed in one of the chemical works, and as compensation he received the magnificent sum of £25 ("shame"). If such an association had existed as he wished to establish amongst them, would they have been satisfied with £25 or even £250? ("No")".

The report outlined Mr. King's references to the working hours of the men at The Greenbank Chemical Works in St. Helens who worked 112 hours per week. He then brought their attention to the London dockers who, by uniting in their actions, had succeeded in gaining an increase in their wages. The gas stokers in St. Helens had also formed an organisation that had resulted in a reduction of the working week and an advance in their wages. The report finished with these words:

"What had been granted to the gas stokers could be granted to the chemical labourers in Widnes and St. Helens, because he believed the chemical works paid much better than the works he had just named. Let them stand shoulder to shoulder in the defence of their own rights, and join the Union. Let them rally round those who were willing to lead them and, if they did, the lot of the chemical labourer would be much better than it was at the

present time ("hear hear!"). He was sure they in Widnes would be willing to accept £2 a week and eight hours work a day rather than £3 and work for 96 or 112 hours a week ("hear hear!"). Until they got the eight-hours movement, they would keep waging a war until the masters were compelled to concede to what they wanted. They would never get it until they made a united effort, and in order to do that they must become members of the United Association of Chemical Labourers (A voice: "Shift the lumpers"). The days of the lumpers were numbered, for the first thing the association would tackle would be the lumpers, and the moment the organisation was formed the lumpers would go to the wall[32]. They would do away with the speckers too. They would find that when the Union was in proper working order the labour market would not be over-stocked, but there would be enough for all. In conclusion he appealed to those present to band themselves together for their common good. So far over 200 people in Widnes have expressed a desire to join the Union."[33]

Shortly after this meeting *The Widnes Weekly News* editorial voiced an opinion that incitement for the formation of *The Chemical Labourers' Union* had given rise to trouble in a number of local works. The dischargers in the employment of Messrs. Golding, Davis & Co., had gone on strike for an increase of between 4d to 6d a day. Some of the labourers at Messrs. Hutchinson's Works had stopped work because their demand for an increase in pay had not been met. The joiners at Muspratt & Sons had gone on strike for an increase of 5 shillings a week in their pay. These men had only been receiving 25 shillings a week while other firms had been paying 33 shillings for the same class of work.

By the end of 1890 Mr. King was claiming that his *Chemical & Copper Workers' Union* had 5,000 members. The Union issued its first annual report in 1891. The report included an impressive list of wage increases gained by the Union in a number of factories. In 1892 most of the alkali workers in Lancashire were said to have joined this union[34].

On 18th March 1892 a *"Royal Commission on Labour"* heard evidence relating to the chemical trades. In the Chair was The Right Honourable A.J. Mundella. Other members of that committee included The Duke of

---

[32] *Lumpers* – a system of contracted gang labour.
[33] *Widnes Weekly News* – December 7th 1889
[34] *A Mersey town in the Industrial Revolution* – T. C. Barker and J. R. Harris

Industry

Devonshire, Thomas Mann and Henry Tait. Among those called to give evidence was Mr. King, the Union Organiser. I have, in my own collection, one of the original documents from that meeting, which was subsequently circulated to members of *The Alkali Manufacturers Association*. I include here some of the interesting points from the evidence given by a Mr. Edward Girling and Mr. King.

Mr. Girling spoke at length about the working conditions in a chemical factory. He had brought with him a flannel muzzle of a type commonly worn by alkali workers. He demonstrated to the Committee how the numerous folds of flannel were worn in order to cover the mouth and nostrils to prevent the worker from being gassed. After a description of some of the hazardous working activities in a chemical factory he criticised the procedures in place for a visit from the Factory Inspector. He said that the employers always knew of an impending visit as this was made by a prior arrangement. As a consequence of this notice, the employers usually ordered a clean-up operation before the visit; so the Factory Inspector did not witness the actual conditions of work or the normal everyday procedures. When it was Mr. King's turn to give evidence to The Commission he included a description of various operations in an alkali factory. He said:

"In what we call the powder-room the lime for the bleaching powder is first laid down on the floor of a chamber (about as large as this room perhaps, sometimes larger and longer) about five inches thick. The doors are then sealed up and chlorine gas is put into the room, and it is left sealed until such time as the lime absorbs the chlorine; then the men, wearing muzzles, such as the one you have seen exhibited this morning, go into the chambers and they put what they call the bleaching powder down through shoots. There are casks underneath to receive the bleaching powder; then underneath all those chambers that I have had an opportunity of seeing, it is an open space. The powder-packing chamber is enclosed, and there is a very slight draught. Sometimes men will have to go in with these muzzles and run out in a few moments, or run out in half an hour; some of them drop down. If they inhale through their nostrils at all it has a very bad effect; they become gassed, and sometimes have to lie up for two or three days. Then they receive no pay.

The sensation they complain of is in the throat – a choking sensation, as if they were asphyxiated. They must inhale through all these rolls of flannel and exhale through the nostrils. But in addition to this muzzle through which they must breathe, they must wear goggles over their eyes; and then, any portion of the skin that is exposed, they put tallow or grease on, and most of these men cannot eat any food until they take a stimulant, whiskey or rum".

Mr. King offered further graphic descriptions of the chemical processes and working conditions. He also remarked upon the damaging effects on nearby residential areas. He told the Committee that those living in a town such as Widnes or St. Helens, in close proximity to factories, were more readily afflicted with bronchitis than people living in other districts.

The hours of work and rates of pay of chemical workers were also subjects on the agenda. Mr. King was called upon again to give evidence to the Committee in these matters. When asked what the hours of labour were in a chemical factory, Mr. King said that the men averaged 84 hours a week. He said this was usually 56 hours one week and 112 in another, or 168 hours in a fortnight, or an average of 84 hours a week. He told The Commission that the working hours were distributed in the following manner:

"The man begins his fortnight's round on the Monday morning; he works, on the Monday, 9 hours; on the Tuesday, 10 hours; on the Wednesday, 10 hours; on the Thursday, 10 hours; on the Friday, 10 hours; and on the Saturday, 7 hours; a total of 56 hours per day-week. Then comes the night-week - which follows the above. He works on the Monday, 24 hours; on the Tuesday, 14 hours; on the Wednesday, 14 hours; on the Thursday, 14 hours; on the Friday, 14 hours; on the Saturday, 13 hours; on the Sunday, 19 hours".

Mr. King was asked if the men were in constant employment during the whole of the 112 hours. He told The Commission that, during the 24 hours, the men would work three charges of 6 hours and 15 minutes making a total of 18 hours and 45 minutes out of the 24 hours. He explained that it took 3 hours solid labour to bring out a charge but the men have to be raking continuously and paying attention to their charges, and working just as hard as if they were actually taking out the charges.

Industry

"The men, to earn their wages, are expected to, and in fact must, turn out three charges in the 24 hours, so that the time occupied in downright bodily labour amounts at the very lowest calculation to 18 hours and 45 minutes in 24 hours".

The questioner, Mr. Mundella, was incredulous. He said *"surely a man cannot do that continuously for a week"* to which Mr. King replied *"It is wonderful what men will do when they are put to it. I am astounded myself at what the chemical workers are able to do under the conditions under which they have to labour."*

On the question of pay, Mr. King said that the wages averaged between 30 shillings and 35 shillings a week for 84 hours a week shift, the year round. He said sometimes they were paid by the amount they do. *"For instance, the salt cake men are paid principally about 3 shillings a ton; the boiler man gets £1.15s. a week"*.

Mr. King then outlined his union's ambitions regarding a reduction in the working hours to 8 hours a day. It was their desire that Parliament should legislate for fixed hours of labour. He cited the Brunner Mond factory at Winnington and the Gaskell Deacon Works at Widnes as two examples of factories that had accepted the 8-hour system. He claimed that the adoption of a "reduced hours system" had had no detrimental effect on production in either of these factories.[35]

Membership of this and other unions continued to grow. For the sum of 6d per week members were eligible to receive strike and lockout pay as well as a death benefit of £3 for the family of the deceased member. The unions accomplished a great deal over a relatively short period of time, including the reduction of the working week, which Mr. King had outlined as one of his main objectives. Thomas Mann, who was a member of that *Royal Commission on Labour* in 1892, was elected Secretary of the new *Independent Labour Party* in 1894. Tom Mann subsequently became a founder member of the *"Eight Hour League"*. This group was influential in convincing all the Trade Unions to adopt the statutory eight-hour day as one of their core policies. Interestingly,

---

[35] *Minutes of Evidence taken before the Royal Commission on Labour (Chemical Trades)* - at Westminster Hall 18th March 1892 - *"Alkali Manufacturers Association Copy"* (Jean M. Morris – personal collection)

the number of hours in a working week appears to have varied according to the type of job. Similarly the wages cover a wide range of payments.

The following list refers to the average working hours and wages paid to employees of The Widnes Alkali Works in 1892.[36]

Job	Hours	Wages
Vitriol Burners	84	36s.2d.
Finishers	66	42s.0d
Chlorine Stillmen	72	44s.0d
Saltcake Men	72	45s.0d
Revolver Men	72	46s.0d
Lime Dressers	56	55s.0d
Bleach Packers	36	64s.0d

It is apparent from the above chart that the Bleach Packer was the kingpin, working least hours for highest pay. The Bleach Packers had special terms of employment both in wages and hours. They did not work shifts and their daily hours were short because of the arduous and unpleasant nature of the job. They were paid accordingly. It should be said that the wages quoted above, taken from The Alkali Inspector's Report, should, I believe, be taken as an approximation as wage differences between various firms were significant. Dr. Hardie in his *"History of the Chemical Industry in Widnes"* tells us that:

"Pyrites burner men at Pilkington Works received 21s.6d, while at the Golding-Davis Works the wage was 32s.8d. Weldon Bleach Packers at these two works received 63s. and 60s. per week respectively. Saltcake men got the highest wages at Gaskell-Deacon Works and the lowest at Golding-Davis`s".

The contrast in wages paid by different employers obviously meant that employment in some factories were preferable to others. On the other hand, we do not know the full picture. The conditions or duties

---

[36] *Alkali Inspectors 29th Report.* (Hours of duty based on average of day and night shifts).

Industry

performed in these works may have differed greatly from factory to factory.

The modern *Health & Safety at Work Acts* and the introduction of "Safety Officers" and employee training in safe working practices, mean that today, thankfully, fatalities and serious accidents at work are almost a rarity. In the 19th and early decades of the 20th century sadly this was not the case. In fact, casualties and fatalities seem to have been accepted as a matter of course. *The Widnes Weekly News* reported fatalities and accidents in local factories with amazing regularity. In the short period between October 1881 and July 1882 there were numerous incidents reported.

Fatal Accident: (WWN - 23rd July 1881)
On Wednesday last an accident of a very serious character occurred at Messrs. Hay Gordon & Company's chemical works. It appears that a youth, aged about 17 years, named Hulse, was engaged hooking some wagons when, owing to some unaccountable reason, he fell under the wagon, the wheels passing over him, mutilating his body in a fearful manner. He was removed with all speed to the Accident Hospital, where he died soon after admittance.

Accident to a Salt Cake Man at Widnes: (WWN - 30th July 1881)
A married man, 38 years of age, employed as a salt-cake man at Messrs. Gaskell & Deacon's chemical works, met with a serious accident on Monday evening. He was drawing the fire out of his furnace when a large quantity of hot cinders suddenly fell into the ash-hole. This caused the hot water contained in the ash-pan to splash onto the man, Brantwood, causing terrible injury to his arms and chest. He was conveyed to the Accident Hospital where his injuries were attended to.

Fatal Accident at a Chemical Works: (WWN - 1st October 1881)
An accident, which unfortunately has proved fatal, occurred to a labourer named John Walsh, 24 years of age, at the works of Messrs. Gaskell, Deacon & Co., chemical manufacturers, on Sunday, 4th September. It would appear that at the time of the accident the deceased was wheeling a barrow, heavily laden with black ash, along a plank over the liquor vats. A piece of ash seems to have fallen off in front of the wheel, which it is supposed the deceased ran his barrow against, causing him to lose his equilibrium and precipitating him into the vat of liquor below. The liquor was very weak,

being only two degrees in strength, but was heated to 140 degrees and this no doubt was the real cause of death.

Horrible Accident at Chemical Works: (WWN - 29th July 1882)
An inquest was held at the Mersey Hotel, Mersey Road, on the body of Peter Kinzie, 19 years of age, who was employed as a labourer at Messrs. Muspratt`s chemical works, and who fell into a caustic filter on the 16th inst., whilst engaged in drawing the liquor from the lime. The deceased was kneeling on the edge of the filter, when the stick he held in his hand went from him, and when attempting to catch it he fell in head first.

Within a space of just a few weeks in 1889 the following accidents occurred:

Hall Bros. & Shaw's Works, a falling object struck a man. He received serious head and neck injuries, knocking him unconscious. Earlier in the same year, this man's brother had lost both his arms in an industrial accident.

The Mersey Copper Works, a labourer had his leg severed when a metal plate fell on him.

The Portland Cement Works, a man fell and received serious injuries.

The Atlas Chemical Works, an 18year old man was crushed to death.

Widnes Alkali Works, an 18year old man was scalded to death by vitriol.

Less than a week after the tragedy at the Atlas Chemical Works a 43year old man called John McDermott, of 20 Victoria Street, was crushed to death by an iron girder in Widnes Foundry. Local Doctor, John O`Keeffe, was called to the scene but the man was dead when he arrived. John McDermott's body was wrapped in a blanket and taken to his home close by *"where a terrible scene was witnessed, the anguish of his poor widow and children being distressing in the extreme".*

Regrettably accidents and fatalities continued to happen with alarming frequency.

Scalding Fatality (WWN - 15th October 1892)
On Wednesday afternoon a man named William Fallon, aged 32, of Nelson Street died at the Accident Hospital from injuries sustained at Messrs. McKechnie's Copper Works, Ditton Road, on the previous day. The deceased was a furnace man. At about 2 o'clock on Tuesday afternoon, together with a man named Patrick Gorry, he was engaged in pouring molten copper into a pan of hot water when it exploded, dashing a large quantity of boiling water onto Fallon.

One of the worst industrial accidents in the area happened at an earlier date, on 6th October 1876. This accident was the result of an explosion at the Ditton Brook Iron Works which killed seven people including a 10year old child. The dead were named as:

> James Crawley, aged 55 years – married
> Patrick Michael Jeffers, aged 18 years – unmarried
> Henry Powell, aged 54 years – married
> John Maddock, aged 27 years – married
> Joseph Plumley, aged 20 years – unmarried
> Joseph Hill, aged 45 years – married
> Joseph Hill (junior) aged 16 years – apprentice
> Phoebe Hill, aged 10 years – child

The Hill family suffered the loss of a father, brother and sister. The little girl had been in the habit of taking her father and brother's breakfast into the workplace every day. All the dead were sitting eating their morning meal in front of the furnace at 8.00 a.m. when the explosion occurred. All except one was killed instantly, unfortunately this man died from his injuries a month later.

In February 1882 a Widnes worker, John Mannion, brought an action against Messrs. Gaskell, Deacon & Company, under the *Employers' Liability Act.* The case against the Company was in its second hearing as the Jury in the previous case were unable to reach a verdict. The plaintiff was a mixer at the Gaskell Deacon Works and part of his duty was to convey materials in wagons along an elevated tramway to the revolving furnaces. This tramway was supported by a number of iron pillars. One of these pillars had been removed and the ground beneath it had been excavated in order to repair the foundations. A wooden pillar had been substituted and placed upon beams stretched across the excavation. During the night shift, while Mannion was riding on a wagon on the tramway, the whole structure collapsed and the plaintiff fell from a height of over twenty feet. He received severe head and back injuries that left him severely and permanently disabled. It was suggested that the collapse of the tramway was due to the negligent manner in which the wooden pillar had been put up. It was also implied that the wooden structure was not strong enough to hold the tramway. At the time of the accident the plaintiff was receiving 5s.5d. a day in wages. The maximum damages, based upon this sum, were to be the equivalent of 3 years wages, a sum fixed at £260. Because this young man was unlikely to be able to work again, it seemed not unreasonable for him to take such action against his former employer.

John Mannion faced a formidable opponent in Gaskell Deacon & Co. The Company produced a long line of eminent witnesses in its defence. The people appearing for the Company included Major James Cross; Robert Carlisle, a Manchester builder; Edward Reed, a surveyor and architect based at Westminster Chambers Liverpool; Mr. J.M. Wilson, a mining and land surveyor; Mr. A.G. Kyle the engineer from Messrs. Hutchinson & Co., Widnes; and Mr. Pritchard the Manager of the Tharsis Sulphur & Copper Co., Widnes. Mr. Deacon himself also gave evidence. All these witnesses gave unanimous testimony that the wooden pillar had been constructed carefully, correctly, and safely. Mr. Deacon however, was unable to account for the accident. It seems odd that representatives from other companies were called to give evidence on behalf of Gaskell Deacon as they were unlikely to have observed this structure prior to its collapse. Perhaps manufacturers were banding together in order to prevent a precedent for future would-be plaintiffs.

In the last stages of the Mannion case the foreman of the Jury said that in the opinion of the Jury there was no gross negligence on the part of the defendants, but that they thought the plaintiff should have adequate compensation for the injuries he sustained. The foreman said that one of the Jury wanted to know whether negligence affected compensation. The Judge said they could not consider compensation until they found negligence. After further consultation the foreman said the Jury were now agreed that there had been *"a little bit of negligence"* and assessed the damages at £50. It was later reported that *"four out of the five Jurymen wished to make the damages £100 instead of £50 but they were "instructed" to do otherwise"*.

Industry

In John Mannion's case there was clearly some fault on behalf of the employer, which was attributable to the unstable nature of the structure. On the other hand, some accidents happened because employees were inexperienced and unaware of the dangers associated with the environment of a chemical yard. The fact that so many employees arrived *"straight from the boat"* with little or no industrial experience, probably contributed to the accident figures. This was certainly a factor in the case of a young boy called James Riley. This 20year old boy had been in England just 10 days when he was killed in an accident at the Hutchinson Works. At the inquest into his death, his uncle, Michael Riley of West Bank Street, told the Coroner that his nephew had only arrived from Ireland 10 days ago. On the Monday he commenced work at Messrs. Hutchinson & Co., and on Tuesday he was crushed between two wagons. He saw his nephew soon after he was injured but he never spoke and died shortly after being removed to the Accident Hospital. A verdict of accidental death was returned. The Coroner remarked *"that it was a pity contractors employed inexperienced men when there were plenty in the town who would do the work efficiently"*.

One accident which received prominent newspaper coverage involved the son of Neil Mathieson who was the owner of Mathieson & Sons. 25-year old Douglas Mathieson was escorting an Austrian friend on a tour of the works when they stopped to watch a massive iron girder being moved into place. The iron pillar was to be the roof support for a new building. It was being raised into position by means of a powerful derrick but unfortunately one of the stakes holding the derrick gave way causing the girder to crash to the ground. Douglas Mathieson was directly below the girder when it fell. He suffered massive internal injuries and died almost immediately. A few months before this his brother, Thomas Mathieson, was almost killed when he tried, unsuccessfully, to save the life of a worker who had been overcome by noxious vapours and fallen into a vat of acid.

The serious accidents and fatalities associated with the chemical and foundry industries in Widnes are far too numerous to list. Nevertheless, we should not think that Widnes alone had more than her fair share of these incidents. All industrial towns had high industrial accident figures. In neighbouring St. Helens an explosion at the Kurtz Alkali Factory killed 5 men and injured 137 in 1890. At nearby Bold Colliery 5 miners were killed in 1905 and on the 18th August 1908 a dreadful explosion occurred at the Maypole Colliery in Abram, near Wigan. That disaster claimed 76 lives, many of them Irishmen.

The disturbing statistics relating to accidents and work related deaths were impossible to ignore. As a consequence, the Government, in an attempt to reduce accidents in the workplace, instituted a number of new measures. *The Factory Acts* which were introduced between 1878 and 1895 began to change the layout of chemical works. Soda vats were to be covered, gangways and gangplanks were to be fenced and dangerous places illuminated. Where Weldon chlorine was used, tests had to be made on the chlorine content of the atmosphere and the figures recorded in a book. Respirators had to be provided for rescue purposes and places were to be set aside for washing down those splashed with caustic[37].

When discussing industrial accidents one naturally assumes that these incidents were confined to workmen. Obviously most accidents in factories did involve workers but contrary to this belief this was not always the case. The absence of "Works Security" or any form of visitor control meant that members of the public were allowed free access to the factories during working hours. An accepted practice was women or children taking the workers' dinners, or brew cans, into the workplace at meal times. Sometimes wives or children would even sit and keep the workmen company during their meal breaks. Now and again wives went into factories on pay-days to meet their husbands in order to obtain money. Some may have feared that unless they did this their husbands would pass a large proportion of his wages across the bar on his way home. Another common occurrence was the habit of taking small children into certain areas of the chemical factory to inhale the fumes from the saltcake process. The fumes were thought to be a cure for whooping cough and numerous other childhood ailments. Unfortunately, this lax attitude contributed to serious accidents that involved visiting women or children. Even from the earliest days instances of children being killed or injured in chemical works were not a rare event.

The following newspaper report from *The Liverpool Mercury* of April 19th 1850 illustrates this type of event. As the mother had gone to meet her husband at the office one might assume that it was pay-day and she

---

[37] *"Dangerous Trades* - T. Oliver (London 1902)

Industry

had gone for money. From this tragic account we can see that the mother of the children seemed totally oblivious to the dangers all around. In fact this may have been a routine procedure for her; something she had done many times before without problem. Although this particular report does not say so, in fact, later reports confirm that the eight year old child also succumbed to his injuries and died shortly afterwards.

> SHOCKING ACCIDENT.—On Monday last an inquest was held before Charles E. Driffield, Esq., the deputy coroner, at the house of Mr. Gerard, the sign of the Angel and Elephant, in Widnes, on view of the body of John Jennion, a child, aged fifteen months. The mother, with another child, aged about eight years, and deceased, went to Mr. John Hutchinson's chemical works, in Widnes, on Saturday evening last, about five o'clock, to meet her husband, and she left the two children standing eight or nine yards from a large fire whilst she went to the office, and just as she returned to them a brick or stone fell into a large panfull of boiling chemical liquid, and caused some to overflow into the fire. An explosion took place, which threw out the whole of the fire upon the woman and the two children. Deceased died almost immediately, the eldest child is not expected to recover, and the poor woman is dreadfully scalded. Verdict, accidental death.

The Victorian journalist, Robert H. Sherard, was able to take full advantage of this ease of access to workplaces. He visited local factories, talked first hand to workers and was able to view, close up, the conditions and operating processes. He said, "*I visited these factories as a trespasser and at a trespasser's risk*". Similar reports from the pen of Thomas Mann, the Labour activist, appeared in a publication called "*The Labour Elector*" in its editions of November 1888 and March 1889. Thomas Mann, who was working at that time as an investigative journalist, took up temporary undercover employment at the Brunner Mond Works in Winnington. His articles described awful working conditions in the factory but, in addition, he also made a scathing personal attack on Sir John Brunner.

The fact that John Brunner, a large-scale employer of labour, was also a Member of Parliament made him a prime target of Socialist critics.

Some detractors thought that Brunner's position in society was incompatible with the ideals he propounded. In response to Thomas Mann's stinging criticism, Sir John Brunner was compelled to issue a pamphlet and write an open letter to *"The Times"*. He strenuously denied the claims made against him personally and disputed allegations relating to employment practices at his Winnington works. It is only fair to say that John Brunner was a very good employer who provided numerous welfare benefits for his workers and also had an extremely enlightened attitude to Trade Unionism. He told his employees *"that nothing would please me better than that you should band together for your common good"*[38]

Working conditions and pay were not the only causes of discontent among workers. Those in positions of power, even of somewhat limited power, sometimes abused their positions. Although the employer or works manager was the main decision maker, foremen also had a certain level of influence. Unfortunately some foremen, especially those whose wives had small corner shops, exploited this minor advantage by putting undue pressure on their workmen. An example of this type of intimidation is revealed in a letter written to *The Widnes Weekly News* on November 5th 1892 by a man called Tom Buckton. Unfortunately, Mr. Buckton did not give the name of the chemical works or the foreman.

A SCANDALOUS IMPOSITION:
LETTER TO THE EDITOR OF THE WEEKLY NEWS
Dear Sir,

To whom it may concern. This morning a friend handed to me a letter he had sent to him from his foreman in the chemical works, who is a tradesman. The letter read to the effect that if you do not lay out your wages in my shop you can look out for a fresh job. Sir, it is an abuse to deprive hard working men of the liberty to spend their hard earnings where they think best. I wonder what chemical masters will allow their foremen to do to the workingmen next.

The numerous *Royal Commissions on Labour,* or formal investigations into the polluting nature of the alkali trade, provide a glimpse of what

---

[38] Stephen E. Koss - *"Sir John Brunner: Radical Plutocrat 1842-1919.* (Cambridge University Press) 1970

life may have been like for workers. Whilst some of these reports show shocking conditions and an apparent lack of protection for the workforce, there is no doubt that the articles written in 1896, by Robert H. Sherard for *Pearson's Magazine*, give us the most explicit and disturbing view of the working environment of the Widnes alkali worker. His observations include not only the appalling working conditions but also the unhealthy surroundings in which the workers and their families lived. I quote from one article:

"In the old days, before the alkali works were established in Widnes, this town was known as Woodend, nor is it very, very long ago since quite a pleasant bit of wood stood on the muddy waste which extends its dismal, swamp-like surface for hundreds of yards to the left of the railway embankment.

Now, except on the heights of Appleton, where the churchyard is, and where a careful farmer has coaxed some grass into being, there is no green anywhere – not one touch on which to rest the eye weary of blackish-brown, and brownish-black, of soot and mud, and the foul slimes thrown up by the sewers or set down by the poisoned air.

So malodorous is this Woodend town that, when the south wind is blowing, its obnoxious presence makes itself felt many miles away. Windows are closed, vinaigrettes are brought out, and evil things are said of the south wind. For miles around the poisonous air kills and kills, and so frequent are the claims for compensation made by neighbouring farmers for their acid-eaten crops against the factory owners, that these manufacturers have found it a matter of economy to buy up the land in the sphere of influence of their sulphuretted hydrogen and other gases".

Robert Sherard also tells us:

"There are nine doctors in Widnes, and there is work for them all amongst the men. The oldest practitioner in the town is Doctor O'Keeffe, who has attended the chemical works in his capacity as doctor to the "Mersey Chemical Works Club" for upwards of thirty-one years. It was thanks to his efforts and repeated applications to the Government that about four years ago a stop was put to the too liberal diffusion of sulphuretted hydrogen gas, which was slowly poisoning the people in the town. That it still breathes its lethal breath over Widnes may be seen in the large patches of metallic bluish

green slime which cover the muddy expanses here and there, but the nuisance has been greatly diminished. "It is a terribly poisonous gas" he said, "and but one of several, which in these alkali works shorten life".

Mr. Sherard also described the awful conditions inside the works, where men were exposed to the great heat of the furnaces while simultaneously subjected to the icy cold of the ill-covered and draughty buildings. He quoted one worker who told him that: *"When you are working, you have one half of your body in the North Pole and the other half in Hell".* One of the salt-cake men, who had been working on the process for over eighteen years, told the journalist that: *"I am standing eight hours on end in front of a fiery furnace, melting with heat, drawing, shoving, and turning the salt with an iron bar, which weighs fifty-six pounds. The heat is so intense that I am perspiring all the time. I have two towels to wipe myself on. One is drying whilst I am using the other. I'm not often hungry, and the gas makes me sick".* He continued by telling Sherard that he was compelled to live for weeks on end on nothing but milk and eggs *"as my stomach won't stand anything solid".* He added *"Not a man of my time but what is gone off or in the workhouse".*

Sherard concluded by saying that:

"The cemeteries where the workers are buried are at Appleton and Wiston (sic), and it is amongst the men a standing pleasantry to say that if these men were dug up they would supply the raw material for a chemical yard. "You could get tons of alkali out of their bones and vats of acid". The laugh goes around. But Roger is their best joke, as Roger is their worst enemy. Roger is their name for the chlorine gas, which, pumped onto slaked lime, transforms this into bleaching powder. Roger is a green gas, and so poisonous that the men who pack the bleaching powder into the barrels, work with goggles on their eyes and twenty thicknesses of flannel over their mouths. They can pack but a few minutes at a time. A "feed" of this gas kills a man in an hour".

We should not imagine that the industrial scene was all doom and gloom. There are numerous reports of works outings to various places. In July 1881 the employees and families of Messrs. Gossage and Sons had their annual workmen's trip. They were given a choice of destinations including Blackpool and Rhyl; they opted instead for Windermere. It seems that, to the Gossage workers anyway, the

Industry

beautiful calming landscape of the Lake District was preferable to the bright breezy attractions of a Victorian seaside town. They apparently had a wonderful day. During the same month a large number of men employed at Messrs. Mort, Liddell & Company's chemical works, together with their families, left Widnes for Blackpool by special train. *"The excursionists arrived in Blackpool in good time, the weather being favourable, they spent a pleasant day amid the many attractions that the town affords"*.

From the 1850s onwards Runcorn's already prosperous maritime business was boosted by the rapid growth of industrial Widnes. Later, the abolition of the "navigation laws" meant that small foreign vessels were able to come into Runcorn Dock for loading salt for export. Directories listed numerous master mariners, sail makers, rope makers, ships chandlers, ship builders and ship broking businesses in that town. The occupations associated with the river were clearly evident in Widnes also. *Slater's Trade Directory* of 1895 lists a large number of West Bank residents employed as watermen; mariners; master-mariners; flatmen and sail makers. Like Runcorn, Widnes also had a number of boat-building enterprises. These included Edward Gandy of Terrace Road and Frederick J. Bibby who had his business on the canal bank. Other Widnes ship-builders of that era were Samuel Stock and William Jamieson. The revitalisation of boat-building in Widnes was due in no small way to the new chemical trade which had brought about an increase in barge traffic. This trade created a strong demand for flat bottom barges to transport raw materials and products. Most of these barges were built locally and were specifically designed to navigate the local canals and the shallows of the River Mersey.

It is worth saying that, despite the fact that the flats were primary intended for canal and river work, many of them sailed further afield and were involved in coastal trade around Britain. In later times some flats were converted to schooners and made long sea voyages. Unfortunately flats that had been transformed into schooners were dangerously instable in bad weather due to having so much extra canvas. As a consequence a great many were involved in accidents and sinkings. One local vessel, reputedly the largest boat ever built at Widnes, was wrecked off the coat of Rio Grande do Sol in Brazil on 26th September 1884. This was a 172 ton vessel named "Janie" which was constructed at the Widnes shipyard of Samuel Stock in 1875.

Into The Crucible

The river, and the crafts that sailed on it, played a vital role in the industrial scene at the south end of the town. The men who worked on the flat bottomed barges, generally known as "flats", collected and discharged raw materials and product to the works along the dock area. The flats also transported sand from the banks off Eastham, on the Wirral, to Widnes Dock where it was unloaded into wagons and transported by rail to St. Helens for use in the glass-making industry. The sandhookers job was difficult and often dangerous. The men would run the boat onto the sandbank and fill her in time to float on the next tide. It was said that in order to secure a cargo the men had to work up to their armpits in water. This must have been particularly hard and unpleasant work in winter. The carrying capacity of the flats varied from fifty tons to one hundred tons. In 1889 there were twenty-five local flats engaged in the sandhooking business. As each boat required three or four men this meant that close on a hundred local men earned their livelihood in this manner. The main owners of the "sandhooking flats" were Messrs. W. Cooper & Co., of Widnes; Messrs. Hill & Gandy of St. Helens; and Messrs. Clare & Ridgeway of Sankey.

There were two places for discharging the sand at Widnes, one in the canal close to the iron bridge and the other in the Widnes Dock. At both these places there was a steam crane provided especially for the purpose of unloading the sand, which was transferred from the boats to the wagons in huge buckets. In the canal the sandhookers were allowed to unload their own flats but in the dock the work was done by the Railway Company's own workmen. The sandhookers wages at this time, apart from discharging, was between 10 shillings and 12 shillings. Obviously the number of trips varied with the state of the tide. Sometimes they only managed to make one trip in a week, sometimes they made two trips and if they were very lucky they might have managed to make five trips in a fortnight. However, sometimes it might have been the case that they would not be able to make even one single trip in a week. This meant that at times they did not earn anything.

Industry

Flats on the Mersey c.1900

In the summer of 1889 the flatmen who worked as sandhookers went on strike. Their main grievance was against The London and North Western Railway Company who employed their own dischargers at Widnes Dock. This was the point of contention. The flatmen claimed they were obliged to stand around idle for long periods while the boats were being unloaded. The flatmen felt that the railway company's workers did not always discharge the sand as quickly as they should and, in consequence, the flats often missed a tide and were forced to lay

Into The Crucible

up in dock longer than necessary. They felt this situation could be avoided if they were allowed to unload their own boats. They had some dialogue with the Company but to no avail.

During the first few days of the strike very few flats went down the river as some of the more resolute strikers had threatened to throw overboard anyone who continued to work. There was a great deal of intimidation and the threats were taken so seriously that extra police were brought into the neighbourhood in case of trouble. The strike of the sandhookers was viewed as potentially very serious because of the possible knock-on effect in other industries. The glass industry in St. Helens relied on the sand deliveries from Widnes Dock, although it was stated that the glass manufacturers usually kept a large stock of sand in hand and would not suffer initially from the effects of the strike. Fortunately, the strike appears to have been short-lived and there was no actual violence. At a meeting between the men and the flat-owners a few days later it was decided that they should take joint action against the Railway Company. However, the ill feeling created by intimidation caused some serious and lasting divisions in the community.

The 1891 census returns for West Bank list a large number of men who worked in water-related employment. Among those whose registered occupation was given specifically as a "Barge Waterman" or "Flatman" were the following men. Interestingly, apart from a few, most come from Widnes or neighbouring regions. There are no men of Irish or Lithuanian origin.

NAME	PLACE OF BIRTH
JOHN STREET	
Thomas Hayes	Widnes
William Day	Staffordshire
William Whittaker	Runcorn
Samuel Hatton	Warrington
John Williamson	St. Helens
William Williamson	Widnes
James Mellor	Widnes
Owen Davies	Abergele
George Holden	Sankey

Industry

LITTLE JOHN STREET
William Fildes   St. Helens

WHITE STREET
John Owen   Runcorn

TERRACE ROAD
Thomas Davies   Widnes
John Mercer   Widnes
William Ashton   Llandulas, Wales

BEAUMONT STREET
Peter Darlington   Frodsham
James Grayson   St. Helens
Edward Jones   Widnes
Daniel Lamb   Widnes
Richard Williams   St. Helens
William Brown   Runcorn
James Mason   Widnes
John Davies   Widnes
Thomas O'Neil   Runcorn

BANK STREET
George Baxter   Runcorn

DAVIES STREET
Robert Carmichael   Scotland

MERSEY ROAD
William Kirby   Sankey

HURST STREET
Enos Beswick   Widnes
Owen Beswick   Birkenhead
Thomas Atherton   Northwich
Frank Atherton   Widnes

OAKLAND STREET
Thomas Williams   Sankey
Walter Abram   Widnes

WRIGHT STREET
George Wymont   Huyton

CHURCH STREET
John Mellor   Northwich
Thomas Albiston   Frodsham

PITT STREET
Joseph Woods   Liverpool

WELLINGTON STREET
John Brawley   Widnes

The subject of alkali waste continued to be a major headache for both the alkali manufacturers and the Widnes Local Board. In November 1884, under the terms of the *Alkali Act*, a number of waste heaps were examined by an Alkali Inspector and some members of the Local Board. They found that several heaps were giving off a considerable quantity of gas and that one heap at West Bank was proving to be particularly troublesome. The deputation also found that an amount of waste, which had only been tipped a few hours earlier, was already hot and emitting an unacceptable amount of gas. By 1889 The Board reported that they were now carrying out daily supervision. They were enforcing more stringent rules on how the waste was deposited and ensuring that there were proper drainage precautions in place. Despite these efforts to control the amount of waste and manage its effects, the troublesome deposits continued to extend in the direction of Ditton to the west.

Part of a Local Board report from 1889 said that:

> *"The piece of ground near Central Station was nearly full up and that such a nuisance had been caused here, and complained of so much by the shopkeepers and dwellers in this part of town, that dumping of waste had now ceased there".*

In that same year some local companies started to use the sulphur recovery process that had been patented by Mr. A. M. Chance. This was to be a means of profitably utilising some of the alkali waste. Messrs. Sullivan & Co. had a prior arrangement with the patentee and thought they had a considerable start and advantage over other firms. Even so, despite this prior agreement, companies like Golding, Davies & Co. were hot on their heels and quick to adopt the process. Other works soon followed suit and of the sixteen works producing alkali waste in Widnes and Runcorn, ten of them adopted Chance's process at that time. Chance's original plan had been to use his process for vitriol production. He had only contemplated the possibility of recovering sulphur when he discovered that C. F. Claus had invented a kiln for the removal of sulphur from coal gas. With the introduction of the Claus Kiln into his own process he was able to recover sulphur from the sulphuretted hydrogen waste.

Apart from the obvious environmental advantages of Chance's process, another incentive to produce sulphur was that the Trade Board of the United States had recently ranked sulphur as a raw material. This meant that they would allow it to be admitted duty free. D.W. Hardie tells us that *"post-Chance waste was practically innocuous, consisting almost wholly of calcium carbonate"*. It was also said that in 1893 the Alkali Inspector was unable to detect any sulphuretted hydrogen from the chimneys of nine principal works in Widnes.

The booming industrial climate in Widnes took a sharp knock in the early 1890s when the town experienced a serious depression. The population figure, which had risen steadily over the previous decades, now started to decline as men moved to other parts of the country where work was more plentiful. The population of Widnes in 1891 was 30,011 but by 1901 it had been reduced to 28,580. Ten years later the town was in recovery and the figure was up to 31,541. The depression of the 1890s was mainly a result of tariffs on exports to the United States and Russia. Cheaper imports also had a serious effect and profits in the alkali trade fell drastically. In 1891 Hutchinson's No.2. Works was almost at shutdown and 400 men were laid off. The United Alkali Company, which had 14 Works in Widnes, reduced their workforce by almost a quarter.[39]

A miners' strike in 1893, which resulted in a coal shortage, caused further job losses adding to the towns rising unemployment figure. The hardship was so severe that local Church organisations opened soup

---

[39] George E. Diggle *"A History of Widnes"* (Corporation of Widnes) 1961

kitchens to feed the hungry and some shops gave away free bread. The local Co-operative Society did their bit by allocating 200 loaves a week to the fund. At a meeting of Widnes Council in September of that year the Councillors discussed the matter of relief work for the unemployed:

> "In consequence of the great distress prevalent in Widnes, caused by the coal strike, a number of men who have been thrown out of work are being employed in doing labour work at the Gas Works and at Stocks Well. None but married men have so far been engaged, and each employed for a period of 3 days. The total number dealt with up to date is 33".[40]

Five weeks later the Council reported that since the introduction of this scheme, work had been given to 114 men and that there were still about 50 men waiting their turn to be taken on. By the end of the strike the total number of men who had been given relief work amounted to 320. Another result of the miners' strike was the shortage of supplies. Council minutes say:

> "Thursday next will be the 10th week since supplies under contract of gas, coal and steam fuel were stopped. During the last few weeks, great difficulty has been experienced in obtaining supplies from any source, even at enormously enhanced prices. In order to economise on the output of gas, district pressures have been reduced wherever possible, and the lighting of a number of public lamps in the less important positions throughout the Borough has been temporarily discontinued".[41]

Those fortunate enough to be in steady employment with the Local Council were anticipating a pay rise. At the same meeting, Councillor Gough moved that the wages of the plumbers and fitters employed at the Gas Works be increased to 8d per hour, and that the charge for their services when hired out be 10d per hour. It was also put to the Committee that the wages of the stokers in the Gas Works be increased by 3d per shift; unfortunately, this last proposal was rejected.

Despite the depression in the alkali trade other industries continued to operate profitably. Gossage's Soap Works prospered and even had a programme of expansion. Widnes Foundry was in full operation and McKechnie's Copper Works, in Ditton Road, was also offering secure

---

[40] Borough of Widnes – *"Minutes of Council and Committees"* 1893
[41] Ibid

employment. In fact this period was the high point of copper manufacture in Widnes. In addition to these existing firms, John Bryson Orr opened a new company in the town in 1896 which he called The Vine Chemical Works. This company, which was located in Moon Street, produced "zinc white" (lithopone) and offered employment to several hundred men. In due course Orr`s Zinc White Ltd. became a well-established and successful firm in the town. A 1948 layout of the Works appears on another page.

The Lancashire Bleaching Powder Association was formed in 1883 for the purpose of maintaining the profitability of chlorine produced by the member firms. It drew up a number of defensive tactics to avoid being undercut by non-member firms. This strategy included the practice of buying up cheap bleaching powder for resale at a price fixed by the Association. Among the original members were the Widnes firms of Muspratt; Gaskell-Deacon; Golding-Davis; Hall Bros. & Shaw; Mathieson; Pilkington, Sullivan and the Atlas Chemical Co. This Association was a forerunner of a chemical alliance that came to fruition in 1890.

In November 1890 a number of the smaller alkali firms amalgamated into The United Alkali Company in an attempt to overcome the competition from the Brunner & Mond Company who were then engaged in the more efficient Solvay process of alkali manufacture. This amalgamation represented over 90% of the British Leblanc firms making it, at that time, the largest manufacturing concern in Britain. A total of 48 companies were incorporated into this merger and 14 of them were based in Widnes. Of the initial 48 firms, 45 of them were chemical works and 3 were salt works. There were 42 works in England, 4 in Scotland, 1 in Ireland and 1 in Wales. To some commercial observers the success of this venture was doubtful. *The Chemical Trade Journal* and *The Times* ran articles claiming that this was nothing more than a collection of old and obsolete works. Within 9 months of its formation the company embarked on a rationalisation programme and began dismantling properties considered to be antiquated. The reason for this exercise was, it was claimed, *"to leave room for the establishment of more suitable plant at a later date".*[42]

---

[42] *Chemical Trade Journal* – August 1891

Into The Crucible

The first Chairman of the newly formed United Alkali Company was John Brock, a St. Helens man who first came to Widnes in 1867 as the managing partner of the British Alkali Works. Sir Charles Tennant, the grandson of the inventor of bleaching powder, was named President. The Company Secretary was Eustace Carey, who had joined Gaskell Deacon's in 1857 as a 21year old chemist, and by 1871 was a partner in that company. The United Alkali Company appointed Ferdinand Hurter the Chief Chemist. Hurter, a Swiss, was a distinguished chemist who had been a pupil of Bunsen. He first came to Widnes in 1867 to work as a chemist with Messrs. Gaskell and Deacon. He was an enormously talented man and further information about his time in Widnes is covered in another part of this book.

The United Alkali Company was, at its inception, the biggest multi-firm merger in existence. The reasons for the merger were obvious. The Leblanc process was in decline because the Solvay method was proving more productive. Solvay had granted a licence to the Brunner Mond Company to start production at Winnington and within 10 years of its start the Company was producing 77,500 tons of soda ash. By 1889 UK ammonia soda production was 219,279 tons, compared with a total production of 584,203 tons of Leblanc soda.[43] It is clear that amalgamation of companies into The United Alkali Company did not produce the profits they had expected or hoped for. In fact, in 1894 The United Alkali Company found it advantageous to enter into an agreement with Brunner Mond Ltd. to form a cartel to fix prices and share markets.[44] By the autumn of 1894 trade conditions had worsened and The United Alkali Company was laying-off men. The number of workers in Widnes fell from 5,760 in 1894 to 4,221 in 1900.

Any effects of the depression of the 1890s would appear to have disappeared by 1900, or at least it had in the Brunner Mond Company. In that year Sir John Brunner told his Board that their accounts showed the continued prosperity of the Company. He also went on to make the following observations regarding productivity and "protection":

"The prospect was held out to the working classes of the country that if they multiplied the cost of their food and clothing by a considerable figure their wages would rise in proportion, and they would have a proportionate

---

[43] *Gaskell Deacon & Co. 1853-1930* –Catalyst Museum
[44] This agreement continued until 1914. *(Barker & Harris)*

Industry

balance left over. He would give them some absolutely accurate figures bearing on this point. The wages paid in England were very considerably higher than those paid in all the highly Protectionist countries of Europe. For every hundred pounds or shillings received in wages by an English workman in a trade about which he (Brunner) knew anything, the wages in France were measured by the figure seventy-seven, and, this was only earned by a daily work half as long again as the Englishman's. In Germany the figure of wages was seventy-eight, and here again the workman had to labour every day half as long again as the Englishman. To his mind there was no hope of raising wages by adopting a Protective policy, and he hoped that what he had said would be carefully considered, and, that the workpeople of the country would not be led into a policy which would raise the cost of their living in a wild and utterly delusive hope that such a policy would raise their wages. From the employers` point of view he wished to speak as to the efficiency of the English workman under a system that induced the whole world to compete in supplying him with cheap food and cheap clothing. What was his competitive efficiency as a producer? Again he took the comparative value at 100, and found that, probably in consequence of low wages and long hours, it took 124 Frenchmen and 131 Germans to do the same work as was done by 100 Englishmen in a trade about which he (Brunner) knew everything".

Sir John continued the meeting with his report on the state of the business. After acknowledging a vote of thanks from the members, he again reverted to the subject of Protection.

"He remarked that the reason why this country had the most honest legislature in the world was because the legislators were not tempted. In every protected country in the world the people who desired Protection were able to offer bribes to their legislative representatives and these bribes were practically irresistible. How much out of a secret service fund could not a great manufacturing corporation in this country afford to offer to members of Parliament every year? At the same time when he entered the alkali trade sulphur pyrites was obtained from Wexford and Wicklow this, however, was put out of the market by the Norwegian, which was stronger in sulphur and cheaper per unit. This also in turn was put out by the Spanish, which, again, contained more sulphur and was obtainable at a lower price. Supposing under these circumstances, Mr. John Redmond, in the House of Commons, proposed that a heavy duty be put upon foreign pyrites in order to bring Irish pyrites into the market again. Brunner, Mond & Company

Into The Crucible

did not use any sulphur pyrites. If it went up in price their competitors would have to pay a highly advanced price for one of their principal raw materials. Would not that be an enormous gain to Brunner Mond? They could very comfortably afford to spend £100,000 in buying votes to carry out that proposal, and they would have every representative from Ireland voting in favour of it. If they wanted to preserve the honesty of their legislature let them beware of import duties."[45]

The new century brought with it *The Factory Act of 1901*. However this Act was a measure merely consolidating and codifying the laws of the previous century, rather than anticipating the policies of the 20th century. The outbreak of the First World War proved to be something of a saviour to The United Alkali Company as demand for all types of chemicals was boosted by the "war effort". During this time Britain had to rely on domestic production for most of her chemicals and industrial materials. Incidentally, before this war Germany had supplied 90% of the khaki dye for the British uniforms. With the onset of war the country had to become as self-reliant as possible. The demand for chemicals like sulphuric acid was insatiable, as the concentrated variety of sulphuric acid was needed for nitration, especially for making TNT.

Despite the earlier rivalries and divisions, The United Alkali Company and Brunner, Mond, & Company were destined to join forces. In 1926 these two firms were merged with two others, Nobel Industries and British Dyestuffs Corporation, to form a new company called Imperial Chemical Industries, which became commonly known by its initials, I.C.I.

---

[45] *Widnes Weekly News* - 30th May 1903

The Irish

Although the nineteenth century witnessed the arrival of a large number of Irish immigrants into Widnes, it is worth noting that the Irish only began arriving here in significant numbers after the alkali industry had become firmly established in the town. Although their presence in our town was in direct response to the development of industry, in fact, there had been a steady flow of Irish immigrants into many parts of England from the mid-18th century. This was mainly in the form of seasonal agricultural labour and was usually dictated by harvest timetables. In our sister town of Runcorn there are records of maritime trade between Runcorn and Ireland as far back as the 13th century and therefore, from time to time, there was often a small Irish presence in that locality. The British Army and Navy were also traditional sources of employment for immigrant Irish. In fact, it has been calculated that in 1830 the Irish accounted for 42% of the non-commissioned ranks of Britain's Army.[46]

In addition to this minor but steady flow of Irish migrants, in later times there were several important developments related to the economy, or famine, which prompted substantial movement of people from Ireland into England. In 1824, after *The Act of Union*, the lifting of duties on the import of woollen cloth into Ireland caused the Irish market to be flooded with cheaper English goods and textiles. This unequal competition resulted in the decline of the Irish textile industry and thousands of workers lost their livelihoods. As a consequence, after 1825 many Irish immigrants into England were handloom weavers seeking work. Most of these came in through the Port of Liverpool and were heading for the textile towns of Lancashire and Yorkshire. During April and May in 1830 the following reports appeared in a Tipperary newspaper "*The Clonmel Nationalist*" [47]

*21st **April**: 50 operative handloom weavers went from Limerick five days ago for Manchester with promise of employment there. Each had £3 from*

---

[46] Patrick Bishop – *The Irish Empire* (St. Martin's Press) 1999
[47] Dr. Patrick C. Power "*Emigration Notes*" 5

the Relief Committee, which held public subscription. In Manchester now there are 50,000 looms. Most of the cotton weavers left Cork for there; where a weaver earns 12/6d a week.

24th April: Perishing weavers from Bandon on Steamer to Liverpool seeking work in Manchester or nearby towns (Report from Manchester Herald).

5th May: Another "colony" of distressed weavers went by canal on 30th April to Dublin to go to Liverpool.

Of course the most renowned wave of Irish migration into Britain occurred during the late 1840s when the population of Ireland was decimated by death and famine. Throughout that dreadful period the north-west of England, particularly Liverpool and its hinterlands, was overwhelmed by an unrelenting influx of immigrants. In 1847 the Irish were arriving in Liverpool at the rate of 700 a day. *The Liverpool Times* of 20th April 1847 states that from January to April that year 127,850 Irish arrived into the Port of Liverpool. At that time the city provided a major entry point from Ireland as there were several Irish harbours with operational routes to Liverpool. These included Dublin, Wexford, Waterford and Drogheda as well as several other minor ports. One afternoon in August 1848 in excess of 1200 destitute people left Waterford Quays for Liverpool.[48] This was a familiar occurrence during the entire period of the famine. This scene was replicated in many Irish ports as countless ships, with their starving and forlorn human cargo, set sail for the Liverpool docks.

The immigrants arriving on the Liverpool quays were desperate, dispirited, hungry and penniless. However, they were among the fortunate ones who survived the treacherous crossing of the Irish Sea. Although there were many natural weather-related shipping disasters on the Irish route in those times, other tragedies were the direct result of malpractice or negligence. Some ships were un-seaworthy and were routinely overcrowded and many passengers never survived the voyage. One vivid description of these so called "coffin ships" says that *"passengers were huddled together without light, without air, wallowing in filth and breathing a fetid atmosphere. They were sick in body, dispirited in heart, living without food and dying without the voice of spiritual*

---

[48] Richard McElwee – *The last voyages of the Waterford Steamers*. Waterford, Ireland.

The Irish

consolation". However it would need another book to relate the awful conditions and all the catastrophic incidents that occurred during this time on routes from Ireland to Liverpool.

One tragedy, on board *The Londonderry,* drew attention to the scandal of overcrowded ships. This steamer was sailing from Sligo to Liverpool in December 1848 with nearly 150 passengers. It was also transporting cattle from Ireland to Liverpool. During the voyage the sea conditions became extremely rough and all the passengers were ordered below deck. The hatch was secured tightly, depriving those below of air or any adequate ventilation. The following is a report from *The Illustrated London News* of 11th December.

"The hatch or companion was drawn across; but the space for ventilation being insufficient the unfortunate people below were subjected to the horrible and lingering death of suffocation. One passenger, more fortunate than the rest, succeeded in gaining the deck, and having alarmed the crew, an effort was made for their relief, but too late, 73 human beings have ceased to exist. It took three hours and a half to get the dead out of the vessel; and as putrefaction had begun, the smell was so offensive that spirits were given to men to get them to go below. The place in which the poor creatures met their fate was about 20 feet long, 14 feet wide and 7 feet high. It had capacity for about 30 passengers; but so crowded was it that the dead lay four deep on the floor."

Naturally the numbers of Irish arriving into the Port of Liverpool caused great alarm. Immigration details for a 2 week period in January 1847 gave the figures as 5737 men, 3497 women, and 1870 children. Such was the volume that the Mayor and local Magistrates were forced to suspend the vagrancy laws in the city. A correspondent for *"The Liverpool Mercury"* wrote on 1st January 1847:

"In less than an hour's drive from Liverpool to Prescot, I counted twenty-one families of Irish labourers, averaging more than 100 souls, evidently fresh from the famine stricken land, seeking subsistence in this most inclement season of the year, and all equally ill clad, hungry, and exhausted".

Another observer wrote: *"These poor people arrive in a state of wretchedness too painful to behold".*

Into The Crucible

In late January 1847 the Mayor of Liverpool, George Hall Lawrence, called a special meeting of the Magistrates to consider the propriety of petitioning the Government. The Mayor told the Magistrates that Liverpool, because of the deluge of Irish poor into the city, could not sustain the burden on the poor rates. He hoped that Parliament would devise some way of relieving Liverpool from bearing more than a fair share of the cost of accepting these destitute immigrants. Things were to get worse. By the end of June 1847 more than 300,000 Irish had landed in Liverpool. The Medical Officer of Health estimated that between 60,000 and 80,000 of these had settled in the city. They were housed in the already overcrowded lodging houses and cellars, most of which were unfit for human habitation.

Irish Famine Migrants landing at Liverpool in 1848

The accommodation situation in Liverpool was so bad that many of the immigrants had little choice but to head inland. The favoured route out of Liverpool was the road to Prescot, from where many headed north to St. Helens or east towards Warrington and Manchester. From Manchester some crossed over the Pennines to Sheffield and south

The Irish

Yorkshire. No doubt some of the famine immigrants travelled through our area and some may have stayed and found agricultural work, however it is unlikely that many famine Irish settled in Widnes *at that time*. Because Widnes was then a sparsely populated area, and our industrial role was in its infancy, this district would have held little attraction for the migrant Irish. They were usually heading for places where there were employment opportunities, or else places where friends or relatives had already settled. Those who took the southerly branch of the turnpike at Prescot went through Bold, while those who took the northerly branch came to St. Helens which was at that time a busy industrial town. St. Helens was only a twelve-mile tramp from Liverpool so this was a natural place to stop and find work. In St. Helens, the registers of St. Mary's Catholic Church, Lowe House, reveal that there were over one thousand Irish in St. Helens in the mid-1840s. This number increased considerably during the famine era. In later years there was a mass movement of Irish labourers from St. Helens to Widnes as industry developed here and employment opportunities were created. It is almost certain that some of these later arrivals into Widnes were *originally* famine immigrants who had previously settled in St. Helens.

Although this is primarily a local history book aimed at Widnes readers, I feel it is important to touch upon the story of the Irish Famine and Irish immigration because it helps us to understand English attitudes and local feelings towards the Irish during the 19th century. It also has a special relevance to our town, as a large percentage of our current population descend from this migrant group. For that reason, the story of the Famine and its aftermath is an important part of our own community history, as well as the history of most Merseyside towns. Although people of Irish famine decent have now been totally absorbed into mainstream society, nevertheless, because of their links to this period of Irish history, I think it would be valuable to understand the many reasons why the Irish were unwelcome on these shores, and why they were the focus of continued prejudice and hostility.

The Irish Famine migration represents one of the greatest and unparalleled population displacements in the nineteenth century, and its causes and effects were major. I have explained in earlier pages how the sheer numbers of Irish immigrants into Liverpool swamped the city with destitute, hungry and despondent people. I have also stated that many of the famine migrants subsequently settled in St. Helens and afterwards relocated to Widnes as industry developed here. Therefore this specific group of ethnic migrants went on to constitute a large percentage of our early industrial population. Before I give a more detailed account of the circumstances which prompted their arrival, I think it is important to explain that these unfortunate people arrived on our shores as refugees rather than voluntary emigrants. Apart from the failure of their potato crops, they were the victims of a feudal system of land ownership which deprived them of a means to earn a living and feed their families. Furthermore, the background to their immigration was predicted by a *Report of the Devon Commission* in 1843 which noted that the main cause of Irish misery was the relationship between landlords and tenants.

The economic and social structure of Ireland in the lead up to the Famine was that of an unindustrialized country, largely inhabited by an indigenous agricultural population who grew potatoes on small patches of land. To place a historical backdrop to these events I include a letter written by the English socialist writer William Cobbett on a visit to Ireland in 1834. The letter may help us to understand how catastrophic the events of a decade or so later were to have on the Irish population.

Cork 17th October 1834.
At the town of Clonmel, I went to see one of the places where they kill and salt hogs to send to England. In this one town, they kill, every year, for this purpose, about sixty thousand hogs, weighing from eight score to twenty score. Every ounce of this meat is sent out of Ireland, while the poor creatures who raise it with such care, are compelled to live on lumpers, which are such bad potatoes, that the hogs will not thrive on them, and will not touch them, if they can get other potatoes. The rooks, which eat the good potatoes, will not eat these, though they be starving. And, yet, this is the stuff that the working people are fed on. There are about eighty thousand firkins of butter, and, perhaps, a hundred thousand quarters of wheat and more of oats, all sent out of this one town; while those who raise it by their labour, live on lumpers! How, will you ask, are the millions of working people made to submit to this? I will tell you when I get back to Parliament House, or to a country meeting at Guildford. It will be better to say it there than here! [49]

---

[49] Molly Townsend   *Cobbett's Writings on the Irish Question 1795-1835*. (London) 1993

Incidentally, the place mentioned in Cobbett's letter, Clonmel, was located in County Tipperary not too far from the borders of Waterford and Kilkenny. This town, and nearby towns and villages including Carrick-on-Suir and Portlaw, were well represented by later immigrants into Widnes. In this area, as in all other areas in Ireland at that time, a landlord system prevailed so virtually none of the labouring classes owned land, they were tenants. The Irish landowners usually acted in their own interests and most tenants were forced to subsist on miniscule plots of land which became less fertile from over production. Despite the limited scope for cultivation, or potential to improve their holdings, the rent demanded by landowners was extortionately high. In 1845 a partial failure of the potato crop was followed by a complete failure the following year, which in turn was followed by a particularly harsh winter. In 1848 the crop failed once again and the hapless tenants were unable to pay their rent and meet other commitments. The hardships suffered by the tenants at this time had little effect on the sentiments of the landlord or his agent. The immediate response was to evict the tenant and his family; the homes were usually razed to the ground in order to prevent them from returning. Starvation and disease became common as tenants and their families were driven penniless from their homes. One report states that some families were wandering the country seeking work and were living on blackberries and cabbage leaves.

English newspaper accounts of the time are filled with countless horrifying stories from Ireland. The vast majority of Irish had depended almost exclusively on the potato crop for existence. In addition, land rents in Ireland were over 80% higher than in England, therefore it was almost impossible for a poor labourer to afford anything more than a quarter acre plot. A quarter acre would yield a potato crop which would feed a family for a year. The potato was the most logical choice to cultivate as to grow grain would require at least seven times more acreage and would also require machinery and knowledge of tillage. Because of the high rents, most of the poorer people were only able to "hire land" by means of a system called *"conacre"*. This was a contract to hire a small section of land, usually no more than a quarter of an acre. The landlord would allow the hirer to grow *one type of crop only* and a portion of this crop had to be given to the landlord in exchange for permission to build a cabin on the land. The hirer would also pay for this permission by giving a certain number of days labour to the landlord. The failure of the crop meant that there was no food and no means of paying "rent".

When the potato crop failed, whole families were obliged to seek the shelter of the workhouse or take the emigrant ship. Workhouses were full to capacity and the mortality rate in them was so great that many workhouse guardians issued orders that no more people should be admitted. Although almost all parts of the country were affected in some way, the distress was most severe in the West of Ireland in the counties of Mayo, Clare, West Cork and Donegal. A report from Mayo says, *"At Castlebar, people lay in the streets with green froth at their mouths from eating soft grass"*. In Roscommon, *"seven skeleton bodies were found in a hedge, half eaten by dogs"*. In County Tipperary *"a man carrying in his arms the body of his child tried to beg enough money for a coffin, but most of those he begged from were themselves beggars, he buried his child himself without coffin or shroud"*.

Reports in English newspapers concerning the terrible situation in Ireland highlighted the appalling system of relief, or lack of it. Of course the Poor Law system relied on rates as well as Government support and there was concern that landowners were not contributing as much as they could or should. One newspaper report of October 1846 said:

"The system of voluntary relief, too, now is pretty generally adopted; but loud complaints are made that some absentee landowners (mainly English) who own large estates in Ireland, are not contributing at all. The workhouse, which two months ago did not contain half the number they are capable of accommodating, are now crowded, and many of the poor, for want of room, are lodged in outhouses."

Barely 4 months later, in February 1847, the following report appeared in *The Liverpool Mercury* under the heading *"Deaths from Starvation"*

"The accounts regarding the situation in Ireland continue to be most distressing. A letter from Shinrone, Tipperary, says "A report has reached Shinrone that a young girl has died at Kilcommon of starvation. Several families at the lower end of Kilmurry parish have been living on cabbages and turnips these past few days, without any other description of food" – at

Borrisoleigh many were living on one scanty meal during the 24 hours, and the forbearance of the sufferers was amazing. A letter from Dungarvan of the 19th instant says "The condition of the people is truly heart-rending. They are starving! One of the Dragoons, a very intelligent man, gave a most deplorable account of the sights witnessed by them as they came along today by the houses with their prisoners. They were followed by frantic looking skeletal women and small children whose cries were unlike anything human – being husky, broken and quite feeble from starvation."

It seems impossible to understand or justify the fact that whilst Ireland was stricken by famine, and hundreds of thousands were starving, huge quantities of food were still being exported from that country to England. If we look at trade statistics we can clearly see that by the late 1830s there was a massive export trade in foodstuffs from Ireland to our shores. Indeed, William Cobbett's letter of 1834 gives an example of this. Ireland was routinely exporting around 80% of its grain production to England. Irish farmers were also exporting pigs, cattle and diary produce. In fact, the industrial towns of north-west England received over half of exported Irish livestock production as steamships facilitated direct transportation across the Irish Sea to our northern ports. It is extremely shocking to learn that this trade in grain and livestock continued almost uninterrupted throughout the whole period of the Irish famine.

Despite the fact that all wagons of food enroute for Irish ports had armed escorts, this callous exportation of food from a starving nation did not always go unchallenged., On 24th April 1846 one convoy, travelling to Clonmel, consisted of *"2 guns, 50 cavalry and 80 infantry"*. Sometimes these convoys were attacked by hungry people, as the sight of food streaming out of the country was too much to bear for starving and desperate people. In Dungarvan, County Waterford, a crowd of people attempted to hold up a boat laden with oats for export. The 1st Royal Dragoons were called out and their Captain gave the order to fire. Twenty-six shots were fired into the crowd and two men were killed while several others, including three women and two small children, were seriously injured[50]. The exporting of food at this time was an act many found impossible to comprehend or defend. The inhumanity of sending food *out* from a famine-ridden country could not

---

[50] *The Great Hunger* – Cecil Woodham-Smith (1962)

be justified or condoned. The blame for this has since been apportioned to greedy landlords and a total lack of sentiment or comprehension by the British Government.

The story of the Irish Famine is a monumental record of abject suffering. This suffering derived not only from the failure of potato crops but also from the mass clearances by landlords, as well as the degradation and failure of relief programmes and the spread of fever pandemics. The result was that over one million people died within a five year span and many more were forced to migrate in order to survive. Those that could physically or financially manage to do so took to the emigrant ships in order to escape certain death from starvation or disease. These unavoidable circumstances compelled them to turn away from their homeland and to leave behind the comfort derived from the familiarity of their native surroundings. They arrived in England in droves; poor, hungry, dispossessed and unwelcome.

Some migrants were half dead when they arrived; or weak from lack of nourishment and ill-clad against the rigours of cold weather. However their arrival here was often the beginning of a new range of struggles and hardships. There are countless harrowing newspaper accounts of the adversities faced by these poor desperate people on their arrival at Liverpool. Many were too feeble to travel far and did not live long after disembarking at the port. An example of this happened not too far from our own town. It concerns the tragic case of 40year old Bridget Callaghan, her young cousin, and four very young children. This small group, newly arrived from Ireland, set off to walk from Liverpool to join a relative in Yorkshire. On the second afternoon of their journey Bridget froze to death under a hedge just outside Bold.[51]

Bridget Callaghan and her little family group had landed in Liverpool on a day in April 1850 and set off at once on the road leading towards Yorkshire. They stopped the first night at Knotty Ash, just outside Liverpool, and late on the second afternoon they reached the Bold area. The following is an extract from a report of the inquest into her death.

---

[51] Barker and Harris *St. Helens: A study of a Lancashire Town in the Industrial Revolution* (Frank Cass & Co.) 1993

The Irish

"Here a local resident allowed them to make oatmeal porridge and also gave them some hot coffee. The poor woman and family left about 5 o'clock in the evening and crept with her children and cousin, under a hedge on the road. They remained there, although it was very cold and rained heavily, until 5 o'clock the next morning; the children began to cry, when a woman from the nearest house came to their assistance; the poor woman was carried to a straw stack and laid down, her limbs being quite stiff, and she died a few minutes afterwards."[52]

This story is not uncommon and in fact may have been typical of the experiences of a large number of immigrants during that period. On 5th May 1847 a Police Constable from Bury in Lancashire found a family consisting of a man, woman and two children lying under a hedge. On stopping to investigate he discovered that they were all weak, cold and hungry. One child was already dead. They had landed in Liverpool three weeks before and were walking to Leeds. At the inquest into the child's death the jury's verdict was *"death from natural causes"*.

Reports in: *The Liverpool Mercury; the Manchester Guardian; the St. Helens Standard; the Leeds Mercury* and *The Halifax Guardian* in 1847 describe countless cases of weak and impoverished Irish immigrants walking long distances. There are several reports of emaciated bodies found under hedges or in outbuildings, their deaths due to hunger and exposure in bad weather. Frank Neal, in his excellent book entitled *"Black '47: Britain and the Famine Irish"*, gives numerous distressing accounts including the story of a man called John Waters who, with his wife and seven children, walked all the way from Mayo to Dublin to take a steamer to Liverpool then planned to walk from there to Yorkshire. The full story of John Waters, as told by Frank Neale, was extremely harrowing and demonstrated the hopelessness experienced by these migrants. John Waters, a 50year old labourer, had previously rented land from a landlord in County Mayo for over 18 years. He paid a rent of £5.10s.a year. During that time he and his wife Catherine had married and raised seven children. By the end of October 1846 the family's health was beginning to deteriorate because of lack of food. They had planted three barrels of seed potatoes and *"did not get one week's supply from them"*. At the beginning of November they decided

---

[52] *The Liverpool Mercury.* 16th April 1850

to go to England. In the words of Catherine Waters *"...the want of potatoes, starvation and poverty obliged us to leave"*.

The Waters sold their only valuable possessions, a horse and a pig, in order to finance the passage to England. They walked all the way from County Mayo to Dublin, a distance of over two hundred miles, at no time asking for Poor Relief. It took them nine days to walk to Dublin from where they took the steamer to Liverpool at a fare of nine shillings for the whole family. On their arrival in Liverpool they decided to head for Sheffield where John had a brother. This would mean making an arduous journey, on foot, across the Pennines with their young children in the depths of winter. On their first night out from Liverpool they reached Prescot where they stayed one night in the vagrancy ward. The next day they walked to Warrington where they stayed for two nights and then set out for Stockport. By this time they were all in a weak state and the children were beginning to show signs of distress. The family survived this section of the route by begging as all their money had now gone. It should be emphasised again that John Waters had been an honest, decent, hardworking tenant for 18 years, providing for his wife and family by working his small patch of land. To find himself and his family reduced to the state of beggars must have been extremely distressing. The Waters family reached Stockport around the 7th December. The journey from Stockport to Sheffield followed a similar pattern with the hapless family having to resort to selling items of clothing, including Catherine's cloak and the boys' clogs, to buy food.[53]

Of course we should not imagine that once they reached our shores the malnourished refugees were safe from the peril of starvation. Many were too weak to recover and, as we saw in the case of Bridget Callaghan, their bodies just gave up the fight. Another case from 1847 concerns the death of a two month old child in Toxteth. The newspaper report provides the following sad account:

"On Tuesday night, a child, two months old, the son of a poor Irishman named Anthony Cawley, died from starvation. From the evidence of Mr. Tomkin, one of the relieving officers for Toxteth Park, it appears that Cawley applied for relief on Tuesday morning, and immediately afterwards he went

---

[53] Frank Neal - *"Black `47:Britain and the Famine Irish"* (Palgrave MacMillan) 1997

to visit the cellar which Cawley occupied; he found the wife of the poor man in bed with (as he supposed) one child; but after asking her a few questions relative to her condition, he saw what appeared to be a bundle of rags, but which, on closer inspection, proved to be the body of a child. Cawley had not alluded to the death of his infant when he applied for relief; nor did his wife draw the attention of the relieving officer to the body when he spoke to her. Mr. Gilmour, a surgeon. Made a post-mortem examination of the body and declared the cause of death to be a general wasting of the system from the want of sufficient nourishment. Cawley stated that he arrived in Liverpool about two months since, when he had a pound in his pocket with which he had supported himself since. His wife and child came over on Sunday last week. The Coroner, addressing the jury said that unless something was done for the relief of this family immediately, the parents would very soon follow their child. The woman was in a very bad state but Mr. Gilmour said that as the woman was not his patient he could not interfere in the matter and nothing could be done. A verdict of death from starvation was returned on the child"

Although there were numerous sympathetic reports concerning the famine in British newspapers, some others were less concerned with humanitarian factors and were openly hostile towards the Irish incomers. Of course, with any historical study, one has to look at the reasons why people react in certain ways and also take into account the historical perspectives of those times. Some historians have claimed that Britain was guilty of genocide because of the failure of State Relief and the fact that food was being exported from a land where people were dying of starvation. To the ordinary citizen things were far simpler; the Irish were placing an unreasonable burden on local funds and causing deprivation among the native population. This attitude, although deplorable and incomprehensible to our modern minds, is more easily understood when we look at the historical background of those times.

The Irish Famine erupted at a time when England was experiencing a trade depression which subsequently resulted in a significant increase in destitution among the English working classes. Many of the indigenous poor were living in extreme poverty. The seemingly unrelenting flood of destitute paupers from Ireland was a constant drain on the Poor Law Unions and the English working classes were suffering great hardship because of this. The effect of unemployment and the huge influx of famine refugees meant that local Poor Law Unions were under enormous strain and many low-income ratepayers were unable to pay the Poor Rate. With the ever-growing competition for work the Irish presence also became a threat to the labour market. It was thought that the arrival of this pool of low-earning toilers held down the standard of living for English workers. All of these things fostered resentment, and resentment has a long memory. Consequently this attitude and a growing bitterness towards the Irish became the accepted norm. Considering these things, we can understand why the sheer volume of Irish migrants, who continued to arrive in great numbers, became an insistent reminder of the huge burden they had placed upon the system. Their mass presence, coupled with the hardships and deprivations of English workers of those times, constantly ignited animosity among the indigenous populations in all the areas they inhabited.

Of course there are two sides to every story. The Irish who arrived here with their families were escaping almost certain death from starvation. Migration to England was often their only choice. However, it was by no means an easy option as life was extremely difficult for the majority of Irish immigrants in the early years after their arrival. They faced poverty and bigotry and became conveniently stereotyped as drunks or criminals, even though their behaviour was no different from the indigenous population. This viewpoint was nurtured by newspapers and other national publications who routinely described them in racially derogatory terms. Editions of *Punch* regularly included offensive and distorted caricatures of the Irish. *Punch* cartoons of the 1880s usually showed the English *"John Bull"* mocking the Irish *"Paddy"* who they depicted as a squat, gruesome "ape-like" man dancing a jig and waving a shillelagh. This particular character appeared in a whole series of shameful front-page sketches. Modern readers might not find it too difficult to equate these images with an unpleasant type of propaganda which occurred in the 1930s in which Jews were depicted as rats.

This brief background to the famine exodus is obviously only part of the story of Irish migration into Widnes. There are other factors which I touch upon later in this book, when I describe the environments some of the Irish and Lithuanian immigrants into Widnes had left behind. However, when considering Irish immigration into our town in those

The Irish

early days we should remember that life was not easy for them. Most had never previously ventured outside their own local areas and were completely unprepared for the change in surroundings. They suddenly found themselves transported hundreds of miles away from a rural landscape into an urban one with an alien social setting. In addition, the native inhabitants spoke differently and were openly hostile towards them.

In England, the immigrant Irish were only able to find work in the lowest and worst paid occupations. Unlike the earlier weaver immigrants, most of the famine migrants had no skills or accomplishments to equip them in the labour market. Generally, the men found work as labourers or dockers, but in those early days many worked as navigators or *"navvies"* as they were commonly known. They were the men employed in cutting the railways and canals that were spreading out in all directions across the country. The women, if they were employed, worked as domestic servants, laundresses or lodging housekeepers. The famine migrants who arrived into our own region were mainly attracted to places where some form of industry or unskilled employment opportunities existed. In Runcorn, the Irish found work as labourers around the docks and in the several shipbuilding yards. They also found employment in the coalmines and chemical industries in St. Helens and in the textile towns of Lancashire and Yorkshire.

Most Irish people left their native land believing that they would find a better life away from poverty and starvation. However this hope, in reality, conflicted with their experiences. The lot of the famine immigrant was usually grinding poverty, unemployment or backbreaking dangerous work for low pay. Many found that they were no better off and in fact, in later periods, some found themselves in worse conditions than those they had left behind. Apart from the tribulation of leaving all that was comforting and familiar, they also had to face the widespread prejudice which was inherent among the indigenous population at that time. As we have seen, most Irish immigrants faced hostility not least because the initial wave of Irish workers threatened to undersell native labour at a time when there was high unemployment in the country. This was a source of bitter and continual recrimination. For the Irish, this open and widespread hostility had a marked effect. It increased the consciousness of their difference and tended towards the

Into The Crucible

perpetuation and cherishing of their Irish separation. This separation, and the preformed attitudes they had carried into exile, fostered a patriotic fervour which flourished in their new surroundings. Several examples of this fervour were patently visible in our own area.

Irish patriotic zeal became a natural by-product of a situation that had created separation. These circumstances formed a *"them"* and *"us"* attitude which shaped extreme partisan standards. An early Irish Republican movement, *The Fenian Brotherhood,* had many followers in both Widnes and Runcorn. In fact Widnes, Runcorn and St. Helens were hotbeds of Fenianism and there were large cells in all of these towns. It should be said that *The Fenian Brotherhood* was not simply a political movement. It was an active rebel organisation which plotted and carried out armed assaults on what they perceived to be "legitimate" targets. On 11th February 1867 there was a plan to attack Chester Castle. This attack was to be part of a series of diversionary raids to take place on English garrisons in various parts of the country. These raids were intended to coincide with a planned uprising in Ireland. However the raid on Chester Castle was a dismal failure. The Authorities were tipped-off and a heavy police presence prevented any serious trouble[54]. The attackers escaped capture but *The Runcorn Observer* reported in the edition of 16th February 1867 that numerous Irishmen from Widnes and Runcorn had been involved in the failed raid. The famous Irish Fenian, Michael Davitt, took part in this attack and is said to have stayed overnight in a house in Caroline Street, Newtown.

During this period there were a large number of Fenian cells not only in Ireland and our area but also throughout England and America. There had previously been a number of failed attempts at an uprising in Ireland and the Fenian Organisation in the north of England was in a state of disarray due to considerable infighting. In August 1867 two of the leaders, Thomas Kelly and Timothy Deasy, came over from Ireland to settle a dispute among local Fenians in Manchester. A month after their arrival both men were arrested. After these arrests the local Fenians decided on a rescue attempt to free the two men. They ambushed the prison van taking Kelly and Deasy to Bellevue Gaol. The two men escaped but a police sergeant, Charles Brett, was accidentally shot dead in the process. The sergeant had been seated

---

[54] P. Beresford Ellis *"A History of the Irish Working Class"* London 1972

behind the van door when the attackers shot at the lock. The police succeeded in capturing some of the rescuers, as well as some others who had played no part in the affair at all. Several were arrested simply because they were Irish and were known to frequent the same pubs as some of the accused.

Kelly and Deasy managed to make their way to America and it is said that they were sheltered there by the German philosopher Frederic Engels, a friend of Karl Marx. As for the captured Fenians in Manchester, seven were sentenced to penal servitude while the remaining five were sentenced to death. After a considerable amount of national publicity, as well as demonstrations, petitions and the pleadings of the radical Manchester MP John Bright, two of the men were reprieved. The remaining three men, William Philip Allen, Michael Larkin and Michael O'Brien were hanged at The Old Bailey Prison, Salford, on 23rd November 1867. Karl Marx wrote at the time *"the political executions at Manchester remind us of the fate of John Brown at Harper's Ferry"*.[55]

Two of those arrested and imprisoned at that time had previously lived and worked in Widnes. They were found guilty on the evidence of a young Widnes girl called Mary Flanagan. Miss Flanagan, the daughter of the landlady of The Foundry Inn in Widnes, was at that time living in Manchester where she worked as a governess. She told the Court that she had frequently seen the two men in the company of a well-known Fenian at her mother's pub in Widnes. Although they strenuously denied any involvement in the affair both men were given sentences of penal servitude for life.

In the shadow of these alarming incidents, the police in Widnes and Runcorn were issued with revolvers and were alert to the possibility of trouble from the Irish communities. Other evidence of Fenianism in Widnes emerged in a number of documents seized by the Liverpool police in 1866. Among the documents was a letter from J.F. McAnliffe, using the alias John Jones. The letter outlined a series of lectures he had given in Widnes in support of *The Irish Republican Brotherhood*. He estimated that he had made, or would make, between 50 and 100

---

[55] Ibid

converts in Widnes.[56] On 23rd March the following year *The St. Helens Standard* reported the arrest of a man in Widnes who was carrying a £50 Bond *"payable six months after the establishment of the Irish Republic"*. Fenian activity continued throughout the nineteenth century in this area and other industrial towns with large Irish populations. From time to time the Lancashire and Cheshire Police considered Widnes and Runcorn to be places of particular interest. Indeed, they were right to assume this as later on in the century there were several incidents which proved this to be the case. On one occasion a large cache of arms was discovered in a house in Market Street and in 1882 a quantity of explosives was stolen from a Quarry site in Runcorn.

An additional element of local unrest was connected with sectarianism. Some historians of the period suggest that prior to the influx of *Famine Irish* the Irish and English workers had mixed freely. However, *The Liverpool Mercury* reports on Liverpool's first Orange-Catholic riot in July 1819, almost thirty years before hungry destitute people from Ireland saturated the city. From then onwards, the battle of the Orange and the Green continued on these shores with both Catholic and Protestant baiting each other. One such event in July 1867 resulted in tragedy at Widnes. Three trainloads of Liverpool Orangemen had made the journey to St. Helens on the 12th July to join a large procession that had been organised by the St. Helens Orange Lodges. The procession provoked spontaneous eruptions of violence in St. Helens that resulted in a full-blown riot, which the local police had great difficulty in controlling. After some form of law and order had been restored, the Orange contingent boarded the train to return to Liverpool. On the way back the train stopped at a Widnes Station. The Orangemen waved their flags out of the carriage windows and sang provocative songs. Some Irish gathered there and jeered the Liverpool men and they, no doubt, sang their own inflammatory songs. Although it was obviously an unpleasant scene it was not violent until one of the passengers on the train produced a pistol and shot an Irishwoman who was standing on the platform.

On 20th July 1867 the *Liverpool Mail* included a report of the St. Helens riot and the shooting of the woman at Widnes. In this report the Irish were referred to as ignorant semi-savages and the overall tone was

---

[56] *"Lancashire Constabulary: report of Head Constable"* - Lancashire Records Office. 325 POL/2/4

offensive. The report ended with the following statement: *"But these English Orangemen unmistakably proved themselves to be semi-savages too – just look at this cold-blooded and most dastardly attempt to murder a fanatic Irishwoman as recorded in a St. Helens print:"*

The following news item from a St. Helens newspaper was then inserted:

"The bloodthirsty fanaticism of Orangeism, which had plunged St. Helens into uproar and conflict, gave, before leaving the district, a most villainous instance of its spirit. As the Orange train was on its way from St. Helens to Liverpool, a delay took place at Newtown, Widnes, to have the carriage shunted. The travellers whiled away the time in cheering and waving their ensigns, and a small crowd of people outside got up a counter demonstration of a similar kind. One woman, however, varied the amusement by burning an Orange handkerchief, upon which a ruffian in the carriage produced a pistol and deliberately fired at her and lodged a bullet in her shoulder. She was at once attended by Dr. Juliott, who succeeded in extracting the bullet, and it is now in the possession of Sergeant Fairley; but the cowardly miscreant who sought a woman's life has gone his way uninterrupted, rejoicing in the deed, and sighing, perhaps, that he has not a few Papists scalps to hang up in his wigwam"

In contrast, *The Liverpool Mail* reported than the 12th July celebrations passed over without any riot or bloodshed in Ireland. The newspaper called for some legislative repression in England that would prohibit "party processions" or "party emblems and tunes". Apparently such an Act already existed in Ireland and was seemingly effective. It also stated that a muzzling order existed within the old limits of the Borough of Liverpool by virtue of a Corporation bylaw. The writer suggested that they be *"similarly put down and muzzled in all other towns and districts"*.[57]

In March 1872 *The Widnes & Runcorn Guardian* reported on a meeting of the Widnes Branch of *The Home Rule Association* that was held in the Public Hall in Widnes. The meeting was chaired by Dr. O'Keeffe and according to the report the room was filled by a decent and well-ordered lot of men. Mr. Gallagher, a local workingman, proposed: *"that*

---

[57] *"Liverpool Mail"* - 20th July 1867

Into The Crucible

this meeting pledges itself to use every legal and constitutional means to forward the attainment of Home Rule for Ireland". The Home Rule Association was a peaceful political organisation that worked in unison with members of the Liberal Party. However, Fenian activity had not abated and it continued to manifest itself from time to time throughout Lancashire. The Fenian organisation flourished in Liverpool and Manchester, which had largest groups. Although these places had significant memberships, as we have seen, there were also strong branches in St. Helens, Widnes, Runcorn and Preston.[58]

The Widnes Weekly News of August 6th 1881 reported the following:

THE FENIAN OUTRAGE AT LIVERPOOL
The trial of James McGrath and James McKevitt for attempting to blow up the Liverpool Town Hall has been concluded. After the evidence as to the prisoners being seen to deposit a bag containing explosives close to the Town Hall, and as to their pursuit and capture, the persons with whom they lodged spoke to their having pieces of iron pipe such as that found at the Town Hall. Counsel for the prosecution laid stress upon the fact that the outrage was instigated by Fenians in America; but the defence was that this was not a political outrage, and that the circumstances had been greatly exaggerated. Both the prisoners were found guilty of the attempt to blow up the Town Hall. A fresh jury was then empanelled to try the charge against McGrath of an attempt to blow up the Police Office. A verdict of guilty having been returned in this case, McGrath was sentenced to penal servitude for life, and McKevitt to fifteen years penal servitude.

For the majority of Irish, who played no part in subversive activity of any kind, they found that the political interests of the new country and that of the old were forced upon them. The subject of Home Rule for Ireland became a significant issue in the General Election of 1885. Several meetings were held at the Drill Hall and the Chairman of *The Irish National League*, local Widnes doctor, John O` Keeffe, endeavoured to get the Irish politician Charles Stewart Parnell to come to Widnes to speak to the Irish electorate in the town. Unfortunately Parnell missed his train and failed to arrive.

---

[58] W.J. Lowe *"The Irish in mid-Victorian Lancashire"* 1990

The Irish

One man who did turn up to speak to the Widnes Irish electorate was Mr. T.P. O'Connor, the then MP for the Borough of Galway. T.P. O'Connor arrived in Widnes in May 1885, his arrival comparable to the razzamatazz of an American presidential election. Mr. O'Connor was driven from Warrington in a carriage pulled by a handsome pair of greys. He was accompanied by Dr. O'Keeffe, Messrs. Fitzpatrick, Quinn and Faulkner of Widnes, Mr. Martin Cox of London and Mr. W.F. Cox of Manchester. The party was met at Halton View by the *Irish National Brass Band*, who were in uniform. They played popular Irish airs as they led the way along Albert Road and Widnes Road to Brendan House, the residence of Dr. O`Keeffe. Large numbers of people assembled in the streets to greet them. Afterwards Mr. O`Connor addressed a large and enthusiastic audience in the Drill Hall. Later that same year Mr. O'Connor was elected MP for the Liverpool Scotland division[59].

The extension of the franchise to "£10 Lodgers" in 1884 meant that in 1885 many Irish received the vote for the first time. Both of the major parties, the Tories and the Liberals, attempted to win their votes. *The Widnes Weekly News* of November 1885 reported that at a meeting in the Drill Hall the number attending was so large that a further meeting needed to be organised. The subsequent meeting was at The Widnes Baths, which was boarded over for the occasion. The editorial congratulated *The Irish National League* on its speaking skills.

When the Government introduced a Parliamentary Bill that would enable the establishment of Home Rule for Ireland, many of the Whigs joined the Unionist Party and formed the *Liberal Unionist Association.* The result of these divisions was that Mr. E. K. Muspratt was asked to stand as the Liberal candidate for Widnes. Mr. Muspratt appeared to be an ideal choice of candidate as he was of Irish descent and he was also a strong supporter of Irish Home Rule. He told the local electorate that he would vote alongside the Irish Party if elected. His slogan for the election was "*Muspratt and Justice for Ireland*". His victory seemed to be assured, especially as the Irish and most working men would have been natural Liberal supporters. However, in Parliament, Charles Stewart

---

[59] In 1916 Mr. T.P. O'Connor became the President of the *British Board of Film Classification*. He was also appointed to the position of official British Film Censor.

Parnell and his Irish Nationalist Party were persuaded to believe that the Tories would be more favourable to their cause than Mr. Gladstone's Liberal Party. Part of the reason for this was that Gladstone himself hoped that with the extension of the franchise in the counties he would be able to do without the support of the Irish Nationalist Party. However, despite wide local support for the Liberals, Mr. Parnell threw a spanner in the works by urging all his followers to support Tory candidates rather than Liberals.

The 1885 General Election was to be a defining event for local voters. Earlier in the year, the provisions of the Reform Bill had broken up the West Lancashire Constituency and created seven separate electoral divisions, thus giving Widnes its very own parliamentary constituency. The successful candidate would be the very first man to represent this town in Parliament. Apart from the significance of the event, this election caused great controversy in the town not least because it appeared that the outcome of the election lay entirely in the hands of the Irish electorate. Parnell's influence on the local Irish voters triggered a great deal of concern. In *The Widnes Weekly News* of 28th November the following article appeared.

> *"Among the nominators and assenters to Mr. Muspratt's candidature were a number of well-known Irishmen of Widnes; but whether this may be taken as an indication that any considerable number of Irishmen will vote for the Liberal candidate, it is impossible to say. The ways of the Irish are at present inscrutable, although up to now the current of the elections would seem to point to the Tories, as the recipients of the Irish support. There are some Irishmen, no doubt, who will be loyal to their Liberal instincts despite the injunction of Mr. Parnell; others may yield a steady obedience to the Uncrowned King[60]. One thing, however, is to be hoped – that in Widnes no pressure will be brought to bear on the voters either one way or the other, and that each may have the opportunity of exercising his vote according to his conscience".*

If the vote of the Irish residents of Widnes was uncertain, no such ambiguity existed amongst the Welsh. A meeting was held at The Baths Assembly Rooms in Victoria Road at which a large gathering of the Welsh community were present. The speeches were, with the

---

[60] Such was Parnell's popularity amongst the Irish, he was commonly called *"The Uncrowned King of Ireland"*

The Irish

exception of one, delivered in Welsh and they resolved unanimously to support Mr. E. K. Muspratt, the Liberal candidate.

On the day of the election two polling booths were open in Widnes from 8.00 a.m. to 8.00 p.m. For electors in North Widnes the base was the Simms Cross Schools while the voters of South Widnes cast their votes at the West Bank Board School. 6977 votes were registered in the election with a majority of these going to the Conservative candidate, Thomas C. Edwards Moss, who was duly elected as the first MP for the Widnes Division. Mr. E. K. Muspratt, although a popular man among the Widnes Irish, was defeated. The Irish voters had followed the orders of Charles Stewart Parnell and voted Tory. However the outcome was different in Northwich, where Sir John Brunner retained the affection and confidence of the Irish Nationalist voters. He was accordingly elected as Liberal MP for the Northwich Division. Sir John had long been a vocal and ardent supporter of Home Rule for Ireland and later donated £500 to *The Irish National League*.[61]

The controversy in Widnes rumbled on for some time after the election. *The Widnes Weekly News* editorial in the edition immediately following the election said:

"Mr. Muspratt's defeat was a foregone conclusion once the Irishmen decided to give their support to Mr. Moss. They have in round numbers 1800 votes in this division and if 85% of these voted (which is the percentage of the total poll) then 1530 went into the polling booth. The local Irish leaders estimate that one fourth of these did not follow the instructions of Mr. Parnell. This would therefore leave 1148 Irish votes given to Mr. Moss. If we deduct this number from Mr. Moss's total and add to Mr. Muspratt's total then our townsman would have been ahead with a substantial majority.

It was publicly remarked that immediately after the result of the election was known, Mr. Moss made good his escape from Widnes and a dissatisfied local Radical was heard to say "Aye, we must expect to see him again about the time of the next election".

---

[61] Stephen E. Koss: *Sir John Brunner: Radical Plutocrat 1842-1919* (Cambridge University Press) 1970

Into The Crucible

The election created some serious and unpleasant divisions among local communities. A Runcorn man was attacked on The Old Bridge as he made his way home late one night. The victim, Edward Hill, the President of the Runcorn branch of the *Irish National League*, lived in The Friendship Tavern, in Fryer Street. It was suggested that during the election he, and some other members of the society, had ignored the directions of Parnell and supported the candidature of John Brunner. The attack on Edward Hill was reported in *The Widnes Weekly News* as "Attempted Murder".

> *"Mr. Hill is the collector for an assurance society, and his business brings him into contact with many prominent Irishmen of Widnes, who have regarded his action with great disfavour. About 7 o'clock on Saturday night, Hill was at the Central Hotel, Widnes, where the recent election formed one of the topics of conversation between himself, Doctor O'Keeffe, and a man named Campbell of 29 Milton Street, Widnes. Shortly afterwards Hill left the hotel and walked through Widnes and on to Runcorn Bridge with a man named John Jones, a newsagent. When they were about 200 yards from the Runcorn booking office, they heard steps behind them. As Jones stepped aside to let these persons pass, Hill was struck with an iron bar. When he fell to the ground, he was kicked about the body and head. As Jones raised the alarm, the men endeavoured to throw Hill over the Bridge. The alarm was heard by several men on the Runcorn side, who reached the scene of the outrage just in time to see two men run back towards Widnes. They were unable to describe these men, as their faces were either masked or blackened. Hill bled profusely from the wounds on his head and face. He attributed the attack to the part taken by him in the Northwich election".*

At the election the following year Mr. Moss was returned, although with a greatly reduced majority. On this occasion the Liberal candidate, Augustine Birrell, had the full support of the Widnes branch of the *Irish National League*. Despite this, the expected Irish vote did not materialise. This is perhaps even more surprising when one considers that Thomas C. Edwards Moss fought that election under the Unionist banner, which was strongly opposed to Home Rule for Ireland. After the election a triumphant Mr. Moss returned to his home at Otterspool where a number of local Orange Lodge bands had assembled to celebrate his victory. One of the bands, *"The Pride of Garston Temple"*, after playing a few tunes for Mr. Moss, marched along Aigburth Road back to Garston. Later, another Orange Band from Liverpool, *"The*

Liverpool Heroes" arrived on the scene. *"The Heroes"* were accompanied by what was described as *"a motley crew"* and very soon a nasty disturbance broke out. The police eventually managed to drive the *"Heroes"* and their mob back along Aigburth Road to the boundaries of Toxteth, where another commotion occurred. It was thought that a territorial dispute had taken place between the Orange Lodges. The result was that a large number of men appeared in court the following day.

Orange and Green tension raised its ugly head in Widnes again that year when a serious disturbance broke out between the two factions. One summer afternoon in 1886 members of the Garston *"True Blues" Loyal Orange Lodge* paid a visit to the Widnes *"Invincible" Orange Lodge*. Their drum and fife band, who were dressed in naval type uniforms, accompanied them. The members of the Lodges, dressed in their regalia and wearing orange lilies, marched behind the band to the strains of *"The Boyne Water"*. There were about 200 men in the procession in addition to the 30 members of the band. Later in the day, after their visit, they marched down Widnes Road towards the London and North Western Railway Station to get the train back to Garston. It was a Saturday afternoon and the area was crowded with local people. When they reached Simms Cross the band allegedly gave a repeat, and somewhat over enthusiastic, rendition of *"The Boyne Water"*. However it seems that this was not appreciated by everyone, as the demeanour of the band and their companions angered a group of local bystanders. It was rumoured that some of the Orange supporters had made grotesque gestures and insulting remarks to the crowd. Within a short space of time numerous people from Newtown and Lugsdale had arrived on the scene and a full-blown fight broke out. A local police officer, who lived in the area, was knocked to the ground and kicked by one of the bandsmen. Very soon a dozen other police officers were on the spot and managed to get the situation under control. Later there were varying and conflicting reports of the incident, each side claiming the other as the aggressor. Some claimed that the Garston men had come armed with spiked sticks while others declared that the local Catholics had thrown stones. The following Thursday fifteen men from Garston appeared at the Widnes Petty Sessions charged with having caused a breach of the peace, all were found guilty and given prison sentences. One Widnes man was summoned for assault and was fined 10 shillings.

It is important to note that for a number of previous years members of the local *Widnes Orange Lodge* had marked their 12th of July celebrations without problem. For the most part, the inhabitants of Widnes co-existed in harmony. Sectarian geography meant that some districts in the town were distinctly Catholic and others mainly Protestant. This meant that it was probably only in the workplace that the two groups merged. Although there were several minor incidents of conflict, on the whole, sectarian violence was comparatively rare in Widnes. However this was not the case in Liverpool where there was a long history of street riots and violence between Catholic and Protestant residents. Although both Widnes and St. Helens had Orange Lodges with healthy memberships, the only violence associated with Orange activities in these towns seems to have involved members of visiting Liverpool Orange Lodges. This was certainly the case in the St. Helens riots and the various incidents recorded in Widnes.

Statistics tell us that in the poorer parts of town excessive overcrowding was the norm. Sometimes three or even four families shared a single dwelling. A survey done by W. J. Lowe[62] tells us that, in 1851, 31 out of 54 Irish households in the town lived in multi-occupancy dwellings. In 1861 the figure was 52 out of 65 Irish households. Most of the immigrant families shared living space with others to economise on the rent. This situation meant that they also economised on their quality of life. The Irish usually chose to share with other Irish families and often this was a kinship or friendship connection sustained by chain migration.

The new factory owners had arranged for housing to be built for their labourers and these houses were put up quickly and cheaply. In 1862 the Newtown area, off Lugsdale Road, was the most densely inhabited and was occupied mainly by Irish families. About this time the Simms Cross district was also developing and shortly afterwards, around 1867, the Moss Bank district came into being because of factory development in that area. Although there were numerous Irish families in Simms Cross and Moss Bank, Newtown was the main concentration.

It has been suggested that James Muspratt may have brought over many of the first Irish chemical workers from Dublin. In 1851 there

---

[62] W.J. Lowe *"The Irish in Lancashire 1841-71"* Thesis Trinity College Dublin 1974 – deposited in Lancashire Record Office

were 520,000 Irish in England and Wales, of which 191,000 were in the industrial towns of Lancashire. This was due to the fact that Lancashire was the most accessible part of England for the Irish arriving in Liverpool. A Parliamentary Commission on patterns of settlement noted, in 1836, that migrations usually settled around ports of entry where jobs were to be found. This pattern of settlement for the Irish remained the same until the period between the 1930s and the 1960s, when London and the southeast of England became the main destination for Irish immigrants.

A census of occupations in Widnes in 1861 shows that among the labourers in the town there were 241 Irish born, 151 English born, and only 23 who were actually born in Widnes. Of those born in Widnes some were of Irish descent. This means that Irish born workers significantly outnumbered English. These numbers provide an indication of the major Irish presence and influence in the town at that time. In a study of Widnes during the period 1841-1871, D Swann gives the following figures for the number of Irish in Widnes as: [63]

1851	250	*7.8% of population*
1861	916	*13.2% of population*
1871	2298	*16% of population*

These figures represent *only* those of Irish birth and do not include children born here of Irish parents. W.J. Lowe, in his analysis of the Irish population in Lancashire, considered this to be an underestimation of the real size of the Irish community in this town. He surveyed 100% of households in Widnes between 1851 and 1871 and he defined an Irish house as one in which the head of the household was Irish born. By using the complete information on the entire Irish population of Widnes for this period, he devised a factor (*the Widnes Factor*) to establish the actual size of the Irish community here and in six other Lancashire towns. W.J. Lowe's figures for Widnes give *minimum* sizes of the actual Irish community, which includes non-Irish born members of the nuclear family (wife and children), and extended families (relatives by blood or marriage).

---

[63] D. Swann *"Changing Morphology of Widnes 1841-71"* (Copy lodged in Widnes Library)

Into The Crucible

W.J. Lowe's figures for this period are defined as the minimum numbers of the Irish community in Widnes for these dates.[64] Using the Widnes Factor *(WF)* which is simply expressed as:

$$WF = 1 + \frac{Other\ Irish}{Total\ Irish\ Born}$$

    1851   WF 1.4   Number of Irish 350
    1861   WF 1.77   Number of Irish 1621
    1871   WF 1.8   Number of Irish 4136

To illustrate the concentration of Irish in the Newtown district I include an extract from the 1871 Census. This is an example of just one street in that area, Victoria Street. All other streets in this district had a similar accumulation of Irish residents. Not all the houses are numbered.

Number	Name	Occupation	Birthplace
1.	Michael Flanary*	Chem. Labourer	Galway
3.	Patrick Caton*	Labourer	Ireland
	James Newnan	Labourer	Ireland
	Gerald Newnan	Labourer	Ireland
	Thomas Kelly	Labourer	Ireland
5.	Bridget Sheridan	Grocer	Ireland
	Martin Purcill*	Labourer	Ireland
	Patrick Mackett*	Labourer	Ireland
7.	William Hays*	Labourer	Ireland
	John Fondler*	Labourer	Ireland
9.	Robert Kelly*	Chem. Lab.	Ireland
	William Cooney*	Labourer	Ireland
11.	Michael Gulligan*	Greengrocer	Ireland
	George Dodd	Stonemason	Cheshire
	Patrick White	Tailor	Ireland

---

[64] W.J. Lowe *"The Irish in mid-Victorian Lancashire"*

The Irish

11 contd.	Thomas Lacey	Labourer	Ireland
	William Hilldridge	Plumber	Salford
13.	William Burns*	Labourer	Ireland
	John Kernan*	Labourer	Ireland
17.	Samuel Hobley *	Labourer	Warwick
	James Furgeson*	Labourer	Ireland
	Edward Burke*	Labourer	Ireland
19.	Thomas Adams*	Labourer	Runcorn
	Christopher Maddon*	Labourer	Ireland
	Cornelius Higgans*	Labourer	Ireland
21.	Alice Thompson	Widow	Ireland
23.	Patrick Dunn*	Labourer	Dublin
25.	John Conley*	Labourer	Ireland
2.	Joseph Peterson	Butcher	Widnes
	Edward Percy	Labourer	Widnes
	Joseph Pinnington	Labourer	Ditton
	John Elleby	Labourer	Widnes
4.	Peter McMan*	Plasterer	Ireland
6.	John Moore	Waterman	Northwich
8.	Matthew Cullen*	Labourer	Wexford
10.	John Gormley*	Plumber	St. Helens
	James Connolly	Labourer	Ireland
	Charles McCana	Labourer	Ireland
12.	Thomas Sunderland*	Labourer	Ireland
	James Cabnor	Labourer	Ireland
14.	Samuel Richison	Joiner	Warrington
	William McConville*	Labourer	Ireland

Into The Crucible

14 cont.	Patrick Cosgrove	Labourer	Leitrim
	Michael McGarray*	Labourer	Leitrim
16.	John Corbett*	Chem.Lab	Galway
	Edward Currin	Furnaceman	Fermanagh
	James Carey	Labourer	Pendleton
	Francis Gillday*	Labourer	Ireland
	Daniel Murphy	Labourer	Ireland
	William Banks	Furnaceman	England
	Simion Corkeran*	Labourer	Ireland
	James Murphy	Cooper	Wexford

Occupants of un-numbered houses in Victoria Street:

Nicholas Clifford*	Labourer	Kilkenny
Andrew Kenny	Labourer	Leinster
Thomas Carroll	Labourer	Louth
James Kelly	Labourer	Cavan
Patrick McGuire*	Labourer	Ireland
Michael Callaghan *	Labourer	Ireland
Michael Kelly	Labourer	Ireland
Joseph Duncan	Labourer	Ireland
John White	Labourer	Ireland
William Walker	Carpenter	Halewood
John Mackim	Labourer	Ireland
John Laughran	Labourer	Armagh
Michael Gahagan*	Labourer	Ireland
Patrick Corbett*	Labourer	Ireland
Luke Whitney*	Furnaceman	Wexford
Peter Hall*	Blacksmith	Cronton
John Ireland*	Blacksmith	Cronton.

The county of birth is only mentioned in a small number of entries; most just give place of birth as Ireland. The names marked with an asterisk were the named head of a household. The names of wives and children are not included here, although they do appear on the original

The Irish

return and the addition of these would add significantly to the list of "Irish" occupants. The grouping (as in Number 16) indicates the level of shared occupancy of a single dwelling. The list also shows that there were a large number of young single men lodging in the town. Immigration statistics suggest that, in the main, the famine period influx came as members of a family unit but after the 1860s a typical emigrant was a lone single adult.

A similar selection for Church Street, West Bank, for the same period contains the names of people from Anglesey; Flint; Lymm; India; Northants; Middlesex; Cardiganshire; West Bromwich; Cornwall; Haydock; Northwich; Frodsham; Tarvin; Sutton; Cronton; Liverpool; Overton; Suffolk; Hampshire; and Rufford. There were no people of Irish birth.

The religious needs of the Irish community, which was predominantly Roman Catholic, was provided by the building of St. Marie's Church (originally known as St. Mary's) in Lugsdale Road in 1865. St. Bede's Church had already been built in 1847 for the Roman Catholics of Appleton, who at the time of building wondered if it was perhaps too large for the then small Catholic congregation. Later another church, St. Patrick's, was erected for the growing West Bank Roman Catholic community.

The Roman Catholic Church, while naturally addressing the spiritual needs of the Irish population, also attended to temporal needs and played an important role in establishing a strong community life. In later post-famine periods, the clergymen themselves were often Irish and were able to offer practical advice and guidance to newcomers. Torn up by their roots, the Priest was the last point of contact with their old way of life. The Church was the one constant and unchanging foundation they were able to refer back to; it offered them stability as well as faith, hope and charity. Perhaps allegations that the Church exerted a far greater influence over this society than was appropriate may have been justified. The Parish Priest had undisputed influence among his parishioners and was probably the only authority the Irish labourers deferred to. He was revered but also greatly feared even by the hardest and toughest of men. The other claim, that the Church had wide political influence, has never been proved. Whether its clout was powerful or persuasive enough to influence the outcome of elections is questionable.

The following names from the *very first* volume of Baptisms at St. Marie's Roman Catholic Church, Lugsdale Road, demonstrates the predominance of Irish names in that parish.

Surname	*Mother's maiden name*
Murtagh	*Leonard*
Cannon	*Ryan*
Murray	*Marrow*
Fox	*Benbow*
Yates	*Leyland*
Regan	*Sweeny*
Nolan	*Dogherty*
Tobin	*Jones*
Rice	*Smith*
Carroll	*Prescott*
Dougan	*Burns*
Loughlan	*Quigley*
Murphy	*Wright*
Reilly	*Dogherty*
Morrissy	*Smith*
Holleran	*Carty*
Mitchell	*Barr*
Doyle	*Kelly*
Gaffney	*Flemming*
Byrne	*Farrell*
Farrell	*Garry*
Canovan	*Burke*
Dunnigan	*Carr*
Tobin	*Goulding*
O`Neill	*Donnelly*
Cunningham	*Toohey*
Plunkett	*Abbott*
McAlhaney	*Owens*
M`Kutchin	*Bryan*

The Irish

By 1875 the Irish were firmly established and dominant in this community. The following is a list of almost entirely Irish names taken from the ***1875 Baptism Register***. These are the surnames of some of the children baptised that year.

> *Rooney*
> *Matthews*
> *Mitchell*
> *Wall*
> *Connolly*
> *Burke*
> *Leary*
> *Ford*
> *Carty*
> *Kelly*
> *McCormick*
> *Hogan*
> *Lynch*
> *Ryan*
> *Boles*
> *Dermody*
> *Daly*

For those Irish who had come here in the hope of improving their lifestyle generally the dream did not live up to the reality. Many lived in abject poverty and as a consequence they were compelled to apply to The Prescot Union for help. In spite of any obvious need, under the conditions of the *Act of Settlement and Removal* obtaining assistance was not an easy process. Poor people who applied for help needed to validate their claim to Poor Relief by proving *"settlement"* within the Parish where the claim was made. If settlement could not be proved, he or she could be forcibly removed back to the Parish of their birth. When a claimant could not prove settlement they were served with a summons to appear before a Magistrate, who would make an order for them to be "removed". It was often difficult for Poor Law Unions to enforce this Act as some summonses were just ignored and people relocated to other places. Of course the other difficulty was that most Unions did not have the resources to ship large numbers of people back to Ireland or wherever they had come from. Nevertheless, for some

Into The Crucible

Irish, the threat of removal was enough to prevent them from seeking help, as they feared being sent back to Ireland.

In 1881 there were controversial plans to reform the "settlement" conditions of the *Poor Removal (Ireland) Bill*. Most Unions were fearful of the financial consequences of this amendment. The following report appeared in *The Widnes Weekly News* of 18th June 1881.

> **THE POOR REMOVAL (IRELAND) BILL**
> *A memorial from the Wigan Union has been forwarded to the Board calling attention to the Poor Removal (Ireland) Bill, which stated that by the Bill it was proposed to enact that no poor person should be removed from England, Wales or Scotland to Ireland from any parish to which such a poor person became chargeable by reason of relief given, provided the said poor person resided in England, Wales or Scotland for five years before becoming chargeable. If the Bill passed in its present form, the memorial stated, very considerable hardship would be inflicted, especially in places where there were many Irish people living. It was therefore a Bill that should be carefully considered by all Lancashire Unions. The practical result of the passing of the Bill as it presently stood would be that an Irish pauper would be enabled to select the parish in which to become chargeable, although he might never have lived or worked for a single day in that parish. The Bill, although not a good measure, would probably receive the support of the Government, unless a strong effort was made to convince them of its injustice. The Wigan Union, therefore, asked to petition against the Bill. The Board were of the opinion that the Bill was one which, if it became law, would affect the Prescot Union very seriously and disastrously, and on the motion of Mr. Hall, seconded by Mr. Meadows, it was unanimously decided that it be petitioned against.*

Throughout the nineteenth century there were several issues associated with Ireland and the Irish which provoked controversy both here and across the Irish Sea. The Landlord system in Ireland stirred outrage not only among the Irish but also amongst decent English people with a social and humanitarian conscience. The evictions which had been prevalent during the famine periods continued all the way through the century, creating great hardship and suffering for those who had been turned out of their homes. Many of those evicted had to witness the sight of their homes being burned to the ground by the Landlords' agents, in order to prevent them returning. As a consequence of these events, a fund was set up to alleviate the suffering. *The Irish Eviction Fund* collected money through their branches in Ireland and England. In England, the Secretary of the fund was the MP Mr. Harrington. In Widnes, not surprisingly, the local Secretary was Dr. O Keeffe who was the champion of the local Irish population. There were several other leading citizens who were moved by the plight of the Irish. In early January 1887 one of our town's worthies, Samuel Sadler, made a personal donation of 10/6d to the Eviction Fund. He wrote:

Dear Doctor O`Keeffe,

I beg to enclose you 10/6d in aid of the poor people of Ireland who are being so cruelly and ruthlessly thrust from their homes by the tyrant land grabbers, at a season which ought to have been to them one of joyous festivity, but which, there is reason to fear, will be to some of them one of distress and sorrow.

You will doubtless know where the distress is the greatest: please forward it to that quarter. Trusting the mite I am able to send may help to alleviate in some measure the distress of some of my less fortunate fellow creatures.

Samuel Sadler.

Dr. O` Keeffe's participation in this undertaking is not unexpected. He regularly involved himself in a whole range of local matters especially those related to Irish issues. He was a complex and fascinating character whose good works and genuine acts of kindness and generosity were countless and legendary. However, despite his undoubted benevolence and compassion, he was not an easy man to deal with. He was single-minded and persistent in his endeavours and certainly not a man to cross. He regularly got *"a bee in his bonnet"* about some issue or other. As a result he sometimes came up with unreasonable and totally preposterous suggestions and stubbornly refused to back down. On one occasion he proposed that *The Times* newspaper should be banned from the Public Library because of its "alleged" libel against the Irish Nationalist MP, Mr. Charles Stewart Parnell. Of course this would have meant bringing politics into an area where impartiality was essential. After what appeared to be a lively and bad-tempered meeting of the Library Committee, his suggestion was, not surprisingly, rejected by the members of The Local Board.

Into The Crucible

Doctor O`Keeffe was famously confrontational when he believed he was in the right, and of course he always thought he was. As would be expected of such a strong character, he was not selective or fearful in choosing his adversaries. In 1889 the good Doctor antagonised and openly challenged the Roman Catholic Dean of Appleton over the timing of *The Irish National League* meetings. Most Roman Catholics of that era would never have disagreed with an appointed religious representative of their church, in fact to do so would have been tantamount to sacrilege. In spite of this perceived irreverence, there was a great deal of aggravated and heated discussion between the two Irishmen on this subject. The Dean objected to The League holding one of its regular meetings on a Sunday. It seems that most of the Irish male population of Widnes, apart from the Dean, were members of this Society or of another Irish organisation called *The Irish Foresters* – both of whom had Sunday meetings. One member of *The Irish National League*, who was possibly emboldened by the Doctor's attitude, wrote to *The Widnes Weekly News* in defence of the decision to meet on Sundays.

> *"The Dean of Appleton does not know the object of the League, how can he when he is not a member? For my part, as a member I think it is a holy society, and just before God and man. I do not think it is harmful to hold meetings on a Sunday – a few hours to hear good lectures on morality and nationality. Now if those lectures were bad and immoral I would very much agree with the Dean. This grand National Society is one of the finest we ever had as Irishmen. We are not afraid of informers being amongst us, and therefore I cannot see why but we should have a few hours on a Sunday afternoon, no more than his young men's society on a Sunday night at the schools. I must also say that the National League has done a deal of good in Widnes for charitable purposes, and I am sure that the Dean is not a member of it, neither did he ever subscribe anything towards it. For my part I would be ashamed of any Irishman that would not be a member of the National League. And now my advice to him would be to keep his wind to cool his porridge for the future and not to interfere with the National League".*

At a meeting of *The Irish National League* in mid-September 1889 the main business of the evening was the selection of Widnes members who were to be delegates to the forthcoming National Convention that was to be held in Manchester. Those present at *The Irish National League* meeting that evening included Messrs. Nolan, Horan, O`Connor, Stafford, Griffin, Tyrell, Kinsella, Behan, McKabe and Delaney. Mr.

The Irish

Horan brought to the notice of the meeting the subject of boycotting some Widnes based Irishmen. This demonstrates that Fenianism, and intimidation associated with it, was very much alive and active in Widnes.

> *"The case of the two (names illegible) whose father is hostile to the national cause in Ireland. His cruel doings in Ireland have created ill will and ill feelings for his sons, who live here, and we were surprised to hear that when these men were turned right out of Ann Street that they could find lodgings in the (omitted), and that shopkeepers in Widnes were still supplying them with groceries. This meeting wishes to give notice to all whom it may concern that in future a very close watch will be kept on shopkeepers who will supply or in any way support the enemies of the Irish cause".*

Newtown in 1891 could almost be described as *"Little Ireland"*. The census of that year shows street after street occupied by predominantly Irish families. While the district was not exclusively Irish they were numerically the largest ethnic group in that locality. In fact, at one point in time they were the largest ethnic group in the town and even outnumbered the English. The information contained in the census also allows us to note a significant number of first generation Irish *"Widnesians"*. There were numerous entries which showed the head of the household and spouse being Irish born, whilst their children's place of birth is identified as Widnes.

In ***Catherine Street***, Joseph Tyrell and his wife Mary were both Irish born but their children James (13), Patrick (11), John (6), Michael (4), and Samuel (1) were all born in Widnes. Their Irish born neighbours, Peter and Charlotte Cullen, had three Widnes born sons, Peter (21), Thomas (17) and James (12). Also in ***Catherine Street*** the same pattern applied to the Hughes, Cosgrove and Leonard families.

In nearby ***Elizabeth Street*** we see the pattern duplicated with the Daley, Mannion, Thomas, Cafferty and Donegan families. This trend is echoed throughout the working-class districts of the town and applies to all foreign ethnic communities. This new generation of townspeople represented a group whose ethnicity became diluted as they and their own children were subsequently absorbed into the general population.

Into The Crucible

The incorporation of the Local Board into a Municipal Borough in 1891 ensured that the months preceding the first election in November 1892 were a time of frantic activity. All the parties prepared to select their candidates and began a vigorous canvassing procedure. The Irish population in the town were anxious for their voice to be heard and wanted their community to be adequately represented. Numerous meetings were organised by *The Irish National League,* all of which were well attended. Even after the elections the campaign for representation continued to be a major theme for *The League. The Widnes Weekly News* printed the following report on 3rd December 1892.

NATIONALIST MEETING AT WIDNES
On Wednesday evening a public meeting in connection with the National League was held in the Baths Assembly Room. Dr. O` Keeffe presided and was supported on the platform by Mr. T.D. Sullivan, MP, Councillor Carsey (Liverpool), Mr. Boyle (Manchester), Alderman Williamson, Councillors Fitzpatrick, Carney, Singleton, Gough, Messrs. H. O` Donnell and Rowe.

The Chairman urged upon the Irishmen of Widnes to continue their strenuous efforts to have their portion of the population fairly well represented on the new Town Council. He hoped their efforts would not be relaxed until they got a number of representatives on the Council equal to their portion of the population. There were a greater number of Irishmen in Widnes than in any town of the same size in England. It did not matter what other people said, he knew the Irish were nearly one half of the population, therefore they must still press on and achieve greater results than those at the recent municipal elections (applause).

Councillor Carsey moved:" That this meeting is of the opinion that the time has now arrived when the Irishmen of Widnes should go shoulder to shoulder in maintaining and improving the proud position they have achieved at the recent municipal elections, and in order to secure success at coming elections we would earnestly urge the necessity of every Irishman to become a member of the T.P. O` Connor Branch of the Irish National League of Great Britain." Speaking of the success of the Liberal Party in Liverpool at the recent municipal elections, he attributed it, mainly to the strength and combination of the Irish Party. It was a great and grand thing to have such a man as Mr. Gladstone on the side of the Irish Party. It was a fine thing to hear such a venerable statesman make a declaration that the remainder of his

The Irish

life would be devoted to the benefit of Ireland and Irishmen (applause). He congratulated them upon the fine representation they had on the Widnes Council, but they must make their Irish organisation strong, and be true to the friends of Ireland, whether they might be English or Irish, so that they would be able to face the enemy. He ventured to say that the Tory party were the enemies, wherever they might be. They were not going to forget the action of the Tories during the last six years. He begged them to claim their proper representation in all public bodies, and stand shoulder to shoulder with the friends of Irishmen (applause).

Mr. Boyle seconded the resolution, and said he was angry to think that such a resolution was necessary in a town like Widnes. He advised them to stand as one solid organisation, and never rest satisfied until Irishmen had gained freedom and self-government. If the Liberals did not work, Irishmen must, for it was an Irish question and must be settled by combination (applause).

Mr. Sullivan, who received a hearty welcome, said it was not too soon to prepare for another battle and a greater victory. It was true that their majority in the House of Commons was not a large one, but he believed it was a true one, each member being true hearted (applause). He urged them to see to registration and their votes. A few weeks hence their grand old leader would place a charter of freedom on the table of the House of Commons.

Alderman Williamson proposed a vote of thanks to the speakers. He hoped that from that time forward the Widnes branch of the National League would be more successful. They did not want all the representation on the Council, but what was fair and just (applause). There were no spiteful feelings against their English friends. With reference to another little gentleman, who by his intrigue and to gain his own ends had robbed the Irish Party of their power in the town, he could only say that when they got the chance they would pay him back in such a manner that his own party would run away from him (applause).

Although I have my suspicions, I have yet to discover the true identity of the *"other little gentleman"* or whether he was ever *"paid back"*. As was evident from the above transcript, the Irish population and the Widnes branch of *The Irish National League* continued to offer their general support to the Liberal Party and to work alongside them.

Into The Crucible

By the autumn of 1897 the Widnes Irish were turning their thoughts to the forthcoming centenary of the *"1798 Uprising"*. In preparation for the event the Widnes branch of the *Irish National Foresters Mutual Benefit Society* had organised a *"`98 Centenary Committee"*. In conjunction with the proposed centenary plans, a series of lectures were held at *The Irish Social Club* in Victoria Road. The Chief Ranger of the Widnes branch, Mr. P. McCann, presided over the first lecture, welcoming the speaker, Professor J.F. Brenerd, of Liverpool. Professor Brenard's lecture gave a graphic description of the `98 Rising. He outlined the background to this troublesome period, the cause, extent and the main characters involved. The lecture was listened to with great interest and was enhanced by the use of limelight illustrations. After the lecture the audience was treated to some musical selections performed by Miss Brenerd and Mr. Mitchell.

During the same period, the Widnes Branch of *The Irish National League* was also offering lectures in connection with the forthcoming centenary. Mr. Thomas Fahey, the local President, welcomed Mr. O`Hagan, whose lecture was entitled *"The land that we love"*. Mr. O`Hagan began his lecture by quoting Sir Walter Scott:

> *Breathes there a man with a soul so dead*
> *Who never to himself hath said*
> *This is my own my native land?*

He continued thus:

> *"Among men of differing nationalities there might certainly be a great number with souls so dead as never to think of their native country, but amongst Irishmen the percentage would be very small for, with the Irish race, next after the love and honour they owed to Almighty God came the love and honour of their native land. In some distant parts of the world it might be that an Irishman acknowledged his permanent resting place, but there were many others in which he would not call his daily house his home. He would in his own mind be desecrating the word by doing so. His home was across the blue water, in that little island which perhaps he might visit no more, which he had left at any rate for half his life, and from which circumstances and the necessity of living had banished him, but his home was still in Ireland, and when he spoke of home his thoughts were there. There was no one who could understand the intensity of this feeling except*

The Irish

those who had felt it. Only those who had been in foreign lands could really understand the meaning of the word home".

Mr. O` Hagan exhibited over a hundred lantern views of Irish scenery during his lecture and was heartily applauded as each new view came on the screen. He spoke of Irish literature, art and poetry and was enthusiastically applauded. His lecture concluded with the following: *"Nature had made the Irish people blithe, frank, and hospitable, pleasant comrades and trusty friends, but hard laws and hard task masters had perverted their disposition and made them quarrelsome amongst themselves but these dissentions of the past few years were dying out and a new era was dawning".*

In April 1898 the Irish community of Widnes were shocked and greatly saddened to hear of the death of the much loved Dr. John McNaughten O` Keeffe. I have remarked in previous pages that Doctor O` Keeffe was a huge presence in the town. As well as having been the champion of the Widnes Irish community for almost 40 years, he was also one of the most well-known characters not only in this immediate area but also within its extended hinterlands. Besides being a master of controversy he was also a dynamic and positive character who got things done. Unfortunately a few years earlier, after a stroke had left him partially paralysed, he had reluctantly retired from his practice in Widnes and relocated to Preston where he had family connections.

John McNaughten O` Keeffe was born in Tralee, County Kerry, on 27th December 1837 and was just 61 years old when he died in Preston on 7th April 1898. He was educated at Queens College in Cork and later took his medical degree in Edinburgh. Prior to coming to Widnes he worked for a few years in Preston where he met his future wife. On his arrival in Widnes he worked as assistant to Dr. Greenup, in Farnworth, before setting up his own practice in Widnes Road. His personal life was marred by tragedy when his wife, Grace, died in 1872 at the early age of 35. Just four months before her death their 5month old son, John, had died. A few years earlier, in 1868, John and Grace had also endured the tragic loss of their baby daughter. After the sad and premature death of his wife and children Dr. O` Keeffe concentrated his time and energies working for the public good. I am glad to say that Dr. O`Keeffe did manage to find happiness again and some years later he married for the second time. His second wife was Theresa Rice the

Into The Crucible

6th daughter of John Rice of Derby and the wedding took place at St. Marie's R.C. Church in Derby.

Almost forty years of Dr. O`Keeffe's working life had been entirely devoted to the people of Widnes. He served on the Local Board, the School Board, the Library and Technical Institute Committee and he was the town's Medical Officer of Health for a great number of years. He undertook all these duties diligently, as well as being a hardworking GP to an underprivileged section of the community. His political views were by nature Liberal and he was an active member of the Widnes Liberal Party. In addition he was a staunch Home-Ruler and regularly spoke about that subject on local political platforms. A short while after Dr. O'Keeffe's death the local Liberal Party paid an emotional tribute to him at a special meeting attended by Mr. Roscoe Brunner,[*] the son of Sir John Brunner. During that evening many moving eulogies were given by several members. There is no doubt that Doctor O` Keeffe was well loved by the local population and a contemporary source stated *"that there was no better-known figure in the town than Doctor O` Keeffe"*. The provision of a Reading Room and a Public Library for the town was a direct result of his efforts and he was instrumental in bringing in several improvements related to public health. During one of his many heated debates he had said: *"I don't care whether I am a solitary individual or not, I will always do what I can for the benefit of Widnes"*. Sadly his name is little known today despite his long and faithful service to the town and its citizens.

Official and personal tributes were also paid to Dr. O` Keeffe in our sister town across the river. Although unrelated, a month after his death, in May 1898, the Runcorn Urban Council called a public meeting in respect of a cause which would have been very dear to Dr. O` Keeffe's heart. The meeting was for the purpose of starting a fund for the relief of the distressed districts in the west of Ireland. Mr. F.J. Norman chaired the meeting and he told a large audience that:

"There is something like 300,000 people suffering in the West of Ireland due to the failure of last season's potato crop. The crops were not equal to half of

---

[*] Roscoe Brunner was to end his life in tragic circumstances. After his failure to secure a place on the Board of the newly formed ICI he fell into a state of depression. He murdered his wife, Ethel, and then committed suicide. For further reading see *"Formula for Murder"* - R.M. Bevan 2003

what they had been in previous years. That being so, the masses were suffering considerably. In fact it was well known that there were thousands of these people who lived upon the soil and who had difficulty in making both ends meet in the best of times; therefore they could imagine what these people were suffering under the present condition of things. The Runcorn people were always willing to help in case of need and those who were unable to help themselves, and on the present occasion he felt that the working people of the town, from the highest to the lowest, would do all that lay in their power to render assistance to these worthy people who were suffering so severely at the present time. Father Gore has received letters of support and sympathy combined with practical actions and he was pleased to hear that among them was one from Superintendent Okell enclosing a sovereign subscribed by the Police Force of Runcorn".

There was a great deal of anger and controversy surrounding an article in *The Catholic Herald* in July 1901. The article referred to a leaflet which was being circulated around the streets of Liverpool and nearby towns, including Widnes. The writer, the Rev. Fr. Kavanagh, claimed that any Irishman who enlisted in the British Army was *"a traitor to Ireland and an offender against the laws of God and the Catholic Church"*. To reinforce his views Father Kavanagh quoted from a letter he had received from an Irish soldier who was fighting in South Africa. The soldier described the hardships he was enduring in the British Army simply because he was "Irish". In fact, it would seem that the leaflet was deliberately misleading. The soldier in question was living under the same conditions and experiencing the same hardships as any other soldier in the British Army, be he English, Irish, Scots or Welsh. The leaflet was said to have had a detrimental effect on the recruitment of Irish into the army, particularly in Liverpool where there was a marked decline in the numbers enlisting. English Catholics were quite naturally outraged at what some described as the *"sinful and seditious advice"* of the Rev. Fr. Kavanagh.

The subject of *"Home Rule for Ireland"* was still simmering away. In October 1912, W.G.C. Gladstone MP, the grandson of the late Liberal Leader, William Gladstone, addressed a large audience of Liberals in The Borough Hall. Among the topics covered on that evening was Irish Home Rule. During his speech Mr. Gladstone highlighted the sectarian divisions in Northern Ireland, giving one a distinct feeling of deja vu. He also drew attention to the general religious prejudice of those who were opposed to Home Rule and pointed out that there were many fine Protestant leaders who had championed Ireland's cause.

"Our opponents are adopting very discreditable methods. They are attempting to prejudice people against the Roman Catholics of Ireland by encouraging the idea that under Home Rule Catholics are going to bring about the ascendancy of their own denomination, and are going to oppress the Protestant minority. I am not a Roman Catholic, and if I may say so without offence to Catholics here, I am glad that I am a Protestant, yet I do feel rather ashamed sometimes at the suspicions and allegations that are made against the Irish Roman Catholics. (cheers). This has so far been the least creditable part of the controversy (hear, hear)

Proceeding, Mr. Gladstone reminded his listeners that the Home Rule policy owed its origin to Isaac Butt, a Protestant, and Charles Stewart Parnell, another Protestant, who brought Home Rule from the propaganda to the legislative stage; that another leader of the Irish Party, Mr. Shaw, was also a Protestant, and that many members of the Irish Party were Protestants returned by Roman Catholic votes. The Nationalist Party had elected a Protestant as their leader three times in succession (applause)".

Mr. Gladstone quoted extensively from a speech given by Ramsey Macdonald on the second reading of the Irish Home Rule Bill. Mr. MacDonald's speech had shown the religious divisions in Belfast and demonstrated the futility of these divisions. He ridiculed the beating of the orange drum and the waving of green flags. He pointed out that both these groups should be uniting in the fight against the real enemy, poverty and labour exploitation in Belfast.

While the Irish population were now able to contribute, as electors, to their new way of life in Widnes they were also beginning to adapt to the new order of things. However this adaptation did not mean the loss of Irish ways and customs that were still strong and evident in many respects. Among the traditions transferred from their old way of life were the rituals associated with death. The Irish wake was an ancient tradition in Ireland and its purpose was to ensure that the person who had died would not be left alone on the night after death. Neighbours, family members and friends would gather to keep the corpse company while it made its journey from this life to the next. Drinks and tobacco were usually provided and the people gathered there would have conversations in which they remembered the deceased in happier times. The inclusion of drink in the proceedings usually meant that there was a certain amount of joviality before the night was over. This was a traditional part of the ritual as the family of the deceased would have considered it important to give the corpse a *"good send-off"* on its journey into the next world. The inevitable drinking and merrymaking that became synonymous with an Irish wake was often found to be distasteful to other sections of local society.

The keeping of up traditions such as the Irish Wake and the celebration of Saints' Days was an important part of Irish communal living which served as a comforting reminder of their old way of life. These reminders helped to ease the process of change as most of the early Irish immigrants into Widnes were overwhelmed by their new surroundings. They also struggled to improve their circumstances and to adapt to a new way of life. Fortunately the road was eased by the succour of their predominantly Irish neighbourhoods in Newtown, Lugsdale and Moss Bank. In addition to the empathy of their fellow immigrants, important support was also provided by the Catholic Church and various Irish cultural societies.

As the Irish gradually began to assimilate and subsequent generations were absorbed into mainstream society, their influence, though diluted, was still present in a variety of ways. A great deal has been written about the development of the Liverpool accent and the impact various ethnic groups had on this. In much the same way we must assume that the predominance of Irish families in this town probably contributed to a gradual change in the local dialect. In fact, the creation of what we have come to accept as the local Widnes accent may owe more to immigrant communities than to the indigenous Lancashire population. Whilst our language still retained many of the original Lancashire words and sounds it became a peculiar hybrid that also, inevitably, included elements of Irish and Welsh sounds as well as sayings and expressions.

Into The Crucible

A rare photograph of Dr. O`Keeffe
(Unfortunately the quality is poor).

The Lithuanians and Poles

In modern times travel between other countries has become commonplace. Journeys from one country or continent to another are no longer the sole privilege of the rich or famous, nor are such journeys considered to be anything out of the ordinary. Today, to some extent, we are all globe-trotters or citizens of Europe and the wider world. During the nineteenth century things were vastly different. The very fact that our town became home to a community of Eastern Europeans, who had travelled from far distant Baltic States, was in itself a situation worthy of note. Their long journey here was not without danger but the pressing reasons for migration outweighed any hardship the journey presented. Moreover, these Baltic immigrants were at that time as much refugees as economic migrants.

Our early ethnic communities played an important role in forming the character of our town. As I stated earlier, when writing about the Irish, it is important to provide some background information on our diverse communities and the reasons why they came here. Obviously the incentives that brought all immigrants to Widnes were connected with employment opportunities. However, the circumstances which prompted their initial departure from their respective homelands were usually created out of necessity. As with the early Irish incomers, the Lithuanians and Poles became a significant element in local society and their presence in Widnes contributed to a rich tapestry of woven cultures which greatly enriched the town. The experiences that prompted their migration are often heartbreaking and the personal histories of many Widnes families would make extremely sad reading. Most of these migrants had endured evil beyond description in their homeland. Apart from economic hardship they had undergone a brutal campaign to destroy not only their national identity but also their religion.

In order to give my reader an insight into the many reasons for their arrival in Widnes I give here a brief summary of the history and environment they were leaving behind. This abstract will also explain why most of these Baltic migrants were described as Russian or Russian Poles when, in fact, the majority were in fact Lithuanians. To start the story one might need to go back as far as the late 14th century when the countries of Lithuania and Poland existed as a double Kingdom but the name Poland was used to describe both. The two countries co-existed relatively peacefully until the end of the 18th century when both Lithuania and Poland were subsequently annexed by Russia and, in effect, their borders were erased. The result of this was that from this period until 1918 Poland and Lithuania ceased to exist as separate political entities. The annexing of the two countries was a brutal occupation which resulted in a process of concentrated colonization and Russification. The main aim of the Tsarist imperial philosophy at that time was to assimilate the non-Russian peoples into the Russian cultural and political system. As a consequence there was a systematic attempt to destroy their national identity, language, culture and faith.

The years 1861 to 1918 are a very significant period in the histories of both Poland and Lithuania. The abolition of serfdom in 1861 and the insurrection of 1863 laid the foundations for a revival of historic nationalist traditions. Consequently, the social and economic effect of these events became a turning point in the history of Polish-Lithuanian relations. At this juncture, the developing Lithuanian nation began to realise its own political goals, not only through confrontation with the Poles, but also in the struggle with the Tsarist regime. This period can probably be defined as the one in which the Lithuanian nation finally detached itself from Polish life and a rise in Lithuanian nationalism occurred.

After the 1861 abolition of serfdom there was an increase in peasant landowning. Landlords, who had previously benefited from the system of serfdom, were compelled to sell off parts of their land in order to pay for the labour that had previously been *free*. The improved conditions of the peasants brought with it a fall in the mortality rate and an increase in the birth rate. However, this advancement in their way of life was to be short-lived. During the 1870s and 1880s there was a serious depression in agricultural prices and this, coupled with the rising population figures, had a severe effect on the economy. The poverty this created heralded the start of a period of mass migration.

The Lithuanians and Poles

At the time these Baltic migrants were leaving their homelands both Lithuania and Poland were still annexed to Russia. This situation caused an external blurring of identity between these two distinct ethnic groups. Most census records did not officially recognise Lithuanians as a separate nationality until the 20th century and as a result most were described as Russian, Polish or Jewish. All of the Lithuanian immigrants who came to Widnes were routinely described as Russian, Russian Poles or simply Poles. Even official Government documents and statistics made no distinction between these two separate nationalities. The *Alien Registration Document* of one Widnes immigrant classifies the person as "Russian" whilst the place of birth is clearly given as Lithuania.[*] Similar registration documents of two individuals who were born in Kaunas, Lithuania, describe them as "Russian Pole"[65]. Further local records and newspaper reports describe all members of this community as "Poles". However, having spoken to a considerable number of their descendants, I am assured that the majority of the early immigrants into Widnes were Lithuanian not Polish. An elderly lady whose parents *were* actually Poles stated that there were *"only a handful of Poles in Widnes – they were mostly Lithuanian.* In the absence of source material that could differentiate between these early immigrants, I accept this lady's statement.

The identification inaccuracy caused irritation to many members of the Lithuanian community who were, naturally, proud of their national origins. Unfortunately this mistake occurred in all the places where Lithuanian immigrants had made settlement. A letter appeared in a Lanarkshire newspaper, *The Bellshill Speaker*, in January 1901 in which the writer complained of this error. He said: *"The mistake is commonly made by the Press and others of speaking about our people as Poles, while, as a matter of fact, the actual Poles in this country do not number more than one hundredth part of the number of Lithuanians. In a country where the "Britain v. England" controversy rages, it is not necessary, I trust, to apologise for intruding to make a correction such as this."* The letter was signed by V. Kisielius who was President of The Lithuanian Educational Society in Lanarkshire.

---

[*] Document in the possession of Mrs. Elizabeth Ellis
[65] Documents in the possession of Mr. Harold McKay

Into The Crucible

Of course there *were* Polish people in Widnes and other areas of the country in the 19th century and the early years of the 20th century. There were substantial Polish communities in Liverpool and Manchester in those early periods. In later years, during the two World Wars, thousands of displaced persons came into England from all over Europe and many Poles did come into Widnes during these times as well. It is estimated that after the last war around 160,000 Poles settled in England. However, for the purposes of this book, my main concentration has been on Lithuanian rather than Polish immigrants. My reason for this is that the Lithuanians were undoubtedly the larger of these two groups in this town.

As we have seen, the economic depression of the 1870s and 1880s had a severe impact on Lithuania and Poland and created an environment which fostered emigration. However, there were obviously many other different reasons why Poles and Lithuanians left their homes. The desire to escape the poverty associated with the dire economic situation was just one reason. Brutal political repression and religious persecution, coupled with a reluctance to be conscripted into the Russian Army, were other reasons. In fact, for many, life under the oppressive and cruel Tsarist regime was intolerable. They had been robbed of their national identity and, as Roman Catholics, they suffered ruthless discrimination and their churches were routinely burned down. Therefore it is not unreasonable for me to describe this ethnic group as political and religious refugees in addition to their status as economic migrants.

In the early days emigration from the Baltic States was usually only on a temporary basis. Like the Irish who took seasonal work in Newfoundland, Lithuanians and Poles often took seasonal work in Germany. This migratory work pattern was cyclical, with the number of migrating workers shifting along with the seasons and economic cycles. Like the Irish, in the main, they came from rural agricultural backgrounds. Their seasonal work in Germany was often their first real experience of commercial industry. The continued comparisons with the Irish are interesting. Although language and cultures were obviously differing factors, the backgrounds, needs and aspirations were almost the same. After spending time in Germany many men were, understandably, reluctant to return to the hardship and repression in their own countries. Like the Irish, they too set their

The Lithuanians and Poles

sights on America. England and Scotland were usually intended to be stepping-stones towards this preferred destination. It is estimated that over 300,000 Lithuanians journeyed to America during the late 19th and early 20th centuries.

Most of the Lithuanians and Poles arrived in Britain through the northeast ports but large numbers also came directly into Liverpool. Although our own area did not begin receiving Baltic immigrants till the 1880s many Poles arrived in Liverpool prior to the early 1870s. At a Select Vestry Meeting held in Liverpool in 1876 it was claimed that there were 65 Poles housed at that time in the local workhouse. Obviously the City was reluctant to place this extra burden on the Poor Rates. During the course of the meeting it emerged that a number of Poles had previously been sent to the Cheshire salt-works. It was suggested that under the terms of *The Act of Settlement* the remainder should be sent back to Hamburg, the port they had sailed from. Despite this, by 1881 there was an estimated 542 "Poles" in Liverpool and by 1891 this number had risen to 630[66]. Although all were described as "Poles" (and most of this group were) it is believed that this number may also include some people of Lithuanian origin.

With the growing number of Baltic immigrants in Liverpool, The Bishop of Liverpool appointed a bi-lingual priest, Father Joseph von Lassberg, a German Jesuit, as a temporary chaplain to the Polish and Lithuanian communities in the city. The Poles and Lithuanians who chose to stay in Liverpool often found work at the Tate & Lyle Sugar Works which was known to be a large employer of Baltic labour. Other Baltic arrivals into Liverpool, who decided to move on, went to work in the coalmines and chemical factories in nearby Lancashire towns. Others moved further afield and went to the Cheshire salt mines; an industry some already had experience of. One Widnes family informed me that their grandfather had worked in salt mines in Russia before coming to England.

One of the earliest Lithuanian settlements in Britain was in Lanarkshire, Scotland. Some sources claim that the first Lithuanians

---

[66] J. Zubrzycki *"Polish Immigrants into Britain"* (Liverpool University) 1956

Into The Crucible

arrived in Scotland in 1855 as prisoners from the Crimean War[*]. These Lithuanians had been forced to fight in the Tsarist army and were taken prisoner. It is not known how many of them settled there permanently. However, from 1870 onwards a small but steady stream of migrants arrived in Scotland under their own steam. By the first decades of the 20th century a substantial number of Lithuanian immigrants had put down roots in Scotland. Interestingly, a sizeable proportion of the Lithuanians who went to Scotland originally came from the Sulvalkija area in the southwest of the country, particularly from the Kaunas district, where they had lived in small rural villages.

The Scottish historian, John Millar, in his book *"The Lithuanians in Scotland"* tells us that the greatest number of Lithuanians arriving in Scotland was during the period 1890-1914. By 1891 there was a sizeable community in Lanarkshire. Records indicate that the number of new arrivals from the Baltic peaked around 1900 and died away almost completely by 1914. Statistical returns for the period 1890-1900 give the number of "Poles" in Lanarkshire as 3000 but John Millar suggests that this might be an exaggeration. Nevertheless their numbers were significant and by 1906 there were about 200 Lithuanians just in the Newtongrange district. Moreover, an official report issued in 1916, possibly connected to *Alien Registration Records*, stated that there were in excess of 4000 Lithuanians working in the mines of Lanarkshire.

The majority of the immigrants arrived through the ports of Leith and Hull. Their journey would have been long and arduous, having made their way westwards through East Prussia to Hamburg from where those who came under their own steam hoped to make the journey to America. However, as the fare to America was equivalent to around £5 and the fare to Leith was only £1 many opted for the cheaper fare. Most planned to resume their journey to America when they had worked to save the additional fare. Some did so, and many sons, daughters, brothers and sisters left their families behind in Scotland and headed off to the New World, never to be reunited. Others remained in Scotland or made their way southwards to areas of Lancashire where there were plentiful employment opportunities, as well as the advantage of close proximity to the Port of Liverpool with its transatlantic traffic.

---

[*] This was a widely accepted claim, although John Millar in his book about Lithuanians in Scotland says this is a myth.

The Lithuanians and Poles

Their arrival in Scotland was no accident, nor was it a place chosen at random. The agents of Lanarkshire ironmasters and mine owners recruited many of these Lithuanians in Germany and the Baltic. They were enticed by an offer of work and financial assistance for their journey to Scotland. Amongst those actively enlisting Lithuanian labour were Merry and Cunninghame, owners of ironworks and coalmines in the Carnbroe area. They were also offered employment in the iron and steel works of Beardsmore`s; Smith & McLeans; and Stewarts & Lloyds. Another important employer of Lithuanian labour was the Lothian Coal Company of Newtongrange. This firm exported coal to the Baltic States via their coal ships from Leith. On the return voyage they imported Lithuanian workers for their pit.

The process of emigration to a foreign land was probably a difficult procedure for immigrants of all nationalities. For the Baltic immigrants into Scotland the language was an additional impediment. Unfortunately, once they embarked upon their journey across the North Sea they were at the mercy of the representatives of their prospective employers. They had no idea where they were going or what awaited them. An edition of *The Daily Mail* in 1887 referred to *"a batch of Poles"* arriving at a railway station in Ayrshire *"with labels around their necks saying "deliver to Merry & Cunninghame, Glengarnock"*. If this was indeed true, one cannot imagine how demeaning this must have been for those poor people. Treated like freight and stripped of their dignity. Of course that was only the beginning of the humiliating and intolerant treatment that was in store for them.

These new arrivals into Scotland were generally robust, healthy and strong agricultural workers. They were accustomed to hard physical work and were seen as a godsend to the ironmasters and mine owners of Scotland who had been hampered by industrial disputes. After their arrival these once rural dwellers, who had no experience of the iron and coal industry, were set to work as furnace workers and underground miners. They were accommodated in Company owned single-storey houses that were uniformly laid out in long narrow rows. The dwellings, like those in Widnes, were in very close proximity to their place of work. In some of these districts the houses were alongside the huge mountainous heaps of coal and waste slag that stretched across the landscape.

Into The Crucible

When describing the general atmosphere of these districts John Miller said:

> "In the villages and towns of Lanarkshire and Ayrshire, where the majority of the ironworks were situated, the smoke and flames from the unceasing fires of the blast furnaces created a perpetual twilight during the day and at night the red glow lit up the area turning night into day – you could read the paper in the street at midnight."

Although comparatively large numbers of Lithuanians arrived in Lanarkshire, it should be pointed out that leaving Lithuania, Poland or other Baltic States at that time was not a straightforward process. Although many did go to Germany for seasonal work, Tsarist Russia did not readily allow them to leave their countries permanently. All sorts of restrictions were applied which meant that most departures were usually of a clandestine nature. This normally involved illegally crossing borders and travelling via the German ports of Hamburg and Bremen to Leith or Hull. As an indication of the great efforts that were made by Lanarkshire employers to entice workers from the Baltic to Scotland, we have only to refer to a book entitled *"Lietuviu Kolumbai"*[67] (The Lithuanian Columbuses). This book tells us that recruiting agents in Lithuania, working on behalf of Lanarkshire employers, led immigrants secretly across the East Prussian border and arranged ship passage from German ports to Britain.

The oral histories of some Widnes families confirm the fact that it was extremely difficult for their ancestors to leave the Baltic States and many of them did so covertly. Although in some instances the methods and routes may have been less problematic, and some may have come under their own steam, there is no doubt that, for many, emigration was only made possible with the help of Lanarkshire recruitment agents. The fact that Lanarkshire mine owners were willing to enable this process confirms the belief that the immigrants were being used as cheap labour. I am sure the mine owners did not go to all that trouble for any altruistic reasons Of course there was benefit on both sides as once they were in Scotland, and had fulfilled their contracts; the immigrants would be free to move south. This was an added attraction as many had hopes of travelling onward to America. As the Lithuanian colonies of Lancashire were within easy reach of the

---

[67] Translated for me by John Millar (Jonas Stepsis)

The Lithuanians and Poles

Port of Liverpool this brought significant numbers of Lithuanians south to places like Widnes, Haydock, Earlestown, Manchester and Liverpool.

Even though we know for a fact that some Lithuanian immigrants were forced to make clandestine journeys in order to leave the Baltic, it would seem that *The North-East Lanarkshire Gazette* was of the opinion that Russia had previously been unconcerned as to whether people stayed in the country or left. *The Gazette* published the following article in December 1904 which informed its readers that Russia was now rounding up its "Lithuanian fugitives" for the purpose of pressing them into compulsory service in the Russian Army. As an unwillingness to be conscripted into Russia's army had been one of the motives for leaving, this must have been a cause of great anxiety, especially for men who had families in Lanarkshire. The article tells us that many of the Lithuanian and Polish men in Lanarkshire were living in fear of being discovered and sent back.

> LANARKSHIRE POLES SUMMONED TO THE RUSSIAN ARMY.—A correspondent writes:— In recent years thousands of Poles have found their way to this country, and have obtained employment chiefly in the mines and ironworks of Lanarkshire. Large colonies of these emigrants are to be found in Hamilton, Motherwell, Carfin, Bellshill, and district, many of the male portions have fled from their country in preference to undergoing compulsory service in the Russian Army. So long as the Muscovite Government had no immediate need of these Polish subjects they seemed to have been indifferent to their departure from the country, but with a decimating war on hand with Japan they are beginning to exercise some concern about the fugitives. A number of them have recently been traced and served with summonses to return to Russia for the service in the army which they have evaded. But loyalty to Russia does not seem to be pronounced amongst the Poles, and very few, if any, have obeyed the summons. Instead, many have emigrated to America and other countries in order to elude their Russian masters, and others who are liable to be called back, are not to be found long in the locality. Dread of discovery is possessing many Poles in Lanarkshire

Into The Crucible

Despite being actively procured by some employers, the Lithuanians were not welcome among the local workforce. The indigenous population looked on the immigrants as serious competition in the job market. They were labelled *"strike breakers"* as they were often, unknown to them, brought in *"straight from the boat"* during disputes. Historical hindsight proves that this was indeed the case. They were used as strike-breakers and a source of cheap labour and they were probably recruited for that specific purpose. An article published in a Scottish journal in 1903 says that they were *"introduced into furnace work by a large colliery during a strike in 1888."* Despite this being a fact, these immigrants were certainly not knowing or willing participants in that situation. They arrived in Scotland as innocent greenhorns with no previous knowledge of industrial relations or company politics. They were simply taking up irresistible offers of an assisted passage, a job and the possibility of a tied house; together with the added attraction of joining a growing Lithuanian community. Records show that most of the new arrivals were young men in their teens or early twenties, but there were also a number of young families and young unmarried women.

Naturally the new Lithuanian immigrants into Scotland faced a great deal of antipathy from the local population who feared for their jobs. However there were a number of other reasons which caused resentment and set them apart from the indigenous inhabitants of Lanarkshire. Not least of these reasons was the fact that the Lithuanians were Roman Catholic. As Scotland was at that time a devoutly Presbyterian country, this influx of nonconformists, who also spoke a different language, sent waves of alarm through the local communities. The fear and suspicion of local populations was fuelled by a long series of unfounded and outrageous articles which appeared in the Scottish press. In 1905 the leading Glasgow newspaper *The Daily Record and Mail* ran the banner headline *"Alien danger: Pole immigrants infected with loathsome diseases"*. Other similarly shocking headlines followed, all of which served to stir up additional fear, as well as a growing resentment and distrust of the immigrants.

Although the recruitment of foreign labour into Lanarkshire caused a great deal of rancour in the local labour market, it would seem that there were plentiful employment opportunities at the time of their arrival. By the 1870s the west of Scotland had in excess of 145 ironworking furnaces with supporting coal and iron-ore mines. The major issue was the fact that the immigrants were used as cheap labour and an instrument to break strikes. There were also viable concerns regarding safety, as they were inexperienced in mine or foundry work. Nevertheless, despite these feelings of disquiet and bitterness, the Lithuanians continued to arrive in significant numbers. Of course every new wave of arrivals created more resentment and hostility. *The Aberdeen Journal* of December 1887 published the following article:

"The question of the importation of foreigners into this country has been set before Parliament with the view to having it stopped so long as a million of our fellow countrymen are without the means of earning a livelihood. In support of this motion, the Chairman said that the importation of Poles by Messrs. Merry & Cunningham was not a new thing, as they had been bringing them over for the past two or three years. When the poor people arrived they did not know a single words of the language, but were delivered over to their importers like a bundle of goods. Messrs Merry & Cunninham had recently made the presence of Poles a reason for reducing the wages below the standard for a particular kind of work. The usual rate of pay of labourers was 3 shillings to 4 shillings a day, but in Messrs. Merry & Cunningham`s establishment it was 2 shillings and nine pence. The number of Poles imported had been increased from time to time and now the wages at Glengarnock were down to 2 shillings a day. That firm provided houses for their employees for which they charged 2shillings and 2 shillings and three pence according to the accommodation provided. They provided medical advice, whether the workmen wanted it or not, for which a charge of sixpence per month was made, and there was three pence a week for the library. Now all that was a considerable tax upon a wage of 12 shillings a week. The Poles, besides being a means of reducing the wages to starvation point, were a nuisance to the locality in which they resided, as owing to their filthy habits their houses were insanitary in the extreme. As they could not return to their own country, they became a buden on the parish in which they resided."

The main concentrations of early Lithuanians in Lanarkshire were in the districts of Bellshill, Coatbridge, Carfin, Newtongrange, Motherwell, Wishaw, Carluke and Larkhall. The earliest settlement was in the Bellshill district but gradually, as they became more established and experienced, they found employment in other colliery centres such as Hamilton, Burnbank, Blantyre and Cambuslang. Small

Into The Crucible

but viable Lithuanian communities developed in all these districts. I think at this point, for the purposes of this book, it is important to mention that a large number of the Lithuanian immigrants who came to Widnes had previously lived or worked in some of these Scottish locations, with Bellshill and Wishaw being particularly relevant.

A family in the Bellshill mining community

Most of the immigrants were young and unmarried but there were also a significant number of married men with young families. It is evident that there were also many extended family connections amongst the new arrivals. These connections became broader as a result of young single Lithuanians marrying fellow immigrants from their newly established Lanarkshire communities. This was a natural occurrence in all ethnic groups as young immigrants usually married other young people from the same ethnic community. This meant that there was no significant Lithuanian integration into local Scottish or Widnes society for several generations.

The unpronounceable Lithuanian surnames caused some difficulty in the workplace. Some were given new Scottish names that, if they were lucky, were slightly similar phonetically to their own. Others had their names changed by minor immigration or employment officials. Some even had their names changed by the foreman at their place of work.

The Lithuanians and Poles

There is a case of a Lithuanian in Scotland who, after signing for his pay with an "X", saw his name converted into Joseph Ecks. The surname "Ecks" was used by him and his family thenceforward. Others were given names like Blue, Black, White, Brown or Green. Some had the first initial of their Lithuanian surname preceded by "Mc" or "Mac" as in the case of a man with the surname Kausiacius who became McKay while others became MacDee and MacTee. In Bellshill, men with the Lithuanian surnames of Domeika, Stepsis, Rusgis, Vasauskas, Navickas, were turned into Brown, Millar, Smith, West and Wallace.

One might presume that these men and their families, and others like them, thought they had no choice in the matter of name changes. The sad fact is that these immigrants were in effect robbed of their ancestral names. Those names were cast away or altered on the dictum of some minor official. Others changed their name voluntarily as changing their name and abandoning tradition seemed like the easy option. Yet, in my opinion, such denials of identity were a high price to pay for social acceptance. Whilst some had their name changed in the manner described, others attempted to anglicise their surname into a more easily pronounceable version that retained an element of their own surname. However, it is important to point out that in almost all cases these name changes were not done through any legal or official channels. Many people with adopted or anglicised names use them now through the process known as *"by habit or repute"*. This is quite legal, although these name changes have not been done in accordance with any official procedure. Obviously, some did opt to change their name legally but in most cases it was done in the manner described[68].

I should make an additional point regarding the anglicising of names. During my many enjoyable conversations with John Millar, the Scottish-Lithuanian historian, I was kindly instructed on some common *"improper"* translations of Lithuanian names. Some of the Lithuanian names still prevalent in Widnes today, and which some families have used for at least the past three generations, were improperly anglicised, probably by some minor bureaucrat or an administrator in the workplace. The names of Lithuanian origin that now use "ski" at the end are *imperfect translations* of the original name. Lithuanian surnames

---

[68] John Millar *"The Lithuanians in Scotland"* 1998

Into The Crucible

should end in AS, IS, IUS or A in family names with AITE or YTE for an adult unmarried woman and IENE for a married woman.

As we have seen, not only were their names changed but often their nationality was altered too. John Millar told me that the majority of Lithuanians were immediately recognisable from their Christian names or surnames but in almost all census returns under the column *Where Born* most entries state "Russia" "Russian Poland" or "Poland; there is no mention of Lithuania. This gives no indication, to anyone unfamiliar with Lithuanian names, of their true nationality. Therefore I have to assume, quite rightly, that the census as a source of nationality must be regarded as defective and fallible.

Interestingly, the fact that many men had their names changed by minor officials in the workplace created problems in identifying them in some records. At one point in time *The Lanarkshire County Miners' Union* were attempting to collate information about the number of "Alien Workers" in the Lanarkshire pits but were hampered by the fact that so many had changed their names. They were no longer easily identifiable by their "strange surnames" as they were now called Black; Brown; White; Smith or "Mac" somebody. Therefore it was nigh on impossible to obtain an accurate number of foreign workers in the local mines.

Language was obviously a difficulty for the majority of these immigrants. Nevertheless, John Millar, in his study of the Lithuanian settlements in Lanarkshire, tells us that it was not as bad as we would imagine. There were so many Lithuanians in the Bellshill area that there was hardly any need to speak English at all. Even at work they were among Lithuanians speaking their own language. However, this led to complaints by the unions who claimed that an ignorance of the English language was a safety issue. Of course this probably *was* an issue, but what we should also bear in mind is the fact that there were mining accidents reported in Lanarkshire almost every week. In reality many of these accidents had nothing whatsoever to do with immigrants, foreign language, or the employment of "Poles". They were down to bad working conditions and the lack of adequate safety precautions in the workplace.

The Lithuanians and Poles

The hostility towards the immigrants took all forms and often came from surprising sources. Keir Hardie, known and greatly admired as one of the founding fathers of the Labour Party, led a fierce campaign against the Lithuanians. As the leader of the Ayrshire miners, Keir Hardie wrote an article for the journal *"The Miner"* in which he stated that:

> *"For the second time in their history Messrs. Merry and Cunninghame have introduced a number of Russian Poles to Glengarnock Ironworks. What object they have in doing so is beyond human ken unless it is, as stated by a speaker at Irvine, to teach men how to live on garlic and oil, or to introduce the Black Death, so as to get rid of the surplus labourers"*

Complaints about the Lithuanian workforce, usually instigated by union officials, continued without pause in Scotland. In January 1897 at the annual meeting of *The Miners Federation of Great Britain*, held in Leicester, Mr. Gilmour, the representative of the Lanarkshire miners, told the meeting that 25% of the men employed in Lanarkshire coal mines were Russian Poles. He claimed they were a danger to all the other workers as they were unskilled, having come straight into the mines without any experience. It was suggested that immigrant workers should not be allowed to work on the coal face until they had three years' experience. Until that time their wages should be greatly reduced. Two years later, in 1899, Keir Hardie, in his evidence to a *House of Commons Select Committee on Emigration and Immigration*, said that the Scots resented immigrants and wanted a total immigration ban. I think it would be fair to say that Keir Hardie's continued campaign against the Lithuanian immigrants was both fierce and xenophobic.

The Lithuanians had been arriving in Lanarkshire since the 1880s and with the passing of years their presence in some areas may have been reluctantly tolerated to a certain extent. By the early 1900s they had become a familiar fixture in the communities around Bellshill and other mining areas. Their numbers obviously had a significant effect, not only in employment terms but also in the ethos of these districts. Their continued presence in the mines was still a cause of contention among the local workforce but at the beginning of 1908 these numbers were considerably reduced. At that time a large number, said to be at least one thousand men, left for Nova Scotia in Canada. A Scottish newspaper reported that:

Into The Crucible

> "John Bulsavage, an alien, residing in Lanarkshire has contracted to supply The Canadian Coal Company with one thousand Lithuanians accustomed to the Scottish mining system. The men are to be employed at the Cape Breton pits, Nova Scotia, and a large batch of them leave next week, their Lanarkshire contracts closing at the end of the year. The home miner is not sorry to witness this depletion of alien labour in Scottish mines, as it may serve to lessen the existing friction and render needless a proposed agitation against the continuance of Polish and Lithuanian immigration to the iron and coal districts of the West of Scotland."

In time, the Lithuanian immigrants that remained gradually became accepted in the local Lanarkshire communities. They themselves began to be actively involved in trade unionism and other local societies and their children integrated into the local schools. They founded their own newspaper *"Jseiviu Draugas"* (Immigrants Friend). The Catholic Church also made provision for them by installing a Lithuanian priest at the parish of Holy Family in Mossend. In the mining villages of Lanarkshire, the Lithuanians enriched the social life with their Lithuanian orchestra, and their choral and operatic groups. Local Lithuanian sports days were organised as though they were Olympiads and these events produced many fine athletes. In fact, Sir Matt Busby, footballer and legendary manager of Manchester United, was born in the Bellshill mining colony, the son of a Lithuanian father and an Irish mother.

The story of the Lanarkshire Lithuanians is of particular relevance to our own community history as there is a strong Lithuanian link between Lanarkshire and Widnes. In the years preceding the First World War there was a marked movement of these immigrants southward to the North of England. A large number of them made their way to Widnes and either remained here or stayed long enough to earn the money to fund their passage to America. Those that came south to Lancashire were attracted here for a number of reasons. The main ones being that there were already established Lithuanian communities in places like Manchester, Earlestown and Haydock and of course there was plentiful work opportunities. Chain migration was obviously an important factor – whereby family members or friends inform others of good employment opportunities and help them to find jobs and accommodation.

The Lithuanians and Poles

Evidence suggests that some Widnes Lithuanians, who had originally come south from Lanarkshire, had previously resided in areas of Manchester, Earlestown and Haydock before coming to Widnes. Some had also gone to districts of St. Helens. Obviously the Lithuanians were not the only transitory workforce at this time. The working population in all the new manufacturing areas was generally mobile. People of all nationalities often left a single imprint on census returns and then vanished from the area completely. Nevertheless it should be said that this process was more pronounced amongst the Lithuanian population who moved fluidly from one area to another in Scotland and the north of England. This migration process is also demonstrated in reverse, as there are indications that there was movement of Lithuanians from Liverpool to Lanarkshire. This is borne out with a claim by the Lanarkshire firm of Merry & Cunninghame who said that some of their workers had come to them *"from the Sugar Works in Liverpool and from the Salt Works in Cheshire"*. One assumes that this was a classic case of chain migration. Of course the downside to this transitory way of life was that it was easy to lose touch with people. The Lithuanian newspaper in Lanarkshire, *"Jseiviu Draugas"*, ran a column with letters from readers in Liverpool, Widnes, Earlestown, Manchester and London who were trying to contact lost relatives and friends.

The information on the Lanarkshire settlement is of great interest to us because it gives an account of the movements of some Widnes Lithuanians before their arrival in this town. We know, from various families` oral histories; that whilst some friends and relatives moved on to America, many Lanarkshire Lithuanians moved to Widnes and stayed here. A considerable number settled in our town and raised their families here. They were involved in the creation of a viable and important Lithuanian community that was destined to thrive in the south end of our town. During the course of writing this book I was fortunate to have been given access to a considerable number of personal family histories, both written and oral. Unfortunately, most of those I have spoken to can only supply a brief account of their ancestors' lives before they arrived in Widnes. However several records and documentations allow us to piece together a vague picture of some of their movements.

Into The Crucible

Lithuanian Women workers at the Carfin brickworks in Lanarkshire

Apart from the people whom we know for certain were in Lanarkshire before their arrival in Widnes, there is also a substantial number of surnames in the Lanarkshire records that later appear in Widnes. These names disappear from records in Lanarkshire around the time they first appear in Widnes. However, due to the lack of accurate source material it is not possible to state with absolute certainty that these were the same people, although circumstantial evidence would certainly point to it being so. It is also interesting to note when looking at census material for Lanarkshire that some names shown on the census appear only for that year. Therefore, it must be assumed that these particular Lithuanians were transient workers, either moving on to the United States or to other parts of England or Scotland.

The following is a small selection of names that disappear from the Bellshill area of Lanarkshire and reappear in Widnes soon afterwards.

Kijauskas (*Keouski*)
Ramauskas (*Ramanauski*)
Matulevicius (*Matalevitch*)
Povilaitis
Karalius
Tupciauskas

The Lithuanians and Poles

Stankevicius*
Derencius*[69]
Klusaitis
Domeika

Among the many people who I know *did* come to Widnes directly from Lanarkshire were two young Lithuanian brothers, Anthony and Stanislaus Karalius. Anthony Karalius's story is one which appropriately finds its place in these pages as it provides a decisive link between Lanarkshire and Widnes. It also provides a personal perspective to the story of emigration. Many years ago during some enjoyable and interesting conversations with his son, the late Branna Karalius, I came to realise the wealth of culture and tradition that was brought to this town by the ancestors of some of our present population. The blending of these cultures through integration with other groups has given this town a unique character and I personally think that we are the richer for it. With the kind permission of the Karalius and Myler families I give a brief account of their Lithuanian history.

Anthony Karalius, the father of the late Branna Karalius, arrived in Scotland from Lithuania in the 1890s and settled into the district of Bellshill in Lanarkshire, which at that time was the largest Lithuanian colony in Britain. Although we do not know for sure, one might assume that he may have been attracted to that particular area by some offer of work from a recruitment agent. In Bellshill, Anthony met the young Mary Vasilouskas (Vasiliauskas) the girl who eventually became his wife. She was also a Lithuanian and she and her family were part of the considerable and varied Lithuanian community that had been established in the town. I use the word *"varied"* by design as it should be said here that, contrary to common belief, not all the Lithuanian immigrants in Lanarkshire at that time were of peasant stock. Some of the Lithuanians who settled in Bellshill and its surrounding areas were university-educated intellectuals who were escaping political repression rather than economic hardship.

---

[69] Names marked * arrived in Britain through the port of Grimsby

Into The Crucible

Among the exiled intelligentsia in Bellshill at that time was Vincas Mickevicius-Kapsukas who was the leader of the Lithuanian Social Democratic Party and who subsequently became the President of Lithuania's first Government when the Republic attained its freedom in 1919. He arrived in Scotland at the beginning of 1915 and although he only stayed for around a year he seems to have spent his time productively, working with *The Russian Political Prisoners` and Exiles` Relief Committee* as well as raising funds for the revolutionary cause in Russia.

Scotland also played host to Dr. Juozas Bagdonas, an important Lithuanian writer, who had published (under various pseudonyms) a number of hard-hitting political criticisms of the Tsarist regime. As a direct consequence of his subversive work and writing he was subsequently forced to flee from Lithuania. He arrived in Scotland in 1905 and immediately involved himself in Lithuanian community affairs and became an influential participant in Lithuanian cultural and educational activities.

Another prominent man in this community was Petras Bancevicius who owned the largest Lithuanian store in Britain (*Varpas Store*) and founded the influential *Lithuanian Information Bureau*. Mr. Bancevicius, who was both an intellect and entrepreneur, had arrived in Bellshill in the early 1890s and from the beginning had proved to be a significant influence on the Lithuanian community there. In 1920 he was officially appointed as an intermediary between the Lithuanian residents in Scotland and the Lithuanian Legation in London. In December 1938 he was honoured by the Lithuanian Government who conferred *The Order of the Grand Duke Geduninas* upon him. He was the first Lithuanian in Great Britain to receive such an award, which corresponded to our O.B.E.

We can see from the honour bestowed upon Petras Bancevicius that he was highly respected among Lithuanian communities of Lanarkshire and indeed throughout Scotland. There are numerous reports of his extraordinary business acumen but that shrewdness was combined with many examples of great benevolence towards his fellow emigres. In 1907 an application was made to The Bothwell Parish Council Cemetery Committee to purchase a large section of land in the cemetery to accommodate 60 lairs (grave plots). It was hoped that this section could be railed off and consecrated for the burial of members of the local Lithuanian community. The application was made by local clergyman, Father Collins, on behalf of the Lithuanian priest, Father Czuberkis. However, on further investigation by The Parish Council, it emerged that the money for the entire purchase was being provided by Mr. Bancevicius. A special meeting was called by The Cemetery Committee to discuss the application. Throughout that meeting Mr. Bancevicius was mockingly referred to as *"That Pole Grocer"*. The application was declined due to the Committee`s fear that *"Poles from all parts of the country could be buried in their cemetery"*.

It is also worth mentioning that Petras Bancevicius was a close friend of the Karalius family and was a witness at the wedding of Anthony's brother, Stanislaus Karalius. It is supposed that this friendship may have pre-dated their arrival in Scotland as Petras Bancevicius was born in Vilkaviskis and Anthony's Father, Vincent Karalius, was born in a village called Pavembriai, which was also in the Vilkaviskis region of Lithuania. Anthony himself was born in a village near Vilnius where his family lived on a farm.

Of course the personal reasons that prompted Anthony to leave his home soil must be supposition, but his son, Branna, believed that his reluctance to be conscripted into the Russian Army was a major factor. Indeed, this specific motive for migration was also suggested by several other Widnes families of Lithuanian origin. In the case of Anthony Karalius, oral family history indicates that this was a strong reason. During Anthony's youth in Lithuania, and up until 1915, the region of Vilkaviskis belonged to the Sulvalkija province of the Russian Empire and consequently all able-bodied men on reaching the age of 21 were conscripted into the Russian army. The compulsory service in Siberia was initially for a period of four years. The service was extremely hard, leaving men in a poor physical condition on their return. However, some reports claim that compulsory military service meant that it could be up to 10 years before men were allowed to return home. Therefore many young men, in an attempt to escape this service, left the country before reaching their majority. An additional consequence of this exodus was that young women, who believed the shortage of young men in the country would leave them condemned to spinsterhood, also left in large numbers.

Into The Crucible

I should point out that it was not only the severity or length of army service that made conscription abhorrent to young Lithuanian men. One of the prime reasons was a reluctance to be involved in maintaining the Tsarist regime. At that time there was a rise in national consciousness and a large nationalist underground resistance movement existed in Lithuania, so there was a great unwillingness among young men to be part of the Russian army. Of course it would be quite wrong to cite the avoidance of conscription as the main cause for emigration. There were several other viable reasons for migration and the real motive for an individual's departure could have been a combination of things. Another major reason was economic necessity caused by the inability of the land to support large families. In addition, there was the oppressive regime which sought to eradicate their cultural and religious beliefs. There was also the common practice of leaving for seasonal work in Germany and then moving on to England or America.

In Scotland, Anthony Karalius and his brother Stanislaus found work as coalminers in Bellshill. Anthony was employed in the mines until at least 1900 and his brother Stanislaus was still employed as a coalminer in Bellshill up until 1904. However, while in Bellshill, Anthony had learned the bakery trade from his brother-in-law, Vytautas, who owned a family business there. In fact this and other Lithuanian bakery businesses were flourishing at that time as they offered familiar foodstuffs to the growing immigrant community. Records show that in 1901 and 1902 Anthony was employed as a journeyman baker in Lanarkshire. Anthony's reasons for moving from Scotland to Widnes are uncertain, but he was more than likely following the example of others who were heading south at that time to the thriving Lancashire industrial towns. There is the possibility that many were attracted to these Lancashire towns because of their close proximity to the Port of Liverpool and its transatlantic route. It is generally accepted that most Lithuanians who came to Widnes still had aspirations of eventually leaving for America, many did so but others decided to remain here.

On his arrival in Widnes, Anthony, with the practical help and guidance of his brother-in-law, Vytautas, opened his own Bakery and Butcher's Shop in Canal Street, West Bank. The Vasilouskas (Vasiliauskas) family may have contributed financially to the setting up of this shop as it originally traded under Anthony's wife's maiden name. The shop focused on selling the traditional black rye breads, sausage meat and other familiar Eastern European foods that were not so readily available in the area. Therefore, as it catered specifically for the needs of the growing Lithuanian community in the south end of the town, the small shop in Canal Street was well supported and the business subsequently thrived. When Branna Karalius had reflected on his memories of the West Bank shop he said that it was a focal point for the Lithuanian and Polish communities alike. However it should be said that the subsequent success of the shop was not entirely due to its West Bank customer base. Through the enterprising endeavours of Anthony and his wife, the shop built up trade among the Lithuanian and Polish communities around St. Helens, Haydock, Earlestown and parts of Liverpool. Regular deliveries by horse and cart were made to all these areas.

In West Bank, the Karalius/Vasilouskas shop, apart from providing the natural elements of business, became a source of help and information for the Lithuanian community at large. Anthony, who was a well-educated man, read and wrote letters for those of the Lithuanian population who were unable to do so themselves. Branna Karalius said that this small but helpful service for fellow immigrants enabled his parents to see both sides of the coin. They were able to see at first hand the daily difficulties people were experiencing. The numerous problems associated with language or the practical challenges associated with life in a new country were all too apparent. Consequently, the shop offered a place of communal support as well as a source of familiar foodstuffs. The importance of maintaining this cultural connection, and Anthony's role in doing so, meant that he was a man of considerable standing within this community.

Anthony Karalius left his business briefly during the 1914-1918 War to work as a coalminer. Many local Lithuanians went down the mines at that time as a way of contributing to the war effort. The well-loved West Bank shop was demolished in the 1930s and Anthony received the princely sum of £100 in compensation. After that time the gradual fragmenting of the Lithuanian community in West Bank came about as the area was cleared of old and decaying housing stock. The residents of the district that had long been associated with the Lithuanian community were relocated to other parts of the town. Some were able to stay together as several families were rehoused close to each other in the areas around Lowerhouse Lane and Moor Lane. Nevertheless, the close Lithuanian community that had existed in the West Bank area for nigh on fifty years had now been fractured and incorporated into general society. Anthony Karalius died in Widnes in 1953, a long way from his roots in that small Lithuanian village. In his lifetime he had become acclimatised to various cultures, from his early associations in Scotland to the varied nationalities he encountered in Widnes in its boom time. This valuable experience, coupled with a natural empathy towards his fellow immigrants, had enabled Anthony Karalius to play a significant role in helping Lithuanians to deal with the trials and tribulations they encountered in the early days of their settlement.

Anthony's story is interesting for the fact that it gives us a personal insight into the history of our communities. It is an account of the ordinary experiences of immigration and his story is probably typical of many. An economic and political migrant, forced to leave his own country and raise a family in an unfamiliar environment, far from all that was comforting and familiar to him. I pay tribute to him and all those like him who overcame the enormous difficulties they encountered in a new and unwelcoming land. In addition to their personal situations, men such as Anthony Karalius were instrumental in creating a stable immigrant community in our town. As this community began to mature in the early and mid-years of the 20th century, and second and third generations assimilated and became anglicised, there was still a conscious ethnic identity within their families. The reason for that is that men like Anthony Karalius, and indeed most Lithuanians, ensured that their children remained culturally aware and proud of their heritage whilst at the same time appreciating and conforming to the environment they lived and grew up in.

Anthony and Stanislaus Karalius had left Lithuania at the end of the 19th century at a time when Vilkaviskis residents were very active in propagating Lithuanian ideas and concepts of national consciousness. If those values and ideals were transposed to Widnes, I do not know. Unlike their ethnic counterparts in Lanarkshire and parts of Lancashire, there did not appear to be any active *formal* Lithuanian Clubs or Societies in Widnes. However, the Polish and Lithuanian fraternities in Widnes certainly socialised among their own ethnic groups and they remained a very close and culturally aware community. There is oral

The Lithuanians and Poles

history of special Lithuanian events in Widnes relating to religious festivals. These events, which were usually preceded by Mass at St. Patrick's RC Church, attracted large groups of Lithuanians from nearby Earlestown, Liverpool and Manchester. Of course the Catholic Church was very important to this community as, indeed, many of them had faced persecution for their faith in Lithuania. In Widnes, the parish of St. Patrick's in West Bank became their spiritual home and they were actively involved in parish affairs. Up until the 1950s some of the young girls of Lithuanian descent proudly wore their colourful national costumes during Church processions in May. I am also told that members of the Lithuanian community held regular dances in St. Patrick's Hall.

During the 19th century England supposedly prided itself on the liberal attitude it displayed towards immigrants. Formal restrictions were only introduced during the first decade of the 20th century after the passing of *The Aliens Act of 1905*. This Act was brought into force as an attempt to control Jewish migration from Russia and Poland. From 1914 onwards it became necessary for aliens (non-British subjects) to register with the Authorities. They were then issued with a certificate *Registration of an Alien*. By the end of August 1914 all Lithuanians in Britain were so registered. Unfortunately, the Police "Alien Files" are destroyed 100 years after the birth date on the named "Alien's" card. This rule has made it impossible to check the original Alien Records for the early Lithuanian and Polish immigrants into Widnes. The registered "Aliens" were subjected to regular police checks, a practice that continued well into the late 1950s. When Anthony Karalius died in 1953 his family forgot to inform the police, who called six months later to carry out their usual checks.

The Poles and Lithuanians originally began arriving in Widnes in the late 1880s and were treated with both curiosity and suspicion by the local population. They were not a welcome addition to the local workforce as it was believed that they would have a seriously detrimental effect on the labour market. Although the Irish were unpopular, they had been able to assimilate more easily and indeed could claim a "right" to be here as they were British citizens under *The Act of Union*. The Poles and Lithuanians, apart from being unable to make any similar claims, had other major disadvantages. The language was a serious impediment, making life more difficult in what was an already a testing and possibly frightening situation.

George E Diggle, in his *"History of Widnes"* describes the arrival of the Poles and Lithuanians in Widnes thus:

"With their beautiful ceremonial dresses, their scrupulous domestic cleanliness, and their meals of cabbage and rye bread, they were the object of great interest for a while. They settled in their new homes, intermarried with local families and became good, solid Widnesians".

Even though we would all have a wish to believe this statement, unfortunately, this is not what *really* happened! Although they did, indeed, become *"good, solid, Widnesians"* sadly, on their arrival they were *not* looked upon simply as "temporary curiosities" and welcomed. The native population was openly hostile towards them. A local correspondent wrote the following derogatory article which, I think, reveals what Widnes inhabitants of that time actually thought about them:

"Among politicians the question is cropping up as to the wisdom or otherwise of longer permitting foreign pauper immigration; and the opinion appears to be gaining ground that low priced foreign labour does not sensibly cheapen, and certainly does not improve the quality of our production. For many years Widnes and the neighbouring town, St. Helens, have been training grounds for the rawest of material in workmanship, in the shape of agricultural labourers and green hands from the Sister Isle,* and the position has been accepted as the natural one; but when the residuum of foreign countries is poured on to us, and some of the best and ablest of our workmen have to seek fresh fields of labour even to the extent of emigrating to America or Australia, then murmurings and discontent begin to prevail among the native population. A fitting comment on this has just been exhibited in an inquest on a Polish labourer who was killed on the railway near Messrs. Muspratt`s Works. The man was trespassing on the line, and appears from the evidence to have walked right into a moving train of wagons. For some time the experiment has been going on in Widnes: the reason appearing to be the great amount of labour they would perform for the lowest of wages. These men are chiefly Poles; and our school-day notions of the chivalry, courage and nobleness of this

---

* This refers to Ireland

ancient nation are rudely shocked by the colony we have of them in Widnes. Their food is extremely coarse – their mode of living and morals appear equally so. This is doubtless the result of the way they are trodden down and kept under in their native country; for the samples we have here are certainly as low, dirty, and degraded a set of creatures as any that bear the name of human being or are counted as men: and our various works managers must be credited with great patience and not a little long-suffering in the training necessary to get out their productions by the aid of this class of labour".

The disparaging sentiments in this, and other local articles of the time, mirror the awful experiences of the Lithuanians in Lanarkshire. Widnes did *not* welcome them nor find them to be simply *"objects of great interest"*. Further details in this chapter will reveal that they were just as unpopular and unwelcome here as they had been in Scotland. In fact, they were unwelcome in all the areas of the country in which they settled. The reasons always included a worry that they would have a negative effect on local labour markets.

Many of the first immigrants were very mobile but slowly a settlement pattern emerged and a stable Lithuanian community was established in the Waterloo region of the town. There were also a number of Lithuanians in Newtown and other areas but the main concentration was in the Waterloo district of upper West Bank. Despite having been thrust into an alien and unwelcoming environment there were several factors which made life more tolerable. Firstly, the comforting presence of so many of their fellow countrymen meant that they had been able to establish a community where they could continue to use their own language and maintain some of their cultural activities. In fact, oral history indicates that the early Waterloo community was practically self-contained and self-sufficient. The only outside influence was their place of work.

Of course, after suffering almost a century of Russian persecution for their faith, their religion was extremely important to them. Therefore the Roman Catholic Church was a major stabilizing factor in their new surroundings. The Latin Mass, which at that time was shared by Catholics universally, meant that they could come together with their co-religionists, of all nationalities, and partake in this sacrament each Sunday. Consequently, St. Patrick's Church, built in 1888, soon became

Into The Crucible

the centre of worship for the Lithuanian and Polish communities in Widnes. However, although the community was able to join their co-religionists in the sacrament of Mass, confession was a different matter. In order to facilitate those who did not have a command of the English language the Diocese made regular arrangements for a Polish priest to come to both St. Patrick`s and St. Marie`s parishes to hear confession.

The Register of Baptisms for St. Patrick's Church began in October 1888. I list below the first twenty names of foreign origin from that first register. The numbers of Lithuanian births for the period up to 1905 is also included. These births represent first generation Widnesians who were of Lithuanian or Polish origin.

First twenty names of foreign origin in St. Patrick's R.C. Church Register of Baptisms

Lukshifis
Valintus
Metacvev
Adamovitch
Comisky*
Walinczius
Martinkiewicz
Busas
Nouelis
Baszkiewicz
Runekis
Maziakis
Bulkousky
Nerkiewiczias
Yochan
Radawicz
Pieczenkis
Mieschute
Miklaszewiecz

---

* Irish

The numbers of Lithuanian births in the first Volume of St. Patrick's R.C. Church

1889	7
1890	7
1891	16
1892	11
1893	11
1894	6
1895	7
1896	3
1897	3
1898	7
1899	7
1900	16
1901	26
1902	31
1903	33
1904	28
1905	22

These births represent first generation Widnes children born of Lithuanian or Polish parents in this town.

The census of 1891 shows a large "Polish" community centred mainly in the area that included Waterloo Road, Water Street, Nelson Street, and Cromwell Street. Of course, as I have stated earlier, the description "Polish" is misleading. I list the names recorded in just those few streets as an indication of the size of this community. In the main, the list depicts the surname of the head of the household or an adult lodger. Where the named is the head of the household there are also additional people of the same surname included in the census. This list is not meant to represent the total number of people but rather the number of single surnames.

Into The Crucible

Surnames of those people classified as Polish in the Census of 1891.

Adamavage
Bassick
Bauledich
Brazowski
Brauzich
Britritka
Chiffiniski
Comerosker
Dovitshi
Dunbavich
Engurich
Garoushia
Granz
Kaloutski
Kenovitch
Lascruner – a Romanian
Lesoiski
Magnis
Maschvich
Matalavitch
Matterlavitch
Mattinckervitch
Matzincavitch
Maziaka
Maroffski
Mauriet
Mercewye
Mercheovitch
Melesha
Messiter
Neski
Paulocaritz
Pellousky
Petter
Phelbs
Prenowski
Ristkoffski
Runneouvitch

Sabadish
Sidouski
Skingich
Sneoutkitz
Stwkitz
Sverouski
Uydgich
Wellinch
Yamkouski
Yermonlouski

The surnames also include Smith, Miller and Mitchell who were reportedly born in Poland (although this was probably Lithuania). The absence of many of the familiar "Widnes" names known to be Polish or Lithuanian in origin, suggests that these families were later arrivals. The majority of names in the above census extract are not found in Widnes today. It is possible that some anglicised their names – while others may have left the area possibly moving on to other places in England or America. *The Anglo-Russian Military Pact,* in 1917, may also have had a significant influence on the absence of many of these men from the town.

It is obvious that the Poles and Lithuanians were able to create a viable community in West Bank and in doing so were able to maintain their ethnic affiliations. John Belcham in his *"Essays in Liverpool Exceptionalism"* defines the necessary components of ethnic affiliation as: *"a common proper-name; a myth of common ancestry; shared historical memories; elements of common culture; link with a homeland; and a sense of solidarity".* The Poles and Lithuanians had all these elements; and also the linguistic difference which set them apart from the native population and other immigrant communities. They also had the shared aim of providing a better life for themselves and their families. Unfortunately the extreme hostility they faced in Widnes did not make this an easy process.

The census of 1891 gives an indication of the sizeable number of Eastern European workers in the town at that time. Their presence here caused continual controversy especially during periods of economic depression when there was strong competition in the job market. The following page from *Hansard* is a part account of Parliamentary proceedings for the 24th March 1892. That day Mr. Edwards Moss, the member for Widnes, SW Lancashire, raised the following question:[2]

PAUPER IMMIGRANTS AND THE WIDNES CHEMICAL WORKERS.
MR. EDWARDS MOSS (Lancashire S.W. Widnes):

I beg to ask the President of the Local Government Board whether his attention has been called to an application which has recently been made to the Prescot Board of Guardians by the chemical workers of Widnes, who have been thrown out of work and become dependent on the workhouse, owing to the employment in their place of foreign paupers at their works; whether he is aware that these pauper immigrants are Poles, 80 per cent of whom arrive in this country quite destitute, and who, by working for starvation wages, are displacing the natural working population of the locality; and whether, in view of the fact that much distress is caused thereby, and as an additional burden is being placed upon the rates of the district, the Government will consider the recommendations of the Select Committee on Emigration and Immigration of 1889, especially the last clause of their Report, and take some steps to put a stop to the immigration of foreign paupers into this country?

THE PRESIDENT OF THE LOCAL GOVERNMENT BOARD MR. RITCHIE (Tower Hamlets, St. George's):

I have been in communication with the clerk to the Guardians of the Prescot Union on the subject of the statements in the question. I learn that distress has existed among chemical workers at Widnes, but this is apparently due to the closing of a number of alkali works in the district. With respect to the immigration and employment of Poles, I am informed that the statement that these immigrants arrive in this country in a state of destitution is misleading. Generally speaking, they appear to be strong able-bodied men who are readily given employment at the works by reason of their fitness and willingness to perform the work allotted to them. The number of Poles employed in the various chemical works, it is stated, does not exceed 50, the majority of whom have been in this country for a number of years. Not one of the men who were relieved by the Guardians with a labour test could, when inquiry was made of them during the present week, say positively that his place had been taken by a foreigner. As regards the allegation as to

---

[2] Hansard (Bound volumes : University of Liverpool)

The Lithuanians and Poles

starvation wages, on inquiry at one of the largest chemical works at Widnes, it was stated that the wages paid to the Poles were exactly the same as those paid to other workmen employed at the works, ten were receiving wages at the rate of 4s. per day, and one at the rate of 4s.3d. It is further stated that not a single Pole is in receipt of relief from the Union, and so far as the experiences of the Guardians and their officers goes, this class seldom or never apply for Poor Law relief. It does not appear to me that there is any sufficient reason at present for the adoption of such a course as is suggested in the last paragraph of the Hon. Member's question[70].

In October 1892 the subject of *"pauper immigrants"* raised its head again when the Prescot Board of Guardians discussed a letter received from the Hackney Union. *The Widnes Weekly News* reported an account of the proceedings in the 29th October issue.

THE GUARDIANS AND PAUPER IMMIGRANTS

On Thursday week, at a meeting of Prescot Board of Guardians, Mr. W. Davies in the chair, the Clerk alluded to the letter received from the Hackney Union, which was read at the last meeting of the Board, requesting the Guardians to join with them in asking the Government to take some action to restrict destitute aliens from entering this country.

Mr. Davies *said that as he moved the adjournment of the subject for further discussion at the last meeting he would now move – "That in the opinion of this Board immediate action should be taken by Her Majesty's Government to check the large influx of foreign immigrants, by establishing regulations as to prevent the landing into this country of persons likely to become a burden to the ratepayers through want of income or friends, and that a copy of this resolution be forwarded to the Local Government Board". He said that the Hackney Union were more or less suffering from that kind of thing and it was very likely that Unions near to places where these people landed did suffer, but those in the Prescot Union had not felt it yet, but from what he had seen he had no doubt that some of these foreigners were supplanting our own countrymen in the labour market, and he thought, looking at it*

---

[70] The name "Pole" was applied to those of Lithuanian birth. There were no specific differences given to these two distinct nationalities in records of those times.

from that point of view, and from the point of view of health, they would be justified in passing that resolution.

Mr. J. Birchall *seconded, and referred to the material that was sent to the Board from Widnes complaining that in consequence of the foreigners having taken their places at the manufactories they were unable to support themselves.*

Major Wareing *This is a free country and you cannot help it.*

Mr. J. Birchall *Inasmuch as people are landed in this country without friends, and without money, I think it is a very reasonable proposition.*

Major Wareing *said that he should talk about pauper immigrants into the country and not foreign labour.*

Dean Finnegan[71] *said he thought Mr. Davies wished, if possible, to prevent the landing of destitute foreigners into the country; Mr. Birchall was speaking to a resolution which would keep out all foreigners and wished to say something on labour questions. There were two facts before them which they could not deny. In the first place Mr. Davies had said, and said with truth, that they had no destitute foreigners in their Union, and this being the case, why need they run into this thing at all. In the second place it had been said that they had foreigners in Widnes. It was true, but what were the facts. From statistics he could produce and from inquiries made he found that not one of the foreigners had ever become chargeable to this Union, and he thought that was a very satisfactory state of affairs. He quite agreed with Major Wareing that this was a free country, and if they saw men among them were they to be the first to rise up in arms against them, and drive them from their shores. He thought they were going entirely out of their way in proposing the resolution. The Poles at Widnes were earning their bread, and if they could get labour it was because they would do labour others would not. He thought there was a great deal in their favour, and if those amongst them would only be as industrious there would be no need for them to come to the Union. Foreign labour was one thing and foreign pauperism another. The Guardians for Widnes were not complaining of the aliens among them as a body, and he thought it should be understood that*

---

[71] Dean Finnegan (St. Bede`s 1875-1906) A member of The Prescot Board of Guardians and The Widnes School Board, was also involved in the welfare of Roman Catholic children in Whiston Institution.

The Lithuanians and Poles

Widnes was excluded from the proposition. They had proved clearly that not one penny had been received by them from the Union. If they rose up in that way and expelled those poor Poles they would have to expel all foreign Princes that came over.

Mr. J. Birchall said the resolution was "foreign or destitute paupers" and, although he was interrupted so much, what he wanted to say was that these people at Widnes, who had been competing for the labour which had been given to the inhabitants of that Union, might have come into the country in a destitute condition originally. If there was some law preventing aliens from landing when they were destitute they would have a better market here for labour.

Mr. Middlehurst said the mover of the resolution had failed to give them any statistics, and therefore he was ignorant on the subject. He was sure that a much larger number of foreigners would have to be allowed to come into this country before any steps were taken in the matter, and as they had no cases in the Union he thought they ought to be the last to move in a matter of this kind.

Mr. Tyrer said he did not know whether the view taken by Mr. Middlehurst was quite a correct one, or, altogether an unselfish one, as he said that because they had no foreigners here they aught not to attempt to assist any other Union (hear, hear).

Mr. Joseph Birchall supported the motion.
Mr. Burt said he had seen in the papers that there were no less than 300 destitute paupers in London alone. Now if that was simply in London, what did it mean, when they came to consider other shipping ports such as Hull, Liverpool etc. There was no doubt that a great many people landed there in a destitute condition, and who, if they did not bear directly did so indirectly upon the working classes of this country, as they drove their workmen out of employment by working for less wages.

Mr. Davies said he did not include all foreigners who came to this country, but only those who are likely to be chargeable to the poor law. The resolution said persons likely to become a burden to ratepayers through want of means or friends.

The resolution was carried by 11 votes to 7.

Into The Crucible

Interestingly, in the above extract Dean Finnegan had said *"The Poles at Widnes were earning their bread, and if they could get labour it was because they would do labour others would not"*. A few years later an article about the so called "Poles" and their work ethic appeared in a publication called *"The People's Journal"*. The writer said:

"I have it from a Works foreman who has over 20 Poles under his charge that he finds them wonderfully reliable. If they are paid by results they work tremendously hard. If they are merely labourers, with a fixed wage, they give conscientious work. They have only to be told to do a thing and they will do it as faithfully as expected, even when the Gaffer's back is turned. They are exceptionally good and reliable workers."

As I previously said, although the majority of Eastern European immigrants into Widnes were Lithuanian, there were indeed a small number of Poles in the town. It should be mentioned that there were also a few Latvians and a handful of Ukrainians. Around the turn of the century several Polish families came to Widnes and settled in the Newtown area. Many of these Widnes Poles had originally come into the country through the port of Liverpool and had afterwards resided for a while in Liverpool and in the Sutton Manor and Peasley Cross areas of St. Helens. After the Second World War more substantial numbers of Polish immigrants came into this town and to other places around Britain. The Kaloski (Koloskeiwick) family were among the early Polish arrivals into Widnes and the following brief passage is from a personal narrative written by the late Felix Kaloski (Koloskeiwick) for his family. The full text was kindly copied for me by his daughter, Helen Cummins, who gave permission for me to use this extract.

Felix Kaloski (Koloskeiwick) was the son of Polish immigrants who arrived in Widnes in the first decade of the 20th century. It is believed that his parents first met on the voyage from Poland to Liverpool. After spending a short time in the city they both moved to St. Helens to join the small Polish community which had been established there. It is possible that one, or both of them, had friends who had already settled in that area. They married in St. Helens where they resided for several years before moving on to Widnes. On their arrival in Widnes his father obtained employment as a *"saltcake man"* at Muspratt's and the

The Lithuanians and Poles

family settled in Victoria Street, Newtown, where Felix and his siblings spent their childhood.

The Kaloski (Koloskeiwick) family arrived in Widnes during a time when there was great hostility against the influx of *"pauper immigrants"*. This could not have been an easy or a pleasant situation. Fortunately Felix and his siblings were too young to have been aware of this animosity and they appear to have had a happy and carefree childhood. One hopes that this was the same situation for the children of all immigrant families in Widnes. Despite the challenges faced by immigrants at that time, the Kaloski family settled into the Newtown area and successfully assimilated into the community. Like most immigrant families, the following generations were totally absorbed into the culture and identity of their new homeland and today descendants of the Kaloski family are well established in Widnes and its surrounding districts. It is a matter of great regret to all that precise details of their Polish origins and the family's life before arriving here have been lost in the mists of time.

Extract from the memoirs of Felix Kaloski

"My childhood days from 1912 onwards were very happy considering my parents were Polish. They married in St. Helens in 1900. In 1905, a year after I was born, we went to live in Widnes six miles away where there was plentiful work to suit everybody.

My mother was a quiet person and got on well with the neighbours and mastered the language problem much sooner than my father, who spent most of his spare time gambling on horses, with a low stake of 3d.

My spare time was spent in the fields and streets around Newtown playing football or anything that kept us occupied, we even spent our spare time climbing on the roofs of houses.

I met my wife, Margaret, who was Irish, and we were married in St. Marie's by Father Barry. When he first came to St. Marie's, Father Barry had the inside of the church renovated and the communicants numbered 500 per month, better still a year later they numbered 800 per week.

The teachers at St. Marie`s were very friendly. They spent much of their spare time helping pupils with their homework and games etc. Incidentally, there were three sisters named Duggan teaching at St. Marie's Infant School during that time, and now and again I received a halfpenny from one of them.

Widnes was renowned for having the cheapest and best gas in the world, the first in the country to use double-decker buses for passengers. They also could boast a first class rugby league team with many trophies.

In summertime, crowds of parents and children played "housey-housey" (bingo) outside the houses on the pavement until darkness fell"...
............unquote

Although, in the greater scheme of things, one cannot consider this to be a tremendously important document, nevertheless some of the points in this narrative are very interesting. One can immediately conjure up a picture of a happy childhood in Newtown as well as a kindly group of teaching staff at St. Marie`s School. Felix also refers to the "language problem" and tells us that his mother managed to master this before his father. The increased number of parishioners at St. Marie's Church in a relatively short space of time is also mentioned. These parish figures, which have been verified, demonstrate how the population of the area was increasing at a great rate during that period. It also compounds the view that not many of the district's inhabitants could claim native origins.

The problems associated with linguistic proficiency, particularly for the older generation, can only be guessed at. I have been told that all of the children of these immigrants were articulately bi-lingual, speaking English at school and Lithuanian at home. It does not appear that they were impeded in their schoolwork by this switching about of thought and speech. Many of the children acted as tutors to their parents, helping them to master the English language. The parents themselves, although unable to speak English, were often multi-lingual. Because they had lived close to national borders many could speak Russian and German, as well as Polish and Lithuanian. I found it interesting that Mrs. Kaloski mastered the language earlier than her husband. John Miller, when talking about the language problem in Lanarkshire, told me that in the early days it was harder for the women. The women

The Lithuanians and Poles

were usually slow to learn English as they were disoriented and isolated, usually only mixing with other Lithuanians whilst the men were in contact with other workers of a different nationality.

Felix Kaloski's description of children playing outside their homes while parents and neighbours played bingo, presents an image of Victoria Street at that time. It offers a picture of a happy and socially integrated neighbourhood. We can see from census records that there were several nationalities residing in this small crowded street of terraced houses. So one can only imagine the atmosphere during those neighbourhood games of bingo, with a multitude of accents and nationalities all happily mingling together in the hope of being able to shout *"housey housey"*.

The campaign against immigrants culminated in the passing of an *Aliens Act* in 1905. This was designed to control the influx of destitute immigrants. Some historians claim that this was aimed particularly at Russian and Polish Jews. However, the wider scope of *The Act* sought to exclude all immigrants *"without visible means of support"*. Initially, *The Act* appeared to have had some degree of success in controlling the numbers of arrivals into English ports. However there were numerous problems with red tape, as in the case of two shipwrecked crews who were refused permission to land in Liverpool. The crews, one Spanish and the other Cuban, after a harrowing experience at sea, were rescued by a liner of the Harrison Line during an ocean voyage. On arrival at the Herculaneum Dock in Liverpool the customs officials refused to allow the rescued men to disembark on the grounds that they were "destitute aliens". After some frantic communications between the Port Authorities, the Home Office and the Cuban Consulate, the men were finally given permission to land.

Eventually, as further problems arose, things became more casual and Port Authorities often lacked the inclination to impose the regulations as stringently as they might. After a while *The Act* seemed to have little effect as new immigrants continued to arrive. However, despite the utter collapse of any attempt to keep out foreigners, the precedent had been set. The outbreak of the First World War put the Government under constant pressure to introduce tougher controls which resulted in the introduction of further new Acts. With the establishment of new regulations the process of assimilation was almost brought to a halt and immigration from Lithuania and Poland was virtually ended with the *Aliens Restriction Act* of August 1914. This was followed some months later by the *British Nationality and Status of Aliens Act* which, according to the official announcement, was designed *"to consolidate and amend the enactments relating to British Nationality and the status of aliens"*. This Act covered the precise definition of *"Natural Born British Subjects"* as well as outlining the method and requirements of becoming officially *"naturalised"*. It also warned those who had already gone through the naturalisation process of how this might be forfeited. The Act also forced Poles and Lithuanians to register as "Aliens" despite the fact that many had been living here for years, had children born here, and some even had sons serving in the British Army.

Of course the outbreak of war and the new alien registration laws meant greater scrutiny of foreigners, particularly those of German or Austrian origin. But all foreigners, especially those who had arrived in this country through German ports, were treated with suspicion. A newspaper report of October 1914 informed the general public that the police throughout the country, acting under the new Government order, had been working energetically in securing enemy aliens in various districts and arresting them for internment in concentration camps. It stated that *"...there had been no partiality displayed, but all coming under the "War Ban" have been duly taken charge of, from Polish miner or chemical worker to Prague professor or business scientist"*. The same newspaper reported that the police in Widnes had been very vigilant and practically every alien in the town had been attended to. It was said that:

"Widnes has been termed the half-way house to America for Russian Poles. They escape military service in their own country and readily find work in the local chemical works. When enough money has been saved they embark for America, but when one Pole leaves the town another arrives on the next train! The police have records of over 200 aliens in Widnes, chiefly Russian Poles."

On the 22nd October 1914 Police Forces throughout the country set about rounding up all unregistered aliens in their districts especially those of German, Austrian or Hungarian origin. Over five hundred people were arrested in Manchester and over a hundred of these were sent to Lancaster for internment. In our neighbouring town of St.

Helens six Germans and two Austrians were arrested. One of the Germans arrested was a Jesuit Priest who was a member of a Roman Catholic Church in the town; another was a German industrial chemist who had lived and worked in the town for several years. In Warrington, six German workers were arrested.

The Alien Restriction Act imposed strictures on residence, registration, travelling and change of abode. It also included further provisions for the deportation of aliens who did not comply with the regulations of *The Act*. The responsibility of registration was placed on "the alien" who was obliged to register at the local police station when he or she took up residence in a town or city. Those who failed to register properly could be fined, interned, given a prison term or even be deported. Apart from the obligations placed on the alien, there was also a liability on the part of lodging-house keepers to inform the police of any "aliens" residing in their premises. I would imagine that for Lithuanians or Poles, or indeed those of other nationalities who did not have a full command of the English language, the registration process may have caused some difficulties and confusion.

A search through contemporaneous newspaper reports relating to the *Alien Registration Act* threw up some interesting cases. In most instances one can plainly see that failure to register was simply a case of carelessness or lack of understanding rather than a deliberate intention to avoid registration. However, some reports tell a more interesting story. A case from January 1915 shows another link between the Scottish area of Bellshill in Lanarkshire and Widnes. It is a further indication that there was a routine movement of people from that area into Widnes and maybe vice versa. This case concerns a Lithuanian couple who had recently moved to Widnes from Bellshill but had failed to register as "Aliens". The newspaper report, on another page, sheds a more personal light on the circumstances of their arrival in the town. The fact that they lied in order to cover their tracks did not go in their favour. They were fined ten shillings each but, fortunately, escaped a prison term.

REGISTRATION OFFENDERS AT WIDNES.

At Widnes, yesterday, Tamocis Zwalanski, a Russian Pole, was charged with failing to register properly, and also with giving false information to the police. Stefana Ralis was also charged with failing to register.

The woman Ralis pleaded guilty, and said it was her fault. Zwalanski said that he did not thoroughly understand the English language.

Superintendent Foster said that as Widnes came under prohibited areas, every alien, friendly or otherwise, had to register. Defendants came to Widnes on December 24, and were discovered by the police. Detective Robinson saw Ralis in Charlotte-street and followed her to a house there. He ascertained that they were moving to 11, Victoria-street, and he went there, and told both to go and register. At the police station the male defendant represented Ralis to be his sister, and signed as such. Later on the same day Inspector Bannister heard of something and visited the house. In answer to the officer, Zwalanski still persisted that the woman was his sister. Meanwhile the police had been in communication with the Scottish police, and it transpired that the couple had eloped from Bellshill, in Lanarkshire, a day previous to coming to Widnes. Ralis was a married woman with a husband and two children. When confronted, Zwalanski admitted the truth of the statement, and said that the woman had told him to say she was his sister. She got to know he was leaving Scotland, and came with him. There was nothing against the man otherwise than not telling the truth.

Mr. Max Muspratt said it was absolutely necessary that these rules and regulations must be strictly observed.

Both were fined 10s each.

The Lithuanians and Poles

Apart from registering as an "Alien", *The Military Services Convention Act of 1916* required all Lithuanians to produce a certificate which proved that they were Russian citizens. This certificate had to be obtained from the Russian Vice-Consulate Office. One assumes that the certificate was needed to account for them not being in the British Forces. It was also proof of a man's exemption on the grounds that *"it was in the national interest that, instead of being employed in military service, he should be employed in other work in which he is habitually engaged."* Of course most Lithuanians, both here and in Scotland, were engaged in vital industries which were important to the war effort. However, although most did *not* enlist in the army, it was estimated that there *were* around 1500 Lithuanians serving in the British Army. This was said to equate to about 12½% of the Lithuanian population resident in Britain at that time. Of course, these numbers did not include the numerous young serving soldiers of Lithuanian descent who were first generation "British born".

During the War years, employers of *"alien labour"* were required to make written reports at regular intervals on all groups of non-national employees. The lists on the following pages are transcripts of those submitted by some Widnes chemical companies in January and February 1916.[72] It is interesting to note that, in fact, many of these men were well over forty and were outside of the military age requirement. In all the lists the majority of men are classified as Russian Poles. Although there *were* certainly several Poles amongst these men, the *majority* described thus were Lithuanian. Despite this inaccuracy, it is obvious that most employers knew that this was not the case. A note on the file says: *"In the attached lists of "Aliens" employed at Widnes chemical works, many are said to be "Russian Poles" although it is certain that they are in fact Lithuanian".* Despite the fact that this important detail had been acknowledged, there is no mention of anyone of Lithuanian nationality on any of the lists.

When studying the following employment lists it might be of interest to note that although some men had just a few years' service, many of the workers had been employed in some factories for a considerable number of years. For instance, a 55 year old man called Bowkowski

---

[72] U.A.C. *"Aliens" File* - /DIC/X10/318 Chester Records Office/ and personal copies owned by Jean M. Morris

Into The Crucible

had 25 years' service at Muspratt's Works and T. Karnsky, who was 48 year old, had 23 years' service at the Pilkington Sullivan Works. Whilst some of the younger men may possibly have been transient workers, many of the older men were obviously steady and reliable workers who had put down roots in the town.

The lengthy service of some men may also suggest that once settled in the town most men did not change their place of employment. In some cases the period of service may give a rough indication of how long they had actually resided in the town. For example we can see that Mr. J. Bowkowski had been living in Widnes since at least around 1890. It is possible that, once established, there was a reluctance to change jobs because they had become accustomed to the working practices in a particular factory. To move to another place of work may have put them at a disadvantage as they would have to adapt to new routines and associate with a fresh set of work colleagues who may not be particularly welcoming to "Poles". It may simply have been a case of *"the devil you know"*.

The Lithuanians and Poles

Marsh Works

Letter to A.Carey from W.F. Murphy (Manager, Marsh Works) 31/1/1916 (including Goldings, Mathiesons & Morts)

Name	*Nationality*	*Age*	*Service*
A. Gerizhey	Swiss	28	18 months
J. Sderavitch	Russian Pole	40	14 months
A. Balanites	"	46	14 months
J. Williams	"	56	2 years
A. Mathvconis	"	47	10 years
J. Yusites	"	18	5 months
J. Strong	"	20	5 years
A. Gowos	"	44	14 years
A. Astrouskas	"	55	13 years
W. Kalbinski	"	53	7 months
J. Gilinski	"	36	6 months
P Sheperd	"	34	2 years
J. Gilinski	"	42	12 years
J. Zakalauckas	"	24	12 months
J. Vincke	Belgian	22	8 months
Urbain Pyck	Belgian	22	8 months
Camille Kemal	Belgian	22	8 months
Gustof Walenus	Norwegian	60+	
T.Carleum	French	35	3 months
Schorel Delaville	Belgian	48	5 months
J. Benitas	Russian Pole	26	8 months
V. Acalosky	"	30	7 months
E. Reynders	Belgian	28	7 months
C. Zanowsky	Russian Pole	35	12 months
J. Milouski	"	40	12 years
V. Bogasky	"	21	11 months

The Swiss, A. Gerizhey is Pro-German. All the Poles say they are Russian, this is doubtful.

Into The Crucible

Pilkington-Sullivan

Letter to A. Carey from W. Narvis Jones (Lancashire Metal Works) 31/1/1916. With reference to your request for a list of Aliens employed at these works. We are not makers of explosives and therefore it is not necessary to dispense with the service of our Polish workmen, as in their absence during sickness or other causes we have great difficulty in filling their places in normal times.

Name	Nationality	Age	Service
J. Kolensuities	Russian Pole 39 Nelson Street.	42	15 months
A. Sutterditch	Russian Pole 11 Victoria Street.	42	12 years
M. Koirlouchas	Russian Pole 17 Sankey Street.	49	18 years
J. Barney	Russian Pole 47 Wellington Street.	45	20 years
G. Anderson	Swede	47	8 months
T. Karnsky	Russian Pole 47 Irwell Street.	48	23 years
M. Bradowskas	Russian Pole	43	2 years
J. Youskovitch	Russian Pole 36 Cromwell Street.	27	9 months
V. Silvarivitch	Russian Pole 50 Irwell Street.	26	18 months
A. Tupshifske	Russian Pole 34 Major Cross Street.	27	3 years

V. Youkowski	Russian Pole 11 Victoria Street	36	3 years
J. Carlouski	Russian Pole 62 Moss Street.	41	4 years
C. Caparvitch	Russian Pole 28 Cromwell Street.	29	2 years
Ino Doran	Russian Pole 36 Major Cross Street.	32	3 years
J. Varnas	Russian Pole 9 Latham Street.	32	2 years
A. Gearitus	Russian Pole 36 Cromwell Street.	23	1 year
J. Frankscovitch	Russian Pole	30	6 years
C. Strang	Russian Pole 8 Water Street.	58	3 years
A. Youvsites	Russian Pole	55	4 years
F. Bower (Father is German)	Born England	34	16 years
J. Slaviskas	Russian Pole Moss Street.	14	9 months
J. Anderson (Swede)	Born England	14	2 days

Yours
W. Narvis Jones.

Into The Crucible

Gaskell-Deacons

Letter to A. Carey from John Smith (Manager, Gaskell-Deacon's Works) 2/2/1916.

Name	Nationality	Age	Service
A. Boreski	Russian Pole 19 Water Street	53	20 year
A. Bartuskos	Russian Pole 24 Water Street	45	12 years
J. Wassilowski	Russian Pole	56	16 years
P. Mataleveitch	Russian Pole 4 Nelson Street	55	20 years
J. Gett	Austrian Pole	60	20 years
J. Gett (Jnr)	son of above	13	6 months
V. Williams	Austrian Pole 4 Nelson Street	19	3 years
A. Yasitis	Austrian Pole	17	2 years
A. Mullovski	Austrian Pole	19	5 years

John H. Smith (Manager)

The last four names were born in England. All have proved satisfactory workmen and have nothing against their character.

Muspratts

Letter to A. Carey from C.E. Tyers (Manager, Muspratt Works) 31/1/1916. Aliens employed at the works.

Name	Nationality	Age	Service
F. Wichitus	Russian Pole 9 Marsh Street	40	2 years
A. Virech	Russian Pole 7 Charlotte Street	40	1 year
J. Gretski	Russian Pole 19 Water Street	50	15 years
F. Savage	Russian Pole 46 Ann Street	37	10 years
J. Grashulis	Russian Pole 47 Nelson Street	25	2 years
S. Keowski	Russian Pole 31 Nelson Street	30	3 years
S. Zalinski	Russian Pole 11 Water Street	45	3 years
J. Bowkowski	Russian Pole St. Michael's Road	55	25 years
A. Guttowski	Russian Pole	40	2 years
J. Miller	Russian Pole 5 Water Street	55	1 year

Into The Crucible

A. Mark	Russian Pole 50 Wellington Street	35	1 year
C. Grashulis	Russian Pole 30 Cromwell Street	30	3 years
W. Mitchell	Russian Pole 30 Cromwell Street	35	2 years
J. Miller	Russian Pole 19 Water Street	35	1 year
P. Miller	Polish Parents	25	1 year
G. Bowkavski	Polish Parents St. Michael's Road	25	1 year

John H. Smith (Manager)

Pilkington-Sullivan Works

Letter to A. Carey, from J.J. Latham, (Pilkington-Sullivan Works) 10/2/1916.

Dear Sir,
Please find enclosed information relating to men of other than British Nationality employed at the works.

Christopher Neilson - *Norwegian (34) has 11 months service. He is a ship's carpenter by trade and has proved a fairly efficient joiner.*

Charles Wieland - *German (23) has 1 years' service.*
He and his father were suspended whilst investigations were made by the Police. The result was that his father was interned and the son allowed to return to work. His mother is English.

Anthony Hulbinskie - *Russian Pole (24) nine months service.*
Very little is known of this man. He says he was born in Russia, but has lived in England for 12 years. He is a bricklayer's labourer.

Carl Ludwig Paulson - *Swedish (33) 1 year's service.*
Employed in the 'Handy Gang'. Paulson was sent to Widnes by the Fleetwood Fishing Vessels Owners Association.

Prosper Barri - *Belgian (36) 5 weeks service.*
Hubert Segers - *Belgian (36) 9 weeks service.*

Both above from the refugee home at Grassendale.

Yours sincerely
J. J. Latham

Into The Crucible

Lancashire Metal Works

Letter to A. Carey from W. Narvis Jones

Name	Nationality	Age	Service
V. Astrowsk	Russian Pole *(Leading Hand – Character excellent)*	39	14 years
Peter Brown	Russian Pole	39	13 years
J. Carparagidies	Russian Pole *(married to an English woman)*	51	20 years
J. Cagdanivice	Russian Pole	29	9 years
V. Cousky	Russian Pole *(married to an English woman)* Runcorn	28	6 years
A. Koparivtiches	Russian Pole 30 Cromwell Street	36	14 years
J. Mazites	Russian Pole	29	3 years
A. Mitchell	Russian Pole	36	14 years
James Powell	Russian Pole 35 Nelson Street	30	4 years
J. Skercav	Russian Pole	36	14 years
John Wilson	Russian Pole 25 Sankey Street	41	2 years

Lancashire Metal Works (continued)

In addition to the above, Frank Pitchilingi (Russian Pole) came to England as a child and has been for many years a naturalized British Subject. His brother was killed in action on the Western Front a year ago. All the above-mentioned keep very much to themselves and seldom undertake work other than their recognised duties.

W. Narvis Jones (Manager)

An additional communication was sent to Mr. A. Carey from Mr. A. Bennett (Pilkington Sullivan Works) on 1st February 1916. In this memo he said that he knew very little of the character or history of his non-British employees *"but they are employed on important heavy work and therefore would be difficult to replace"*.

I would like to mention a further point regarding the brother of Frank Pitchillingi, who was mentioned in *The Lancashire Metal Works* report. This young man was killed in action in France on 19th May 1915. He was just 25 years of age. He enlisted under the name of Frank Kennedy and was a member of *The King's Liverpool Regiment*. On reflection, I think most people would find it rather sad that Lithuanians and Poles were treated with hostility and suspicion at a time when some of their sons and brothers were fighting for their adopted country. Indeed, some, like young Pitchillingi, were paying the ultimate price for their loyalty.

In July 1917 Britain signed the *Anglo-Russian Military Convention*, a reciprocal agreement between the two countries regarding military service of British subjects in Russia and Russian subjects in Britain. The Lithuanians were classed as Russian Poles and as such were liable for service in the Russian army. This meant that in Britain large numbers of Lithuanian men age 18 to 41 were given the choice of returning to Russia to fight with the Russian allies, or to enlist in the British army. Many chose, albeit reluctantly, to return to Eastern Europe but by the time they arrived in Russia the country was in the grip of revolution. The

Into The Crucible

dependants of those who had elected to go were left in dire straits. At first neither the Russian nor British authorities would accept responsibility for their maintenance and refused to pay any form of allowance. In December 1917, after a number of petitions to Parliament, the British Government relented and agreed to make payments to the wives and children of these men.

Unfortunately many of the Lithuanian men who opted to go to Russia were not allowed to return to their homes and families in Britain after the War. Many historians are of the opinion that these men were prevented from returning to Britain from Russia because the Government feared that Bolshevism was on the rise and could spread to this country. It was subsequently decided that the dependants of those not allowed to return had become an unsustainable burden on the system. As a consequence, the British Government suspended dependants` allowances and brought in a repatriation scheme in order to deport the families. Initially it was said that the repatriation scheme would be voluntary but, once the Treasury had withdrawn dependant payments to the families, it became virtually compulsory. These families, many British born wives with British born children, had the impossible choice of leaving or remaining here with no means of support. In Lanarkshire the Lithuanian community was catastrophically reduced. The Lanarkshire Parish Council asked for the registration of the number of Russian/Lithuanian families who were still resident in Lanarkshire. The report finished with the words *"the removal of these people will release a fair amount of accommodation"*.[73]

In the absence of relevant source material it is not known if many, or indeed if any, Widnes based Lithuanians were involved in this type of removal. *The Widnes Weekly News* for 1917 makes no mention of repatriation orders for Lithuanians or of the departure of Polish men from Widnes and there is no oral history of this happening. However, during 1918 at a hearing of *The Widnes Tribunal Court*, the case of eight Russian Poles was referred to. It was stated that they had been given "permission" to return to Russia under *The Military Service Convention*. As they did not do so they were therefore deemed to be in the British Army Reserve and had the rights of British citizens. This leads one to believe that the regulations of *The Military Service Convention* were open to different interpretations.

---

[73] Newspaper - *"The Bellshill Speaker"* – 13th September 1918

The Lithuanians and Poles

Despite the undeniable poverty and hardship experienced by the Lithuanian community during their early years of settlement in Britain, many Lithuanians gave generous donations to the *Lithuanian Relief Fund.* The fund had been set up in Lanarkshire in 1914 for the purpose of providing financial aid to relatives and friends who were suffering hardship back in Lithuania. As chain migration clearly linked Lithuanian communities in Scotland with those in North-west England the organisation soon started to receive donations from other districts. As a consequence, branches of the fund were established in the areas of England and Scotland where Lithuanians had settled. The amounts raised give an indication of the sizes of Lithuanian communities in these places. Below is an extract from a record of Branch Collections*.

Scotland
Bellshill	£148.8.8d
Glasgow	£129.1.9d
Mossend	£68.10.1d

England
Clockface	£2.11s
Earlestown	£14.13s
Haydock	£13.19s
Liverpool	£17.2s
Manchester	£61.10s
St. Helens	£1.9s
Widnes	£7.14s

While this book was primarily intended to deal with the period up to 1920 only, the following translation from a Lithuanian publication is included because of its relevance. The sparse information about later Lithuanian or Polish community activity makes this article particularly interesting. The translation is literal and names are spelt in the original Lithuanian. This information was given to me by Vida Gasperas of *the Lithuanian Cultural Society* who located this information in the Society's archives and also kindly translated this short passage for me.

---

* There were numerous other areas mentioned in the original report

"Britain's Lithuanians 1947-1973" edited by Kazimieras Barenas.
WIDNES

Zmuidzinas, in his book "Pasaulio lietuviai" published in 1935 (World Lithuanians 1935) gives the number of Lithuanians in Widnes as 450. Another source reduced it to 60. Yet another source in 1950 says that there were 35 Lithuanian families in Widnes. This information is in line with "Britanijos lietuvis" published in 1949 and given information that in Widnes lived about 100 old immigration Lithuanians. So the main Widnes Lithuanian colony was pre 1947-1948 Lithuanian immigrants. The new immigrants were few who lived there only temporarily. The source mentions a few notable names: Joe Guy past Mayor and restaurant owner. His grandparents came to Britain around 1888 and their name was Gutauskas, his parents were born in England. Another Vince Karalius was known as a community worker and rugby player. Two brothers, Lukoseviciai[74] were distinguished as boxers.

In 1949 a priest, J. Steponaitis, lived there for 3 years reviving the activities of the colony. In 1949 Widnes organised National Day celebrations and also Bishop P. Bucys`s 50th anniversary of priesthood which drew about 250 Lithuanians from nearby colonies of Liverpool, St. Helens, Earlestown, Haydock, Sutton Manor and others. The festivities were organised by the Widnes Lithuanian Community Committee of S. Karalius, K. Grazulis and P. Valinskas. During the celebratory Mass a male voice choir was led by F. Ramonis, and the Jolly Brothers, J. Vasiliauskas, J. Pilipavicius and P. Nekrosius performed later and Mrs. Makeliene organised the National Dance group.

In 1949 Widnes Lithuanians organised a local convention that was attended by a few hundred Lithuanians. Greetings were received from S. Karalius and P. Klezas.

In January 1950 a Children's Party (Eglute) was held and on 8th July 1950 there was a big religious procession.

After this brief revival there is very little known as to what happened to the Lithuanian community in Widnes".

---

[74] Known as Luckovitch

The Lithuanians and Poles

Although this chapter has been specifically dedicated to the story of our Lithuanian and Polish immigrants, I thought it might be useful to add the names of a few more Widnes citizens who came from other parts of the world. The following list includes men who settled with their families in Widnes. It provides their places of origin as well as the date of their arrival in Britain. Of course there were numerous other people as well, but I add these few names simply as an indication of the multi-cultural composition of our early industrial society.

Name	Place of Origin	Address	Arrival
Henry Auer	Hungary	Appleton Lodge	1892
John Boner	Germany	69 Mersey Road	1902
Alfred Bronchemite	France	64 Widnes Road	1889
Nathan Cornberg	Austria	31 Frederick Street	1910
Harris Corran	Russia	33 Albert Road	1912
Frederick Gandolfo	Italy	29 Victoria Road	1903
Louis Lautenberg	Russia	74 Waterloo Road	1901

Of course those who are listed as being of Russian origin may have come from countries which had been annexed by Russia, such as Lithuania or Poland.

Into The Crucible

Girls of Lithuanian descent – St. Patrick`s May Procession

The Welsh

Apart from the large number of immigrants from across the seas, people from other parts of Britain were also attracted to the abundant employment opportunities in Widnes. In 1861 there was a substantial number of Scottish people living in the Farnworth and Lunt's Heath areas. These were mostly employed as flax spinners working in the canvas and sailcloth industry in that part of the town. Thirty years later the census of 1891 provided us with information on the places of origin of other new citizens. I list below a selection of "P*lace of Birth* locations that appear for that year.

Derbyshire
Durham
Lincolnshire
London
Macclesfield
Norfolk
Northampton
Oxfordshire
Scotland
Shropshire
Staffordshire
Tyne and Wear
Warwick
Yorkshire

In addition to the above, William Gossage was responsible for bringing a large number of workmen from Worcestershire into the town. These men had previously worked in his Stoke Prior Factory where washing soda was produced using the Leblanc process. There were also large numbers of early settlers from Cornwall and other south-western regions. Workers also came from the Midlands when Thomas Bolton & Sons set up their copper works in the town in the 1880s. Among other numerous and varied workers who moved to Widnes special mention should be made of the Welsh workforce. The

Into The Crucible

Welsh came to Widnes in significant numbers many of them coming from areas of Flint and Anglesey. In fact the Welsh were among the first immigrants into the town, arriving as early as the 1830s. Runcorn also had a sizeable Welsh community which was linked to the stone quarrying trade. It is supposed that most of the early Runcorn Welsh were quarrymen who had originated from North Wales. A Welsh church, under the leadership of The Rev. John Jones, was established in Runcorn in 1829 when the Welsh Calvinist Methodists opened their chapel in (Back) King Street. In 1856 another Welsh Chapel was opened in Rutland Street to accommodate the growing Welsh community.

It is probable that some of the Flint men came to Widnes because they had previous experience of working in the chemical trade. The chemical industry was well established in Flint as early as 1842, with Messrs. Roskell, Williamson and Co., being the main employer. This factory produced hydrochloric acid and, like other chemical factories of that era, had provoked numerous complaints relating to the unavoidable escape of noxious vapours. In 1850, following these complaints and numerous claims for damages, Roskell was forced to close his works. Amazingly, the factory was taken over by James Muspratt who had a long history of complaints and legal actions against his own chemical operations in Liverpool. Despite his dubious reputation in respect of atmospheric pollution, it seems Muspratt acquired this factory without any real opposition from Flint Corporation. It was said that he had given the Corporation firm assurances regarding control of escaping vapours.

James Muspratt bought the Roskell & Williamson works in 1852 for £7000 and brought in his two sons, Richard and Frederic, to run it. The Muspratt brothers were assisted in the management of this operation by John Kingsby Huntley. Almost immediately James Muspratt transferred Frederic to Widnes to oversee the establishment of The Wood End Works, leaving Richard in sole charge of the Flint Works. It is probable that some of the Widnes Welsh, who originated from Flint, came here around that time as a result of the Muspratt connection, or at least because of their previous industrial experience in that chemical factory.

Prior to the development of Widnes as a centre of alkali manufacture, St. Helens was already an up and running industrial town which had

The Welsh

attracted a substantial amount of Welsh labour. Our neighbouring town of Warrington also had a significant Welsh community. The Welsh populations in both these towns were associated with the presence of the copper industry in these locations. Since the discovery of copper at Parys Mountain in Anglesey in 1768[75] there had been a significant increase in copper mining on the island. Subsequently, in the latter years of the 18th century, copper ore was shipped in considerable quantities to both St. Helens and Warrington. Evidence suggests that the Welsh had been employed in St. Helens as early as 1779 when copper smelting works with links to Welsh copper mines became established in the Ravenhead district. Most of these workers came either from near Holywell in Flintshire, or Amlwch in Anglesey where the Parys Mine Company mined on Parys Mountain. [76]

The establishment and rapid development of the alkali industry in Widnes prompted the movement of a significant amount of labour from St. Helens to Widnes. This mobile workforce included large numbers of Irish but also substantial numbers of Welsh workers who were attracted by the growing employment opportunities in the new chemical industries. In addition to the transient workers from St. Helens, there were also Welsh workers who came directly from Wales to work in the new alkali factories of Widnes. As a consequence, by 1860 a sizeable Welsh community had become established in the town. The number of Welsh residents was sufficient to merit the provision of three Welsh chapels. The Welsh Wesleyan Chapel in Cromwell Street was opened in 1866. In 1887 this congregation had increased considerably prompting a move to a new larger building on the corner of Lacey Street and Luton Street. The Welsh Congregationalists also had a substantial flock, and they subsequently established their chapel in Moor Lane. The third chapel, the Welsh Presbyterian Chapel, was sited in Milton Street.

In 1871 John Street in West Bank was home to numerous Welshmen and their families. The following men were named as the heads of their households. Each had a spouse and a number of children.

---

[75] Copper was also discovered in the lead mine of *Penryn Du* on the Lleyn peninsular in 1764.
[76] For more information on St. Helens Welsh – see *"Across The Gap"* Jean. M. Morris (2016)

Into The Crucible

> Robert Roberts from Flint
> John Evans from Abergele
> John Riorden from Denbigh
> Hugh Hughes from Anglesey
> Edgar Lowe from Flint
> John Davies from Flint
> John Owens from Mold

In February 1882, prior to the building of the new larger Wesleyan Chapel, the following article was published in *The Widnes Weekly News*. The article highlights the fact that immigrants of all nationalities felt the need to join together, either socially or in a religious environment, with people of their own ethnic group. In this respect the Widnes Welsh were no different from the Irish, Poles and Lithuanians. The full article outlined various fund-raising activities. It reported a pleasant concert that was held in the Lacey Street schools and it also congratulated the friends at Cromwell Street for their praiseworthy endeavours.

"The Welsh Wesleyan Methodists in Widnes, as may be generally known, are now a considerable body, and by their rapid growth have come to be looked upon as of importance. True, like some of their religious brethren, they have not this far been able to raise a temple of imposing appearance or of large dimensions, nor, indeed, have they aspired to this. Some twenty-five or thirty years ago, their numbers here were exceedingly few, but as the extensive manufactories grew up others were tempted to leave their native mountains and lovely valleys to engage in more lucrative and no doubt more arduous employment, and gradually Welshmen came to number no insignificant portion of our population. In the early days of their settlement, religiously they formed part of the then existing churches, but, as we know the home-feeling and the natural longing for home associations is strong, and consequently they did not "neglect the assembling of themselves together" in order that they might converse in their mother tongue, and worship in their native language. Time sped on, numbers increased, a meeting-room was eventually engaged where for a considerable time the services might be held in the Welsh language, and some years since an unostentatious chapel was erected in Cromwell Street, where for a considerable time, the services have been conducted by a Welsh minister. The surroundings, however, are anything but inviting, and the inhabitants of the neighbourhood, as a rule, belong to the Roman Catholic Church, while

The Welsh

those attending the Welsh chapel principally reside at some distance from their places of worship. The edifice too has become too small, and it has long been felt that a more commodious building was necessary".[77]

In July 1889 the Widnes Welsh were reading a report in *The Widnes Weekly News* about the sale of Snowdon. The mountain had been put up for sale by public auction in London and was described as a *"freehold state in the parish of Beddgelert".* The estate comprised of 1500 acres of land with cottages, buildings, hotel and beacon with an enjoyable rental of £216.10s. The large demesne contained mineral wealth, including copper and other metals, and valuable slate quarries. The first bid of £2000 was made by a clergyman but the final bid of £5750 was placed by a Mr. Perks of Lombard Street, London, who secured the mountain with mineral rights, fishing rights, property and slate quarries, for an unknown client. Today's readers will no doubt find it inconceivable that the whole mountain with its rich mineral sources, quarries, land and buildings could have been purchased for less than the price of a second-hand car!

Other reminders of the Welsh community in Widnes are some street names in the area around Moor Lane. Near to what in later times became the Hugh Lewis Camping Store, we find Rhyl Street and Ellis Street. The houses in these streets were built by Mr. J. Griffith, a Welshman, and were occupied mainly by Welsh families. Part of the building that became the Hugh Lewis Camping Store was actually The Welsh Congregationalist Church in earlier days. Until relatively recent times a memorial stone was still on view inside that building to commemorate one of the members of this community who fell in the First World War. Evan Llewellyn Thomas was just 23years old when he was killed in Palestine on 26th March 1917. Known as Eddie, he played football for the Wesley Guild and was the organist in the Welsh Congregationalist Chapel, where the plaque in his memory was inscribed in Welsh.

As we have seen in chapters relating to the Irish and Lithuanians, most separate ethnic groups were clustered in their own distinct localities. In the case of the Welsh it would seem that West Bank and the area bordering Victoria Road and Moor Lane were mainly home to

---

[77] *Widnes Weekly News* – February 1982

Into The Crucible

the Widnes Welsh communities.[78] In the Census of 1891 we find a considerable number of Welsh people scattered in these locations. Although there were numerous Welsh families residing in the West Bank area at that time, the streets around Victoria Road and Moor Lane had the largest concentration of Welsh residents. An extract from the 1891 census covering streets in those neighbourhoods is given here:

Victoria Road
Grace Jones from Anglesey
Robert Davies from Mostyn
Joseph Roberts from Gresford
Hugh Jones, his wife and family from Corwen
Isaac Edwards, his wife and family from Holywell
John and Sarah Jones from Caernarvon

Lacey Street
Joseph Platt, a Blacksmith, and his family from Wrexham
John Jones from Denbigh
David Thomas from Montgomeryshire
John Platt, a Fitter, from Wrexham

Luton Street
Fred Jones, a tailor, from Corwen

Eleanor Street
David Ogborn, a copper worker, and his family from Swansea
Ann Davenport from Bangor
Jane Griffiths, a stay maker, a widow, from Mostyn

Market Street
Mr. Davies, an engine driver from Denbigh
Patrick Hannery from Flint
Winifred Williams (who takes in lodgers) from Llandudno
Margaret Evans from Anglesey

---

[78] Census Returns 1891

The Welsh

Witt Road
Mr. Williams from Rhos, Denbigh
James Durbin, wife and 4 sons all from Rhos, Denbigh
George, James and John Rees, nephews of James Durbin (all from Monmouthshire).

Ellis Street
Hugh Jones and family from Anglesey
William Gallagher from Flint
Evan Griffith from Llanelli
Thomas Leigh from Holywell

Moor Lane
The Kenyon family from Flint
Thomas Coleman from Flint
William Jones, an engine fitter from Holywell.
William Owen from Penmawr
John Griffiths a Grocer, from Flint

Egypt Street
The Lewis family, with eight children, from Wales

Rose Street
Thomas Martin and Charles Martin from Merthyr

Moorside Terrace
Owen Hughes from Pwllheli

The fact that sizeable numbers of Welsh had moved northward to Merseyside and Lancashire was evident from a statement made at a meeting of *The Welsh National Society* in Liverpool in October 1890. The Chairman on that occasion had said, *"There was so large a number of Welsh people settled in Liverpool that it had been described as the metropolis of Wales"*. It is worth saying that the Welsh presence in the City was varied and noteworthy. It included not only labouring workforces but also craft and professional people. Some of the most beautiful old churches and buildings around the City of Liverpool were the creations of talented Welsh born architects, stonemasons and stained-glass artists. On October 15th *The Liverpool Daily Post* made a full report of *The Welsh*

Into The Crucible

National Society meeting. The guest speaker was Sir Robert Cunliffe and also present were a number of Welsh councillors and clergymen. It was stated that there was a large company of Welsh people, not only from Liverpool but also from surrounding districts including a considerable number from Widnes.

The address by Sir Robert Cunliffe had a theme of friendship and unity. He criticised the anti-English attitude he claimed was prevalent at that time in Welsh newspapers and publications. He said:

"Clearly there are faults on both sides, and I am not desirous of apologising for one or the other. My point is that those who can and do use influence with either are performing the most patriotic work when they seek to soften and not to emphasise points of difference. Now, if translations which have been published can be trusted, it is undeniable that some of the Welsh papers have printed references to England and the Government of the country which certainly do nothing to create that better understanding which, I think, we all agree is desirable. In one widely circulated paper I read "They (the writer is referring to the Irish) have long enough been under the destroying hoofs of the English. My belief is that it is high time for the Welsh to do something of the same kind. We have suffered patiently for hundreds of years, and it is full time for us to be delivered from the oppressive yoke and grievous English chains"

Sir Robert's address went on to outline more examples of what was, in his opinion, a misplaced sense of extreme patriotism.

"Now I have been led to this conclusion by noticing what I think cannot have escaped the observations of anyone who lives in or knows much about the Principality – viz., a tendency in some of those who speak or write, and who may be presumed to lead or reflect on Welsh opinion, to dwell with too much complacency on Welsh virtues, or too much severity on English shortcomings. Is there not a disposal to extol the ancient language of Wales to a degree which might be construed by enthusiasts (we have plenty of them) to mean that the acquisition of English also is a desirable thing?"

The report of the meeting did not indicate whether or not this speech was favourably received by the audience. It states simply that a vote of thanks was given to Sir Robert for his address.[79] From this account we

---

[79] *Liverpool Daily Post* – October 15th 1890

are led to believe that there was a fair degree of anti-English feeling among sections of the Welsh population. This is not too surprising as, like the Irish, the Welsh had strong nationalistic tendencies. As a consequence there were several key points of contention with the British Government. One of these was the question of the disestablishment of The Church of England in Wales. Another concern was the anglicising of Welsh place names and the spread of the English language. In fact the preservation of the Welsh language was an important topic. From contemporaneous reports in *The Widnes Weekly News* we are able to see that the Welsh language was still widely used amongst our own Welsh population. Local church services were conducted entirely in Welsh and it is believed that the language was in common daily use among the community until well after the turn of the century. Sadly, with the passing of time it vanished from the lips of the majority and only the few ardent may have retained something of its lovely lilting tones in their households.

The election of councillors for the first Town Council in 1892 was of great importance to the ethnic communities who were keen to have their own representatives. *The Widnes Weekly News* of October 22nd 1892 tells us of a meeting organised in support of Welsh candidates.

THE PROGRESSIVE CANDIDATES` CAMPAIGN
WELSH MEETING
Last Friday evening a meeting of the Welsh ratepayers was held in the Welsh Wesleyan Chapel, Lacey Street, in support of the candidates, Messrs. Brown, Lewis and Shaw. The weather was very inclement but despite that drawback there was a good attendance. Mr. Robert Roberts, who presided, opened the meeting in a Welsh speech, and other Welsh speakers all spoke in their native language. The resolution affirming that the representatives of educationalists upon the School Board is inadequate and ought to be increased was proposed by Mr. Owen Owens, supported by Messrs. Brown, Shaw, Poole, and the Rev. J.T. Thomas, of Llanrwst (who had kindly given his services to the cases) and carried unanimously.

The report also gave details of the entertainment provided that evening. The audience was treated to a performance of Welsh songs sung by Miss Lizzie Owens and accompanied by Miss Thomas. The meeting ended with the following statement from Mr. Roberts: *"We*

Into The Crucible

understand that the Welsh vote, which is pretty strong, will be given solid for the progressive candidates. A Welsh committee has been formed and an energetic and thorough canvass is being made".

In the same month the MP for the Widnes Division, Mr. Gilliat, attended a Welsh concert at Garston where there was a large Widnes Welsh contingent present.

There was feverish activity among the members of two Welsh chapels in September 1898. The Welsh Congregational Church in Moor Lane celebrated an anniversary and jubilee by inviting a preacher from Kensington Chapel in Liverpool to preach. The Rev. J.O. Williams, known as "Pedrog" preached a powerful sermon to a large assembly. Pedrog was well known, not only as a preacher but also as a Bard. He was the possessor of no fewer than thirteen *"Bardic Chairs"*. A number of other eminent speakers were in attendance. It was said that *"not often did the Welsh people of Widnes have the opportunity of hearing such talented speakers at the Moor Lane Church"*. The speakers congratulated the congregation on finally removing the debt on the chapel. They also spoke encouragingly on the subject of *"The Eisteddfod"* that had been organised by the church over a number of years. Not too far away, on the opposite side of Victoria Road, the Welsh Wesleyans were saying a sad farewell to their minister Rev. Owen Hughes who was being moved to the Holyhead circuit. A farewell tea was served in the Lacey Street Sunday School followed by a meeting in the Welsh Wesleyan Chapel. A number of speakers paid tribute to Rev. Owen Hughes and presented gifts to him and his wife.

Members of *The Welsh Congregational Church* in Moor Lane were the prime motivators in establishing *The Widnes Eisteddfod*. As we have seen, most of the early ethnic groups found ways of keeping their own cultures active. It was an important way of maintaining a link with their old way of life and the things that were familiar and dear to them. For the Welsh community who had settled in Widnes in those early days, apart from their churches, music was also an important part of their national custom. In an effort to replicate the ancient musical traditions of their native land, they established their own Welsh music festival in Widnes in 1894. *The Widnes Eisteddfod*, which was usually held at the end of February, subsequently became a significant event in the social life of the town. It was an important annual occurrence which was enjoyed not only by the Welsh citizens but by all sections of local communities on both sides of the river. Such was its perceived importance that in February 1904 the local Education Committee, on the application of the Eisteddfod Committee, resolved that the afternoon of Thursday 25th should be regarded as a half-day holiday at all council schools.

Perhaps it should also be said, in relation to *The Widnes Eisteddfod*, that the event was renowned for its high standard of competition. Entrants for the various categories came not only from the two towns, but from far and wide across the north of England. Interestingly, in the latter years of the Eisteddfod's existence, in the male voice choir section, there was reluctance by choirs from outside the area to enter the competition. It seems that Runcorn's leading male voice choir, who usually won the trophy, was considered to be "unbeatable". There was certainly no suggestion that the Runcorn choir was favoured in any way; the fact was that they were *"simply the best"*.

Following the *Education Act of 1902* the Widnes Education Committee was formed. The first elections to this committee caused a great deal of interest and all the ethnic communities were anxious to have their own representation. However this was not a simple case of wanting an Irishman to represent the Irish or a Welshman to represent the Welsh. I'm afraid it was far more complex than that – religious allegiances were brought into play! The following letter to the editor of *The Widnes Weekly News* might explain.

> Sir,
> "Referring to last week's meeting of the Town Council upon the education question, it appeared to me a little misleading that Mr. Councillor Owens when supporting Mr. Evan Thomas` claims for election on the committee, should have included an appeal for the sake of the Welsh community.
>
> Mr. Owens said "the claims of Mr. Evan Thomas were paramount", but he need not say anything in his favour more than had already been mentioned. He would remark however, that it would be fitting to elect him, "if only as some recognition of the Welsh people of this town".
>
> Would Mr. Owens think it very fitting to elect a Nonconformist (such as our friend Mr. Thomas is) to represent the whole of the Welsh community?

Into The Crucible

It would certainly have suited the Nonconformist section of the people, but what about the Welsh members of the Church of England? Is it supposed that everybody with Welsh blood in their veins belongs to the dissenting bodies? This supposition may be prevalent in Widnes, but not so in Wales, where the Welsh Protestants are very fond of the Established Church, and the services are conducted in the Welsh tongue.

The Welsh churchmen in Widnes, (of whom there are a fair proportion), would most strongly protest against being represented by a Nonconformist of the Welsh or any other nation. That is of course over the new Education Act.

Now the fact of the matter is this, Mr. Evan Thomas is a Nonconformist, and naturally it is inferred that his sympathies lie in that direction regarding the Education Bill. Hence he had to go. It was decidedly not a question of considering the claims of the Welsh or any other nation, but it might have been a ruse on the part of the Nonconformists to keep their ranks intact.

Personally, Mr. Thomas has my greatest respect and esteem but, as a Welsh Churchman, I feel compelled to repudiate the idea that the whole of our community would have calmly submitted to being represented by a Nonconformist in respect to the Act. I voice the sentiments of a number of my countrymen (of the Established Church) when I say that we should not have entertained it for one moment. We resent the idea, without prejudice to Mr. Thomas, who certainly is a capable man to represent the Welsh Nonconformists, but then they do not compose the entire Welsh community.

Signed: "CYMRO" *May 18th 1903".*

In October 1912 the grandson of the late and much loved Liberal, Mr. William Gladstone, attended a Liberal Rally in the Borough Hall in Widnes. The Rally had opened with a male voice choir singing various songs including a rousing rendition of *"Men of Harlech"*. Mr. Gladstone Junior addressed a packed audience of around a thousand people. He spoke on a number of topics including Irish Home Rule and several times during his speech he touched upon proposals to disestablish the Church in Wales. Following this, a Mr. Ellis Roberts put the case for Wales, and was given a very favourable reception. The newspaper reported the event thus:

The Welsh

"Mr. Ellis Roberts, B.A. was cordially received and prefaced his address by remarking that he had come there that evening to place the case of Wales before them. He had come to address an English audience but the first thing that met his ear on entering that spacious hall was the sound of vocal music, which was such good music that he really thought that it must be a Welsh choir (laughter) – and that a Welsh meeting (renewed laughter). He listened to the choir's excellent rendering of "Play the Man" but they put their foot into it afterwards by singing "The Men of Harlech" (laughter). They did not sing it with the spirit of a Welsh choir, and if that had been a Welsh meeting the people would have been on their feet and joining in the singing straight away (laughter). However he was glad he was speaking to English people, for he generally found that all the English people wanted was a little education on the Welsh Disestablishment Bill. The English did not see the Welsh bill as the Welsh saw it; they did not feel it as the people of Wales felt it. The Church of England was the Church for the English people, and it was doing good work, but the people of Wales were asking that the Church of England, the church which had not proved itself the national church of their land, should be disestablished and disendowed in Wales. That had been a burning question in Wales for the last 40 or 50 years. They had heard that evening how strong a demand Ireland was making for Home Rule, but let him invite them to hear what little Wales was doing (hear, hear)".

On concluding his speech Mr. Roberts was loudly cheered by the audience and the Widnes Liberal Association voiced their support for this Bill. It should be mentioned that *The Welsh Disestablishment Bill* was strongly supported by the Welsh community in Widnes.

During the years of the First World War, the Welsh community did their utmost for the War effort. Welsh "flag days" were a regular occurrence in the town. The annual *"Widnes Eisteddfod"* also continued to be an important event for the Welsh people of the town and its surrounding areas. Although it is evident that the War had a diminishing effect on the competition, nevertheless, the event continued uninterrupted throughout the entire period of the conflict. The 1917 *Eisteddford* was reported thus:

"Though war effects were noticeable in the programme and proceedings of the 23rd Widnes Eisteddford held in the Borough Hall yesterday, it was a matter for felicitations on the part of the local Welsh community that this annual event has so successfully and vigorously survived the war period.

Into The Crucible

There was some falling away in the number of contests as compared with happier years, this being most marked in the chief choral competition, where the prevalent man shortage asserted itself and reduced the contest to one choir, and that the Garston Presbyterian Church. In the children's events, which were as popular as ever, competition was as usual strongly marked and keenly demonstrated, especially during the afternoon"

In much the same way as the Irish and Eastern European communities slowly lost their ethnic distinctiveness in the town, the Welsh too were subsequently absorbed into mainstream society. It is perhaps not too surprising that the Welsh integration came much easier and faster than the other groups. It is obvious that the Welsh had far more in common with the indigenous population than the other two groups and therefore assimilation was easier and more acceptable.

The Welsh Arch at Irwell Street - 1902

What they left behind

There are countless written histories of the countries represented by immigrants into Widnes so I shall not concern this reader with an in depth account. Nevertheless, to maintain the tone of this book and to give at least a flavour of the type of environments these immigrants left behind, I include a picture of provincial life in parts of Ireland and Lithuania in the mid to late 19th century. Some people might question the relevance of this chapter in a local history book but I make no apologies for including it. Many of today's Widnes citizens have no knowledge of the circumstances that prompted their ancestors to emigrate, or the type of lives they lived before they came here. Indeed, most people I spoke to regretted that they were never told anything about their roots and all wished they had asked more questions. For those reasons and those people I include this chapter.

During the nineteenth century the Irish were a significant presence in Widnes and they were by far the largest immigrant group in the town. Their arrival here in the early days was connected to the Great Irish Famine of the 1840s, which was one of the most seminal events in Irish-English history. This catastrophe brought about a period of abject suffering and degradation for countless families, and prompted one of the most dramatic waves of migration in European history. The Irish who arrived on our shores during that awful time were unfortunate refugees rather than voluntary migrants. Regrettably, as emigration was often their only hope of survival, many hundreds of thousands were compelled to leave their native land and venture into an uncertain and alien situation.

As we have seen in an earlier chapter, the Famine immigrants arrived in vast numbers into the Port of Liverpool. From there they spread out to neighbouring towns or walked long distances to other parts of the country in search of work and shelter. Many, after working for a period in other places, eventually relocated to Widnes where there were plentiful employment opportunities in the chemical trade. As a consequence of their substantial numbers in the town the Irish were able to create a viable community which was subsequently absorbed into our early industrial society. Most had come from rural areas of Ireland and were virtually penniless when they arrived. They were also unskilled an inexperienced in factory work. The only ability the Famine migrants possessed was a willingness to do hard work.

Although the Famine era brought the greatest number of Irish to these shores, immigration from Ireland continued throughout the nineteenth century. During the remaining decades of that century the largely agricultural economy of Ireland never fully recovered from the effects of famine and there was a great deal of deprivation throughout the entire country. The 1801 Act of Union, which had such a detrimental effect on several areas of Irish trade, meant that Ireland was ruled from Westminster rather than Dublin. Therefore Irish people were legitimate citizens of Britain. As British subjects they felt at liberty to move to England in order to provide a better life for themselves and their families. This meant that migration from Ireland to England was a continual process throughout the century.

The Irish immigrants into Widnes came from all counties of Ireland and in most cases their native environments and experiences, whatever the province or county, were similar. If they were lucky, some small towns and villages may have provided limited opportunity for work in minor types of cottage industry; but in most cases employment was usually of an agricultural nature. Of course none of the rural labouring classes actually owned land, if they worked their own patch of land they were always tenants not owners. Their employment or tenanted land was invariably connected to large estates which were owned by landlords, most of whom lived abroad. The estates were usually left in charge of a "land agent" who managed the land and property on behalf of the absentee landowner. Historians generally agree that the main cause of Irish misery at that time was connected to bad relations between the landlords and tenants.

Although Irish immigration into Widnes did involve "famine" migrants who had transferred from St. Helens and other places, the immigrant trail from Ireland to Widnes continued well into the 20th century. Furthermore, there were few places around England that did not have Irish communities composed of exiles from all corners of Ireland. Certainly our neighbouring towns of St. Helens and

What they left behind

Warrington, as well as the cities of Liverpool and Manchester, played host to significant Irish communities. As a consequence, back in Ireland there was scarcely a town or village that had not had their populations greatly reduced by emigration. In fact there were hardly any families in Ireland who did not lose relatives, friends or neighbours to the emigrant trail. Those who did remain in Ireland grappled with another kind of distress. They were coming to terms with a significantly emptier landscape and the knowledge that they would probably never see their emigrant sons, daughters or relatives again.

The surroundings and circumstances emigrants left behind were similar, no matter which village, town, county or corner of the country they came from. Therefore there was plenty of scope when deciding on a location to demonstrate the type of environment some Widnes immigrants had left behind. However I chose as my model the small town of Carrick-on-Suir, which is located in County Tipperary in the south-east corner of Ireland. Its neighbouring villages are bordered by the counties of Kilkenny and Waterford and within easy access of the counties of Wexford and Carlow. Census information shows that Carrick on Suir and all of these south-eastern counties were well represented by immigrants into Widnes.

The Main Street of Carrick on Suir c.1900

Into The Crucible

Today Carrick-on-Suir is a modern thriving town with a wealth of cultural amenities including two superb theatres which house an award winning Operatic Society and an outstanding Drama Group. However things were vastly different in the 19th and early 20th century when young men and women were forced to leave the town in search of work and a better life. In this area, as in all other areas in Ireland during the 19th century, a landlord system prevailed so virtually none of the native population owned land, they were tenants. The tenant usually paid £1 per acre, which was a large amount in those days. The rent was paid twice a year on *"gale days"* which were usually in May and November. The majority of tenancies were on a yearly basis and hardly any had leases, which meant they could be thrown off their land and out of their homes at any time. Most tenants had little or no rights apart from the right to cultivate their small patch of rented land. A tenant was not allowed to cut or prune trees, make or repair existing roads, drains or watercourses, and he certainly did not have game or fishing rights. This meant that he was not allowed to shoot birds, rabbits or hares or take fish from nearby streams and rivers; if he did so he faced severe penalties. In addition to this, the rent paid by the tenants was hardly ever of benefit to the local economy as the money usually left the country in the pockets of absentee landowners.

The landlord class, which was generally comprised of members of the English aristocracy, usually lived abroad whilst maintaining an estate or landed establishment in the area. In the village of Piltown, in County Kilkenny, which is just a few miles from Carrick-on-Suir, the main landowner was Lord Bessborough. It is significant to note that the children in the local school were taught how to salute Lord and Lady Bessborough. The "salute" was a profound bow on one knee with fingertips touching the ground. Not too far away, Lord Clonmell's agent expected his tenants to display a picture of his lordship in their homes![80]

Whilst the landowner was generally absent, an agent was employed who was in total charge. The agent deputised for the landowner in personal matters or disputes. His permission had to be sought and given in order for a person to marry. Permission was also needed for a tenant to be able to give lodgings to a visitor, even for just one night! The agents' power was enormous and many tenants were ground down

---

[80] Dr. Patrick C. Power – *Carrick-on-Suir and her people* (Dublin 1976)

What they left behind

under their tyranny. Those who fell foul of the agent, or fell behind in their rent, were treated mercilessly. Evictions were commonplace, whole families were dispossessed and often had their houses pulled or burned down as soon as they left. In these evictions the agent usually brought in a group of men from elsewhere known as "emergency-men". These men were employed to guard the crops from being harvested by the evicted tenant or his friends. The emergency-men were, naturally, hated by everyone and considered to be the lowest of the low.

Apart from the potato blight which created a mass exodus at the time of the Famine, there is no doubt that the landlord system in Ireland was also directly responsible for a large number of emigrations. The repressive conditions and high rents demanded by landowners was highlighted in *The Widnes Weekly News* of August 27th 1889 when Irishman, Thomas Delaney, of 37 Major Cross Street, wrote a letter to the editor, which was published under the heading *"Landlordism in Ireland, Persecuted Shelburne"* Mr. Delaney started his letter thus:

Dear Sir,
Kindly allow me a space in the columns of your widely circulated journal to bring under the notice of the English people the doings of certain landlords in Ireland. My object in writing this letter is to bring before the bar of public justice the action of the present Tory Government in aiding, helping and encouraging, by every means in their power, the doings of bad and vindictive landlords, in order to banish the people of Ireland from their native land, and to blacken if they can the justice of their cases before the eyes of the world. I therefore wish, with your kind permission, to show that on the estate of landlords, who listen and agree to the fair claims of their tenants, peace and goodwill exists, whilst on the estates of bad and persecuting landlords, in the same locality, who are deaf to the calls of reason and justice, and who are supported in every cruel act by a coercionist Government, on these estates and on these alone are to be found misery and desolation, as is the case in parts of the County Wexford, namely, the Barony of Shelburne, which is situate in the west of the county and bordering on the Rivers Barrow and Suir.

Thomas Delaney's letter named specific landlords and the amount of rents they were demanding from their demoralised and struggling tenants. Although in most circumstances the landowners were absentee

Into The Crucible

English aristocrats, in one case this was not so. Among those named by Mr. Delaney was a woman, Mrs. Byrne, who he described as a tyrant of the worst type. She was a resident landowner and was Anglo-Irish. The letter alluded to the case of a man who was a tenant on her land:

> "The land in his occupation was purchased by the Byrnes from the Colclough`s of Tintern Abbey, and ever since the Byrnes became owners of that part of the Colclough property, the rents which were till then considered fair, have since been raised by the Byrne family from year to year until they now stand at 52% over the gross valuation; and not satisfied with raising the rents, the Byrnes took every possible opportunity to persecute and bring to ruin every poor tenant who chanced to be under their control. The Byrnes in their day, especially in Black `47 evicted and banished from their native land no less than 29 families, numbering I believe 120 human souls. The tumbledown homesteads of these poor people are still visible to the eye of the traveller. What a pity to see the land of those poor tenants turned into sheep and bullock walks, simply to gratify the greedy inclination of a persecuting woman."

It has to be said at this point that not all the landlords were bad. Some were very fair with their tenants and were held in high esteem by them. Lord Ormonde, who owned large sections of land in County Tipperary, was extremely considerate towards his tenants and did much to improve their standard of living. Others, such as The Marquis of Waterford, who owned the Curraghmore estate in Portlaw, a few miles from Carrick on Suir, were infamous for the heartless and harsh behaviour they displayed towards their tenants.

In 1879 a society called *"The Land League"* was founded in County Mayo by Michael Davitt. Its purpose, among other things, was to obtain some security of tenure and to get a fair rent system. Branches of *The Land League*, not surprisingly, spread quite quickly throughout the country and were usually organised through parish clubs. Incidentally, the founder of *The Land League*, Michael Davitt, had links with Widnes as it is believed he had taken part in the ill-fated Fenian raid on Chester Castle in 1867. At that time he was supposedly lodging in Caroline Street, Newtown, before he was compelled to make a covert escape from the area. In May 1878, the year before he founded *The Land League*, Davitt attended a huge meeting at the Theatre Royal in St. Helens under the chairmanship of local Widnes Doctor, John O' Keeffe. Joining him

What they left behind

on the stage at that event were some of the foremost Irish political figures of the day, including the leader of the Irish Nationalist Party, Charles Stewart Parnell MP.

The downtrodden tenants and impoverished workers of Carrick on Suir were avid supporters of *The Land League*. In October 1880 a meeting of *The League* was held in the town and drew large crowds from neighbouring villages. In Westminster, Charles Stewart Parnell, who was himself a landlord in County Wicklow, voiced his support for *The Land League*. His public support and speeches resulted in his arrest and trial in December 1880. He was charged with *"creating ill will among Her Majesty's subjects"*. The publicity surrounding Parnell's trial encouraged the growth of *The Land League* in Ireland and mass meetings were held all over the country. In Carrick-on-Suir, in 1881, John Dillon, MP, made an impassioned speech attacking the proposed Land Bill that was being debated in Parliament at Westminster. The following day John Dillon was arrested for his *"violent speech"*.

Despite much disappointment among the Parnellites, because of its watered down and unsatisfactory components, *The Land Act* became law on 22nd August 1881. The Act, although not encompassing all the desired elements, did provide facilities to arbitrate on rents and also under certain conditions granted tenants some security from eviction. Although it was not entirely satisfactory it was a step in the right direction. Throughout this time Parnell and his Irish Party continued to voice their opposition to *The Land Bill* and actively encouraged people to ignore the provisions it had given. In October of that year Charles Stewart Parnell was arrested again and imprisoned in Kilmainham Goal, Dublin. By the end of 1881 *The Land League* had been totally suppressed.

In the wake of the demise of *The Land League* a new organisation emerged in October 1882. *The Irish National League,* unlike the Land League which had appealed mainly to the farming communities and the clergy, drew its membership from a wider section of society. *The Irish National League* was also more political in character than *The Land League*. Carrick-on-Suir was the first town to have a branch of this society and, no doubt, later Carrick emigrants to Widnes would have become members of the Widnes branch of *The Irish National League*[81] which was headed by the inimitable Dr. John McNaughten O`Keeffe.

During this period the economic situation in Carrick-on-Suir and the surrounding villages was in serious decline. The high rents demanded by the landowners meant that families were barely able to exist. The town itself had few employment opportunities and its only real strength was as a market town offering sales of pigs, calves, butter and general farm produce over four days of the week. There was also an annual *"hiring fair"* where able-bodied men sold their labour to farmers for a year, or young girls were taken on as domestic servants in farms or on the large estates known as the *"big houses"*. The harvesting of woods belonging to Lord Ormonde on the southern and eastern slopes of the mountain, *Slievenamon*[82], also gave employment to a small number of people. The wood from the trees, mainly oak, went into the making of barrels at the coopers of Carrick and nearby Clonmel. The bark of the trees was used for the curing of hides. Tanning and Brewery industries did exist in the town but these were not sufficiently large enough to offer any significant amount of employment for the population. Slate quarries in a village to the north of the town also offered limited employment, but many of the men who worked in this industry found more profitable employment by moving over to North Wales to work at Penrhyn and other quarries. Some travelled further afield to the slate and marble quarry regions of Vermont in America.

The lovely river *Suir* (pronounced Shure) that ran through the town also offered natural employment opportunities for a few inhabitants. Fishing provided income and some men were employed in a commercial Salmon Fishery. This work was seasonal during the months February to August. In late August these men usually travelled to Wales to work in Welsh mines and quarries until the following January. The willows (known as sallies) that grew along the river-bank proved a valuable commodity for the local basket makers who sold their wares locally and also exported baskets to England. In addition to these natural assets, which created a small degree of employment, the farming communities had the benefit of a number of creameries based

---

[81] Dr. Patrick C. Power – *Carrick-on-Suir Town and District 1800-2000.* Ireland 2003
[82] Pronounced "Sleeve-na-mon"

What they left behind

in and around the town that made butter for export.[83] Another small business, a locally owned saw-mill, operated in the town but this was taken over in 1909 by a Liverpool firm called Lovell & Company. There were numerous problems with machinery and the mill eventually closed down in 1922. So, all in all, there were few real employment opportunities either in the town or its outlying districts.

The village of Portlaw, a distance of barely five miles from Carrick-on-Suir, and situated beside the Curraghmore Estate of the Marquis of Waterford, was more fortunate as it was established as an industrial village in the early 19th century. This village, like Carrick-on-Suir, deserves mention as there were several families in Widnes who originated from this small rural district. The Malcolmson family, who were English Quakers, were responsible for bringing the cotton industry to Portlaw in the early nineteenth century. Like most Quakers they were extremely benevolent employers who were honest and fair and respected the rights and dignity of their employees. They also built cottages in the village for their workers, which were laid out in five small streets, like the fingers of a hand. The cotton industry thrived in Portlaw until the American Civil War, when a shortage of raw cotton supplies occurred due to an imposed blockade by Union forces. The village industry struggled on until 1876 when it finally went bankrupt. The reasons for this failure were numerous but mainly the slower introduction of power looms and cheaper imports caused an inability to compete. The failure of this employment was catastrophic to the village and after 1876 many emigrations followed, including a number of families who relocated to Widnes.

The lack of employment opportunity, and the high rents demanded by the landowners from their tenants, meant there were large numbers of poor both in the town and the surrounding countryside. *The Saint Vincent de Paul Society* offered as much assistance as it could, and the Poor Law System provided workhouses, but as the workhouse often meant the breaking up of families many were reluctant to avail themselves of this relief. The emigrant trail was often the only practical choice. The talk of plentiful work and opportunity in England was a huge enticement for people living in such dire economic circumstances.

---

[83] Ibid

Those attracted by these stories and who were able to scrimp together the money for their fares, naturally, chose that path.

Although Widnes became home to a large number of Irish immigrants from the south-east corner of Ireland, emigration from that area was not confined to England. In the areas around Wexford, Waterford and Kilkenny there was a tradition of taking migratory seasonal work in the quarries and mines of Wales, which was a relatively short voyage away. In addition, some men from Waterford and its hinterlands, including Carrick on Suir and people from nearby Wexford, travelled further afield for their seasonal work. Ships that arrived periodically into Waterford harbour en-route for St. John's, in Newfoundland, often took on seasonal workers from Ireland to work in the Newfoundland cod-fisheries.[84] Most men returned home after their customary few months seasonal work, but many settled there. Interestingly, today, the descendants of these 19th century Irish workers still populate certain areas in Newfoundland. Some regions are almost entirely inhabited by families whose origins stem from just a few small villages in south-east Ireland. I am told that most speak with accents similar to those of County Waterford.

The plight of the Polish and Lithuanian immigrants into Widnes was not dissimilar to the Irish in many ways. They each shared a history of deprivation and oppression. The Irish were ground down by poverty and a tyrannical landlord system that kept them subjugated; and English laws meant that their native Irish language was gradually and systematically erased. The only solution for young people in search of a better life was to emigrate. Of course, in addition to the fact that these emigrants were economic migrants who were desperate to escape crushing poverty at home, we have established that some Poles and Lithuanians were leaving their homeland to avoid conscription into the Russian army. Under Russian rule both Poland and Lithuania became subject peoples, impoverished and repressed. However, to completely appreciate their plight it would be necessary to fully understand the complex histories of both countries; sadly I must admit that I am ill-equipped to offer this reader more than just a glimpse.

---

[84] Jean M. Morris -*The Honey Meadow and Beyond* - (Greengage Press - Peterborough 2002)

It is important to remember that at this time the ethnographical territory of Lithuania was fragmented into various parts, some in Eastern Prussia, each with its own complex history. The Lithuanians of Lithuania Minor, estimated to have numbered about 156,000 in the middle of the 19th century, were involved in a different process of social development than those in Lithuania Proper. When serfdom was abolished in Russia in 1861, the formation of a class of free peasant landowners was already complete in Prussia. As a result of this, there emerged a wealthier and better-educated class of Lithuanians in East Prussia.

As we have seen, most people in this country did not make a distinction between Lithuanian and Polish immigrants and assumed that they were *"all the same"*. Indeed, perhaps the complex histories of both countries made this error understandable. Although these nations were distinct and separate Kingdoms, each proud of their individual identities, the two nations forged an alliance in the mid-14th century and the two crowns were subsequently united into a Polish-Lithuanian State. Although Lithuanian peasantry remained staunchly loyal to their native heritage, and Lithuania was still considered a separate entity, the fact that their borders were fairly fluid meant that there was a strong Polish influence on Lithuanian life. However in later times Polish cultural dominance was challenged and Lithuania began to regenerate its own territorial and cultural autonomy. Unfortunately by the end of the 18th century both countries had been annexed by Russia and their borders were subsequently obliterated as they became part of the Russian Empire. However, in spite of this, there is no doubt that Lithuanians always saw themselves as people separate from Poles and Russians.

When looking at the Polish/Lithuanian relationship we see that, whilst not always friendly, the two countries did band together several times in the interest of freeing themselves from Russian rule. They united in a number of large-scale but unsuccessful rebellions against Russian occupation. Unfortunately the result of these failed uprisings, especially the one in 1863, was an increased and intensified repression. This was particularly harsh in Lithuania where the Commander of the Russian occupation forces ordered the mass executions of captured Lithuanian freedom fighters. Many were publicly executed by hanging in the market places of towns and villages. To add to this horror, villagers were forced to witness the harrowing scenes.

The abolition of serfdom in 1861 and the rebellion in 1863 appears to have marked the beginning of the period in which Lithuania began to separate itself from Polish life. After the suppression of the insurrection of 1863-4 the process of unifying the Russian lands gained strength and the Kingdom of Poland also lost the last remnants of autonomy. In Lithuania, the policy of "Russification" increased in intensity and stringent laws were imposed on the native population. These laws included the prohibition of the Lithuanian language and the printing of books other than those printed in the Russian Cyrillic alphabet. The banning of books and the total suppression of all Lithuanian literature, including newspapers and journals, brought about an underground movement in book smuggling and a renewed resurgence of nationalism. Amazingly, though hard to believe, carriers of these forbidden books faced severe penalties. They ran the risk of being shot at the border or being banished to Siberia if they were caught with any form of Lithuanian literature. The Lithuanian author, Romas Sadauskas,[85] in one of his articles on Lithuania says:

> ...that nowhere in the world was a nation forbidden to use its native language to pray, teach its children, and publish and read newspapers. It was like tearing the tongue from the mouth or the heart from the chest, the heart which can love not only one's neighbour but also one's native country. We are the exception unknown to the world; for several generations our ancestors experienced the prohibition of their native language. Lithuania alone smuggled books, an activity completely unknown to the rest of the world. For whom did the book publishers, despite great danger to themselves, bring books published abroad in this forbidden language? The books were for ordinary villagers, ploughmen read them under their thatched roofs during the autumn and winter evenings.

Religious anti-Catholic discrimination also caused serious and violent clashes as Lithuanians were forced to resist the measures imposed upon them by the Russian government. Catholic churches were routinely closed as attempts were made to impose the Orthodox Russian Faith upon the population. The closing of churches provoked organised peasant resistance that was only conquered by floggings,

---

[85] Romas Sadauskas *"The Road Travelled by the Lithuanian Book"* - (1990)

What they left behind

arrests and deportations to Siberia. One of the most dramatic events of this kind was one that has become embedded in Lithuanian history, the *Kraziai Massacre* of 1893. Kraziai was a small Lithuanian town with a population of around 1700. When a series of petitions failed to save the local church the people began to gather to prevent the removal of sacred objects. A force of Police Gendarmerie and Cossacks arrived and invaded the church, destroying religious artefacts and brutally beating the people and driving them out. The mounted Cossacks drove the fleeing Catholics into the nearby Krazante River, where a number were drowned. A large number of the townspeople were publicly flogged and about 70 were brought to trial. Various accounts either exaggerate or minimise the number of deaths, nevertheless, this incident became entrenched in memory and enhanced the development of both national consciousness and the Lithuanian alienation from the Russian influence. The intense anti-Russian feelings that arose from the Kraziai incident, and other similarly brutal occurrences, lay bare the reasons why Lithuanians were reluctant to enter the Russian army.

The Vilkaviskis region of Lithuania has previously been mentioned in connection with immigrants into Widnes. Among the small towns and villages in this area is Pavembriai, which was the birthplace of Vincent Karalius. Vilkaviskis (Vilkovishk) is located in the south-western part of Lithuania on the shores of the Seimena River, a tributary of the River Sesupe. It is about 18km from the border with Prussia (now Russia) and 3.5 km from the St. Petersburg-Berlin railway line. During the period of Prussian rule (1795-1807) the residents were encouraged to build stone or brick houses, instead of the traditional wooden ones, for which they were granted a third of the cost. Despite the large number of stone houses, in later years the town suffered a number of extensive fires which destroyed countless homes. Another interesting fact about the area relates to Napoleon and his infamous retreat from Moscow. In the summer of 1812, Napoleon, with a huge army of about 250,000, based themselves in the Vilkaviskis area for four days, causing a great deal of damage to the town. After his defeat and retreat from Moscow, many of the French soldiers froze to death and drowned in the lakes around Vilkovishk and twenty French soldiers and three Generals are buried in the vicinity.

Into The Crucible

A Lithuanian Village with wooden houses

In 1866, after Lithuania was annexed to Russia, Vilkovishk became part of the Augustowa Region. Following this the Russians built large barracks near the town as well as several factories. One factory produced spirits and a number of other factories were involved in oil extraction. The district was also a centre for processing pig bristles that were eventually used in the production of brushes. At its height there were around a thousand people employed in this industry. Vilkovishk also had a few large warehouses where locally produced goods were stored for distribution to neighbouring towns and villages. However, although the land was not generally profitable enough to support large families, the main source of employment was in the growing of agricultural products, timber and grain, all of which were destined for export to Germany.

In the 19th century a large percentage of the population of this area was Jewish. In the middle of the 18th century a cholera epidemic hit the town of Wizajny(Poland) about 35 km south of Vilkovishk. The Jewish refugees from there, who were not allowed to enter Vilkovishk for fear of infection, settled in a forest nearby and the community of Vilkovishk supplied them with food. Many of them died and were buried near the forest. Descendants of these Jews later settled in Vilkovishk and lived there till the Holocaust. In the 1880s and 1890s Jews from Russia headed for Vilkovishk in order to smuggle across the border into Germany without a passport. From Germany they would endeavour to sail to America. It should be said that both the Jews and the Catholics suffered great abuse and oppression by the Russians.

In 1915 Vilkovishk was captured and occupied by the German army who remained there till 1918. An independent Lithuanian State was established after the First World War and Vilkovishk became the district centre. However, when looking at the migration of Lithuanians into Scotland, and subsequently into Widnes, we are dealing mainly with the period which spans 1880-1914. During these years economic poverty, resulting from a depressed farm economy drove both Lithuanian and Polish peasantry off the land. Employment opportunities in their native lands were limited or almost non-existent, especially in rural areas where traditional occupations had been associated with agriculture. In addition to economic hardship and lack of opportunity, another key factor which brought about a surge in emigration was the increased Russian oppression.

We can see from the descriptions of the places and conditions that the Irish, Poles and Lithuanians left behind, that life was not good in their homelands. It is hard for us modern readers to imagine existing under such tyrannical conditions; living in an environment in which we were not allowed to follow our religious beliefs, or even speak or write in our own language. However, despite the huge hardships and oppressions, they were probably *reluctant* emigrants as they were leaving behind their families and all that was comforting and familiar to them. Nevertheless these emigrants bravely headed off into the great unknown, in the hope of creating a better life. Unfortunately, the grass was not too green on the other side either. They were all unwelcome and resented and were, without exception, subjected to astonishing levels of racial abuse and discrimination.

Into The Crucible

Widnes Brass Band

The National School, West Bank.

Everyday Life

The township, in the early years after the establishment of the first chemical factories, was composed of the villages of Farnworth, Appleton, Hanging Birch, Crow Wood and Widnes Dock. However, the speed with which the area transformed itself from a rural idyll into a hub of continuous industrial activity resulted in the rapid spread of residential building. Houses and streets hurriedly sprung up on once open spaces and green fields, swallowing up the beautiful terrain in the south of the town. Furthermore, these dwellings were constructed unbelievably close to the newly built factories with their unhealthy emissions. Of course, not only did the physical landscape alter, as once verdant areas became crammed with industrial development and grim tightly packed streets, there were also huge and important changes in our society.

At the beginning of the 19th century most people were farm workers or rural craftsmen. By the end of that century they had become factory workers. This was the result mainly of the effect of The Industrial Revolution which had started in Britain around 1760. This event brought far-reaching changes to the working lives of the entire population. The process of industrialisation and change which occurred in Britain during the 18th and 19th centuries subsequently became a dramatic feature in the history of this country. For not only did the Industrial Revolution bring about great progress in manufacturing and invention, it also had a major influence on the traditional nature and structure of social order. As a consequence, the fairly rapid change from an agrarian to an industrial society impacted upon the behaviour of all sections of society and there were few people, rich or poor, who were unaffected.

The huge volume of labour that flooded into our area created a new social phenomenon which turned cultural and social attitudes and conditions of life upside down. The newcomers, wherever they came from, were mainly country-bred and had the traditional outlook and character of country folk. Despite this shared characteristic, there were numerous marked differences that set groups apart. Not least of these were nationality and religion. The blending together of these groups into a common working and living environment was never going to be easy. However this new working society was forced to adapt to a new system of social relations, as well as a new lifestyle that was far removed from their previous existence and customs. Unfortunately this new way of life was accompanied by the twin evils of crime and poverty, as well as intolerable living and working conditions.

Quotes from a book written by Charles Booth in 1889 established the fact that all our new industrial towns contained, chiefly in families of unskilled workers, a mass of people *"who never had a chance to live even physically satisfactory lives"*[86]. Sadly, this must have been true of the majority of people who lived in the cramped streets in the south end of our town. The new townscape that represented the town's industrial progress had given rise to deplorable living conditions. Uncontrolled development resulted in huge areas of jerry-built housing in streets of mud, un-served by sewers or piped water. In addition to this, the atmosphere in the immediate vicinity of their homes was polluted and harmful. Furthermore, countless tons of industrial waste[87] was dumped throughout the town in toxic mounds, often perilously close to residential buildings.

By the mid-1860s Widnes ratepayers had recognised the need to provide essential services such as drainage, water, gas, paving, lighting, and health provisions for the welfare of the rapidly rising population. On 15th June 1865 a meeting of Widnes ratepayers was held at the Public Hall in Hutchinson Street for the purpose of considering the propriety of adopting the Local Government Act of 1858. Amongst those present at that meeting were Mr. Gossage, Mr. Deacon, Mr. Barrow, Rev. Smythe, Dr. Greenup, Mr. Powell, Mr. Woodhouse, Mr. McClellan, Mr. Cowley, Mr. Davies and Martin Taylor. During the meeting Mr. Gossage said:

"Many gentlemen present would remember the time, as he did himself, when there were not twenty houses in the place; and looking at the number crowded together now, he thought that everyone would admit that proper sanitary regulations were required. If left to individuals, sewering etc. got

---

[86] *"Modern Britain"* - (London 1979). - T. K. Derry & T .L. Jarman -
[87] Known locally as "Galligu"

neglected – what was everybody's business was nobody's – but after adopting the Local Government Act they would appoint a Board of Commissioners to carry into effect its provisions, a Board consisting of their own neighbours, gentlemen who were interested equally with themselves, and who would doubtless be sufficiently conversant with sanitary matters to make that little city – for he could not help calling it a little city – more healthy than it was now. Looking to the future, he might not see it but he thought there were gentlemen present who would see it ten times its present size. The Local Government Act was capable of application to towns very much greater than Widnes at the present time."

The Act was unanimously adopted and the first meeting of the newly constituted Local Board of Health was held at the Public Hall on Tuesday 3rd October 1865. William Gossage was elected Chairman of the Board and the other members were John Knight, Robert Barrow, Edward Young, Henry Deacon, Thomas Gleave, John McClellan, Richard Kent and George B. Shute.

Profiles of William Gossage, Henry Deacon and John McClellan have been recorded in this book and elsewhere. I found scant information on some of the other members of the Board and was unable to uncover anything at all of interest on Thomas Gleave. John Knight was, in partnership with John Baker Edwards, one of the proprietors of the Lancashire Manure Company which was based in Moss Bank in 1855. Ten years later, on 15th May 1865, his partnership with Mr. Baker Edwards was dissolved and John Knight set up another works near The Horns on the site of what used to be, in recent years, the *"Laporte"* factory. Robert Barrow, who died in 1881, was a watchmaker from Farnworth and his address is recorded as Farnworth House. Edward Young was a farmer, also from the village of Farnworth. He was the person responsible for a proposal to develop the footpath from Derby Road to Pit Lane into a highway. George Shute was a local landowner.

Richard Kent was originally a watchmaker who settled in Widnes sometime around 1842. In 1851 he married Sarah Morrison, the daughter of Mr. Alex Morrison, landlord of the Boat House Inn, in West Bank. In 1855 Sarah Kent was conducting a school in their home at Bradley Cottage in Albert Road. After running a "paper stall" at the Runcorn Gap Station, Richard Kent subsequently opened shops in Waterloo Road and Ann Street. In 1857 Mr. Kent was appointed the first postmaster of Widnes. In later years, when he became Chairman of The Widnes Local Board of Health, Richard Kent presented a lamp to the town. This lamp, known locally as "Kent's Lamp", stood for many years opposite the old Police Station in Victoria Road. Richard Kent died in 1899.

The expansion of the town had been accompanied by the removal of the better-class homes to the outskirts of the town, distant from the homes of the factory workers. This was an age of contrasts. For the factory worker, his home was far removed geographically and in every other sense from the homes of the middle-class sections of Widnes society. Unfortunately, when building houses for the Widnes labouring classes, little consideration was given to comfort or providing adequate space for life and leisure. A new urban wasteland was created without thought for anything beyond speed and cost. On what now appear to be incredibly small areas of land, there were numerous streets of hastily thrown up terraces of cheap houses intersected by a warren of narrow passages. These cramped streets were located conveniently, but unhealthily, close to the factories and were often tainted by smoke and noxious gases. The whole area would have been a study in shades of grey, without greenness, the sky often obscured by a haze of smoke from the factories. The only concessions to leisure were the numerous pubs that were positioned at handy intervals on street corners.

Shortly after the setting up of The Local Board, a surveyor was appointed who was given the dual role of Surveyor and Nuisance Inspector. The new officer, Mr. Shufflebottom, was asked to make a report on some of the streets in the Waterloo and Newtown districts. He found that, without exception, they were all in an appalling condition. They were without drainage or sewers and the surface of the streets were just a mass of mud and water. The streets were also receptacles for every kind of filth. Some years later Councillor David Lewis wrote about the passages (back entries) that divided the streets:

"...the back passages were detrimental to public health. The surface being filled up with cinders readily absorbed the foul matter deposited upon it in the process of emptying the privies and middens. Unfortunately, it is the custom of many of the poor people to keep their front doors locked. Entrance to the house is by the back door. Children made the filthy passages, lined on either side by a series of privy middens, their habitual

playground. Hawkers of food brought their carts up these narrow lanes exposed to contamination by dust and emanations from privy middens. It is not surprising, therefore, to find that the town suffered at times from serious outbreaks of fever, and that the death rate was comparatively high".

The number of houses under construction in 1871 gives us some indication of the population concentrations in the town during that period. There were 73 houses under construction in Enumeration District 11, which comprised of Cholmondeley Street, Church Street, Bank Street, Davies Street, Hurst Street, Irwell Street, John Street, Mersey Road, Viaduct Street, West Bank Lodge and White Street. This was in marked contrast to the Enumeration Districts that covered Cronton and Farnworth where a total of only seven houses were being built. The greatest period of urban development in Widnes was in the mid-1870s as this era saw the large-scale development of West Bank. Newtown was the earliest concentration of housing but by the late 1860s and early 1870s some of the original parts of this district were already being demolished to make way for the railways.

Building plans submitted to The Local Board from 1865 onwards provide us with the names of the main builders of our town. Some builders were immortalised in what were once familiar street names, Wood, Kershaw, Carlisle, Travis and Midwood to name but a few.[88] Edwin Wood appears to have been the most prolific of these builders, having constructed 850 houses in the town. Lagging behind him were James W. Carlisle and William H. Kershaw who built in the region of 300 houses each. An additional point of interest regarding Mr. Kershaw is that he was one of the first tenants to obtain a lease on Hutchinson's West Bank Dock Estate. The lease, which was at a cost of £50 per annum, was taken out in January 1865.[89] At that time he was described as a Timber Merchant. His lease was extended in October 1874 and the company continued at this site until its closure in 1897 following the death of Mr. Kershaw.

---

[88] *Planning Registers Vols. 1 & 2 December 1865 - Feb 1928* Chester Record Office – LBWd. 2557

[89] *"Across The Gap"* - Jean. M. Morris (Springfield-Farrihy – 2016)

Into The Crucible

Below are details of some of building activity in Widnes during the 1870s.

Year	Description	Builder	Street
1870	31 houses	T.F. Butler	Pepper St., Cross St.
1870	31 houses	Samuel White	John St., White St., West Street
1870	41 houses	J.W. Carlisle	Joseph St., William St,
1871	51 houses	F. Brotherton	Irwell St. Bank St., Beaumont St; Terrace Rd.
1872	36 houses	J.W. Carlisle	Grove Street
1875	19 houses	H. Travis	Travis Street
1877	27 houses	W.H. Kershaw	Muspratt Street
1877	26 houses	T. Sadler	Vine Street
1878	22 houses	T. Leicester	Kent Street

The Widnes factory worker's house was small, measuring maybe 12' in width and 20' in depth. It usually consisted of two rooms upstairs and two rooms downstairs, with a steep dark staircase going up from the kitchen to the upper floor. It had an outer yard that contained a small shelter, a midden, which was emptied during the night by the night-soil men. The inside walls of the house, separating it from its neighbour, were so thin that family rows could be heard half a dozen doors away. The front door generally opened directly onto the street, this door providing the only barrier between the occupants and the neighbourhood. When the door was opened, the distinct noises and smells of the district confronted the residents. The sound of factory hooters and trains shunting, and the smoke and stink from the nearby factories immediately invaded their senses.

Everyday Life

The men's lives were regulated by work times and the opening and closing times of nearby pubs. The women's main purpose, apart from rearing the children, would be to stretch the meagre income to provide food and clothing for the family. It would have been a constant struggle to put food on the table. The grocer sold *"on tick"* and would have to wait for weeks for his money, but if he failed to provide this service then he wouldn't have customers. Some of the people lived in perpetual poverty. In order to provide for extras at Christmas those who could manage it joined slate clubs and loan clubs that were mostly administered from public houses. The shadow of deprivation and continuous debt hung over most of them. As a consequence they were the prime targets of the *"tally man"* who sold clothes and other things to them on their doorsteps, whilst offering endless credit from which they never escaped.

The pawnshop too was an integral part of community life. Anything of value would be pawned – from a wedding ring, bedding, an item of clothing or anything at all that might be of some small value. In addition to the pawnbroker, moneylenders, often operating from their own homes, would lend money without security but at hugely inflated interest rates. This often meant that the loan would never be paid back and the debt increased rather than reduced.

Worrall's Directory of 1876 lists the following Pawnshops

John B. Imison	*Waterloo Road*
Horatio Syred	*Waterloo Road*
Union Loan Co.,	*Church Street*
Joseph Newton	*Marsh Street*
John Ward	*Victoria Road*
William Jameson	*Ann Street West*
Charles Neill	*Ann Street West*

As an additional note of interest, and as an indication of the level of this practice, it has been stated that in 1855 there were 129 pawnbrokers in Liverpool taking an average of 50,000 pledges a week.[90] There is no record of the number of pledges in any given period in Widnes but one

---

[90] Anthony Miller – *Poverty Deserved? Relieving the poor in Victorian Liverpool* – Liver Press 1988

would assume this was also relatively high. In 1872 an Act of Parliament was introduced to ensure that all pawnbrokers required a certificate to trade. The Minutes of Widnes Town Council name several local pawnbrokers who had applied for certificates. In 1895 these included the following:

James Carroll	Waterloo Road
Redmond Carroll	Widnes Road
William Houghton	Victoria Road
Mary Imison	Waterloo Road
John Smith	Mersey Road
William Harvey	Mersey Road

Other means of raising or providing money was by joining one of the many Tontine Clubs or Friendly Societies in the town. Of course these were savings related and not many people had spare cash to put aside. For those that did, the dividends would usually be shared out among the members in time for Christmas, thus providing a welcome boost to the family budget at a time when extra spending was needed. Apart from the pleasing pay-out, the declaring of the annual dividend appears to have been an enjoyable social event with music and song reported in almost every instance.

In December 1889 the following clubs declared their dividends.

Blackburne Arms Tontine Society
Mr. Daniel Lloyd (President) announced that after deducting all expenses for the year each member would receive £1.6s. dividend besides leaving a balance of £1.8s.10d to begin the new year.

Page Lane Tontine Society
The amount each member received was £1.4s. The evening was an enjoyable occasion. Songs were rendered by Messrs. Lee, Perks, Travis and Dale with Mr. Bagley presiding at the pianoforte.

Mersey Hotel Tontine Society
Issued a dividend of 13s.6d for each of the 95 members.

Obviously most members of our local society were not in a position to save money. In fact most were barely able to keep the wolf from the

Everyday Life

door. Poverty knocked on countless doors in Widnes and for some it was a permanent state. At a meeting of the members of the *Widnes Distress Relief Committee* in 1879 serious concern was expressed. The Committee unanimously agreed that cases of real hardship in Widnes were multiplying by the day. As the Committee had limited funds at their disposal, it was feared that there would be *"great privation in many houses in Widnes unless there was greater philanthropic and charitable endeavours"*.

The Chairman said:

"It is an easy matter for those who have not felt the pressure of adverse circumstances to be sceptical about the existence of deep distress, but those who have the best opportunity for judging assure us that the destitution in Widnes at the present time is appalling. While efforts of the committee have done much to alleviate the distress, it must not for one moment be considered that the relief afforded has been anything more than sufficient to keep body and soul together".

Over the following years there are numerous reports which show that poverty was not alleviated. Numerous inquest verdicts report starvation as a supplementary cause of death and in some cases this was cited as the prime cause. In addition, the impoverished were often unable to pay for medical treatment and this dire situation frequently produced tragic results. In 1886 the following case appeared in the local press.

"Margaret Doyle, wife of John Doyle, labourer, 74 Timperley Street, died during confinement. Before her illness Doctor McCambridge was called in to attend the woman, but as the husband could not afford to pay the fees he was directed to call in the parish doctor. By the time the husband had complied with these instructions it was too late, the child and mother were dead".

In the grim narrow streets everyone knew everyone else with an intimacy of detail; which women donkey-stoned their steps each day; who owed what or pawned what; which men were known to beat their wives or spend all their money on drink. Everyone and everything was so near that it was hard to keep things private. The houses opposite were literally just a stone's throw across the cobbled roadway,

Into The Crucible

windows directly facing each other allowing the occupants little privacy. However, despite this lack of privacy, in this collective experience of community people were prepared to rally round in times of trouble or need. The fact that almost everyone in the neighbourhood had shared experiences and backgrounds helped to create an identity which became a form of mutual kinship among the inhabitants. Neighbours worked and lived in the same environment and worshipped at the same church, and most had the same ethnic origins. Therefore, when needed, they all pulled together and provided help and support. Some people took on specific roles in the community, such as the people who read and wrote letters on behalf of those who could not do so; or the army of capable women who assisted at births; or the people who could be called upon to sit-up with the sick or dying and the women who washed and laid out the local dead.

To the inhabitants of Newtown, Lugsdale, Moss Bank or West Bank, these close-knit neighbourhoods became a small world as homogenous and as well defined as a village. Life centred on this small group of streets and on their complex and active group life. The inhabitants of all these neighbourhoods shared a special bond which was forged by work and hardships. The closeness and intimacy of this environment, where people were thrown together in common circumstances, living and working in a mutually shared experience, contributed to a sense of "belonging" which probably lasted until the last bricks of Newtown, Moss Bank and parts of West Bank were pulled down.

If one were to stroll along Lugsdale Road today it would be hard to imagine that this was once the gateway to a vibrant and swarming locality. In those days, if you had turned from this road into Ann Street, you would have found yourself in Newtown's chief commercial thoroughfare. This street was the main artery of the district and its shops provided all the day-to-day necessities for the crowded community. In *Worrall's Directory of 1876* we can see that Ann Street could boast no less than five butchers, seven grocers, five drapers, three confectioners, two pawnbrokers, a hairdresser, a milliner/dressmaker and an insurance agent. In addition, some of the neighbouring streets had small shops[91] and of course there was an abundance of public houses. Today, looking at this relatively small area of land, it is almost

---

[91] Some people operated small shops from the "front rooms" of their homes.

Everyday Life

impossible to visualise the cluster of streets and the small tightly packed houses that were once home to hundreds of families.

Following the provision of three new schools in the town in 1877 and 1878, which included the building of Warrington Road School, the residents of Halton View saw the start of further building work the following year when the foundation stone was laid for St. Ambrose Church. It had been agreed by The Church of England that a new church was needed to ease the accommodation situation for the fast growing local communities. The foundation stone for St. Ambrose Church was laid by the Home Secretary, Mr. R. A. Cross[92], in October 1879. At the ceremony, local luminary Mr. J. Sutton Timmis told the congregation that *"there were over 9000 Widnesians who claimed allegiance to the established church"*. Although St. Michael's Church at Hough Green had been opened under licence early in 1870, the two existing "Widnes" churches at that time, St. Luke's in Farnworth and the original St. Mary's Church, in West Bank, could only accommodate around 1900 worshipers. In response to this situation a committee was formed in the hope that funding could be raised for the construction of two additional churches. Incidentally, it was not only members of The Church of England who saw their congregations grow at that time. Shortly after the foundation stone had been laid for St. Ambrose Church, another religious group, the Primitive Methodists, started work on building a small chapel in Princes Street to accommodate their increasing numbers. This structure was replaced by a new larger building in Frederick Street in 1905.

The resolve by members of The Church of England to provide a further two churches in the town was given a boost when two local residents, Mrs Lee and Mr. Bibby, said they would each be prepared to donate an acre of land on which to build the churches. Although the committee had hoped to raise £10,000 for the new buildings, donations fell short and only reached £7,000. Nevertheless, despite the shortfall, this sum was enough to build the churches although the original plans had to be trimmed back accordingly. It was decided that £3,000 would be used to build a church at Halton View and the remaining sum would

---

[92]Mr. Cross was appointed Home Secretary by the Prime Minister, Benjamin Disraeli, in 1874.

be used to build a church at Simms Cross, which was the most populous area. The latter church would be dedicated to St. Paul.

St. Ambrose Church was opened on 28th March 1881 although it was not officially consecrated until 6th December 1883. The second church, St. Paul's in Victoria Square, was dedicated in 1884. At the time of building, St. Paul's did not have the tower which we see today; this was added later and completed in 1907. Interestingly, despite the church being dedicated in 1884, the first marriage to be solemnised in St. Paul's did not occur until eleven years later. At the beginning of October 1895, Caroline, the daughter of Henry Deacon, married the Rev. W. Hodgson. At the end of this ceremony Gossage's Prize Band played Mendelssohn's *"Wedding March"* and the happy couple were presented with a bible by the churchwarden, Mr. Lowe, in recognition of the fact that they were the first people to be married in the church.[93]

Of course the established Church of England, whilst having a large following in the town, was not the only religious institution in Widnes. As with the multi-faceted society who lived and worked side by side in our town, there were also huge numbers of differing types of non-conformist worshippers. These numbers included Roman Catholics; members of the Welsh churches; Presbyterians and Methodists. All these groups had a significant presence in the town and each built their churches and chapels almost entirely with the financial help and support of their congregations. Although some did have generous benefactors to ease the burden, others had to rely solely on the goodwill of their congregations to maintain their edifices and support their religious ministers.

The *"Mother Church"* of Widnes Methodism at that time was the Victoria Road Chapel which was opened on 20th July 1864 by the Rev. Marmaduke C. Osborn. It should be said that this beautiful building may not have materialised in such a magnificent form had it not been for the benefactions of Thomas Hazelhurst, the Runcorn soap manufacturer. Mr. Hazelhurst, who also contributed to the construction and maintenance of Methodist chapels in Runcorn and Frodsham, had offered to fund the cost of building this church if the Methodist Society would pay for the land. The Victoria Road site was subsequently bought for £500 and a splendid building was erected at a

---

[93] *"Across The Gap"* – Jean M. Morris (Springfield-Farrihy – 2016)

Everyday Life

cost of £3,354. By 1878 the Methodists had raised enough funds to be able to buy land adjacent to the chapel, on which they erected a new building for their Sunday school.

The Victoria Road Chapel (later the site of The Queen's Hall)

To explore the beginning of Methodism in this area we need to go back as far as the early 1780s. During this period pioneering travelling preachers arrived in Runcorn to spread the Methodist philosophy. However, for the history of Methodism in our own town, we need to go back to October 1835 when divine service was held for the first time in the home of Mr. John Palin, the dockmaster at Widnes Dock. Mr. Abraham Leach of Runcorn conducted that first service. Mr. Palin continued to open up his home for the religious instruction of local boatmen and dock labourers for a number of years after this. As the congregation expanded it became clear that this venue was no longer viable. Subsequently the loan of an upper room was offered by Messrs. Cooper & Hudson, the sailmakers, at their establishment on the canal bank. This room was used for many years until, by the determined efforts of William Hartland[94], the building of a dedicated chapel and school in Sutton's Lane was commenced in 1850. This building served

---

[94] William Hartland, known as *"The Father of Widnes Wesleyanism"*

Into The Crucible

the congregation, which had now grown considerably, until the new Victoria Road Chapel came into existence in 1864.

I found an interesting piece from May 1857 which refers to the building of the Sutton's Lane Chapel. This gives an indication of the extraordinary generosity of this congregation and their determined efforts to provide a fitting place of worship for their members.

> *"The Wesleyan Methodists at Widnes Dock have been in the habit of holding their services in a small room over a cottage. Being found too small, efforts were made to obtain further accommodation, and they have resulted in the erection of a neat little chapel, capable of seating about 300. On Friday last, the new place of worship was opened, when two sermons were preached by the Rev. J.S. Workman, of Manchester. Two sermons were also preached on Sunday by the Rev. J. Wheeler of Altrincham. During each service the chapel was crowded to excess, many of the more affluent and influential members of the society from Runcorn and vicinity being present. After the close of Sunday's services, the Minister announced from the pulpit that the chapel had cost, completed, £556.5s.; that the subscriptions given by friends amounted to £277.14s.9d., including £100 from Mr. Hazelhurst; that the collections at the services on Friday were £113.9s.3d., and on Sunday £174.1s.; amounting altogether to £556.5s., thus, to the very shilling, clearing the whole cost of the chapel. On the announcement of such unprecedented success, the congregation gave vent to their feelings by loud acclamations and clapping of hands, which the Minister had some difficulty in suppressing. It may be added that the members of this chapel are almost entirely working men."*

Of course, when chronicling the history of Methodism in Widnes, it is important to point out that the Sutton's Lane and Victoria Road Methodist chapels had drawn their congregations mainly from the south end of the town. However we should not forget that there was also a significant Methodist presence in the northern region of the township. Whilst William Hartland had been a driving force for the building of a chapel in the south, Samuel Kelsall, who introduced Methodism into Farnworth, was influential in persuading Thomas Hazelhurst to finance the building of a chapel at the other end of the town. Mr. Kelsall, who led a "Society Class" at a venue in Appleton village, had originally wanted to build a Methodist chapel on the site of an old schoolroom near Page Lane. However this proved to be

Everyday Life

impractical so land at Derby Road, owned by his mother-in-law, Mrs. Swift of Ditton Brook Farm, was chosen instead. The original Derby Road chapel,[95] which consisted of a worship room and two small vestries, was opened on 23rd April 1849. The inaugural service was conducted by the President of the Methodist Conference, Rev. Robert Newton. The entire building costs of £320 were generously donated by Thomas Hazelhurst of Runcorn. During the early years of the chapel's existence, the congregation included many Scottish weavers who lived in the Farnworth area. These internal migrants were mainly employed in the sailcloth factories which had been established in Farnworth and Lunts Heath.

Much has been said and written of the excessive drinking habits of ordinary workingmen in Victorian manufacturing towns. The dire living and harsh working conditions are often cited as being contributory factors to this problem. In our own town, the nature of work in the alkali trade often meant that men became dehydrated; particularly those who were continually exposed to extreme heat and gas. The conditions in the bleaching department were described thus:

"The bleaching department was said to be undoubtedly by far the most trying of all of those employed in the chemical works. Here men had to enter the Weldon chambers, which had been filled with chlorine for four days, and shovel out the powder while it was still intermixed with the gas. They wore goggles over their eyes, and muzzles over their nose and mouth and smeared any exposed parts of their bodies with tallow as a protection. Sometimes, despite these precautions, they were overcome by gas and had to be revived by a dose of whiskey. Some took to whiskey as a regular antidote; one of them claimed that he needed a glass three or four times a day and usually took another before he went to bed at night in order to sleep off the gas"[96].

Most households kept a quart of beer in a jug under the kitchen slop-stone, in readiness for the man of the house returning from work. This would probably have been more of a necessity than an indulgence. Even men who were not considered to be heavy drinkers were often in

---

[95] The original chapel was located fronting Derby Road at the corner of Beaconsfield Road, almost opposite the present chapel.

[96] T.C. Barker & J.R. Harris - *St. Helens: A Study of a Lancashire town in the industrial revolution* (Frank Cass & Co.Ltd.) 1993

the habit of drinking a lot more than that amount each day. Their daily occupation was "thirsty work" and, as a consequence, they drank copious amounts of beer in order to replace the fluid they had sweated out during the day. In addition, as many historians have pointed out, in those days it was considered much safer to drink beer than water! Nevertheless it should be said that it was not simply the taste and thirst quenching allure of beer that contributed to a high level of alcoholism amongst workers. In fact, Public Houses themselves were part of the appeal and the problem. The inns and taverns that were generously scattered throughout the neighbourhoods became an important social and economic element of town life. The pubs were an attraction not only for the beer, warmth and company, but because they also served as meeting places for workingmen. Gatherings of workmen in public house environments often created a forum for debate and an outlet for grievances.

Contemporary amateur anthropologists sometimes attribute the heavy drinking to the consequences of exchanging the wide-open spaces of field or bog for the cramped streets of a Victorian town. Whatever the reason there is no doubt that there was a major drink problem in our town. As a result, Widnes gained an unenviable reputation as a brutal and unruly place. One of the major issues associated with the high level of alcohol consumption was the fact that an intolerable portion of a man's weekly wage was spent in the pub. Naturally this added to the existing deprivations of family life. Of course there were additional alcohol related issues that caused concern; not least of these were the various types of violence associated with heavy drinking. For instance, there were the usual acts of aggression that followed an evening of heavy boozing; or the violent behaviour that occurred between drunken spectators during secretly organised bouts of bare-knuckle prize-fighting. Regrettably, alcohol-fuelled domestic violence was also widespread in working class communities. However the victims of this sort of abuse did not often make formal complaints because domestic violence was generally tolerated, it was almost an accepted fact of life. Of course, although I refer to working class communities, this cowardly type of behaviour was most certainly not confined to any one class or group of people. Domestic violence occurred amid all sections of the population, although amongst the so-called "upper" classes the publicising of such behaviour, especially in a

Everyday Life

court of law, would have been regarded as bringing a family's name into disrepute.

The demand for alcoholic beverage meant that there were a large number of public houses in areas of dense population. In 1900 an estimated 125,000 places were licensed to sell alcohol in the United Kingdom. The fact that pubs only shut between the hours of 1.00 a.m. and 4.00 a.m. meant that men often drank on the way to and from work. Drink was also sold from carts outside some factories which meant that alcohol was readily available in a variety of locations. This probably reveals the true extent of the habit, as it would appear that vendors set up their stalls and off-licences in any place where working men were likely to gather.

In *"Worrall's Directory of 1876"* a list of local Public Houses gives us an idea of how numerous these establishments were in relation to land acreage.

NEWTOWN
The Commercial – Ann Street East
The Crown Vaults – Ann Street West
The Kings Arms – Ann Street West
The Liverpool – Ann Street East
The Market Gate – Ann Street West
The Market Hotel – Lugsdale Road
The Norton Arms – Lugsdale Road
The Queens – Lugsdale Road
The Rams Head – Caroline Street
The Stanley Arms – Lugsdale Road
The Star – Elizabeth Street
The Three Tuns – Ann Street East
The Victoria - Ann Street West
The Vineyard – Lugsdale Road

MOSS BANK
The Golden Bowl
The Rose and Crown

Into The Crucible

WEST BANK
The Albion – Waterloo Road
The Angel - Mersey Road
The Arch – West Bank
The Bridge – Church Street
The Britannia – Irwell Street
The Commercial – Widnes Dock
The George – Waterloo Road
The Mersey – Mersey Road
Northwich Vaults – Waterloo Road
The Railway – Widnes Marsh
The Royal – Hutchinson Street
The Sportsman's Arms – Canal Bank
The Swan – Waterloo Road
The Vine – Waterloo Road
The Wellington – Wellington Street
The West Bank – Mersey Road
The White Star – Queen Street

Perhaps as a way of indicating the density of pubs in small areas, this list shows that there were no less than 5 pubs in Ann Street East, a stretch of road that was barely 120 yards long. In 1876 there were a total of 57 public houses in Widnes and by 1903 there were 108 licensed houses in the town. That equates to one pub to every 288 inhabitants.[97] In D.W. F. Hardie's *"History of the Chemical industry in Widnes"* he gives the following information:

"Bleach-packing, as may be readily understood, was a particularly thirst-creating job. Straight from the dust and odour of the chambers, still wearing their brown paper leggings and paper hats, the packers would resort to their favourite inn, where, in order not to give offence to the other patrons, they drank apart in the "packers` hut".

Of course not all men were drinkers. At the opposite end of the spectrum there were several local *Temperance Societies* and *Improvement Societies* who steadfastly lectured their followers on the iniquities of drink. From the mid-1870s "temperate" individuals in Widnes were able to avail themselves of alternative types of Public Houses, known as

---

[97] George E. Diggle *"The History of Widnes"* 1961

Everyday Life

Cocoa Rooms. These establishments were part of a privately run company known as *The British Workmen's Public House and Cocoa Rooms*. They had sprung up around the country, especially in manufacturing towns with large populations of working men. The Cocoa Rooms provided an alternative social gathering place where tea, coffee and cocoa, as well as light snacks, replaced the "evil drink". Every effort was made to make these places appealing; some even made stoves available for those who wished to cook for themselves, provided they purchased a hot drink. At a meeting of the Directors of this Company, which took place in Liverpool in 1876, it was said that they were offering the working men of the country a substitute for beer. They were providing Public Houses *"where men could enjoy that wholesome and cheap beverage, cocoa, in surroundings suitable to the neighbourhood in which they were placed"*. The Company owned two establishments in Widnes, one in Ann Street and the other in Hutchinson Street. In later years, when the popularity of Cocoa Rooms had petered out, the Ann Street building became a *"Model Lodging House"*.[98]

Despite the high level of alcohol related problems in the town, the Temperance Movement did constitute a major presence in Widnes. The Movement, which emerged nationally in the 1830s, became a key source of social reform. When studying the subject of alcohol abuse we can see that the problem became more widespread and reached almost epidemic proportions during the nineteenth century. This state of affairs was more noticeable in the new manufacturing towns with large working populations. There were numerous reasons for this, the main one being that living and working habits had changed dramatically as industrialisation had taken hold. The new populations were still adapting to an unfamiliar lifestyle and their behaviour was being shaped accordingly. Unfortunately, for some people, the lure and opportunities for excessive drinking were irresistible. The Temperance Movement had been formed in response to this, with their main focus being an attempt to fight intemperance among the working populations of the country.

In 1876 a group of local abstainers formed a "Company" with the intention of building a Temperance Hall on land leased from the trustees of the Hutchinson estate. It was estimated that the project

---

[98] Jean M. Morris *" Across The Gap"* 2016

Into The Crucible

would cost in the region of £2500 with the sum being raised through the issue of £1 shares. The Company was to be managed by nine directors: John Griffiths, Samuel Hughes, William Hunt, Thomas Jones, James Watterson, David McKay, John Powell, Thomas Reay and Abraham Speakman. The first registered subscribers to The Widnes Temperance Hall Co. Ltd., were John William Coxton, a manufacturing chemist; Thomas Reay, blacksmith; Thomas Hulse, dockmaster; Thomas Hughes, teacher; Thomas Stanley, chemical works foreman; and Thomas Steele Swale, a printer. Each of the above named took up one share at a value of £1 each.

Initially there was a fair amount of interest and support for the Widnes Temperance Hall scheme and a considerable number of people were willing to invest. However, despite this, at an extraordinary meeting of the shareholders, held in the Hutchinson Street Cocoa Rooms in May 1881, it was decided to abandon the scheme. During the course of the meeting a resolution was passed to wind up the affairs of the company by voluntary liquidation. It was said that *"despite the Institution having such worthy objectives it was realised that it could not be carried out in Widnes with any commercial success"*. The Chairman of the meeting thanked those who had invested money, especially those members of the working classes who had taken up shares *"in the hope that their investments might not only prove remunerative, but also assist in promoting the comfort and sobriety of the community."*

Despite the failure of the Temperance Hall Company, Temperance meetings were prolific in several parts of the town. Numerous Temperance Lodges operated throughout the district, each catering to the needs of local members. Several societies were linked to churches, such as *The Farnworth Church of England Society; St. Ambrose Gospel Temperance Mission* and *The Moss Bank Wesleyan Band of Hope*. Other lodges included those with more interesting names like *The Star of Widnes; Hope of Appleton; Haste to the Rescue* and the more ordinary named *Independent Order of Good Templars*. All these organisations worked extremely hard to dissuade men from becoming drunkards. One meeting was reported in *The Widnes Weekly News* in January 1882:

Everyday Life

ENTHUSIASTIC MEETING OF THE TEMPERANCE MISSION IN WIDNES

The local lodges of the Independent Order of Good Templars in conjunction with the Sons of Temperance held their weekly mission at the Lacey Street Wesleyan School when Thomas Horrocks of Darwen, well known throughout the country as "the converted clown", preached two sermons to crowded congregations who listened with rapt attention to the thrilling discourses.

Although most proceedings of local Temperance Societies were conducted in an extremely serious and sober manner, some occasions were more entertaining. Several events were family orientated and junior members and small children were allowed to take part. In the summer months, picnics and demonstrations were held at various fields around the district. These events were usually preceded by processions of members and children parading through the town. Sometimes there were musical gatherings which included the singing of hymns and temperance songs. In May 1882 the *Farnworth Church of England Temperance and Total Abstinence Society* had their last meeting of the season. The evening was a jolly occasion with songs and recitations and later *The Band of Hope* sang some temperance songs. In 1884, at a meeting of the *Farnworth Wesleyan Band of Hope,* Mr. John Bray had delivered a lecture *"full of sound and wholesome advice. He urged them to still greater exertions on behalf of the temperance cause, and warned them against the reading of impure literature".* The lecture was followed by a musical programme that included a solo by five-year old Maud Hollins who sang *"Jesus loves the little ones".*

Of course, as I stated earlier, it is frequently said that it was safer to drink beer than water in Victoria England. In Widnes, in the 1860s, the quality of drinking water was certainly suspect. In 1856 the ever-enterprising John Hutchinson had founded *The Widnes Gas and Water Company* with the intention of supplying these services to the town. The Company, which had its premises in Earle Street, Newtown, held its first meeting on 24th November 1856. The members present on that occasion were: John Hutchinson, Chairman; James Trevelyan Raynes, Arthur Sinclair and Oswald Earle. Shares in the new company were taken by Robert Daglish (100); Edward Greenall (50); William Lupton (50); William Wright (100); William Gossage (50) and William Pennington (50). By November the following year the Company had erected 180 street lamps which were being paid for by various individuals and companies at a rate of £2.12.6d. per year. There were also 141 water tenants who paid 1d per week. By 1859 the business was buoyant and it was decided to employ a surveyor/land agent to oversee operations. The new surveyor, Mr. Joseph Carruthers Routledge, was also contracted to do work relating to the Hutchinson works.

After four years of successfully supplying local residents with gas and water, the Company decided to apply for official permission to become the sole provider of these services. In May 1860 *The Widnes Gas and Water Company* was officially authorised by an *Act of Parliament* to supply gas and water to the township of Widnes. At that point the Company was reformed with John Hutchinson as the Chairman. The other directors were Oswald Earle, Rev. E. Carr, Arthur Sinclair, James Trevelyan Raynes and Major James Cross.

Later that same year John Hutchinson agreed to supply the railway with water and the Company quickly set about installing further improvements and additions to their systems. A water main was laid along Ferry Road and a new gasholder was purchased. There were also a number of new street lamps erected in the area around West Bank. Seven additional lamps were installed on the Ferry Road between the Toll Bar and the Ferry; four of these were paid for by The Railway Company. Hutchinson & Earle paid for a lamp to placed outside their new office building; John Wright paid for one opposite West Bank House and a further lamp, opposite The Snig Pie House, was to be paid for by John Wright or the tenant. Gas was also supplied to the Lambert Works, the Police Station, the Vineyard Public House, the Wesleyan Chapel and St. Mary's R.C. Church in Lugsdale Road. The gas supply to Gossage's Works was piped from Waterloo Road over the footbridge through Mr. Gossage's garden.[99] Muspratt's Works was supplied with gas through a meter, but they experienced several problems with leaking gas pipes. As a remedy, the leaking pipes were normally plugged with wood.[100]

The water being supplied by *The Widnes Gas and Water Company* to the town was being extracted from a well in the Hutchinson Works.

---

[99] Publications of *The Lancashire & Cheshire Historical Society*.
[100] *"Across The Gap"* – Jean M. Morris (Springfield-Farrihy 2016)

Everyday Life

Unfortunately, because of the hazards associated with its location, the quality of this water was not good. On one occasion the water supply was polluted by caustic soda which had leaked into the source from a tank in the works. On another occasion Mr. Henry Deacon had a sample of the water analysed in his laboratory. He reported to The Local Board that it contained 171.5 grams per gallon of solid matter, mainly salt. As further problems emerged, grave concerns were raised regarding the water source. In November 1865 The Local Board wrote to the Company to say that the quality of water was not acceptable. They also complained that, apart from the water being bad, there was also an insufficient amount to supply the township.

As a result of these worries The Local Board made a formal demand to *The Widnes Gas and Water Company*, under clause 70 of *The Public Health Act*. The Board ordered the Company to improve the water supply or surrender the right to provide this service. The Board indicated that they would be willing to purchase the Company's works and water mains. After a series of protracted negotiations an agreement was reached. This agreement allowed the Local Board to petition Parliament to supply the township with gas and water. The Bill was duly promoted and subsequently passed as *The Widnes Improvement Act 1867*. This Act empowered The Local Board to supply gas and water to the town. Under the assorted provisions of *The Widnes Improvement Act* the Local Board was also authorised to abolish the tolls levied by William Wright (of West Bank) on every vehicle passing along Snig Lane (Mersey Road). Subsequently, arrangements were made to purchase the Mersey Road tolls from Mr. Wright's trustees. The purchase price was £50.

Apart from the problem of water quality, the other difficulty had been the insufficient amount of water available from local wells to supply the town. In response to this, and under the provisions of *The Widnes Improvement Act*, The Local Board set about building new waterworks and a reservoir at Pex Hill. Work on the reservoir started in May 1868 and in July the following year the new waterworks were officially opened. The overall cost was estimated to be in the region of £40,000 which was to be repaid by The Local Board over a period of thirty years. Following the successful provision of a first-class water supply for the residents, it is clear that The Local Board were actively working towards building a town to be proud of. Five years later, in

Into The Crucible

August 1873, provisional plans were in place for the development of Victoria Square as a civic area. Around 4000 yards of land, adjoining Alforde Street and Brook House Lane, were purchased from Mr. John Shaw Leigh for the site of a Town Hall and Market. Later, additional land was purchased from the Leigh Estate for the improvement of Victoria Square. In November 1877 The Local Board purchased two semi-detached houses in Terrace Road from Mr. Midwood at a cost of £1,250. The houses were to be modified and used for hospital purposes and the Widnes Accident Hospital was subsequently established there in 1878.[101]

Brass bands were prolific in the town in the nineteenth century. Bands associated with Temperance Societies and church organisations were a regular feature of local parades and religious events. Although there is no recorded date for the formation of the band associated with St. Marie's R.C. Church, in Lugsdale, it is believed that their first official performance was at The Volunteer Hall on the occasion of the visit of Cardinal Manning in 1879. On that occasion the band, dressed in their distinctive garb of green suits and slouch caps, were given an enthusiastic reception. In West Bank, The Church of England Temperance Band was formed around 1883. They practiced in the National School until they broke up in 1887. That same year The Jubilee Band was formed with the majority of the members coming from the old Church of England Band. Also in West Bank, The Oakland Street Wesleyan Band was formed under the leadership of Mr. J. H. Harper. When this band was eventually discontinued many of the members joined Gossage's Works Band and later some became associated with The Widnes Subscription Band.

Adverts from *The Widnes Weekly News* of July 1881 give us a flavour of the medical obsession with the state of one's liver. There were numerous adverts for remedies for cleansing or purifying such as, *"Pepper's Quinine and Iron Tonic"* or *"Doctor King's Dandelion and Quinine Liver Pills"*. For those more concerned with the effect of baldness *"Lockyer's Sulphur Hair Restorer"* was available. As there were no controls over false claims in advertising, or over the composition of medicines, there were countless "quack remedies" on offer. In the same edition we saw that Thomas Tebbutt had a summer sale at his premises

---

[101] This building was reconstructed and enlarged by Widnes Corporation in 1914.

Everyday Life

in Ann Street West, he was offering bargains in ladies' hats and bonnets. There were also a number of adverts for *"an amazing electric corset"* and other mind-boggling items.

The fact that firearms could be easily purchased in Widnes at that time led to a number of fatal incidents and crimes. Among the most disturbing crimes was the murder of Patrick Tracey, which appears in another chapter. Another terrible incident involving a firearm occurred in Milton Street, in West Bank, in 1881. This resulted in the deaths of a young boy and a young woman. The following account of the incident is extracted from a newspaper report:

"The greatest consternation was caused in Widnes on Saturday night by one of the most melancholy accidents with which the pages of Widnes history has been marked, and from which it is to be hoped an important lesson will be drawn, resulting in the death of a servant girl, and an errand boy named James Hague. The boy, it appears, has been in the employ of Mr. Birchall, draper, of Waterloo Road, only a fortnight, while the young woman, who was to have been married within a fortnight, had for the last eight weeks been employed as a domestic servant at the house of Mrs. Rowlands, in Milton Street, where Mr. Birchall lodged.

One of the local policemen, called Stott, was on duty in Waterloo Road and called casually at Mr. Birchall's shop to pay for some clothing he had recently purchased. A conversation took place, in the course of which Mr. Birchall expressed a wish to present this officer with a revolver, and sent his errand boy to fetch it from his lodgings. The message was duly delivered to the servant, who forthwith proceeded to fetch it from the bedroom, and it would appear that either by accident or in fun – without the knowledge that the gun was loaded – she pointed it at the boy and he was shot in the face. Another boy named James Atherton had accompanied Hague and was waiting outside when he heard the report, and on going to the back door was met by the servant, who told him an accident had happened and asked him to go for Mr. Birchall. The report was also heard in the next house, where the girl immediately ran for assistance. Mr. Overton, the neighbour, on seeing what had happened said he would fetch or send for someone else, and as he turned to do so, the girl picked up the revolver, said she would show him how the boy had shot himself. He had, however, by this time got to the door and did not see what occurred, but it is quite evident she placed the revolver into her own mouth and pulled the trigger, for he immediately ran back and found her on the floor bleeding with a wound in her mouth and the revolver lying beside her. Mrs. Rowland's nephew had arrived at the scene just prior to this and had gone in search of a doctor. When the Doctor arrived both were alive but died shortly afterwards. No survivor saw either of the bullets fired, and there must ever, therefore, be some slight doubt in the minds of many how, at least, the accident to the boy was caused".

In 1879 members of The Widnes Local Board were both shocked and humiliated to discovery that The Board's accountant, Mr. Pierce, had been systematically "cooking the books" to the tune of £1200. There had been such a degree of confidence in this man that the accounts had never been properly audited. Mr. Pierce absconded and was never brought to justice. The funds were never recovered. However, this incident prompted the scrutiny of the accounts and unearthed further fraudulent behaviour by another employee, a Mr. Burgess. Burgess was arrested and received his just desserts. These incidents, no doubt, brought about a change in the way money matters were conducted by the gentlemen of The Widnes Local Board. However, the following rather philosophical statement was made at the time *"It is no good crying over spilled milk, it will be much better to look at the silver lining to the cloud. The ratepayers have every reason to expect that The Board's loss by the absconding of Pierce, will be the ultimate gain of the town".* In another book, *"Across the Gap"*, I mention several other cases of fraudulent behaviour committed by local middle-class offenders. It is clear that this type of crime, and the opportunity to do it, was present in a number of situations.

In November 1881 Major Cross, as Chairman of The Local Board, had been petitioned by a number of ratepayers, the most vocal being the instigator of the petition, local practitioner Dr. John O' Keeffe. The petitioners desired The Board to establish a Free Library under the provisions laid out in *The Public Libraries Act*. A public meeting was held in The Drill Hall when a vote was taken. Of the estimated 250 people present only eight were in favour. In the absence of a "Free Public Lending Library" other establishments filled the void. A Reading Room was open on Saturday evenings in the Science School in Major Cross Street. A couple of fee-paying lending libraries also operated in the town, such as the one based in Farnworth at Mudie House, 16 Derby Road. This establishment was relatively well stocked and offered nearly 300 volumes to select from, as well as an ample

Everyday Life

supply of magazines. The books could be borrowed for 1 week and the magazines for 3 days. Subscriptions to this library were charged at 1 shilling per week or 15 shillings per annum. There were Mudie Libraries in most of the major towns around the country. The proprietor, Charles E. Mudie, set himself up as a bookseller and publisher in the 1840s and shortly afterwards branched out into lending books. The development of the railway network meant that he could send boxes of books to numerous parts of the country. He was very successful and a powerful figure in publishing circles in the 19th century, as more than half the run of novels published at that time went to his libraries. Mudie's Libraries inevitably died out in the early years of the 20th century when Local Authorities began to set up Free Public Libraries.

"*Local Notes*" in *The Widnes Weekly News* of December 1885 made the following statement with reference to Dr. O` Keeffe and the subject of the Library. "*He has taken in hand the question of the provision of a reading room and library for the town, and it seems probable that we shall have a reading room and library as a result of his persistent endeavours and proposals*". A second petition, once again instigated by Dr. O` Keeffe, was presented to The Local Board. As a consequence a second public meeting was held, resulting in the adoption of *The Public Libraries Act*. Our Public Library was finally opened on 16th May 1887. Miss Proctor, the schoolmistress from Halebank School, was appointed as our first librarian at an annual salary of £65. As a note of interest, Warrington was the first town in Lancashire to establish a Free Library supported out of the rates, this was in operation from as early as 1848.

The new Library proved to be a great success with the townspeople. In April 1889 it had 3577 volumes on its shelves and no less than 2065 library cards had been issued. It was estimated that over 45,000 books had been issued to borrowers during the first year. The number of daily visitors to the reading room was over 400. In order to support this facility the ratepayers were charged a penny extra on their rates. Other support came from John Brunner, whose generosity was renowned. He donated money and also presented a considerable number of books to the new Library.

Dr. O` Keeffe`s role in obtaining a Library for our citizens was only the beginning of his endeavours to make Widnes a town to be proud of.

Into The Crucible

His next project was to build a Town Hall. His unrelenting activities on behalf of the people of our town should certainly be commended. Even today, almost one hundred and thirty years later, we still enjoy the benefits of some of his accomplishments. *"Local Notes"* in *The Widnes Weekly News* of January 1886 give an insight into the Doctor's tenacious personality.

> *"The result of the ratepayers` meeting held on Tuesday evening is very gratifying to a certain extent. That we shall have a free library and reading room is now a certainty, but as to its character and locale we shall be left in the dark for some time. With regard to the question of a Town Hall for Widnes, a spirit of utter niggardliness seemed to pervade the meeting, and for once I could enter into the spirit of Dr. O` Keeffe`s righteous indignation. His love of Widnes is equal to his patriotism for Ireland, and it did one's heart good to see him as he hurled his metaphorical missiles right and left. If certain persons did not feel a little uneasy during the worthy Doctor's oration I am very much mistaken".*

Although there were numerous pressing matters for The Board to deal with, public health was one of the most a serious causes of concern. The lack of an adequate sewage system, or any laws compelling landlords to provide reasonable sanitary arrangements, was an obvious hazard to the health of the population. Smallpox, cholera, typhoid, diphtheria and scarlet fever outbreaks were not uncommon, and the infant mortality rate was very high. Typhus was a particularly dangerous disease due to its high contagiousness and cholera was also a killer disease and there were regular outbreaks of both. Because people lived in overcrowded conditions diseases of this nature were extremely hard to contain. Unfortunately, because in those times the primary methods of disease transmission were not fully understood, the medical establishment of the day was completely unequipped to handle these epidemics. It was some time before it was discovered that some infections were transmitted through contaminated water and, at that time, there were no proper public purification systems in place. In an attempt to address these problems *The Public Health Act* of 1872 had divided the country into sanitary districts, with each district having its own single Public Health Authority. In towns this was The Municipal Authority. Each authority was required to appoint a Medical Officer of Health and a Nuisance Inspector for the purpose of combating

Everyday Life

preventable disease. The role of Medical Officer for the town was subsequently undertaken by Dr. O` Keeffe.

In March 1885 Dr. O` Keeffe was in the headlines once again and, as usual, he was at the centre of controversy. Throughout his long career in Widnes Dr. O'Keeffe's reputation swung between saint and devil, depending on which side of the fence you were on. There is no doubt that this man was dedicated to Widnes and his work for the town knew no bounds. He always acted in the best interest of its citizens, even though sometimes this was not an easy or popular path. On this occasion a serious epidemic of measles in Runcorn caused alarm and consternation among the population of Widnes. Dr. O` Keeffe, in his capacity as the town's Medical Officer, raised the matter at a meeting of The Local Board. The Doctor informed The Board that he felt *"duty bound to do his utmost to shield the inhabitants of this town from incurring the danger of acquiring infectious diseases and having them spread in our midst"*. The Board, obviously alarmed and fearful of infection, raised the subject of Runcorn workers coming into the town each day. It was said that over 700 footbridge tickets were issued each week to men employed in Widnes who resided in Runcorn. As a direct result of Dr. O'Keeffe's unease about infection being brought into the town, the members of The Board voted six votes to three to instruct their clerk to write to all Widnes employers who employed Runcorn men. The Board's letter appealed to employers of Runcorn men to issue instructions to compel their workers to live in Widnes or else dismiss them from their employment.

The measles epidemic continued to rage in Runcorn, as did the controversy over The Local Board's foolish interference in business matters. However, despite the growing indignation of employers, *The Widnes Weekly News* published a number of letters from Widnes workmen who seemed to agree with The Board. Although the original subject of employing Runcorn men had been associated with the spread of measles, some writers took the opportunity to air their grievances from a different angle, one man said:

"It is a great injustice that men from another town should be employed who do not pay a single penny to our rates but take something like £1,800 per week from those who would willingly pay if they had employment, but who are excluded. I do not for a moment say cease employing these men, but

compel them to live in the town in which they earn their bread, drink its water, use its gas in the streets, and other things the Widnes ratepayers have to pay for".

The controversy and the measles continued to rage for a number of weeks. During this time Dr. O` Keeffe was both applauded and pilloried for his stance. I assume that the hullabaloo abated with the end of the epidemic. I do not know if any employer complied with The Local Board's request

In May 1885 the Guardians of the Prescot Union issued a list of persons in receipt of parochial relief in several townships of the Prescot Union. The Union was divided into five districts and the list gave the total number of paupers receiving relief in each district and the amount received. This is the list for the period ending March 1885.

Sutton	*269 paupers*	*£786.2s.11d*
Windle	*305 paupers*	*£744.1s.4d.*
Eccleston	*293 paupers*	*£777.17s.8d*
Prescot	*244 paupers*	*£645.0s.2d.*
Widnes	*352 paupers*	*£572.5s.*

An explanatory note says that although Widnes has by far the largest number of persons in receipt of relief *"it expends upwards of £200 less than two of the districts, and that its outlay is far below that of the remaining two. In the Widnes expenditure is included the cost of providing 300 vagrants with temporary lodgings, and this fact causes its figures to compare all the more favourably with those of the other districts. The list is published and circulated amongst the ratepayers with the view of detecting and preventing imposition".*

Because the chemical industry attracted a transient workforce of young single men, as well as the family men who found settled accommodation, lodging houses became an essential part of the local environment. In response to this, there were countless lodging houses scattered around the Newtown and West Bank areas of the town in close proximity to places of employment. These establishments were mostly inhabited by single men. However men who could not get a place in this type of accommodation usually found lodgings in the homes of local families. As a result of the high demand for accommodation, and in order to make ends meet, it was customary amongst most working families to sub-let rooms in their already overcrowded houses. In most cases a small sub-let room would be occupied by several people. In some instances men who worked night shifts would occupy a bed during the day and those on day shift would sleep in it at night. One record from the late 1870s shows that one small two bedroom house in the Newtown area had twelve occupants of which only four were children. One cannot imagine how unhealthy, uncomfortable and unpleasant that type of existence must have been. In 1884 *The Widnes Weekly News* ran an article entitled *"The Danger of Keeping Lodgers"*. However the danger in this instant was not connected with the odious hazards of overcrowding, but something of a different nature. The article demonstrates a satirical but rather caustic sort of journalism. The author was careful not to name individuals but I am sure the clues scattered throughout the article were sufficient for local people to recognise those mentioned.

THE DANGER OF KEEPING LODGERS

An elopement which took place on Saturday night from the neighbourhood of Simms Cross, Widnes, has given rise to a good deal of tongue exercise and a corresponding amount of scandal on the part of the gossips. An Irishman, whose name would rhyme with "work"; who is employed at one of the local chemical manufactories, and who resides in a street named after the primary letter of the Greek alphabet[102], married, after a too hasty courtship of a few days, a buxom Saxon woman, whose vision, though somewhat defective physically, was sufficiently astute to show that she is "skilled in the ogle of the roguish eye". Her amorous glances induced an individual, whose name is similar to that of an important Yorkshire town not many miles from Leeds, though he hails from Cheshire, to leave his abode on the opposite side of the street, and to take up his residence in her husband's house. Immediately after he did so, their "billing and cooing", which had been previously observed by some of the keener sighted people, became most marked, and they partook of the loving cup together with regularity and frequency. As the two men worked alternate shifts, the husband was unaware of the attentions which the lodger was paying to his wife. After matters had proceeded in this way for a short period of time with an everyday sameness, the neighbours determined to make the husband acquainted with the true state of affairs, and this they did on Saturday evening. What followed can better be imagined than described. The

---

[102] Alpha Street

enraged husband first gave the lodger a bit of his mind, and then ordered him to leave the house instantly, and as he went out at the front door, the wife made her exit at the back. They were quickly at each other's side, and they hastily determined to unite their fortunes. They accordingly departed the scene of their budding love, and went their way "basking in the sunshine of each other's smiles". Before proceeding to his work the following day, the deserted husband nailed up the door and windows of his domicile, being determined that if "the false and fickle one" returned she should not have a chance of appropriating any of his property. On Monday evening, the lodger returned for some articles of clothing which he had left in the house in which he abode before he became "stricken, smitten and afflicted", and amidst a good deal of rough "chaff" he was asked to state the locality of the bower to which he had borne away his lady love; but this he positively refused to do, and said that they had determined to cleave unto each other until death parted them.

Before the days of radio and telegraphic communications, and long before the internet had been conceived, the newspaper was usually the sole source of national news. Local publications, in addition to reporting on the local scene, were also the heralds of national and international news. Scandal, melodrama and horrific stories from all parts of the country found their way into the pages of our local press. The strange stories of *"Spring Heel Jack"* made periodic appearances at various locations around England throughout the 1850s, 1860s and 1870s. Was he simply an *"urban myth"* or did the sightings of him actually take place – who knows?

The creepy story of *"Spring Heel Jack"* probably goes back to before 1850 but the first reported sightings of him occurred in that decade. In the following two decades he was seen at a number of places around the country. He was described as a Dracula-like person who possessed amazing acrobatic skills, namely being able to jump to great heights to evade capture. According to one report, the army authorities set traps for him after it was claimed he had slapped sentries with his icy hands and then jumped on top of their Guard boxes. The last reported sighting was in Liverpool in 1904, where he was, supposedly, seen by a large group of people in Everton. He was observed jumping from street level to rooftop and back. The group tried to corner him but apparently he simply leaped away into the darkness.

His appearance in Widnes was reported in *The Weekly News* of November 1887.

"Spring Heel Jack" first appeared in New Brighton and caused great terror by his nightly visits, he crossed over to Liverpool and succeeded in causing considerable alarm in the suburbs of the city in Aigburth, Mossley Hill, Garston, Woolton and Allerton. "Spring Heel" has now begun to expand his sphere of operation to Halebank, Tarbock, Ditton, Widnes and Farnworth. Numerous people have been afflicted by his presence, and a woman at Ditton received such a shock by the sight of his person that she is said to have been rendered seriously ill in consequence. He appears dressed in a long cloak, with his face illuminated, and wearing springs, which give him extraordinary powers of locomotion. There is widespread fear of him in the district, and it is a thing devoutly to be wished for that he should fall into the clutches of the law and a stop be put to his deeds of nightly prowess".

There were numerous alleged sightings of *"Spring Heel Jack"* at various places around the country right up until World War II. One would assume that this legendary creepy tale is simply a classic folk myth, as stories of a comparable nature have occurred in other cultures. There were similar appearances in America and India in the 1960s, though the individual in these cases was given a different name.

In March 1889 the subject of public health became a serious issue again. There was a great deal of dissatisfaction in the town regarding the management and operation of The Local Board's "Night-Soil Department". As a consequence Dr. O` Keeffe told Board members *"that it was vital that immediate improvements should be implemented for the health and cleanliness of the town"*. Furthermore, he made an effort to persuade the Nuisance Inspector to follow up complaints regarding "soil removal". He also asked him to compel landlords to improve sanitary arrangements on their properties. His pleas seemed to fall on deaf ears and he received little support from The Local Board or The Nuisance Inspector. Shortly afterwards the death of a toddler in the Simms Cross area was directly linked to diseases carried from the effluvia from the contents of middens near to the child's home. The night-soil contractors had frequently "forgotten" to remove the contents. In April, the mortality rate for Widnes was 27.6 per 1000. *The Widnes Weekly News* editorial said:

"We venture to think that if the present sultry weather continues, combined with the filth which is unfortunately always too abundant in certain parts of the town, the rate for May will not be much lower. At the meeting of The Local Board last week an interesting discussion took place in regard to the system of removing the night-soil, and it was gratifying to note that under the present contractor there had been a marked improvement. We do not wish to enter into the vexed question as to whether The Board could not do the work better and cheaper themselves than by contract. We believe it will be more expensive for The Board to do the work themselves, but it should be done more satisfactorily, and no doubt the ratepayers will not object to paying a little more if they know that they are paying for work which has been done well. At the present juncture we would urge upon The Board's officials, and upon the night-soil contractor as well, the importance of their work being done with the utmost possible speed. Already we hear of numerous cases of scarlet fever and measles, and in the almost tropical heat now prevailing these isolated cases may, unless the greatest care is exercised, develop into an epidemic. In this month of April last year there were more deaths than in any other month except August.

These reports and statistics paint a grim picture of the town in those days. It was not uncommon to read of children dying through neglect, hunger or substandard accommodation. In June 1889 another child died as a result of poor housing. The owner of a house in Eleanor Street was heavily censured for failing to maintain the house. The child was struck by a falling downspout. The parents of the child had repeatedly asked the landlord to repair the pipe and frequently told him it was in a dangerous condition. The child was under two years of age and was in the arms of her mother when the accident happened. Only a short while afterwards another child, aged 3months, starved to death in Midwood Street. The parents were charged with manslaughter.

Everyday Life

Two views of Appleton village

Top image (1) Tithebarn Street - archway in centre is the archway visible in picture (2). Also in (2) the low front wall of St. Bede`s on right.

Into The Crucible

In Liverpool in October 1890 a debate was held in The Public Rooms, the subject was the sanitation and housing of the poor. The Bishop of Bedford opened the debate with a paper on *"Acquaintance with and Obedience to Sanitary Laws a Christian Duty"* in his speech he spoke of a Dr. Carpenter:

".....who traced to unsanitary habits and surroundings and the neglect of sanitary laws much of the crime, pauperism, lunacy and immorality that prevailed, and held it to be the duty of the Church to make the principles of sanitation known throughout the land".

Whilst the Bishop of Bedford rightly mentioned the presence of unsanitary habits and surroundings, we should remember that the lack of clean running water in dwellings meant that in many cases personal cleanliness was not easy to achieve or maintain. Water was usually obtained from a standpipe in some streets or else by going into factory premises. In some areas there was no proper drainage or facilities to remove sewage. Naturally this appalling situation created opportunities for germs and infections to flourish. Records from the 1890s show that the number of typhoid cases treated at the local hospital far exceeded that of scarlet fever.[103] As I stated earlier, diseases such as cholera, typhoid, typhus, smallpox and scarlet fever were endemic during the nineteenth century. Unfortunately the poorer classes were less resistant to contagion because they were underfed and continually exposed to conditions in which infection thrived.

Needless to say that Widnes was no different to other towns with large populations and dense overcrowding. An epidemic of smallpox in the neighbouring towns of Warrington and St. Helens caused serious concern in September 1893. At a meeting of The Widnes Council it was agreed that the Market Inspector be instructed not to allow the sale of old clothing or similar articles in the market or market places. The Borough Surveyor also produced and explained plans prepared by him for the erection of a temporary "Wooden Hospital" for the treatment of smallpox.[104] Some years later, when a letter from The Local Government Board was circulated to members of the Council, the town was made aware of other shocking possibilities. The Local Government Board required that all Medical Practitioners in the town be urgently

---

[103] *Ibid:*
[104] Widnes Borough Council *"Minutes of Council & Committees"* 1893

Everyday Life

reminded of their duty to give immediate notification of all cases of *Plague*. It was impressed upon them the importance of complying with this regulation.[105]

By the beginning of the 1890s the general sanitation arrangements, although now slightly improved by the installation of various sections of public sewers, still left a great deal to be desired. In 1892 the Sanitary Inspector reported to the Council that he had received a complaint about the oozing of offensive matter from houses in Appleton Street, near the Post Office. He said he had previously recommended that all the closets in Appleton village should be converted into water closets but nothing had been done to rectify this situation. By 1893 a large numbers of houses in the town were classed as unfit for human habitation. Six houses in Milton Road and a number of houses owned by Thos. Bolton & Sons, in Cromwell Street, were condemned. The Town Clerk had a meeting with representatives of Thos. Bolton & Sons, who promised to either improve or vacate these dwellings. During the same period the Council, adhering to *The Housing of the Working Classes Act 1890,* found it necessary in relation to dwellings *"so dangerous and injurious to health as to be unfit for human habitation by reason of dilapidated, ruinous, and unsanitary condition"* to recommend that proceedings be taken against the owners of some dwellings in the Newtown area. These included 12 houses in Caroline Street and 3 houses in Margaret Street. At the other end of the town some houses in Birchfield Road and Joseph Street were earmarked as causing a public nuisance due to the condition of the privies. During that same period the members of the Health Committee were called upon to inspect properties at 69 and 71 Lugsdale Road.

Although there is no confirmation of this, I would assume that the visit of the Health Committee to the mentioned properties in Lugsdale Road was probably connected to a tragedy that had occurred earlier that year. A 5year old girl had died as a result of being badly burned in an accident at 71 Lugsdale Road. At the inquest into the child's death some upsetting details emerged about the family's living arrangements. The parents of the dead child told the Coroner that they and their three children, the eldest being the deceased 5year old, rented a single storey

---

[105] *Ibid* – September 1900

two-roomed cottage in Lugsdale Road for a rent of 3s.6d. per week. In order to pay this rent they found it necessary to sub-let one of the rooms to another family. The second family consisted of seven persons, father, mother and five sons, aged 6years, 9years, 11years, 13years and 24years. This family had only one bed in which the parents slept at one end and the four younger children at the other. The 24year old slept on a table by the window. The dreadful overcrowding, brought to light by this case, in which twelve people lived, ate and slept in two small rooms was not unusual. When asked by the Coroner why they did not find more suitable accommodation the mother of the dead child said, *"because we cannot afford anything better"*.

In addition to the discomfort of shared occupancy, there was also the detrimental effect on people's health when so many of them were packed into overcrowded houses with inadequate sanitation.[106] The custom of keeping corpses for "waking" also presented serious health issues, as coffins were usually kept in the same room where people lived, slept and ate their meals. In June 1869 a man who had died from typhus fever was kept in the house for several days after his death. This presented a serious health risk to the other inhabitants. In this case the Local Board ordered that the body be removed and buried, and the house cleansed and disinfected to prevent further spread of disease.

An additional and continuing cause for concern was the unhealthy atmosphere caused by the release of noxious vapours from the factories. One man wrote to *The Widnes Weekly News* in 1893:

WHERE IS THE ALKALI INSPECTOR?
To the Editor, Dear Sir,
I beg leave to ask through the columns of your paper, who is the above named gentleman and where does he reside? One thing, however, is quite apparent; he does not live anywhere near to the works on the Marsh, in fact he does not live in the slums – I beg pardon, I mean Waterloo Road and the streets off it. Heaven knows, Sir, the above district at its best is not a very desirable locality for health, but bad as it is, it is made worse night after night by dense clouds of noxious vapours from the adjoining works. It has been going on for some considerable time and seems to go worse instead of better. Children playing in the streets, and weary toilers, more dead than

---

[106] For further reading: *"Across The Gap"* – Jean M. Morris (Springfield-Farrihy 2016)

Everyday Life

alive after a hard day's work, have to seek shelter in their miserable tenements from its poisonous ravages. Surely Sir, this is too bad. Who is to blame? Evidently either the Inspector or the United Alkali Company's officials! But I suppose they both live at a respectable distance from "the madding crowd" and the gas."

In 1870 the actor, J. B. Preston, came to Widnes and opened a theatre. Prior to this the townspeople had used The Public Hall in Hutchinson Street as their entertainment venue. The Public Hall was not, as might be assumed from its name, in public ownership but was owned by The Public Hall Company Limited. It opened on Tuesday 18th October 1864 when a huge inaugural Ball was held in the new building with the benefit proceeds going to The Mechanics` Institution. It was a glittering event with tickets selling at ten shillings for gentlemen and seven shillings and sixpence for ladies. The band was composed of musicians from Liverpool and St. Helens and was conducted by Mr. R.L. Burrows. The evening opened with a lively polka and dancing continued well into the early hours. In contrast, Mr. Preston's new theatre, which was adjacent to the Wellington Hotel in Wellington Street, was on a less grand scale than The Public Hall. In fact it was built of wood and as a result it became known locally as "the old wooden shed". Despite this rather undignified nickname, the proprietor had given it a more formal name, *"The New Alexandra Theatre".* Mr. Preston employed a resident company of actors, actresses and comics who performed Shakespearean plays and popular Victorian melodramas. Although Mr. Preston usually took the lead in performances, from time to time he engaged travelling players. Among those who appeared on his stage in Wellington Street was the legendary Dan Leno. Preston's little wooden theatre provided entertainment for good number years but, sadly, it all came to an untimely end when the building accidentally burned down.

In fact, even if Mr. Preston's little theatre had survived, it would soon have been eclipsed by a new theatre which opened in the town in 1887. The new theatre was called *"The Alexandra"* and it seated 1400 people, 1000 in the pit and a further 400 in the gallery. The architect, Mr. James Rimmer, said this theatre was *"to be erected regardless of expense".* In reality, the final building costs were in the region of £5000. The building was lit by gas, the brackets protected by wire gauze. In the event of fire, there were three hydrants and two lengths of hose. The new theatre was immediately successful. Two years after opening, in

Into The Crucible

the first week of September 1889, the management stated: *"...this week has been one of the most successful in the history of the Alexandra Theatre. Mr. Montague Roby`s Midget Minstrels performed for the public. Altogether the entertainment is the best of its kind ever witnessed in the neighbourhood"*.

"The Alex", as it was affectionately known, offered its patrons a variety of entertainments ranging from dramas and musical plays to the popular musical hall acts of the day. Among the people who appeared on its stage in the early days of their careers were Charlie Chapin and Stan Laurel. In fact these two "legends" appeared together on stage at *"The Alex"* in November 1906. The two men, although little more than boys at that time, appeared with a group of travelling players in a performance of *"Casey's Court"*. Although *"The Alex"* was extremely popular there was still a demand for other places of entertainment. On 28th July 1890 another theatre opened in Widnes. This venue, known as *"The People`s New Theatre of Varieties"*, was owned by Mr. D. Cohen, who had previously managed *"The Alexandra Theatre"*. An advertisement from *"The Era"* tells us that this was a neat wooden structure offering accommodation for about 1800 people. It also gave additional information which tells us that the stage was 33ft deep. Obviously, in the days before film and television, in a town with a population of around 30,000 there was scope for several entertainment venues. In February 1894 there was an attempt by Mr. George Mellon to open a Music Hall in Ditton Road. He applied to the Magistrates for a licence to permit music and dancing in a wooden structure which had previously been occupied by a company called *"Ohmy's Circus"*. The application was refused after an objection had been raised by Messrs. Gerrard, Bray and Kiddie, who were the owners of The Alexandra Theatre. It might be construed that they didn't want any more competition.

Over previous years, and indeed for centuries before, crossing the river from Widnes to Runcorn had been a major problem. Journeys had been undertaken via the Old Ferry which was neither a convenient nor a pleasant way to get from one side of the river to the other.[107] When the Railway Bridge opened in the late 1860s it became possible for residents of the two towns to cross via a toll footbridge that ran alongside the railway. However this was only a pedestrian crossing

---

[107] For further reading see– *"Across The Gap"*- Jean M. Morris (Springfield-Farrihy 2016)

Everyday Life

and other traffic, such as commercial items or cattle, were still being transported via the old and dangerous ferry. By the late 1880s it had become obvious that another means of access was necessary between the two towns. Subsequently, the Runcorn Improvement Commissioners approached the Widnes Local Board asking them to consider the possibility of connecting Widnes and Runcorn by means of a vehicular bridge. They believed that the two towns should approach the county councils of Lancashire and Cheshire with a view to inducing them to build such a bridge over the river.

Sir John and Lady Brunner at the opening of The Transporter Bridge

In 1889 a company was formed by an *Act of Parliament* to build and operate a Transporter Bridge to supplement the toll footbridge that ran alongside the railway. The following year The Bill received royal assent and construction work was started. Sir John Brunner was the Chairman of the Bridge Committee and he was given the honour of performing the opening ceremony when the structure was completed some years later. There are conflicting accounts of the total cost for the construction of the ingenious piece of engineering known as The Transporter Bridge. Some reports say it was £100,000 while others say the real cost was £137,663. However, it is believed that Widnes Corporation was responsible for £25,000 and Runcorn Urban District Council £10,000. In an article in *The Times* in April 1911 it was said that Sir John Brunner subscribed £25,000 towards the construction of the Transporter Bridge. He also provided a further loan of £12,000 and a personal guarantee on a bank loan of £31,000. When it became obvious in 1911 that the Bridge would operate on a perpetual deficit, Brunner assigned his interest to the Widnes Corporation: "a virtual gift" *The Times* reckoned of £68,000.

The Transporter Bridge

As one would expect in a town with a large and varied population, there were a number of clubs and organisations that catered to political, religious and social groups of all persuasions. There were The Oddfellows, The Foresters and The Brotherhood of Shepherds, as well as several Welsh and Irish social and political societies and, as we have seen, there were also numerous Temperance Groups in the town. In addition to all these societies, a Masonic Lodge was formed in the early 1870s. It is believed that the inaugural meeting of The Widnes Lodge of Equity (1384) was held on 10th November 1871 at the Simms Cross

Everyday Life

Hotel. Among the first members were: R.D. Simpson; J.W. Fowler; H.S. Oppenheim; W. Jamieson; J.W. Wareing; W.I. Thompson; James White; A Borthwick; A. Tippett; R.D. Simpson; J. Raven; W. Newsome; R. Neill; J.W. Carlisle and George Brown. Their early meetings were held at Walker's Commercial Hotel in the town. It is evident that the majority of these organisations did not have their own venue. Therefore most were obliged to hold their meetings in local hotels or church halls. However, in October 1889, when a group of townsmen came together for the purpose of forming a Widnes Conservative Club and drawing up a constitution, their new club premises had already been completed. The building, in Victoria Road, was owned by shareholders of the "Conservative Club Building Committee". That committee included Mr. R.W. Parnell; Mr. W.T. Husband; Mr. R. Lewis; James White; Mr. J.B. Imison; Mr. T. Knowles; Mr. G. Pryde and Mr. G.E. Sayce.

As we saw in reports about *"Spring Heel Jack"*, newspapers of those times provided a picture of life both in the town and in other parts of the country. *The Widnes Weekly News* included Garston and Woolton in its regular circulation area. It reported widely on activities in those districts, as well as on current national and international events. Because of the large Irish population in this area all the local newspapers, including the Liverpool daily and weekly newspapers, reported on events and happenings in Ireland. National news stories also found their way on to the pages of our local press. In *The Widnes Weekly News* editions of 1888 and 1889 we see numerous reports concerning the Whitechapel Murders, known to us today as the *Jack the Ripper* crimes. These gruesome murders gripped the country with fear, particularly as the police seemed unable to find the perpetrator of these shocking crimes. The September 28th 1889 edition of *The Widnes Weekly News* reports:

THE WHITECHAPEL MURDER
An inquest was held into the death of a woman. The jury after considerable consultation, returned a verdict of WILFUL MURDER by some person or persons unknown

Throughout the autumn of 1888 the Whitechapel murders continued to be a major news item in our local press. The shocking details were printed in each issue and it became apparent that Scotland Yard were no nearer to solving the crimes. The following year readers of *The*

Into The Crucible

Widnes Weekly News were engrossed in reports of the trial of Florence Maybrick who was accused of poisoning her husband in nearby Aigburth. The Maybrick case created a huge amount of public interest and was reported in great detail. The trial took place at St. George's Hall in Liverpool and a verdict of murder was returned by the jury. Mrs. Maybrick, who was an American, was sentenced to death. Despite the verdict, some believed her to be innocent and after a series of public petitions and demonstrations her sentence was commuted to life. After serving a period of nearly fifteen years in prison she was released and returned to America in 1905. Coincidentally, one of the latest in a long line of theories regarding the identity of the Whitechapel killer is that James Maybrick, the victim, was actually *"Jack the Ripper"*.

I would like to provide another rather interesting fact relating to Florence Maybrick. In 1917 whilst in America, Widnes man, Jack Carney, had an interesting encounter. Carney, who was at that time working as a journalist with a left-wing publication, was an unsuspecting guest of this lady. As she had by this time reverted to her maiden name of Chandler, and she had been back living in America for twelve years, he had no idea who she was. He and his friend, who was an acquaintance of Mrs. Maybrick, were invited to her home for tea. They had an enjoyable afternoon which was made all the more pleasing for the fact that Mrs Chandler said she knew of Widnes, as she had spent time in Liverpool. Carney only learnt the true identity of his hostess some time later. He subsequently described her as a gentle and gracious lady.[108]

In October 1890 the Widnes Local Board made application to borrow £3,000 for the building of a new Fire Station and fourteen cottages on land belonging to The Board in Lacey Street. Of the fourteen cottages, eight were to be for the use of firemen and the remainder for other council workmen. Mr. J. Carr, Superintendent of the Fire Brigade, said *"at that time the Brigade was scattered over the town and when fire broke out only one or two men could be got to go in charge of the engine"*. He thought this was a very unsatisfactory state of affairs. He told the meeting that in the past five years The Brigade had had to attend 24 fires.

It is clear that religion played a large part in the lives of all sections of Widnes society. The numerous church organisations and social groups,

---

[108] *"Portrait of a Revolutionary"* – Jean M. Morris (Springfield-Farrihy 2011)

Everyday Life

of all denominations, generally functioned in harmony throughout the town. Generally, members of the indigenous population adhered to the established Church of England whilst the newcomers who were of Irish, Polish or Lithuanian origin were, almost without exception, members of The Roman Catholic Church. The presence of these immigrants in the town increased the Catholic population significantly. The most populous Catholic area was the Newtown district and the expanding congregation in that neighbourhood created an urgent need for a church. Up until that time it had been necessary to use the school building for the celebration of Mass. Because of the expense involved in building a new church, the parishioners were asked to subscribe to the costs. Early in 1865 the Parish Priest told his congregation:

"I trust I have said sufficient to induce you all to do your best towards subscribing towards the new Church. I hope that no one will be unwilling to subscribe a little. The men at the respective works will do their duty. I have spoken to them on this matter last Sunday. I shall expect a day's wages from every man and, at their works, in future, a shilling, sixpence or threepence a week." [109]

Obviously the expectation that men would contribute a percentage of their weekly wage, in fact, a whole day's wage, was a huge ask. Nevertheless the contributions were made and sufficient funds were raised to build their new church, although there was still a substantial debt remaining. The new Roman Catholic Church of St. Mary (St. Marie's), in Lugsdale Road, was duly opened in September 1865. To mark the opening a solemn High Mass, with an orchestral accompaniment, was celebrated by the Bishop of Liverpool.

In Victorian England pew rents were the standard way to ensure a regular church income in order to meet the bills and maintain the clergy. In the new St. Marie's Church benches were to be let on a quarterly basis. On 24th September 1865, shortly after the opening, the Parish Priest informed the parishioners that:

"Benches in the church are to be let from this day, and as the quarter will commence the first of October I hope you will lose no time in taking them. The front benches will be three shillings a sitting – the middle ones two

---

[109] St. Marie's Parish Archives

shillings and sixpence and the lower ones and aisles two shillings a quarter. They will be paid for in advance. I trust there will be no complaints for persons not coming to Mass – there is plenty of free ground for all to come and hear Mass without paying anything. Those who can afford to ought to pay, in consequence of the heavy debt on the Church".[110]

Although the coming of industry into the area caused the local Catholic population to increase considerably, the origins of Roman Catholicism in Widnes actually date back to much earlier. Of course, if we go back to the pre-reformation times we would see a significant Roman Catholic presence in the district. Naturally, after this time, numbers diminished drastically and very few of the indigenous population followed the Church of Rome. In the early years of the 18th century a room in Lower House Farm was used as a chapel. Sometime around the mid-1700s this room was abandoned when a small dedicated chapel and presbytery was built at Appleton village on land donated by the Dennett family. The Rev. Marmaduke Wilson was the first priest in charge of the small chapel at Appleton. He was also the last priest to say Mass in the room at Lower House. Father Wilson continued as priest at Appleton until his death in 1822, aged 82. During his time in Widnes he was assisted in his duties by a number of other priests including Father Thomas Pinnington, Father John Rigby and by Father Henry Gillow who succeeded him as Parish Priest in 1822. In September 1847, during the pastorate of Father Gillow, St. Bede's Roman Catholic Church was opened. Father Gillow was succeeded as Parish Priest in 1848 by John Hutchinson's friend, Father Fisher*.

As you have read earlier, the Irish presence in the town was considerable. The fact that there were also a number of established Orange Lodges in the district could have created a certain amount of tension. Nevertheless, generally, our inhabitants seem to have lived and worked in harmony. On the few occasions when friction did occur, the antagonism was created by members of visiting Orange Lodges, not by local men. Obviously there were strong sectarian feelings amongst some members of the population but, generally, these did not develop into serious conflict. It would seem that in small town communities

---

[110] Ibid.
* Father Fisher came to St. Bede's in 1848 just a short while after John Hutchinson's arrival in Widnes. He was born in Manchester in 1810.

Everyday Life

these divisions were less evident than in larger towns and cities. For instance, sectarian violence was quite common in Liverpool especially during the period leading up to the 12th of July when Orangemen celebrated the anniversary of *"The Battle of the Boyne"*. There are newspaper reports detailing some dreadful incidents in the city, with neither side being entirely blameless. As we have seen, in Widnes, apart from a few isolated incidents, the event usually passed off without much disturbance. The 1885 parade demonstrated this. *The Widnes Weekly News* reported on the occasion:

"On Sunday morning, the members of the Widnes Orange Lodges assembled in fair number to celebrate the "auspicious 12th of July". Meeting in their Lodge Room in Victoria Road, attired in the insignia of their order, and wearing orange lilies, they walked in procession to Widnes Parish Church. A large number of people assembled in the streets, and although the Orangemen, Nationalists, and Salvation Army were in close contingency to each other, and the former had to walk a considerable distance along streets chiefly peopled by Irish Roman Catholics, there was no evidence of ill feeling, and certainly no indication of a disturbance, which says much for the law abiding and forbearing spirit of the people".

Unfortunately the scene was a little different the following year when a group of visiting Orangemen from Garston were involved in a nasty disturbance with local Catholics near Simms Cross. On that occasion the Orangemen had come armed with spiked sticks and were openly provoking and aggressively inviting trouble. Sectarian violence returned to the streets of Widnes in 1888 when Orangemen from Garston and Widnes Roman Catholics encountered each other again. On this occasion there was little credit to either side as both groups baited each other and were equally belligerent. This resulted in several arrests from both sides. Fortunately the normal peaceful and tolerant behaviour resumed the following year. That year, 1889, the 12th July celebration had something of a carnival feel about it. Huge crowds of Orangemen, along with their supporters, arrived in Widnes from Liverpool and other areas for their annual gathering. The venue for this particular event was the Farnworth Athletic Grounds. The members of 115 lodges in the Liverpool Province joined the Widnes Lodges on what was apparently a bright sunny day. In addition to the Widnes and Liverpool Lodges there were representatives from Warrington and St. Helens. It was estimated that the final number of

Into The Crucible

attendants was well in excess of five thousand people. This is an extract from the report of the event.

> "From eight o'clock till after ten in the morning, Central Station, Liverpool, and the vicinity were crowded with men, women, and children sporting orange lilies and wearing the vari-coloured regalia of the Order. Five special trains left at intervals and conveyed between three and four thousand persons to Hough Green Station, where they were received by the Widnes, and other Orangemen. It was after eleven o'clock when the last train arrived from Liverpool. As soon as possible the lodges were marshalled in a procession which was about a mile long. Among the lodges were four female lodges from Liverpool and one from Widnes, the dispensation of the latter being carried by Mrs. Taylor and Miss E. Rogerson.
>
> The procession was headed by the grand lodge car, containing Brothers Harry Thomas (Grand Treasurer); R.Murray; W.Shaw; J.W.Ballard and James Lynch. Twelve drum and fife bands were in attendance, their music enlivening the processionists in their three-mile walk from Hough Green to Farnworth, while their naval and military uniforms were striking features in the procession. Most of the lodges had beautiful banners, some of which were really works of art.
>
> The route taken to Farnworth was through the Ball of Ditton, Highfield Road, Birchfield Road, and Derby Road. It was rumoured that they would not go through Widnes, but that course was not decided upon. The show field was reached at one o'clock after a quiet and orderly march".

Although members of various religious groups in the town generally afforded a reasonable tolerance to people of other creeds, occasionally there were small pockets of discord. Sometimes the dispute was not with other denominations but within their own ranks, as will be seen from a report that appeared in *The Weekly News* of 12th November 1892.

WIDNES INVINCIBLE LOYAL ORANGE ORDER
The annual meeting and tea party in connection with the above Lodge were held on Monday evening at the Conservative Club. The tea was provided by Mrs. Coupe in her usual efficient manner. The meeting was under the chairmanship of Mr. R. Lewis who was supported on the platform by Mr. Touchstone of Manchester. The speaker, Mr. Touchstone, was loudly cheered on rising. After explaining the first principles of Orangeism, he

said it was to the benefit of the country to have an established Church and that a Protestant one (applause). He contended that the Church of Wales was a part and parcel of the Church of England. They did not want imitations of Roman Catholics in their church but unfortunately such men have found their way into it. He could not understand how any vicar, rector or curate, who was guided by the Bible and Prayer Book, could countenance high ritual that was practised in some of the churches. They were eating the bread of the Church of England but were rank Romanists at heart. He would rather see them honest and upright, and go over to Ireland and be Romanists. He was pleased that they in Widnes had recognised their duty at the contest in July.

In a similar tone, we find that some readers' letters to *The Widnes Weekly News* were often quite openly sectarian. It should be said here that our local newspaper was fairly even handed with the space given to all letters, no matter from which denominational or political standpoint they were written.

LECTURE ON ARCHITECTURE AT WIDNES
Sir,
I regret to take exception to any remarks of the highly instructive lecture on the above by Dr. Larkin at the Free Library, but I noticed in speaking of the various kinds of architecture of English cathedrals and different parts of the same he called the communion table an "altar" which is quite contrary to the teaching of the Church of England. The prayer book mentions "table" (I think about 16 times). "Altars" were destroyed at the Reformation by command of Archbishop Grindal and tables substituted. A Protestant Primate of the same stamp is needed these days.
Yours truly, A PROTESTANT

The following letter was from the same edition in March 1899

A PROTESTANT SOCIETY FOR WIDNES
Sir, Permit me through your columns to ask cannot a branch of the Church Association, Evangelical Protestant Union, or Protestant Alliance (the latter is composed of Churchmen and Nonconformists) be inaugurated in Widnes. I think it is important for Protestants in every town and village to be "up and doing" for the ritualistic traitors who are trying to overthrow our Protestant heritage, secured to us "by the blood of the martyrs". Bishops Ridley and Latimer and others were burnt alive for refusing to

accept the blasphemous Mass, which with other English doctrines, is actually being taught in the Church of England, by clergy who have subscribed to the 39 articles, and I regret to say evangelical clergy are imitating them by introducing tasting communion, singing and intoning prayer contrary to Scripture and prayer book; decorating churches, and sometimes placing a floral cross on communion table; surpliced choirs, and surplices in the pulpit, thereby following the advice of Dr. Pusey(?), one of the instigators of the tractarian movement which has developed into full blown Popery.
Yours .. ANTI-PROTESTANT

The signature, or nom-de-plume, on the last letter could be confusing. The writer was not in fact saying that he was against the Protestant religion, but rather against the rituals that had been introduced to Anglican services. There had been some controversy within the Church of England during the previous year when evangelical anti-ritualists had attacked practices in some Anglican churches. They were opposed to the wearing of vestments and the use of incense in some Anglican parishes, claiming that they resembled Roman Catholic ceremony. The anti-ritualists also began to push for Government legislation to enforce Orthodox Church Discipline. This presented huge problems for some MPs as it became clear that their support, or maybe their lack of support, for the *Church Discipline Bill* became a test of their Protestant solidarity.

The number of churches in the town, of all denominations, suggests that the population in general were devoutly Christian in their outlook. The Protestant groups in particular put much emphasis on "self-improvement" and "temperance" and encouraged their young people to join these movements. Some of their churches provided gymnasiums; in fact these groups were the forerunners of the modern day "youth clubs". Among the many groups of non-conformists who were based in the town I think that The Salvation Army is one that deserves special mention. Members of The Salvation Army were a familiar sight on the streets of Widnes and the group also had a healthy following in Runcorn. In fact, General Booth, the founder of the movement came to the area in 1886 to open a new Barracks in Runcorn which was to be known as *"The Citadel".* The Widnes Salvationists, who had their Barracks in Hibbert Street near Simms Cross, held their regular meetings in Victoria Square where they usually attracted

Everyday Life

substantial crowds with their lively singing and tambourine shaking. They also frequently held dinnertime services in some of the works, particularly Bolton's Copper Works where their services were well attended. Although, as we have seen, there were sometimes feelings of antagonism or resentment amongst other religious groups, it is probably fair to say that the Salvation Army did not attract the same degree of hostility. Most people appreciated the fact that Salvationists practiced their Christianity in a practical way. They were liberal with their help and compassion and were always to the fore when either or both were needed. Their relief was always distributed without prejudice. It was simply given when needed, irrespective of the recipients` religion, nationality or political leaning.

Poverty and its consequences were familiar company in the narrow congested streets of Widnes in the nineteenth century. *"What is the cost of "living" or simply "subsisting""?* was a question often asked by politicians. How much money did a person need to exist in Victorian Britain? *The Widnes Weekly News* raised the question of *"the cost of food per head"* in its *"Notes and Queries column"* of November 1892.

> *"A queriest asks a rather singular question as to what is the cost of food per head – I presume in this country. I have some figures by me which give this at 9pence per head on the average, but whilst the residents of a mansion may cost 5shillings or 10shillings a day per head the residents of many a cottage do not cost 6pence or how could a labourer with 24shillings a week, with a wife, and perhaps 5 children, live and pay house rent, fuel, and clothing? Some statistics in my possession profess to give a daily expenditure in pence, of each person in several countries. This of course includes every cost. It will thus be seen that we of the UK cost most in living, rent, taxes, clothing etc."*

United Kingdom	20
United States	15
France	15
Belgium & Holland	13
Germany	13
Spain	8
Italy	7
Russia	6

Into The Crucible

If these statistics are to be accepted, and taken in comparison with the average weekly wage as outlined in *The Alkali Inspectors 29th Report,* it is apparent that most families suffered great hardships. In 1892 a young girl called Catherine Case, of Pitt Street, was prosecuted and fined 5 shillings for stealing 28lbs of coal from a wagon in a siding in West Bank Dock. In another case a young woman called Mary Cunningham appeared in the dock with a baby in her arms. She was charged with stealing a pair of boots, valued at 2s.11d, from the Public Benefit Boot Co. Ltd., in Victoria Road. Later she pawned the boots at the premises of Mr. H. Syred, in Victoria Road, and then spent the money on basic provisions at a local grocery. She was sent to jail for fourteen days. As in the case of Catherine Case, stealing coal from wagons, factories or tips was a regular occurrence. There were countless other instances where food items, such as bread, eggs, cheeses or hams were stolen from shops. It was also quite common for children to be caught stealing poultry or other produce from outlying farms. All these offenders were punished with heavy fines or imprisonment. Even fairly young children received harsh punishments which usually involved an extremely long term in a reformatory or an industrial school. These appear to be pitiful crimes committed in desperate circumstances. It is obvious that hardly any were carried out for financial gain; but were simply an effort to put food on the table, warmth in the hearth or clothes on their backs.

Perhaps, in retrospect, we should view these convictions alongside the historical background of that particular time. During this period Widnes was in the grip of a serious economic depression. 400 men had been laid off from Hutchinson's No.2. Works and The United Alkali Company were making serious reductions in their workforce. The unemployment situation in the town was causing a great deal of concern. As a consequence, local church organisations considered it necessary to open soup kitchens in various locations around the town. Poverty was banging loudly on the door of most homes in the working class districts, and the majority of families were in dire circumstances. It was in these conditions that crime found a willing partner. We have only to examine statistics relating to offences of stealing and poaching to appreciate the fact that poverty played a significant part. It is apparent that these types of crime were prevalent during times of economic depression. Figures also show that this category of crime decreased considerably when there was plentiful employment.

Everyday Life

Over a period of time the question of Widnes becoming a Municipal Borough had been raised by various parties. Not least of these was the inimitable Doctor O`Keeffe who ardently supported the plan. In 1890 there is mention in the minutes of The Local Board of a letter from Mr. T.E. Delaney, who was writing on behalf of the members of *The Irish National League*. Mr. Delaney urged The Board to give the matter some serious consideration. Another communication on the same subject was received from *"The Owner's and Occupiers Association"* in September of that year. The Board, after a great deal of caution and deliberation, organised a canvass of the townspeople. The result of the survey was that three quarters of those canvassed were in favour of The Local Board petitioning Her Majesty the Queen to grant a Charter of Incorporation. After making the customary enquiries the Board was asked to submit a draft Charter. This Charter was subsequently approved in June 1891. In June the following year The Local Board received the Letters Patent under the Great Seal of the United Kingdom granting a Charter of Incorporation to the Borough of Widnes. The Widnes Local Board was dissolved later that year and held its final meeting on 8th November 1892.

In July 1893, the youthful Borough of Widnes received a magnanimous donation which was intended to be a permanent and historic symbol of the honourable status of its leading citizen. His Worship the Mayor (Mr. F.H. Gossage) made a most generous gift to the people of the town. He submitted and presented to the Council, for the use of the Mayor of Widnes, a gold chain of office and pendant. He expressed the hope *"that this mayoral chain might always be honourably borne by the gentleman selected as Chief Officer of the Corporation"*. The members of the Council placed on record their appreciation *"of the great care which he has exercised in selecting the appropriate devices, symbolising the staple industry to which the Borough owes its present position, which having been approved and embodied by the authorities of the Herald's College the grant of Arms recently made to the Borough"*[111] The Widnes Borough Coat of Arms, which is mentioned here, was prepared by the officers of the College of Arms on the occasion of the town's Incorporation. The device was a shield divided into four quarters. Two sections contained a hive with bees and the remaining two contained the red rose of Lancaster, taken from the arms of Henry VII. The crest, in its entirety,

---

[111] Widnes Borough Council *"Minutes of Council & Committees" 1893*

was a symbolic reminder of the town's history and influences. The hive and bees represented industry and the red rose was the emblem of Lancashire, the county in which Widnes was then located. Beneath the shield was a motto bearing the words *Industria Ditat;* the literal translation being *Industry Enriches*.

By 1896 hundreds of acres of the Widnes and Ditton marshes, known as the "Ditton Alps", had been buried under an estimated 8 million tons (to a depth of 12`) of alkali waste, known locally as galligu. By marked contrast, the newly created Town Square displayed a cluster of elegant and imposing buildings which were a joy to behold. The visual impact of this new civic area had created an ambience befitting a town which had just been granted Borough status. The pseudo French Renaissance architecture of the Town Hall, the equally beautiful St. Paul's Church, the new Library and Technical College and the new Market Hall; all of which were in keeping with the town's newly acquired importance. Alas, only a short distance from the splendour of these buildings the scene was less inviting and somewhat depressing.

The industrial waste tips located around the town became an accepted part of the landscape and the inhabitants learned to live with them. However, despite the population becoming resigned to their existence, they posed a serious risk to health because of the presence of sulphur in the waste. The obnoxious effects on health and the environment were noticeable in a number of ways. In wet weather, rainwater on the waste caused it to give off sulphuretted hydrogen. In dry windy weather, the waste became heated and combustion took place. As a consequence, waste heap fires were not uncommon and on one occasion it was reported that one such fire had burned continually for a year. The fires produced unpleasant smells, fumes and irritant gases. On foggy or damp nights the escape of sulphuretted hydrogen from the tips created a blue tinged or lead coloured bloom which hung over nearby streets. All in all, it was a most unpleasant and unhealthy situation.

Despite the unpleasant smells and fumes emanating from these waste heaps, the heat they gave off sometimes proved to be an irresistible attraction to vagrants, especially in the cold weather. It was not uncommon for the homeless to be found sleeping on the tips, snatching some degree of comfort from their warmth on bitter winter

Everyday Life

nights. This was obviously a dangerous practice and one which resulted in the death of Michael Carr, a 45year old labourer of no fixed abode. *The Widnes Weekly News* made the following report:[112]

> "Michael Carr, of no fixed abode whose body was discovered on a waste heap in the vicinity of Ditton Road on Thursday morning. A witness says the body was found on the property of the Ditton Land Company. The man had previously been observed on the waste heap and warned that it was dangerous. His body was found the following day. The Coroner asked the witness, "are there any fumes from the heap?" The witness replied "it is on fire!" The Coroner concluded, "I suppose he would go to sleep there sometimes so as to get warm".

> Dr. Creighton Hutchinson gave the following evidence from his post-mortem examination. Externally the man was fairly well nourished, but very dirty. His fingers were slightly burned. No marks of violence were evident. His right lung was inflamed and left one slightly congested. Death was due to inflammation of the lung accelerated by exposure. He would not have died from inflammation of the lung had he been in bed.

In 1896 the town's most famous Ice Cream Maker, Mr. Gandolfo of Victoria Road, was proudly advertising the purity of his ice cream. Copies of certificates of analysis were published in *The Widnes Weekly News*.

The Laboratory, Chapel Street, Liverpool. July 19th 1896
Analysis of sample of ice cream obtained by us at Victoria Road, Widnes, the shop of Mr. F. Gandolfo on July 8th 1896.
We have analysed this sample of ice cream and find that it is free from poisonous metals or any injurious ingredients.
Signed: Edward Davies and Sons.

A further glowing recommendation was supplied by J.A. Webster of Wigan who declared:

> *I have frequently watched the making of ice cream at Gandolfo's, and have inspected each ingredient. Every part of it is of the best, and it is soundly*

---

[112] *Widnes Weekly News* – November 22nd 1902

wholesome, and nourishing, and I frequently find it beneficial in cases of illness.

The local drinks manufacturer, Mr. A. Cooper of West Bank, also published similar testimonials for his products.

Mr. Granville H. Sharpe, late Principal of the Liverpool College of Chemistry

I hereby certify that I have submitted to careful chemical analysis samples of ginger beer, ginger ale, cider, lemonade, soda-water, brown beer, hop ale etc., aerated and fermented beverages manufactured by Mr. A. Cooper, West Bank, Widnes, and I find them to be perfectly pure in composition, of excellent quality, and certainly free from contamination or undesirable admixtures in any form. These provide a pleasant and inviting flavour and taste. I have analysed also a sample of the water used in production of these beverages, which I find to be of good purity and well suited for the purpose.

The Town Council sounded a note of discord in their meetings of mid-November 1897. Councillor Charles Hemingway, who represented the West Bank Ward, moved that the Council go into committee to consider the constitution of the various committees. Mr. Hemingway who was an immigrant of sorts, having come to Widnes from Everton in Liverpool, said *"several gentlemen were not satisfied with the committees they were placed upon"*. Councillor Hemingway, a local builder with premises in Church Street, was the builder of houses in Witt Road, Moor Lane and Hibbert Street. As an experienced builder he believed he would be more use on one of the Building Committees; but instead he had been assigned to two committees which did not appeal to him (The Cemetery Committee and Library Committee). He stated that it *"was no use putting square men in round holes"*. Of course some might have thought, in view of his own business interests, that a place on a building committee would not have been appropriate. Charles Hemingway was also on the Health Committee and the Highways Committee. Minutes of Council meetings show that he was a rather forceful character with immoveable views on a variety of subjects. His main claim to fame is that during his time on The Council he managed to get his face on almost every *"official photo"* (in a prominent position of course).

Everyday Life

In the winter of 1897 the residents of the town, especially those in West Bank, were saddened by the circumstances of some a dreadful accidents that occurred. In November, 7year old Ellen Case of Wellington Street was killed by a runaway horse. Six other people were injured, one of them, 3year old Henry Gandy, of Cholmondeley Street, sustained serious injuries. The owner of the horse was a Fishmonger & Greengrocer from Mersey Road. The horse and cart had been left in charge of a 14year old boy who was employed to hawk fish, rabbits and greengrocery around the streets. Unfortunately, the horse bolted and ran among a crowd of people causing the death of one young child and the serious injury of another. There is no doubt that the winter of 1897 was a bad one weather-wise and an unlucky one for some of our residents. A few weeks after the death of young Ellen Case in West Bank, there was more dismal news. In the first week of December storms raged over most parts of England and Wales. Widnes and Runcorn, although relatively lucky to have escaped the worst of it, did however have several instances of damage and injury. A young man called William Farrell, of Victoria Street, was hit by flying masonry and needed urgent medical treatment. The gale force wind also brought down several chimney pots, one of which hit Thomas Roberts of Luton Street, causing concussion and deep cuts to his head and shoulder. The assistant Borough Surveyor, Thomas Hughes, also sustained a serious injury when walking along Albert Road. A large hoarding at the corner of a side street was blown by the severe wind and struck Mr. Hughes, causing severe bruising to his head, a dislocated shoulder and a fractured shoulder blade.

Although there were several other weather related incidents which left people in need of medical attention, the storm damage to buildings was relatively slight, apart from the loss of slates and chimney pots. However the effects of the flooding that followed had more disrupting effects. Water collected in considerable volume on wasteland at Lugsdale causing flooding to some nearby houses, and the Gas Works was flooded to a depth of 3feet in the yard, storerooms, and retort houses. Although the fires in the Gas Works were not extinguished, it caused a great hindrance to the normal working procedures. The water also invaded the nearby works of the Widnes Foundry causing some damage but a higher degree of inconvenience. Runcorn was similarly affected and traffic on the Ship Canal was brought to a complete standstill. Of course this stoppage caused major disruption as any interruption in canal and river traffic had a negative impact on local industry. Any type of slowdown on the canals meant that products and materials could not be moved in or out efficiently.

The town's first Mayoral Car – with the Mayor, Samuel Quinn. Councillor Charles Hemingway is seated in back.

The weather that winter was indeed a topic on many lips but other more cheerful matters were also up for discussion. Preparation and funding for the celebration of Queen Victoria's Diamond Jubilee were subjects the on the agenda during a meeting, chaired by the Mayor, in the Town Hall in December 1897. Also attending that meeting were managers and senior representatives of local works. The Mayor had invited them for the purpose of organising a system of collections from local workmen to fund a public park and an extension for West Bank Promenade. The Mayor, having explained the object of the meeting, went on to suggest that all works should be issued with subscription sheets bearing the names of all their employees. A special day was to be set aside to receive the contributions and he suggested it be called "Jubilee Saturday". He believed that this would result in a much larger contribution being given than by mere box collections. Mr. Carr,

Everyday Life

representing the works managers, endorsed these remarks and added a further suggestion that the men be encouraged to state what they would give, and then be allowed to pay this amount in instalments.

Victoria Park – Opening Ceremony
(Councillor Hemingway front left in light trousers)

It would seem, if the above proposal is correctly interpreted, that most men were placed in a position where it would have been tricky to decline. They were to be "encouraged" to contribute and to pay a fixed amount from their pay each week. Nevertheless, despite any additional hardships this may have incurred, it is obvious that working men did contribute as expected. These public subscriptions, together with donations from leading companies and individuals, enabled the Borough Corporation to purchase 34 acres of the Appleton House estate. As a result Victoria Park was officially opened on 31st May 1900. The extension to the West Bank Promenade did not materialise until some three years later. Both the park and the promenade became positive features of town life and provided pleasant spaces in an

281

Into The Crucible

otherwise gloomy environment. I think it is worth reminding today's residents that we, and those countless generations before us who have enjoyed these public spaces, are the beneficiaries of the unselfish financial help of hard-working men and women.

While plans for the Jubilee celebrations were occupying some members of the Council, there were obviously other more pressing issues to be attended to. The quarterly report on the health of Widnes and district was issued in December 1897. During the 3 months ended September 30th 320 births and 191 deaths were registered in the town. Among the 191 deaths were 91 infants under one year of age and only 12 persons over 60 years of age. Cited among the causes of death were diarrhoea, fever, whooping cough, measles and diphtheria. There were also 8 violent deaths recorded. Although many causes of death were given as the types of sickness and diseases that were to be expected at that time, records show that an additional cause of death in some cases was given as "starvation".

Details of one of the saddest and most disturbing cases emerged during an inquest in 1898. The inquest was concerned with the death of 55year old Catherine Mulligan of North Street, near Waterloo Road, who died of starvation in June that year. Her husband, James Mulligan, told the Coroner that he had been in the workhouse for five weeks and after he came out he resided with his wife and daughter in the house in North Street. There was no furniture in the house except for a straw mattress on which he, his wife and his daughter slept. The husband was employed as a stonebreaker at the Gaskell Deacon Works and he usually earned 11s.6d for 3 weeks work, but during the last 3 weeks he had only earned 10s. The Coroner asked the man how his wife spent the money, to which the husband replied *"she used to buy a bit of chuck and one thing and another"*. The Coroner then asked if the wife drank, to which the husband replied that his wife had been a most sober woman and did not like drink. After further questioning he asked Mr. Mulligan how much the rent was for his house and he was told it was 4s a week. The Coroner, clearly moved by the appalling poverty experienced by this family, asked the man if he had applied for poor relief. A short transcript of some of the questions asked at the inquest appears here:

Everyday Life

Mr. Borthwick: *Have you ever made an application to the relieving officer? - No Sir.*

Mr. Borthwick: *I think you ought to have done so. It is a very sad case. We pay very big poor rates here and they ought to be applied in such a case.*

The Coroner: *My experience of poor rates is that they are not for the poor but for the officials. About ten pence in every shilling goes for officials and 3d for the poor.*

Mr. Borthwick: *If I had information of this I would have given them food.*

The Coroner: *The case shows quite a shocking state of affairs apart from that.*

It is obvious that not all needy people sought relief from the Poor Law Union. The inquisitorial method adopted, and the air of grudging charity that permeated its activities, probably made it a last resort for all but the desperate. However, we can see from this sad case that even the desperate were deterred from applying. This was plainly a tragedy waiting to happen. The Mulligan family did not have enough money for food, or anything else. In fact the man's weekly wage did not even cover the rent on the poor hovel they called home. Sadly this was not an isolated case, there were numerous other hunger related deaths recorded in Widnes. Nevertheless, whilst there was obvious deprivation all around, the Victorian attitude towards poverty was not always a charitable one. It is clear that the middle classes were often of the opinion that the plight of the poor was their own fault. Many thought poverty was a result of intemperance and indolence and not of poverty itself. Social conditions such as low pay, dreadful housing and inadequate public health provisions, were never considered to be a contributory factor. Some even attributed poverty to failings in the character of the poor themselves and placed much emphasis on the "improvement" of the individual rather than the actual causes of poverty. Unfortunately, as we have seen in the case of Mrs. Mulligan, she was neither intemperate nor indolent, she was just poor.

There was much sadness in the town when the death was announced in March 1898 of Dr. Ferdinand Hurter, The United Alkali Company's head chemist. Dr. Hurter was well-known and respected locally and was considered to be a brilliant man in his field. His death was all the more shocking when one considers that he was only 54 years of age. However, although he continued to work up until the time of his death, it is believed that he never entirely recovered from a serious bout of illness that occurred at the beginning of 1894. This illness left him weak and debilitated and as a consequence he spent three months convalescing in his native Switzerland. His dismay at his increasing lack of energy was expressed in personal letters to friends and associates. In one letter he said that ill health was coming between him and his work and that he felt *"old and worn out."* In another letter, written just weeks before his death, he says *"my health for the past two years has not been good, and life has become sour for me."* Despite the debilitating nature of his illness, and the fact that his powers of concentration were failing, Dr. Hurter continued working to the best of his abilities. On the morning of his death he had spent a few hours in his laboratory at the United Alkali Company in Widnes. In the afternoon he attended a concert a St. George`s Hall in Liverpool and then returned home to take tea with his family. While sitting at the tea-table he collapsed and died.

Although a native of Switzerland, Dr. Hurter had been involved both professionally and socially with Widnes for over thirty years. After achieving a Ph.D. degree at Heidelberg University in 1866 he came to Widnes the following year. On his arrival in the town was employed by Messrs. Gaskell, Deacon & Company where he acted as chief chemist and scientific adviser. Later, in 1890, following the amalgamation of several smaller firms into the United Alkali Company, he was appointed chief chemist to that organisation. Among his numerous initiatives was the setting up of a main laboratory in order that research and analytical resources could be controlled in a central establishment. This led to the creation of the Central Laboratory, which eventually became known as *The Hurter Laboratory* when the building was taken over by the General Chemicals Division of I.C.I many years later.

From his arrival in Widnes in 1867 up until his untimely death, Ferdinand Hurter`s career span saw both the development and ensuing deterioration of the Leblanc method of alkali manufacture. His investigations into every factor of the Leblanc process made him one of the leading authorities on this method of production and gained him a worldwide reputation throughout the alkali industry. Whilst there is

Everyday Life

no doubt that Dr. Hurter's contribution to scientific research and development in the alkali industry was impressive; we should be aware that it is not only in that sphere of study is he remembered. We should bear in mind that Dr. Hurter's long-time collaboration with his friend and colleague, Vero Charles Driffield, led to important discoveries and advancements in the science of light in photography.

Ferdinand Hurter

Into The Crucible

These two brilliant men met for the first time in 1871 when Driffield came to Widnes to work as an engineer at the Gaskell Deacon Works. Driffield had previously served an apprenticeship with a photographer in Southport but, whilst still retaining a love of photography, he decided to change course and take up engineering. His arrival in Widnes marked the beginning of a long friendship between him and Hurter, which had originally come about through their mutual love of music. Although Driffield had abandoned photography as an occupation he was still an enthusiastic amateur and subsequently urged his friend Hurter to take it up as a hobby.

Vero Charles Driffield

Everyday Life

Unsurprisingly, considering Hurter's analytical mind, the *"hobby"* and its many technical processes soon became a matter for scientific research. Many years later Driffield, when discussing their collaboration in photographic research, said of Hurter *"to a mind accustomed like his to methods of scientific precision, it became intolerable to practice an art which, at that time, was so entirely governed by rule of thumb, and which of the fundamental principles were so little understood"*.

After almost twenty years of study into the disciplines of photography, which resulted in eight published papers on the subject, Hurter and Driffield's attempts to rank photography as a quantitative science was finally acknowledged. In 1898 they were jointly awarded *The Progress Medal of the Royal Photographic Society* in recognition of their enormous contributions to photographic science. Sadly, the death of Ferdinand Hurter on 5th March 1898 marked the end of this lengthy friendship and collaboration. Nevertheless their combined research into the science of photography had a major impact on this art and gave them an important place in the history of photography.

Obviously, Ferdinand Hurter did have other interests outside of science; he had a great love of music and regularly attended recitals in Liverpool and elsewhere. Furthermore, during the decades he lived and worked in Widnes, he was involved in local social and political affairs. In 1885, in the lead up to The General Election, he appeared on campaign platforms in support of Mr. Muspratt's candidature, and spoke robustly in support of education. During the many years of his residency in Widnes, living first at Prospect House in Crow Wood, then later at Wilmere House, he was a regular member of the congregation of St. Luke's Church in Farnworth village. Although he had relocated to the Cressington Park area of Liverpool some time before his death, he still retained links with the church at Farnworth. Sadly, his final return to St. Luke's was on the occasion of his funeral. Following the service his remains were interred in Farnworth churchyard.

I mentioned earlier that there were high numbers of single men in the town who had no family homes to return to at the end of their working day. These men were accommodated either as lodgers in other people's homes or in the many common lodging houses that were scattered around the south end of the town. The common lodging houses were, ostensibly, strictly regulated and applications were required for official registration. Among those who made application in 1892 were:

> Patrick Cain for House at 2 Oxford Street
> Mary Walsh for House at 2 Marsh Street
> Patrick Anderson for House at 7 Nelson Street
> P. Fitzgerald for Houses at 2 and 4 Lugsdale Road

The Sanitary Regulations Act 1847 had made it a criminal offence to run a lodging house without official registration. A general guideline issued in 1851 gave the following information regarding the licensing of Lodging Houses.

> "Every person who intends to keep a lodging house must now apply for a license. In his application he must state the number of rooms in his house, the number of his family's and domestics and the number of lodgers which he wishes to accommodate. The house is then inspected and measured by the Inspector of Nuisances and he is followed by the Medical Officer of Health, who reports as to the sanitary condition of the dwelling. Upon the certificate of The Medical Officer, a license is granted for the number of lodgers the house is calculated to receive. The keeper is furnished with the rules, regulations and bye-laws under which he is placed and a copy of the license should be suspended in each room. The Inspectors and Sergeants of Police are appointed to visit the lodging houses by day and night, and in the event of overcrowding or refusing to register the houses, summonses are issued against the keepers, and fines inflicted."

Although there was a duty to register any enterprise that operated as a lodging-house it is obvious that there were numerous unauthorised establishments in the town. Our guide to that conclusion is via the nineteenth century census records. It is fairly easy to identify illicit lodgings from census data as these records provide details of the number of inhabitants in each dwelling, as well as their names and ages. From these entries we can see that in some houses there were abnormally large numbers of unmarried male occupants who were unrelated to the head of the household. One does not need to be Sherlock Holmes to deduce that these houses were being used as lodging houses.

Everyday Life

Whilst many lodging-house keepers were meticulous in acting within the law, others flouted the rules relating to registration. Obviously registration brought with it certain legal obligations towards the residents. There was also a requirement to submit the premises to regular inspections to confirm that it was in good order and fit for human habitation. It should also be pointed out that there were additional restrictions which applied to morality. Persons of different sexes were not allowed to share the same room unless they were a married couple. This rule was to discourage premises being used as *"houses of ill-repute"*. Clearly, some owners did not want to register their properties because of the additional hassle or responsibility this created. One assumes that in order to satisfy the requirements of registration the lodging-houses needed to be clean, well-run and of a certain standard. Therefore, as unregistered establishments did not need to comply with any regulations, they were probably of a rougher and less salubrious nature.

Although I did not find any detailed description of conditions in Widnes lodging houses, one would expect that they were similar in most respects to those portrayed in a Liverpool newspaper report from 1849. The details refer to a case in which eighteen people were fined for over-crowding in their lodging-houses. The offending houses were described as:

> *"Most unhealthy and filthy places and the people taken in as lodgers were herded together in a manner which could only result in producing fever and every kind of disease. The lodging-houses were in narrow and contracted streets and in eighteen of these houses against which information has been laid, the total number of inmates amounted to 338."*

Despite the fact that there was a legal responsibility to register, the law in Widnes seems to have been surprisingly cavalier in its application. Although it is obvious that there were a large number of unregistered houses, the number of prosecutions seems to have been relatively low. I suspect that because of the scale of the problem the authorities simply turned a blind eye.

As with lodging houses, slaughterhouses/butchers were also required to be registered. However, the licensing of these premises was quite strict and in this case there was no question of turning a blind eye.

Into The Crucible

These establishments were regularly inspected, as were local bake-houses. Any contravention of the law relating to hygiene or other conditions of registration could lead to prosecution or even the loss of a licence to operate. In December 1899 the following slaughterhouse proprietors were issued with permits.

Sarah Johnson	119 Mersey Road
Kate Most	63 Widnes Road
J. Bower	69 Mersey Road
W.J. Hedley	John Street
L. Pfister	47 Waterloo Road
R. Potter	Ann Street
Charles Bill	Ann Street
R. Bailey	Albert Road
J. Fletcher	160 Widnes Road
G. Coupe	Croft Street
James Rawson	26 Victoria Road
Robert Taylor	Farnworth Street

When we think of nineteenth century Widnes we generally conjure up images of gloom and drudgery. Of course we are right to do so as in many respects the town was a bleak and unforgiving place. Fortunately, in spite of the numerous negative aspects, there were other less depressing features which helped to reduce the dreariness. Sporting activities brought some light relief to members of the population who had opportunities to pursue leisure. Needless to say, that in the streets and houses at the south end of the town leisure time was probably a rare luxury. Therefore, in the beginning some sports were generally thought to be the domain of the more affluent but, as the century progressed, working men became more involved both as participants and spectators. Numerous local football and cricket clubs were established and there was also a lot of interest in boxing and athletics. As we will see, some groups, such as cricket and athletic clubs, were formed quite early on. One of these, *The Widnes Athletic Club*, came into being in the early 1860s and their early activities took place at *The Grapes Running Ground* near to Widnes Dock. A report of an early Sports Day in May 1864 is reproduced here.

Everyday Life

GRAPES RUNNING-GROUNDS, WIDNES DOCK, NEAR WARRINGTON.

Entries for Mr. Hunt's 140 Yards Handicap, to be run at the above grounds, on Saturday, May 14, and Whit-Monday, for a silver cup, and £5 in money-prizes—J. Phillipson, Newcastle, scratch; J. Neary, Hulme, 5 yards' start; M. Burke, Salford, 6; R. Charnock, St. Helens, 7; H. Holland, Cheshire, 7; R. Quaile, Liverpool, 7; H. Stapleton, Hulme, 7; W. Brown, Newcastle-on-Tyne, 7; P. Canavan, Newton, 7; R. Davis, Liverpool, 11; W. Lea, St. Helens, 11; T. Pottear, St. Helens, 12; J. Gorse, St. Helens, 12; J. Travis, Farnworth, 12; R. M'Keshall, Liverpool, 12; C. Walton, Liverpool, 12; W. Lawless, Liverpool, 12; W. Lowe, St. Helens, 13; A. Davis, Widnes, 13; J. Hulme, Prescot, 14; T. Fernley, Newton, 15; W. Joley, Stretton, 15; J. Rutherford, Widnes, 16; T. Boardman, Widnes, 16; J. Heyes, Widnes, 16; W. Woods, St. Helens, 17; J. Carr, St. Helens, 17; T. Rught, Widnes, 17; J. Jones, Sutton, 17; T. Banks, Parr, 17; R. Banks, Parr, 17; S. Mason, Widnes, 17; J. Leadbitter, Prescot, 17; E. Unsworth, Farnworth, 18; H. M'Cawley, St. Helens, 18; S. Broom, Appleton, 19; J. Wright, Farnworth, 21; T. Heyes, Appleton, 21; R. Lomax, Widnes, 21; J. Boardman, Upton, 21; L. Thompson, Widnes, 21; R. Harrison, Widnes, 22; J. Walin, Widnes, 22; J. Daniels, Widnes, 23; C. Broom, Appleton, 24; J. Anderson, Widnes, 24; P. Capehon, Widnes, 24. Acceptances, 1s. each, to be made at Mr. Hunt's, on or before Wednesday, May 11. Heats to be drawn on Thursday, May 12. Any man winning a handicap after this day, will be put two yards back.

May 1864

Common belief and previous local writings have suggested that the *Widnes Cricket Club*, which had evolved from the *Woodend Cricket Club*, was founded in 1869 by James White. However, contrary to this long held view, we now know that it was established as early as 1851 by two of the Gossage brothers. This information is derived from a speech made by the President, Mr. T. H. Gossage, at the annual dinner in November 1872. At that dinner, which was held at the Simms Cross Hotel, the President remarked that the Club had just attained its majority having been formed in 1851 by his two brothers. He also

Into The Crucible

stated that their first game was played at Hill Wood[113]. The Club became known as *The Widnes Cricket Club* in 1874. During its early years the club played its games at various temporary locations in the town. Some early games were played in Ditton Road on a site later occupied by McKechnie Brothers Copper Works. Following this, they transferred their play to a field belonging to Lockett's Farm in Peelhouse Lane (near to the present day Lockett Road). Later they played on a field behind the Drill Hall in Victoria Road before moving to a site in Lowerhouse Lane. Interest in the game of cricket steadily grew in the town and as a result several other clubs were formed. These included *The White Rose Cricket Club*; the *Hough Green Club*; *Widnes Tradesmen*; *Widnes Excelsior Club* and the *Farnworth and Appleton Cricket Club*.

LIVERPOOL ATLAS (SECOND ELEVEN) V. WOODEND (WIDNES) (FIRST ELEVEN). — Played on Saturday at Widnes. Score:—

ATLAS.		WOODEND.	
W. Marsden, b Carr	2	R. Gardner, c Drinkwater, b Hooton	16
W. E. Miners, b Carr	19	W. Bibby, b Hooton	0
T. Drinkwater, c Carr, b Taylor	0	F. Harrison, c W. Miller, b Hooton	8
W. Miller, b Carr	3	J. Jenkins, b Hooton	1
Jno. Hooton, b Carr	2	J. Nunn, run out	0
W. Woffenden, b Carr	3	J. Carr, c Marsden, b H. Miller	18
C. K. Pattison, b Carr	0	J. W. Wareing, c W. Miller, b Hooton	0
H. Miller, run out	9	W. Taylor, run out	3
J. A. Hutton, b Carr	10	J. Gardner, c Lee, b Hooton	2
J. Lee, not out	4	D. Foster, b Hooton	1
E. Evans, absent		S. Kenrick, not out	0
Extras	17	Extra	4
Total	69	Total	56

A clipping from *The Liverpool Mercury* of 5th July 1869 is reproduced here. This refers to the early *Woodend Cricket Club* and gives details of players of that era.

---

[113] *Runcorn & Widnes Guardian* – November 9th 1872

Everyday Life

FARNWORTH AND APPLETON CRICKET CLUB.

The members of the above club held their fourth annual evening party in the Drill-hall, Widnes, on Friday, the 5th instant, when about eighty persons sat down to tea, the room being adorned with numerous flags, appropriate mottoes, &c. After tea, Mr. H. H. Lea, chairman of the club, proposed the health of the Queen and Royal Family. "The Army, Navy, and Volunteers," proposed by Mr. J. Farrant, was responded to by Corporal W. Upward, of the 47th L.R.V. The secretary then read his report, which showed the club to be in a flourishing condition. The highest batting averages during the season were made by Messrs. R. Scott and J. Farrant, and the best bowling average by Mr. N. Farrant. Mr. S. Upward proposed "The Farnworth and Appleton C.C.," and Mr. H. Lea responded. "The Officers and Committee" was proposed by Mr. W. Holt, and responded to by Messrs. J. Farrant (capt.), N. Farrant (sec.), J. Heyes (treas.), and H. Lea for the committee. Other toasts followed. The company afterwards adjourned to the large hall, where they enjoyed themselves with dancing to the lively strains of Mr. Powell's efficient string band until a rather late hour in the morning.

The above cutting appeared in a St. Helens newspaper in November 1875. It refers to the *Farnworth and Appleton Cricket Club,*

This club should not be confused with *Widnes Cricket Club* as both clubs were operating at the same time. Two further cuttings detailing matches played by both teams on the same day in July 1875 are also included here.

WESTMINSTER V. FARNWORTH AND APPLETON.—This match was played on the ground of the latter, at Widnes, on Saturday, and resulted in favour of the visitors. The fielding was very close on both sides, and for Westminster Messrs. Hewitt and Greenwood played well for their respective scores, as did also J. Farrant for the Farnworth. The bowling of Messrs. Lawton and Watson for the Westminster was excellent, the latter taking three wickets with three consecutive balls.

Westminster.		Farnworth.	
Bond, c Ireland, b Bibby	0	Bibby, c Ankers, b Lawton	3
Leatherbarrow, c Farrant, b Bibby	3	Critchley, run out	0
Watson, b Ireland	3	J Farrant, not out	11
Lawton, run out	1	Upwards, b Watson	0
Rogers, run out	0	Scott, b Lawton	0
Hewitt, c Ireland, b Bibby	17	Mason, b Watson	0
Greenwood, ht wkt, b Bibby	9	Latchford, c Allan, b Watson	0
Ankers, c Farrant, b Bibby	2	Ireland, st Rogers, b Lawton	0
West, b Ireland	3	Turton, b Watson	0
Walker, b Ireland	0	Williams, c Hewitt, b Watson	2
Allan, not out	2	N Farrant, b Watson	1
Extras	6	Extras	1
Total	46	Total	18

JULY 1875

WIDNES (2nd eleven) V. PEASLEY CROSS COLLIERY.—This match was played at Widnes on Saturday last, and resulted in a victory for the visitors.

Widnes.		Colliery.	
Pritchard, b Mearns	3	Grimes, b White	12
Parks, c & b Mearns	2	Duxberry, b Cozier	3
Cozier, b Grimes	3	Bamber, c Gerrard, b Cozier	0
White, run out	2	Mearns, not out	55
Scott, c Swift, b Mearns	10	Swift, b Cozier	6
Gerrard, b Grimes	7	Fairhurst, b Cozier	0
Calander, b Mearns	6	Foster, b Cozier	3
Johnson, st Mearns	8	Hunter, b Cozier	0
Horton, b Mearns	14	Burton, stumped	1
Mitchell, st Mearns, b Swift	2	Leyland, b Parks	5
Davies, not out	1	Sephton, run out	19
Extras	6	Extras	14
Total	64	Total	118

Everyday Life

Like the *Widnes Cricket Club, Widnes Football Club* also materialised from small beginnings. Its origins lay in *The Farnworth and Appleton Football Club* which was founded in 1873 by Mr. W. Ireland. Early reports show that the star players at that time were Beveridge, Tilley and Kendrick. In the beginning this club played their games on unfenced fields where Ross Street now stands. Later they moved to a field on which The Widnes Technical College and Library were built in Victoria Square. In 1875 the club moved their games to an enclosure in Mill Brow, off Peelhouse Lane. At this time it was decided to change the name to *The Widnes Football Club*.[114]   In 1895 *The Widnes Football Club* became a founder member of the Northern Union and their first fixture under the direction of the Northern Union took place on 7th September 1895. This was an away fixture against Runcorn. Unfortunately, the game was lost 15 points to 4. At this time a team consisted of 15 players and they were all local men.

An early photograph of Widnes Football Club

---

[114] Information kindly given to me by Tom Fleet from his *"History of Widnes Rugby League Football Club"* (unpublished)

295

Into The Crucible

Communities in all districts of the town usually had a number of social groups and activities affiliated to their local churches. These included brass bands, temperance leagues, football clubs and athletic clubs. As we know, generally, the Newtown district was largely populated by Irish Catholic residents who belonged to the parish *of St. Mary (St. Marie`s)*. This parish had several groups which provided recreational interests for the young men of the district. These included *St. Marie`s Brass Band* and the *Young Men`s Catholic Society*. In addition *St. Mary's (Marie's) Football Club* was formed in the parish sometime around 1885. However, as might be expected in an area as densely populated as Newtown, there was more than one football team in the district. Another team known as *The Newtown Wanderers* also had a large following.

Perhaps it is not too surprising, in view of the overwhelming ethnic composition of the district, that these Newtown clubs had adopted a strong Irish ethos; although it was said by both clubs that anyone of any nationality or religion would be welcome to play. Despite this friendly statement, in 1889 some people claimed that the Committee of *St. Mary's Football Club* were racially discriminating against English players. In spite of claiming to be welcoming to anyone who had a genuine interest in playing football, there were some who said that the club discouraged English men from joining. The club's Committee strongly disputed this and pointed out that two of their leading players, Burgess and Wailing, were "English". Amid the controversy, the Secretary of the Club was forced to issue a statement saying that *"it matters not what nationality a man is, if he wishes to become a member of St. Mary's F.C. he can do so simply by paying his entrance fee. I also state that it is false to say that anyone was refused to be admitted as a member because he was an Englishman"*.

Among the players who appeared for *St. Mary`s Football Club* that season were: Farrell; Donohue; Kelly; Brennan; Whelan; McGarry; Manning; Connolly; Daley; Mannion; Burke; Hughes; Rushton; Broome; Wailing; Burgess; Gordon; Coutts and Hartles. We can see that there was a predominance of Irish names on the list but this was natural as the majority of residents in that area were Irish. Although it is clear that most of the players had Irish origins we can also see that there were a number who did not. Therefore I would think that accusations of discrimination were tenuous. As an additional point of interest

Everyday Life

concerning *St. Mary's Football Club,* the Chairman of the club at this time was Dan Garghan. Dan Garghan was a bold and courageous man who holds a noteworthy place in the history of Widnes. In later life he was the Mayor of our town but some years earlier he was involved in a major dispute which received national interest and put our town to shame.[115]

As with all sports, each era has its own heroes. During the late 1890s the name of Dan Brennan would have been familiar among Widnes football fans as he was the captain of *Widnes Football Club* for several seasons. In a rare interview from 1899 we are given a potted biography of the man and his football career.

AN INTERVIEW WITH DAN BRENNAN OF WIDNES FOOTBALL CLUB

A Manchester contemporary remarks: Dan Brennan has long been a popular favourite among the football enthusiasts of the sweet-smelling town on the Mersey, and has been an important factor in the rise of Widnes from a second or third rate club to the front rank of Northern Union organisations, having been captain of the club for the past three seasons, and also for a similar period earlier on. He is the most modest and unassuming of men, but this week an interviewer succeeded in eliciting from him some interesting reminiscences of his football career.

Born in Widnes on June 21st 1869, Brennan is now in his 30th year. As a lad he displayed considerable prowess at the game, and when about 15 years of age he won local fame as a smart halfback for Simms Cross Amateurs, and afterwards for Newtown Wanderers. Shortly afterwards Widnes St. Mary's – a one time flourishing junior club, was started and Brennan took the position of full back. While playing with St. Mary's, Brennan gained a reputation as a reliable full back, and he played in the match at Wigan for West Lancashire against South East Lancashire. He was also asked to play for St. Helens towards the close of the season 1888-9 and his play in that team against Widnes on the Saints' ground riveted the attention of the Widnes Committee, who at once invited him to enter the town's club; and in March 1889, he made his debut in the Widnes ranks against the Maoris, who were then touring in this country.

---

[115] See *"Where Spring Never Came"* (Jean M. Morris - 2007)

Into The Crucible

In 1890 he was appointed sub-captain of the first team, the captaincy being held by that veteran forward J.H .Smith, the present President of the Lancashire section of the Northern Union. In the following season he was appointed captain, and retained that office for three years. Then a change was made but three years later Brennan was again put in command of the team, and he still stands on the roll as captain. This season, however, owing to a severe attack of typhoid fever in the autumn, by which he was laid up for three months, he has not been able to follow the game much, and when he did turn out he was not in good condition. Therefore he was quickly placed hors de combat in the rough handling he received in the match with Wigan on February 11th, when his ribs were injured giving rise to an attack of bronchitis from which he has only recently recovered.

Under these circumstances, a week ago he sent in his resignation as captain, but placed himself at the disposal of the Committee if his services were required as a player. It is probable, therefore, that this season will be his last, and it is fitting that his sterling services to Widnes football should now be placed on record and appreciated at their full value. Brennan is the true type of a sportsman. He plays for the love of the game, and his ambition has always been to enhance the honour of his native town in the football world. Under his command the Widnes team in the present and past seasons have won a distinguished place in Northern Union circles[116].

We are told that Dan Brennan was unmarried at this time and living in Ann Street. He was also a talented musician who played the euphonium in *St. Marie's Brass Band*. On consulting the record of his baptism at St. Marie's Church, I discovered that Dan Brennan was in fact older than stated in this article. He was born on 21st June 1867, the son of Daniel and Anna Brennan (nee Moran).

Two matches against the touring Maori team were held at Widnes in 1889. Dan Brennan made his debut for Widnes in the second of the two visits of the Maoris to the town. *The Weekly News* said that:

"The Maori team were so inspired by the cordial friendship and welcome they received here that they felt a strong desire to return to the chemical metropolis before they left England for their native land".

---

[116] *Widnes Weekly News* – March 25th 1899

Everyday Life

Unfortunately the Widnes team lost the game, the score being one goal and three tries for the visitors, and one try and two minors for the home team. The Widnes team members on that occasion were:

Hartles, back; Barker, Parkinson and Brennan, three-quarters; Farrell (captain) and Howard, half-backs; J.H. Smith, Hughes, Partridge, Hardman, Gandy, Williams, Hewitt, Kiddie and Gordon, forwards. Umpire Mr. A. Hufton; Referee, Mr. F.T. Parry, secretary of the West Lancashire Union.

After the match the teams sat down to a "knife and fork tea" at the Railway Hotel. Later that evening a Ball was held in the Baths Assembly Room in honour of the Maoris. The dancing commenced shortly before eleven o'clock and went on until half-past four the next morning. There were about 100 persons present, although only four or five of the Maori team had remained as they had to leave Manchester at 10 o'clock the following morning for London.

In the mid-1880s Tom Wright opened a gymnasium and boxing club behind a pub in Wellington Street. The members were issued with a cotton singlet which bore the motto of the club *"Nemo me Impune Lacessit"* (no one strikes me with impunity). Boxing was a popular sport, although bouts did not always conform to Marquis of Queensbury rules. In 1885 the famous bare-knuckle fight between Wailing and Donnelly drew large crowds at Cuerdley Marsh; the purse for the fight was the enormous sum of £10. This did not appear to have been an even match as Wailing weighed 14 stone while Donnelly was barely 12 stone! The match went five rounds with Wailing the victor. On another occasion two men, Patrick Kennedy and Edward Merrigan, were charged with breach of the peace when a fight was broken up by a Police Constable. The men claimed they were just *"amusing themselves – fighting for fun"*. The case against them was proved and they were both sent to jail for one month. This form of entertainment, although illegal, had been going on since the early years. In May 1869 a particularly brutal and gruelling match took place on the outskirts of Bold Heath. A report of the event gives the following details:

"On Saturday morning last a disgraceful and brutal prize fight for £10 took place near to St. Helens between Michael Brannan and John Burns of Widnes. The fight had been arranged for some time previously, and was to

have taken place in Widnes, but was prevented by the vigilance of the police from coming off in that district. It took place near to the borough of St. Helens and lasted over two hours during which time some 60 rounds were fought. Both men were severely punished, but Burns had much the worst of it. He fought until he was unable to stand and had to be carried away, after his backers had thrown up the sponge, to a public house in the neighbourhood."

In 1885, six men appeared before the Magistrate charged with prize fighting in a field at Crow Wood. The fight was broken up by the police at 3 o'clock in the afternoon. The policeman involved described the scene:

"William O`Connor and William Kelly were fighting together in a field where a regular ring had been formed. Thomas Kelly was picking his brother up as he had been knocked down. Peter McCabe was standing watching and inciting them. There was a crowd of about fifty persons assembled. The men fought between 8 and 9 rounds. The onlookers were making a noise and encouraging the principals. There was some money staked. The men were fighting without their shirts and there were seconders for the principals, and there was a bottle and a sponge. One man had said there was going to be some kicking "Lancashire fashion" and a lot of men shouted to the principals not to engage in that".

Apart from "local" prize fighting, the male residents of Widnes also had an interest in events further afield. In July 1889 the local press reported on a marathon fight held in America between John L. Sullivan and Jake Kilrain. *The Widnes Weekly News* gave a detailed account of the "fight" which lasted two hours and eighteen minutes and went to 72 rounds at which point Kilrain, after having taken a heavy beating, threw in the towel.

In November 1889 a buzz of excitement spread through the town as word circulated that *"The Hero of Runcorn Bridge"* would once again perform his amazing feat. 23year old Tommy Burns was the son of Irish parents. He had been born in Liverpool but spent most of his life in Widnes where he attended St. Bede` School. The family lived in Midwood Street and his father was employed as a baker with Mr. Wolsencroft in Newtown. The following is a report of the event. It

Everyday Life

supplies not only a graphic description but also gives us a flavour of the thrilling atmosphere of the occasion.

"Last Friday night considerable interest was aroused in Widnes and Runcorn by the statement that Tommy Burns would dive off Runcorn Bridge at noon on Saturday. This was to be done, according to the announcement, to convince Mr. McHugh, vice president of the Sefton Swimming Association, that the previous jump was accomplished. There were thousands of incredulous people beside Mr. McHugh, but Burns thoroughly convinced them as to the dive on Saturday. Long before noon people began to assemble on either side of the river, anxious to catch a view of the daring diver, but as the time wore on, and no Tommy appeared, the cynically disposed began to button-hole their friends and say that the whole affair was "another sell". Just about noon however, the hopes of the crowd were raised by the appearance of a small gig, manned by four men, coming up the river, and flying a light blue broad pennant, which, it transpires, is Burns` favourite colour. The crew of the gig came on shore and proceeded to The Mersey Hotel, stating as they went that the dive would be made at one o'clock. It was twenty minutes to eleven when Burns reached the Hotel accompanied by his trainer, Professor Boston. He there put on a diving suit, and afterwards blackened his face, and donned some old clothes, to give him the appearance of a coal-heaver. He also placed a hump on his shoulders, under his overcoat, and if there had been any opposition to the feat the officials would have been rather more cute than usual to detect the "champion all-round athlete" in the dirty and ugly looking vagabond who followed Mr. S.H. Kenrick on the bridge. At this time there was a large crowd on either side of the river, and also on the bridge, and at the very lowest computation the feat was witnessed by three thousand people. The tide was at the full 1-5, and it was so far in the diver's favour that it was the highest evening tide of the month, the water rising 24 feet 2 inches. There was now a lull in the passing vessels, and the gig, accompanied by four other small boats, put out to prepare for the dive. Meanwhile Burns arrived on the bridge, without meeting the slightest opposition. He at once took off his boots and overcoat, and climbing over the iron rails of the footpath, on the span nearest Widnes, he gazed for a second at the rolling flood, 75 feet below, and then, exactly at 12.59, made a splendid dive. Every eye was strained and for a second the crowd held its breath in terrified anticipation, but it was only for a second. Burns divided the water with his extended arms, and, according to his own statement, he only sank four or five feet. He could not have sunk much more, for it only appeared a second before his

Into The Crucible

head reappeared above the water, and then the crowd gave vent to a tremendous burst of applause. While under the water Burns had divested himself of the clothes he wore as a disguise, and then proceeded to give a short exhibition of ornamental swimming, after which he climbed into the boat and was rowed ashore. He made the best of his way through an enthusiastic and cheering crowd to the Mersey Hotel, where he was at once placed in the bath by his trainer and after fifteen minutes ablutions he dressed, apparently none the worse for his dive. Subsequently, Burns and several friends were entertained to dinner by Mr. Herriman, and in the afternoon Tommy witnessed the football match between Widnes and St. Helens."[117]

The truly amazing Tommy Burns was to delight the crowds again the following year when he faced Carlisle D. Graham, an American, in a remarkable contest. The pair dived off Runcorn Bridge into the river, swam ashore then ran 136 laps around the bowling green at The Snig (Mersey Hotel). The distance run equated to ten miles. Burns, winning the contest, made a time of 83 minutes and received £25. Apart from these daring feats, Tommy Burns performed numerous other audacious deeds which included jumping from The Clifton Suspension Bridge and the Forth Bridge. He also jumped from a moving train into the docks at Liverpool and on another occasion he leaped from a train as it was crossing the Thames. A report of some of his amazing feats appeared in a London newspaper and included the following text:

"Dived off Vauxhall Bridge and then ran to Brighton, dived off West Pier and ran back to London in nineteen hours and four minutes, in January 1896. Dived off Lambeth, Vauxhall and Chelsea Bridges inside twenty minutes and then ran to Epsom Town Hall inside two hours on Derby Day 1896. Dived off London Bridge and ran to Yarmouth, dived off the pier and ran back to London a distance of two hundred and sixty miles in forty-six hours and fifty-nine minutes, in September 1896. There are many other daring athletic feats, which space compels us to eliminate."

Unfortunately the intrepid Tommy lost his life performing a diving feat in Rhyl in July 1897. He was just 29 years old and was penniless when he died.[118]

---

[117] *Ibid – November 9th 1889*
[118] *"Across The Gap"* – Jean M. Morris (Springfield-Farrihy – 2016)

Everyday Life

THE DEATH OF TOMMY BURNS.

ARRIVAL OF REMAINS IN LIVERPOOL.

Immediately after the inquest it was publicly stated at Rhyl that the wife of the late diver Tommy Burns was absolutely penniless, and that she was unable to remove the body without assistance. Mr. Tom Wood and Mr. F. Geary, of the pier, at once opened a subscription list, and collected £3 18s., the balance of which, after paying the charge for conveying the corpse to Liverpool, was handed to the widow. The pier proprietors provided an oak brass-mounted coffin, which was made by Mr. H. T. Roberts, who took charge of the funeral arrangements. Yesterday the remains were carried by Mr. T. Wood and the members of his minstrel troupe from the pier to the railway station, the widow and a lady friend being the only mourners. The corpse was placed in a special coach, and left Rhyl by the 8 45 train. There was a large number of people in attendance at the railway station, and every mark of respect was shown. The widow stated that, according to present arrangements, the deceased will be buried on Saturday, at four o'clock, at West Derby Cemetery. The widow is absolutely unprovided for. The train bearing the coffin arrived at Lime-street Station at ten o'clock, and the remains were conveyed in a hearse to the deceased's late residence in Farnworth-street. Only the undertaker's people seemed aware of the event, and there were few spectators beyond the mourners.

The Death of Tommy Burns "Hero of The Runcorn Bridge"

The name Tom Burns appears again in 1903, however this is not a reference to *"The Hero of the Runcorn Bridge"*. This was another Widnes person of the same name who achieved an astonishing degree of success in the boxing ring. This Tom Burns fought and beat several impressive opponents and, when his own career in the boxing-ring ended, he became a very successful trainer. Despite his fearsome reputation in the boxing world, outside the ring he was known to be a very modest and mild-mannered man. An interview which is included here gives a little more detail of the man and his entry into the world of boxing.

INTERVIEW WITH A NOTED WIDNES BOXER

Ever since Widnes began to boom as a manufacturing town its inhabitants have always been true lovers of sport of all kinds, and many famous athletes have sprung from its midst. For some time the centre of attraction has been a young fellow named Tom Burns who has achieved great fame as a light-weight boxer. In fact, he may be regarded as the light-weight champion of England, and at the present time he is open to meet anyone at 8st.8 lbs.

Burns is a very unassuming young fellow, and like many personages who are well up in their profession, he has a great aversion to talking about himself. He is 22years of age and has lived in Widnes since he was a child. He is a staunch teetotaller and non-smoker. Although Burns has attained a high position in this particular line of sport, he has not a great liking for such a calling, and if it were not that he is heart and soul in the art of boxing he would sever his connection with it.

It was purely through unforeseen circumstances that Burns became a boxer. Some years ago when the United Alkali Company used the Baths as a recreation club Burns attended one night more as a spectator than anything else and during the evening he was induced to put on the gloves with a young fellow who had gone in for boxing. At that time a man called Phythian was the instructor, and on being told that this was the first time that Burns had had on the gloves he was quite taken up with the way he shaped, and expressed the wish that he would like to have Burns for a pupil. Under Phythian`s instruction he progressed very rapidly, and for two seasons he won the local competition. He later boxed opponents from other areas and each time he gained first honours. It is very likely that in the near future Burns will be matched to meet George Justice of New York who is at present residing in Newcastle."

Everyday Life

Tommy Burns (standing) in his later role as a Trainer.
The surname of the young boxer was Pheysey.

Into The Crucible

In January 1899 some Widnesians made a special trip across the river to our sister town to see the *"Son of Buffalo Bill"* perform at Novello's Hope Hall. Young Cody, who claimed to be the son of Colonel Cody, aka *"Buffalo Bill"*, was giving an exhibition of rifle shooting and lassoing. He was assisted in the performance by his sister Madame Rosselle. During one part of the act Madame Rosselle held an object on her forehead and Young Cody aimed with his rifle. Just as he pulled the trigger the lady slipped and the bullet entered the side of her forehead. She was immediately taken in a cab to the surgery of a local doctor. Her injuries were not life threatening, although she had an ugly wound that bled profusely. A local report of the incident ended with the words *"She was not able to resume the rifle-shooting performance"*.

The Circus arrives in Town – Sanger's Circus, Waterloo Road, 1903

The usual places of entertainment were often forsaken during the first week of May each year when the "Fair and Circus" came to town. A regular and popular visitor to Widnes was Sanger's Circus. This travelling show offered the workers of Widnes and their families something out of the ordinary. Like most touring entertainment companies the Circus stuck to a regular calendar and usually visited towns on their circuit around the same time each year. Their

Everyday Life

weeklong engagement in Widnes generally came after their visit to Knutsford. The theatrical publication *"The Era"* made the following observation in 1893:

> *"From rural Knutsford to manufacturing Widnes is not very far as the crow flies, but oh! the difference! Not a scrap of green verdure whereon to rest the eyes, the very air we breathe redolent of the chemical works, soap works and the kindred trades which make Widnes the murkiest town in the Liverpool district. Yet even at Widnes the people gather in crowds to keep May Day. To amuse them at the fair were Lord J. Sanger's Circus and Hippodrome; Sedgwick's wild beast show; Chippendale's living pictures and menagerie; Walsall's living novelties; Marcus, the lion-pawed man; George Payne's Storm at Sea; Wilden's living curiosities; and the penny novelties of Messrs. Yates, Hales and Butterworth. T. Gledhill's steam horses; Green's tunnel railway and Montgomery's horses were the machine novelties."*

Illegal gambling games of "pitch and toss" drew large crowds of men. One game in January 1899 finished in a less than sporting manner. A Sunday afternoon session at West Bank Dock ended up in a fight over the betting money. Punches were thrown and a number of people were called upon to appear in court. One man summoned two others for assault and they, in turn, summoned him. A number of witnesses were called and all those involved were heavily fined. A local headline was *"Sunday Gambling and its results"*. Though illegal, gambling games of this type took place regularly in various locations around the West Bank and Newtown districts. They usually took place on weekend afternoons and always involved large groups of men. As the police were always alert to the likelihood of games occurring in certain places, the gamblers usually posted a "look-out" to warn them of approaching danger.

Billiards, which in earlier times was a pastime enjoyed by the more affluent, had by the late 19th century become a popular sport among the working classes. In February 1899 a match took place at St. Mary's Catholic Club between the Club members and a team from The Sacred Heart Club from St. Helens. The members of the local St. Mary's team on that occasion were: *J. Leonard, S. Quinn, M. Flanagan senior, R. Whitty, J. Carroll, W. Murphy, M. Murphy, H. Fitzgerald, J. Smith, J. Ryder, and M. Flanagan.* Unfortunately the home team were well beaten The

Into The Crucible

popularity of this game went from strength to strength and there were several teams in the town. In later years after the Drill Hall, scene of so many great occasions, both political and social, was made redundant[119] the building became home to a Billiard Hall known as *"The Black Cat"*.*

Sport and entertainment was put aside in May 1898 when the death of Mr. William Gladstone was announced. The Mayor, Alderman Wareing, asked all the inhabitants of the Borough to show their respect to the memory of Mr. Gladstone by lowering the blinds of their houses, or by demonstrating their sympathy in other ways at the time of the funeral. A memorial service was held at St. Paul's to coincide with the timing of the funeral. The Mayor invited members of public bodies to join him at the Town Hall at 2.30 p.m. in order to accompany him across the Square to the church.

Despite the fact that many had been persuaded by Charles Stewart Parnell to desert the Liberals in the election of 1885, the Irish population in Widnes received the news of Gladstone's death with genuine sadness. In many Irish homes he was a hero and his photograph was often displayed on walls along with that of Parnell. Most Irish were Liberal because of that Party's support for Home Rule. However, it was noticeable that after Gladstone's retirement the Liberal's strategy on Ireland diminished, and by the early 1900s the Liberal Party's policy on Ireland was not unlike that of the Conservatives. As a result of this, the emergence of the Independent Labour Party in Widnes, in the early years of the 20th century, attracted many Irish who had become disenchanted with the Liberals.

Because of their large numbers, the Irish vote was very important in the town and the Nationalists were well represented on the Town Council. In July 1893 a vacancy occurred in the Victoria Ward due to the sitting councillor being declared a bankrupt. The candidates up for election were Mr. Hugh O'Donnell, (Nationalist) a baker and grocer from Widnes Road; and Mr. Charles Hemingway (Independent) a builder from Church Street. Mr. O` Donnell was nominated by the Rev. James Clarke and Mr. Hemingway was nominated by Mr. James Chapman. Dr. O` Keeffe was the agent for Mr. O` Donnell and Mr. Hemingway was represented by J. K. Hughes. A crowd of around 500

---

[119] Following the building of The Barracks in Peelhouse Lane.
* *In 1912*

Everyday Life

assembled outside the Town Hall at nine o'clock on the night of the election, to hear the result. Mr. O`Donnell won by a majority of 62. After the customary vote of thanks to the returning officer, Mr. O`Donnell said that *"the contest had been a fight between English and Irish and the Irish had won"*.

The provision of a new Municipal Cemetery in 1898, to provide burial space for all denominations, was enabled by the Corporation's purchase of the Moss Brook estate. Subsequently a section of the estate was laid out for that specific purpose. Prior to that date all burials had taken place in the three churchyards in the town. By 1898 the accommodation in these churchyards had almost been exhausted and two of the graveyards were due to be closed. It was decided that it was *"better to provide a cemetery away from town rather than to extend the burial grounds in the town"*. In December the previous year there had been a rather unfortunate incident when a section of the wall of St. Bede's burial ground fell into Deacon Road, leaving a number of coffins and their contents exposed. The wall, which was partly composed of stone and rock, had been damaged by a period of exceptionally heavy rain over the previous few weeks.

Deacon Road Quarry and St. Bede`s Graveyard

Into The Crucible

The first interment in the new Municipal Cemetery took place on 3rd October 1898 and the officiating clergyman was the curate from St. Ambrose Church, the Rev. Mr. Thompson. The provision of a cemetery had been a significant undertaking because, in addition to planning, it had involved the construction of two chapels. To mark the completion of the cemetery chapels the Corporation and contractors gave those workers who had been involved in building them, a celebratory dinner at the Railway & Commercial Hotel. 56 men sat down to dinner that evening and among those present were the members of the newly formed Cemetery Committee. Of course in those days nothing was simple when religion was involved. Prior to the consecration of the chapels, the Cemetery Committee received a deputation at the Town Hall from the Non-conformist Free Church Council who raised objections regarding the consecration of the Church of England portion of the cemetery. The deputation included Councillor Owens, David Lewis and Mr. A.E. Calvert. They told the Committee that the purpose of their visit was to:

> "Respectfully, but strenuously, object to the consecration of the allotment of ground apportioned to the Church of England. If consecration was simply a religious rite, they as non-conformist ratepayers would have no objection, but they knew that the rite was a legal form as well as a religious one, carrying with it the freehold of the land and giving to a section of the Church that which every ratepayer had helped to pay for. Another consequence of consecration was that it conferred on the Bishop of the Diocese an authority that should be exercised by the Local Government. This cemetery too, having been provided under the Public Health (Interment Act 1879) also gives the Bishop the right of appointing a chaplain, the salary of whom must be approved by the Bishop and provided by the ratepayers. To prevent the inequality and invidious distinctions between the churches and great injustice to the heavily taxed ratepayers is the purpose of this deputation".

The General Purposes Committee of Widnes Council received a letter from the Commanding Officer of the 6th Lancashire Volunteer Artillery in March 1900. The Officer was enquiring whether, in the event of his deciding to apply to the War Office to move the Hale Battery to Widnes, the Corporation would be able to provide a suitable drill shed. He also requested that assistance be given in the formation of Volunteer Rifle Ranges by the acquisition of suitable sites. The finding of sites for

Everyday Life

various purposes was a priority at that time. The Council was also looking for a suitable site for the provision of an "Open-Air Baths" for the town. Land fronting Davies Street and Beaumont Street was identified as being the most suitable site available for this type of facility. Clearly, at some point in time this idea was abandoned as the "Open-Air Baths" failed to materialise.

In August 1900 the first meeting of the newly constituted *Lancashire Inebriates Board* was held in the County Hall in Preston. Various Acts of Parliament had been introduced to deal with habitual drunkenness throughout the country. This in itself indicates that Widnes was not unique and no worse than any other densely populated area at that time. "Inebriates Reformatories" were located around the country and the Board advised that *"These reformatories were working well and seemed to be serving their purpose admirably"*. A total of 22 authorities had contributed to the reformatory scheme. The Board created a sub-committee to select possible sites for a *Lancashire Inebriates Reformatory*. It was stated that the separate sites, one for men and another for women, should not be too close to each other but it was suggested, for economical purposes, that they should be only a few miles apart. It was also desirable that they be placed close to the centre of the County about ten or twelve miles from Preston.

When reading about alcoholic abuse in Victorian England, particularly in the new manufacturing towns where the problem was the greatest, it is easy to forget that many women were also habitual drunkards. The fact that sites for "Inebriates Reformatories for Women" were also being sought illustrates the level of this problem. In fact during this same period one Widnes woman appeared in court on charges of drunkenness and disorderly behaviour twelve times within the space of a month. In cases such as this *The Inebriates Act,* which was brought in during 1898, allowed magistrates to send inebriates to a licensed reformatory. If they had been convicted of drunkenness four times in a single year they could be held in a reformatory for up to three years. In 1905 the guidelines for magistrates said that to be classified as a "habitual drunkard" one had to be incapable of managing ones affairs when sober as well as drunk. The result of this was that most of the people being sent to "Inebriates Reformatories" after this date were classified as "mental defectives". With the introduction of the later

Into The Crucible

"Mental Deficiency Act" the function of some of these reformatories changed and they became certified institutions for "mental defectives".

It is impossible to look at Widnes during this period without the constant reminder of the frightful environment and lack of decent housing for the poorer sections of Widnes society. A letter to *The Widnes Weekly News* in June 1902 demonstrates that there *were* people with a social conscience who wished to see improvements in these conditions.

SQUALID COURTS OF WIDNES
To the editor,

Sir,
Our town is marred here and there by miserable looking streets and alleys, which are comparable with large blots of ink one sometimes sees in a scholar's writing book. Signs of filth and decay are on every hand and one wonders how a human being could comfortably exist in such gloomy quarters. Some homes are in the immediate vicinity of our great works, whose processes fill the adjoining streets with obnoxious odours, yet a certain class of people run their whole course of life amid these surroundings. Little children, barely clad, may be seen bounding along in their youthful sport, and from one year's end to another they breathe the foul atmosphere of a confined area bordered all around by tall, grim looking factory chimneys. In this particular instance, one reflects on the Waterloo Road district. Can we not place them in better houses, and try and improve their method of living? Can we not raise them to a higher standard of citizenship? One cannot expect a child living in such circumstances to develop into a healthy human being: their present mode of living tends to lower their physical scale of the human race! Of course Widnes is no exception to other towns, but we hope that our representatives in the municipal chamber, in the course of time, will clear away the filthy parts of the town. One does not expect to complete a change at once, but let us make just one step in that direction. Other towns are carefully and seriously considering the "Housing Question" and we hope that ere long Widnes will follow their example.

Signed : "Desideratum"
Widnes, 9th June 1902.

Everyday Life

Clearly the Corporation was acutely aware of the deficiencies surrounding housing and they did make great efforts to improve the sanitary and health provisions in the Borough. Although things did progress rather slowly there was a gradual but steady decrease in the death rate during the years 1906 to 1910. Further developments in healthcare occurred in November 1903 when the Mayoress, Mrs. W. Winwood Gossage,[120] established the *Widnes Queen's Nurses Association*. At the start there were just two nurses but by 1910 they had six nurses and two midwives and a Nurses Home had also been provided. At this time too, the town had a Medical Officer of Health, a Sanitary Inspector, an Accident Hospital and an Isolation Hospital at Crow Wood. The Isolation Hospital had a *"Branch small-pox hospital erected in a detached situation far from dwellings of any kind and kept for any emergency that may arise"*[*]

As early as April 1899 the subject of providing electricity was discussed. The Gas and Water Committee asked the Borough Engineer to obtain information as to the cost of providing an electrical installation suitable to the needs of the Borough. In April 1901 The Board of Trade granted the provisional order, which was called the *Widnes Electric Lighting Order 1901*. However, there was no real progress until early in 1903. By December 1903 three companies had made application for the right to supply electricity to the Borough. The Mersey Electric Supply Co. Ltd. was chosen but by the time the transfer was ready the company had gone into liquidation. After considerable delay, and numerous amendments to the provisional order, the Corporation entered into an agreement with Salt Union Limited. The Salt Union then formed a new company, which they called The Mersey Power Company. This company continued to supply Widnes with its electricity until the industry was nationalised decades later.

The new century brought with it changes in political ideas and philosophies. This produced support for new groups and many Irish electors deserted the Liberal Party in favour of the Labour Party and the Independent Labour Party. In January 1906 the newspapers were saying that the most remarkable feature of the General Election had

---

[120] Mrs. Winwood Gossage was a member of the Tate family who gave the Art Gallery of that name to the nation.
[*] David Lewis *"Widnes a Review and Forecast"* (T.S.Swale) 1911

Into The Crucible

been the phenomenal growth of the Labour Party. Daniel Garghan was among the founder members of the Independent Labour Party in Widnes. Their meetings, held in a room above a shop on the corner of Victoria Road and Eleanor Street, attracted many eminent speakers such as Sydney and Beatrice Webb, Thomas Mann, Mrs. Pankhurst and her daughter Sylvia, and also the enigmatic Victor Grayson who was to vanish, supposedly murdered, some years later.

Daniel Garghan went on to become a Town Councillor and, despite an unfortunate run-in with the police almost twenty years earlier, he became the Mayor of Widnes in 1925.[121] His brush with the law was connected to incidents which occurred in Victoria Square in 1906. These incidents, related to the banning of public meetings by the Independent Labour Party and the Salvation Army, started off as a minor protest but developed into a national "cause". The situation arose from what now appears to have been a rather childish and spiteful act by a member of the Town Council. It is believed that one of the Councillors resented the increasing support for The Independent Labour Party and attempted to curb their activities by banning their public meetings. He claimed that meetings in Victoria Square caused nuisance to worshippers at St. Paul's and disruption to traffic. Unfortunately this meant that if The Independent Labour Party was to be stopped then The Salvation Army could not be allowed to hold meetings either. To allow them to do so would have shown bias, therefore they became innocent victims of this vendetta. It was a silly situation which spiralled out of control. The police, who attended in unnecessarily large numbers, were heavy handed with the protesters and a substantial number of people were arrested and fined for obstruction. Some people refused to pay the fines and were sent to prison; among those imprisoned were Dan Garghan and several other local men including Patrick Hooligan and Peter McCarthy.

The Salvation Army had been holding Sunday evening meetings in the Square for a long time, in fact for well over twenty years! As this was the recognised venue for public gatherings, The Independent Labour Party also applied to the Council for permission to hold meetings in the Square and approval was subsequently given.

---

[121] Daniel Garghan was Mayor when King George V visited the town briefly on his way to Cheshire on 8th July 1925.

Everyday Life

However, despite having received official permission, shortly afterwards the police decided that both these meetings were illegal. As stated earlier, The Salvation Army had been meeting in Victoria Square for almost twenty years without the slightest problem or opposition. Their meetings were well conducted and peaceful, indeed The Salvation Army services were typical joyful *"happy-clappy"* events and certainly not a danger to public order. Nevertheless, the police arrived in force and attempted to close down their meetings as well as the meetings of The Independent Labour Party. A number of arrests were made and the situation escalated. Needless to say, that even those who were not politically inclined were incensed by the conduct of the police towards The Salvation Army.

When the first meeting was broken up, the indignant members of both The Salvation Army and The Independent Labour Party vowed to fight the decision. It seemed inconceivable, particular to a kind and laid-back religious group, that anyone could suddenly raise an objection to something that had been happening unchallenged for years. As a consequence, the following weeks saw more and more people turning up to encourage them, some even travelling great distances to show their support. In response, the police presence was strengthened and each Sunday there were more arrests and dozens of people were fined for simply being in the crowd. Henry Ackerley of Bold, a well-known member of the Independent Labour Party, was summoned for having obstructed the highway in Victoria Square. In fact Mr. Ackerley emphatically denied having been in the crowd on the afternoon in question. He said he did not attend the meeting in the Square that day because of a resolution having been passed to the effect that those members who had already been fined should not take part in subsequent demonstrations. Furthermore, he declared that he was a law-abiding man and he did not wish to do anything illegal. Evidence in support of Mr. Ackerley`s statement was given by Daniel Garghan, Leonard Boyle, Stephen Boden and Thomas Wood. The Bench said they were more inclined to believe the police than these witnesses. Henry Ackerley was fined one shilling and costs.

Into The Crucible

The Lamp, Victoria Square

Daniel Garghan had defiantly attended most meetings and was fined a number of times. He was a man of strong principles who steadfastly refused to accept a ban on what he believed was a matter of "free speech". In a further act of protest he made an application to the Mayor, Alderman Quinn, and Alderman Major W. J. Wareing for a commitment order against himself, in respect of fines inflicted upon him. He stated that he desired either to be committed to prison or to be exonerated. He was adamant that he would rather go to prison than pay the fines. A number of reporters from various newspapers also had their names taken and were fined. *The Liverpool Daily Post* wrote an article describing one of the events in Victoria Square. I include extracts from that article:

"The representatives of the local branch of the Independent Labour Party are still bent on contesting the rights of the police to move them from obstructing Victoria Square near the big lamp. They congregated on Saturday evening when a goodly number assembled. Mr. Millar, who took the chair, complained of the action of the police of arresting three of their party at the unearthly hour of three in the morning. The police had gone at that hour and taken out of his bed an old man of sixty years and taken him

Everyday Life

to the lock-up because he had not paid his fines. It was a scandalous thing to do, and their action has been condemned by all right-thinking people. If such things were done in Russia they did not want them done in Widnes. The battle was not waning. In certain quarters it was said that the first round would finish the Labour Party, but he was glad to say it was not so. It was a fight to the finish, and the working men must win. They had offers of financial aid from all over the country. The fight did not concern Widnes alone, but the whole of civilised England and, in the future, Widnes would be noted for the strong stand it made for liberty of speech."

The article went on to say that the guest speaker was the Rev. W. Schofield Battersby, known as the Workingman's Parson, whose arrival was greeted by cheers. The Rev. Gentleman spoke at length about the action of the police at previous meetings and of the support for the Widnes Independent Labour Party from all over England. The report continued thus:

"The remainder of his speech was confined to socialistic principles. In conclusion, he said that these prosecutions were the matches that were going to set fire to the whole of England in the cause of liberty and free speech. What was socialism? Instead of being brothers in England, they were all living like cats and dogs and in hatred of one another. The socialists had the knowledge that they were members of one family, and that workingmen ought to have their share of the pleasures of the world."

The newspaper outlined the rest of the speech and continued with a summary of the proposed actions of the Independent Labour Party. Interestingly, the report gives credence to Mr. Ackerley's claims:

"The present policy of the Widnes branch of the Independent Labour Party is to import speakers and chairman, and the local members to absent themselves from the meetings in order to avoid the accumulation of summonses. They also made a decision to hold meetings in other places besides Victoria Square and an overflow meeting was held simultaneously with the other, on some waste land adjoining the London and North Western Railway Station. This other meeting was addressed by Alexander Despres, Liverpool, who will appear at next Thursday's sessions upon charges of obstruction and inciting to a breach of the peace on the 8th inst"[122]

---

[122] *Liverpool Daily Post* - July 1906

Into The Crucible

That meeting had been a lively one. The arrival of the police on the scene was greeted with the singing of an anthem which had been composed by a member of the Boyle family, to the tune of "The Red Flag" – the words of this anthem were distributed and sung at all subsequent meetings and became known as *"The Widnes Whisper"*. The song was further popularised by being printed in national as well as local newspapers.

> *Some men have tried to crush this band*
> *But still through all the more we stand*
> *They've tried to move us from the Square*
> *But we mean to hold our meetings there.*
> *Then, come join hands in this great fight,*
> *We must be free, our cause is right*
> *These people we must never fear,*
> *But keep the Red Flag flying here.*

A large number of people were charged with causing an obstruction. Amongst them were James Boyle, an elected member of the Council, and other members of his family who lived in Waterloo Road. A number of Salvationists were also charged, including Catherine Martin and Thomas Crawford. The Salvation Army, like The Independent Labour Party, had a huge number of supporters who travelled from outside the area to swell the numbers and to lend their support to the principles of free speech.

Amongst the personalities who arrived in Widnes to join the stand for "Free Speech" was the MP for Newton, Mr. J.A. Seddon, who later raised a question in the House of Commons regarding the actions of the Widnes Police. Although because of his status he was immune from arrest, on his arrival in the town Mr. Seddon had immediately been cautioned by the Widnes Police. The cause was further enhanced by the appearance of the renowned suffragettes Christabel Pankhurst and Annie Kenny, who joined the speakers in Victoria Square one Sunday evening in August. On that occasion the Independent Labour Party councillor, James Boyle, handed the meeting over to his wife, Mrs. Boyle, who was making her "maiden speech". Mrs Boyle apparently

Everyday Life

spoke with great eloquence and was given a rousing reception. Miss Pankhurst, who spoke after her, made the following comments:

"You have just seen a living example of what women can do. Which of the men present could have made a better first speech than Mrs. Boyle has done? Mrs. Boyle is a working woman and has had no university education – men`s foolish laws denied her the right to educate herself – but, just as the working man is as good as the rest of the community, so is the working woman".

The famous suffragette, Annie Kenny, who had just endured six weeks imprisonment in Holloway Prison, told the crowd that she was more determined than ever she had been before. She said she was proud to stand alongside them in the cause of free speech and that "right" was on their side. She subsequently entertained the crowd with an account of her earlier arrest and incarceration saying:

"The working women of this country had sent a deputation to see Mr. Asquith, the Chancellor of the Exchequer. He had refused to see them, saying that the Chancellor of the Exchequer had no connection with the granting of the franchise to women. Then six of them went. Three got at the front door and three at the back, but the Chancellor of the Exchequer was afraid of six women and came out from his back door in a covered motor car. She had got six weeks for ringing the Chancellor's doorbell. All the time they were at the house Mrs Asquith and the maids were laughing at these working women from behind the blinds".

The appearance of such newsworthy people in Widnes served as useful propaganda for The Independent Labour Party. The Salvation Army also had huge support not only locally but also around the whole country. *The War Cry*, the Salvationists publication, sent special investigators to Widnes to look into the persecution of their co-religionists. Issue after issue of *The War Cry* were dedicated to the Widnes situation, and their nationwide meetings were dominated by the news of the shameful persecution of their comrades in Widnes. Their publication branded the local Police Superintendent, Superintendent Strickland, as *"one of the most notorious police officers in England"* and as *"the evil genius behind the scenes"*. At a meeting of the Salvation Army at their London Headquarters, The Regent Hall, it was agreed to ask the Home Secretary to take measures to preserve Victoria

Into The Crucible

Square in Widnes as a meeting place for their local members and other groups wishing to hold public meetings. Whilst supportive meetings of Salvationists were called all around the country, locally, the Salvationists held a mass meeting at a very packed Alexandra Theatre on Sunday 11th November, where they put forward a resolution that read:

> *"That this meeting of the inhabitants of Widnes protests against the Police prosecution of members of the Salvation Army, whereby innocent persons, seeking only the good of their fellows, are subjected to the indignity and cruelty of imprisonment.*
>
> *This meeting also declares its clear conviction that there is absolutely and emphatically no legitimate reason whatsoever for the prosecution, no private or public inconvenience ever having been experienced during the past 25 years from the Army's meetings in Victoria Square.*
>
> *This meeting therefore claims, in the interests of public liberty and not less of good government, that these prosecutions should cease, and appeals to those in authority to interpose to put an end to them.*
> *Further copies of this Resolution will be sent to the Home Secretary, the Chief Constable of the County, and the MP for the division".*

The Provincial Commander of the Salvation Army, Richard Wilson, corresponded at length with Councillor David Lewis asking him to intercede on their behalf. They approached David Lewis in his dual role as a Town Councillor and the President of the Widnes Free Church Council. Councillor Lewis was sympathetic and did the best he could, but to no avail. He was also canvassed by various other local religious organisations, imploring him to use his influence and good judgement. He received the following letter, dated 7th November 1906, from a man in Gladstone Street.

> *To D. Lewis, Esq.*
> *President of Widnes Free Church Council*
>
> *Dear Sir,*
> *At a meeting held on Tuesday the 6th inst. Of the Young Men's Mutual Improvement Society, Frederick Street Primitive Methodist Church, the*

following resolution was proposed and unanimously carried, also that a copy of same be sent to the President of the Widnes Free Church Council.

That this meeting is of the opinion that the incarceration in jail of members of the Salvation Army for "obstruction" is a disgrace to the town, and respectfully suggest that steps be at once taken to secure their release.

We therefore propose that a petition be forwarded to the highest authorities praying for the withdrawal of the sentences. This class pledges itself to render all the aid possible to secure this end.

Yours sincerely,
Charles Sage, Jr.,
Secretary

It is evident from this letter that The Salvationists had massive public support both here in the town and nationally. Local and national newspapers ran regular headline features. The situation intensified and as a consequence became completely out of control. On 13th November 1906, the Provisional Commander of the Salvation Army wrote to David Lewis informing him that local Salvationists, Catherine Martin, Thomas Crawford and Miss Kershaw had been released from jail, but warned that others were ready to take their place:

"Councillor Lewis,
Dear Sir,

I have information from Liverpool to the effect that the two officers and Miss Kershaw have been removed from Walton Jail.

So far as I can understand the position, a Birkenhead gentleman who has been following the case down, has not been able to sleep for 3 nights; he could not rest any longer, and went to Walton Jail to pay the fines for our Comrades. He is independent, and not at all connected with the Army. No doubt he has done this out of the kindness of his heart – but paying fines, we do not consider, will help the case. It is certain the Salvation Army will not pay any! While we have a measure of pleasure in knowing these Comrades are free – others will be committed and have to take their place. Those who go in the future, I expect will be going in for 7 days, and I do not think even

Into The Crucible

the kindness of friends will lead them to come to the decision that they will pay their fines.

I am arranging for the above named Comrades together with Mrs. Wynn and her little boy to go into our Southport Holiday Home, where they will remain until the 26th when I expect to bring them back to a large Welcome Meeting at the Drill Hall in Widnes.

Possibly by that time, other Comrades who have been convicted will have been in and out of prison again.

I go down to London today and shall be there till Friday. I hope to be down again in Widnes on Saturday, and thank you for all your interest and kindness.

Yours faithfully,
Richard W. Wilson
Provincial Commander"

Of course it was a ludicrous situation and one which had spiralled completely out of control. The Town Council had become a national laughing-stock and their actions were seen as petty and vindictive as the motive behind the ban was abundantly clear to everyone. Happily by the end of the year the matter was eventually resolved. The Town Council made the following ruling at "The General Purposes Committee" meeting on 20th December that year:

That all proceedings against the Salvation Army and others should be withdrawn.

That meetings would be allowed provided they are confined to the part of the Square near the lamp.
That meetings would be allowed provided they do not interfere with traffic or cause annoyance to the worshippers at St. Paul's Church.

The above decision might very well have been a direct result of a letter sent to the Council only three days before, on the 17th December. This previously unpublished letter, which I include here, was from the Under Secretary of State. It looks to me very much like a rap on the knuckles.

Everyday Life

Whitehall,
17th December 1906

Sir,

I am directed by the Secretary of State to say for the information of the Town Council, that his attention has been drawn by questions in Parliament and otherwise to the proceedings in connection with meetings held in Victoria Square, Widnes, and that, although questions of street obstruction and of Police action with respect to it do not strictly come within his jurisdiction, but belong to the Local Authorities, in this case the Town Council and the County Police authority, he is much concerned on account of the numerous cases in which members of the Salvation Army and others have been arrested for obstruction, and in default of payment of fines have been committed to prison to undergo sentences of imprisonment. He would be very glad if some arrangement could be suggested which would render these criminal proceedings unnecessary; but, before he can take any step, it is essential he should be fully informed of the views of the Town Council, and particularly of the reasons which, in their opinion, render it necessary that the small meetings hitherto held in the Square should now be prohibited as obstructing the traffic. He will therefore be glad if you will bring this matter before the Town Council and move them to favour him with a full statement of their views at their earliest convenience.

Should the Council prefer to discuss the matter in conversation, Mr. Gladstone would be happy to make arrangements for anyone who may be deputed by the Town Council as able to speak fully on its behalf to have an interview with the officials of the Home Office.

I am Sir,
Your Obedient Servant,
C.E. TROUP

Obviously the situation was preposterous and the Town Council could not justify their decision, especially as the above letter asked why *"small meetings hitherto held in the Square should now be prohibited as obstructing the traffic"*. The fact was the ban on The Salvation Army had fuelled outrage all around the country and the protests that followed had left The Council with egg on its face.

George E. Diggle in his *"History of Widnes"* said that the whole sorry saga began with the wish of a prominent Tory in the town to curb the activities of the Independent Labour Party. Of course, this was also the generally held view among the townspeople. This assumption is given some credence as it appears that in April 1906 "The Market and Baths sub-Committee" were happy to grant permission to the Salvation Army to hold meetings on the westward side of the Town Hall. On 18th July, Thomas Woods, Acting Secretary for the Independent Labour Party had also made application for permission to hold open air meetings nearby. The Committee, which consisted of Councillors Clarke, Hemingway, Wood and Peters, agreed to permit this as long as the meetings were conducted in an orderly and lawful manner. The fact that only a week or so later the committee changed their mind makes one think that there was indeed interference from some internal quarter.

Ultimately, and despite attempts to restrict their activities, the Independent Labour Party thrived in the town. Their growth was due mainly to the change of allegiance of the Irish electorate from the Liberal Party. The Independent Labour Party eventually affiliated itself to the Widnes Trades Council and this was later absorbed into the Labour Party. I would like to add a further anecdote relating to the Victoria Square Incidents and Dan Garghan. In 1925 when King George V briefly visited Widnes, Dan Garghan, as Mayor, was responsible for welcoming him to the town. Unfortunately the King was delayed and arrived much later than expected. When the King apologised for keeping the Mayor waiting, Dan Garghan amiably replied *"It is not the first time I have been detained at Your Majesty's Pleasure"*. No doubt this was a reference to the 7 days he spent in Walton Gaol for his part in The Victoria Square incidents.

As a new century progressed, the immigrant and the rest of the Widnes population saw the town change rapidly. Theatres and Picture Houses, Skating Rinks, Cycling, Football, Cricket and Athletics were all providing a release from the demands of factory work. The coming of the bus service[123] and improved railway links, as well as the now popular bicycle, gave them opportunities to travel further afield. Their leisure hours were now being spent in new and exciting ways. In May

---

[123] The first "covered" double-decker buses in Britain came into operation in Widnes.

Everyday Life

1903 the American "Wild West" showman, *"Buffalo Bill"*, brought his famously colourful show to Liverpool and many travelled from Widnes to enjoy this spectacular event. Among the stars touring with this legendary show was the St. Helens man, Tom Colquitt, from Fingerpost. Colquitt was billed as the *"Human Kangaroo"* because of his remarkable acrobatic feats.

Daniel Garghan

Into The Crucible

In 1910 the members of the Anglican Church in West Bank saw the building of a new and impressive St. Mary's Church, which was a replacement for the previous building which had developed structural problems. Like many of the early buildings in that area the first church, which was built at Widnes Dock in 1858, was erected on a levelled alkali waste tip. Regrettably by 1901 the foundations of this church were crumbling and the building was considered to be unstable. A scheme to build a new church was initiated and donations poured in. The new church was estimated to have cost in the region of £16,500. It had walls of red sandstone and the roof was covered by Welsh slate tiles. At the official opening and consecration, on 12th November 1910, the Bishop of Liverpool, The Reverend Dr. Chavasse, declared that this was the most beautiful church he had ever consecrated.

Mr. Valentine with his plane in Widnes

In July 1911 the first aeroplane to be seen in the district made a forced landing in a field of corn near the Ball O` Ditton. James Valentine, the pilot, was engaged in an *"All England Air Race"* sponsored by *The Daily Mail*. Despite the lack of widespread communication systems, it seems that the Widnes bush telegraph of those times worked remarkably well. Within a relatively short space of time the whole of the township knew of the arrival of James Valentine and his flying machine. The police,

Everyday Life

who were hastily summoned by telephone, mounted a guard around the plane while James Valentine was entertained to supper by Mr. Kelly, of Upper House, on whose property he had landed. After what was probably a welcome meal and rest break, the aviator left Widnes by car to spend the night at his brother's home in Alderley Edge. He returned in the morning and resumed his flight, but not before signing dozens of autographs for the crowds who had gathered to see him off. The race was subsequently won by Lieutenant Conneau who was flying under the name Beaumont. Frenchman, Emile Vedrines, was second and James Valentine came in third.

The improved regional railway links increased the popularity of this mode of transport. Regardless of the fact that there had been a number of minor crashes, which resulted in some fatalities or passengers being injured, most people were undeterred. In November 1872 there was a bad collision at the Carter House Junction, near Moss Bank, which involved the Manchester to Liverpool and the Stockport to Liverpool trains. In that incident the engine driver was killed and a number of passengers hurt. Although such incidents must have had some effect on the confidence of local rail travellers, nevertheless, the railway was still the most popular and convenient form of transport. In view of this, and despite a number of other incidents which may have given rise to some feelings of unease, the local travelling public were completely unprepared for what was to happen in our area in September 1912. On this date a railway disaster of a magnitude previously unparalleled in South Lancashire occurred just beyond Ditton Junction. An express train, full of holidaymakers returning from North Wales, fouled the points when coming down the incline of Runcorn Viaduct into the Junction.

"...about forty yards from the bridge which carries the roadway over the line the engine left the tracks and after ploughing up the permanent way hurled itself against one of the brick buttresses of the bridge. The entire train propelled forward at a frightful speed, first caught the opposite buttress and then crashed forward into the centre platform."[124]

The newspapers gave extensive details of the horror in which 15 people were killed and 42 were injured, some seriously. The first

---

[124] *Widnes Weekly News* – 20th September 1912

Into The Crucible

reports gave eyewitness accounts with disturbingly graphic details of the crash scene. An appeal for assistance had been sent by telephone to all medical men and women in the area and local doctors and nurses speedily responded to the call. Clergymen from all denominations and Nuns from the Sisters of Charity Order also arrived at the scene. Along with these spiritual supporters, numerous ladies from charitable organisations arrived to provide practical help to the dying and injured. Hundreds of railway workers and labourers from the district worked with feverish energy to extricate the dead and dying, and the large waiting rooms on the two platforms were turned into an emergency medical centre and mortuary. Although people did what they could, unfortunately, rescue work was almost impossible as the railway coaches were smashed like matchwood and had burst into flames. One of the more horrific reports described how passengers had been slowly roasted to death.

Workers at the scene of Ditton Rail Crash

In the weeks following the disaster various theories were put forward as to the cause. Among them was the fact that most of the engine drivers were in the habit of speeding, to make up for lost time. The train, at the time of the crash, was doing upwards of 50 miles an hour when the speed should have been just 15. The Station Master at

Everyday Life

Ditton Junction claimed that he had thought of reporting the driver on previous occasions. The ensuing enquiry found the cause of the accident was human error. The driver, from Llandudno Junction, who also died in the crash, was held to be responsible.

Despite the dreadful sadness which hung over the district in the weeks following the crash, the Liberals of Widnes found time to divert their attention to an important local political event. The previously mentioned visit to the town of the Liberal MP, Mr. W.G.C. Gladstone, the grandson of the late Right Hon. W.E. Gladstone, caused great pleasure and excitement among the ranks. About a thousand people assembled at the Borough Hall for a Liberal Rally. Mr. Gladstone was given a rousing welcome that almost verged on adulation.

> *"A male voice choir in the balcony struck an inspirational note with renderings of such pieces as "Play the Man" and "Men of Harlech". The appearance of Mr. Gladstone was hailed with prolonged cheers, as accompanied by the leaders of the party in the division he took his seat on the platform, to which an oil painting of his distinguished grandfather was a noticeable background"*[125].

Of course large gatherings of people were not confined to political rallies or activities connected to protest. Events related to religious denominations often drew large crowds from the ranks of their own faithful followers. An event, on a Sunday in November 1912, attracted Roman Catholics from the Lugsdale district and surrounding areas. Thousands gathered to welcome Dr. Whiteside, the Archbishop of Liverpool, who had been invited to lay the foundation stone of the new St. Marie's School. The new school was urgently needed to accommodate the growing number of pupils in St. Marie's parish. The building, which was erected in Lugsdale Road opposite the church, was to cost £4500 and would accommodate 344 scholars. On the day of the event the vicinity of St. Marie's Church was colourfully decorated for the ceremony. The occasion was enlivened by a procession, headed by the band of the Farnworth Nautical School, who were followed by members of various guilds of the church and Ditton Young Men's Society.

---

[125] *Ibid*....25th October 1912

Into The Crucible

Charles Glover Barkla

The period 1914-1918 was not a happy one for the residents of Widnes, especially those who had menfolk caught up in the terrible conflict of that time; nevertheless, there were several bright spots. In November 1918 the town was celebrating the news that a Widnes born man, Professor Charles Glover Barkla, was to receive *The Nobel Prize* for physics. The value of the prize at that time was £8000. Dr. Barkla, the son John Barkla who was the Secretary of The Atlas Chemical Company, was born in Widnes in June 1877. As a child he attended the Simms Cross schools before moving to Liverpool Institute and University College where he studied maths and physics. Following a period at Trinity College, Cambridge, he returned to Liverpool University in 1902 as *Oliver Lodge Fellow*. Following his successful period at Liverpool he left in 1909 to become Professor of Physics at Kings College London. In 1913 he accepted the Chair in Natural Philosophy at the University of Edinburgh and held this position until his death in 1944.

Education

Considerable advances took place in education in the 19th century. As early as 1811 the Church of England was active in many aspects of educational promotion. In October that year *The National Society* was formed with the main purpose of founding a church school in every parish in England and Wales. The Society funded, or helped fund, the construction of schools, the purchase of equipment, and it also trained the teachers. These schools were originally known as "National Schools". The State was also mindful of its obligations and from 1833 gave grants towards school building costs. After 1846 grants were also awarded for teaching purposes. In 1869 two other societies were formed, *The Education League* which was secular, and the *National Education Union* which was Anglican. However, it was not until the passing of the *Education Act of 1870* that education became a priority. It is believed that it was mainly due to these two societies and their continued endeavours that this Act was passed.

The earliest established school in this area was *Farnworth Free Grammar School*. This endowed school was originally founded on 20th July 1509 by William Smythe, the Bishop of Lincoln, and placed, at that time, under the control of the Mayor and Corporation of Chester. A *"Schools Inquiry Commission"* in 1867-8 stated that the school was at that date under the control of ten Trustees. Most of these trustees were farmers who did not appear to take much interest in the school. A further observation from the same report informs us that:

"The principle function of the Trustees, besides receiving and paying over to the Master the endowment, seems to be the appointment of the 10 foundationers, who are taught free of charge except for materials. They are usually the sons of small farmers, and are not selected on the grounds of

intellectual merit. Most of them, as I was told, could have afforded well enough to pay the usual fee".[126]

The original school, near to Farnworth Parish Church, was little more than a cottage. Over time, with the help of monetary bequests from local dignitaries, a house was purchased in Farnworth Street. During the period 1733 to 1758 the headmaster was the Rev. John Wilcoxon. Unfortunately the Reverend Wilcoxon was a notorious drunkard. As a consequence of his inebriated conduct the number of children on roll fell considerably during his tenure. At one point the number of pupils on roll was as low as three. One of his successors, William Binns, seemed no better as he was dismissed in 1851 for *"moral laxity"*. When the house in Farnworth Street was demolished the first purpose built school was erected on the site. During the 1860s Mr. James Raven was appointed headmaster and by 1876 there were more than 90 pupils on roll. Mr. Raven spent a considerable amount of money out of his own pocket to improve the school. James Raven retired in 1878 and was succeeded by Walter Angus Watts. Mr. Watts had come into teaching fairly late, he had previously worked as a chemist at Hutchinson's works. The following decade saw the reconstitution of the school on more formal lines. As the school flourished, the accommodation in Farnworth Street proved to be inadequate and it was decided to move the school to a new building in Peelhouse Lane.

There was also a Sunday school in Farnworth which was located near to the Church. In addition, a number of Dame Schools were operating in both the Farnworth and Appleton districts. These Dame Schools were usually for the education of working class children. They were mainly run by elderly ladies in their own homes. In Baines Directory of 1825 we see that there was also a *School for Young Ladies* in Farnworth village owned by a lady called Susan Pierpoint. In addition, directories of 1855 inform us that there was a well-attended private school at Crow Wood conducted by Mr. William Moss, and a boarding school at Bradley Cottage run by Mrs. Sarah Kent, the wife of the town's first postmaster.[127]

---

[126] P.R.O. Kew - British Parliamentary Papers – *Schools Inquiry Commission (Session 1867-8)*

[127] It is believed that sometime during this school's existence it was honoured by a visit from the eminent Victorian, John Ruskin.

Education

The first Roman Catholic school in Widnes was *St. Bede's*. This school was erected in Appleton village in 1823 with Mr. John Glover being appointed the first headmaster. By 1852, during the time of the Rev. George Fisher, it was necessary to replace the old schoolroom with a larger building because of the considerable increase in the Roman Catholic population in that district. In 1863 the staff of this school consisted of two nuns from the *Notre Dame Order* and two pupil teachers. There were 80 children on the roll which comprised of 54 girls and boys in the mixed department, and 26 infants.

Appleton Academy, Highfield Road

The next Roman Catholic school to be established was *Appleton Academy* which was located in Highfield Road. This school was opened in 1830 by Mr. James Eccles and taken over in 1834 By Mr. Richard Bradshaw.[128] Appleton Academy was a private school which provided a broad sphere of education for all young boys. In 1865 the Academy was offering a wide range of lessons including Drawing; Dancing; French; Latin etc. for a fee of £35 per term. The average age of pupils

---

[128] Richard Bradshaw, who was originally from Chorley in Lancashire, married Margaret Eccles, the daughter of the previous owner, in June 1848.

was between 11 and 13 years of age but it also received students as young as 8 years. The school had a strong Roman Catholic ethos and earlier supposition was that it served as a seminary for the education of students who were preparing for the priesthood. However, despite that long held view, later evidence suggests that although some of its pupils may indeed have gone into the priesthood, it was primarily a private school with a robust Catholic culture. The running of Appleton Academy appears to have been a real family concern. The teaching staff included Mr. Bradshaw and his wife Margaret, along with his brother-in-law, Robert Eccles. Mr. Bradshaw's sister, Miss Elizabeth Bradshaw, was responsible for domestic care. Richard Bradshaw, apart from running his own successful school, was prominently involved in other areas of education in the town. He was the manager of St. Bede's School and also a member of the Widnes School Board. Following his death in 1890 the Academy was sold and the building was eventually converted into private dwellings.

By the end of the 1830s the settlement around Widnes Dock had expanded and a school was needed to educate the children of the workers who lived in that district. To satisfy that need the first "National School" in Widnes was built there in 1839. *The National Society* donated £20 towards the building of the schoolroom and additional expenses were met by private subscription. The original promoters of this school were the Rev. William Jeff, vicar of Farnworth, Thomas Kidd, Esq., and Mr. Thomas Shaw. Shortly after the opening of the Dock School, The Church of England National Society provided a second "National School" for the village of Farnworth. The Farnworth School opened sometime around 1842.

The National School at Widnes Dock was sited beside the St. Helens & Runcorn Gap Railway. Unfortunately this proved to be a regrettable choice of location as numerous chemical factories soon began to inhabit the area. In 1858 this school was closed and replaced by a new building in Waterloo Road. The old Dock School building was sold on 21st March 1859. The new Waterloo Road School, *St. Mary's National School,* was allied with St. Mary's Church in West Bank. The Trustees of the new school were named as John L. Wright of Runcorn; Robert Reed of Farnworth; Thomas Johnson of Runcorn; Thomas Shaw of Farnworth; John McClellan of Widnes and William Brundrit of Runcorn.[129] Mr. J.C.

---

[129] *Dock National School correspondence* – Lancashire Record Office

Education

Crawford was appointed headmaster of *St. Mary's National School* in 1867 and remained at the school until his retirement in 1911.

Sometime prior to 1861, under the direction of Father Fisher of Appleton, a schoolroom was opened in Newtown. This room was also used for celebrating Mass before the building of the Church in 1865. In 1861 a new school, *St. Marie's Roman Catholic School*, was built adjoining the old schoolroom at the corner of Margaret Street and George Street. A classroom attached to the old school and a house in the same street was demolished to make room for the new building. The land on which the new school and the earlier schoolroom were built had been donated by Mr. John Hutchinson. The building cost £1000 and voluntary subscriptions raised £794. The Parish Priest at that time was Rev. Thomas Walton. He was pessimistic about the future funding of the school in such a poor locality.

In the years between 1861 and 1871 industry expanded and the population of the town literally doubled. This growth in populace brought about a considerable increase in the number of Roman Catholic residents at the south end of the town. This expansion necessitated the provision of another school to provide for the growing numbers of Roman Catholic children in the area. To respond to this need a school was opened in West Bank in November 1872. The new school, *St. Patrick's School* in Hutchinson Street, offered accommodation for 622 pupils. Twenty years later, in 1892, this building was sold to Messrs. Thomas Bolton & Sons who were expanding their Hutchinson Street works. The earlier school was subsequently replaced by a new *St. Patrick's R.C. School* which was built in West Bank Street. The new larger school was able to accommodate 750 scholars.

Although the precise date of the establishment of the Roman Catholic school at Ditton Hall, known as *St. Mary's*, is not known; it is generally believed to be circa 1860. In *Slater's Directory* for 1869 the teacher is named as Eliza Hagan. In 1876 the school was listed as *St. Mary's R.C. School*, Hale Lane, Ditton and the mistress at that date was Ellen McGinty. The school at Ditton Hall was not the only educational establishment in the Ditton area. Sometime around 1866 a school was opened by William Thorburn who was the owner of *Ditton Iron Works*. This school, which was attached to the ironworks, was provided specifically for the children of his employees. The teacher was Miss

Mary Hind. The opening of this school caused a drop in attendance at the Ditton Hall School, as the owner of the works insisted that the children of his employees attend his school. There was also a "National School" at Ditton that had originated from a Dame School. Later, as the population of this region of the town expanded, a committee, under the direction of the Rev. Jeff, Vicar of Farnworth, was set up to canvass subscriptions for building a new Anglican Church and school in that district. As a result, *St. Michael's Church* at Hough Green was opened under licence early in 1870 and the school opened two years later. Other Christian denominations also set up schools in the town. A schoolroom was provided in the Wesleyan Methodist Chapel in Suttons Lane in 1868. By 1870 it was providing accommodation for 162 children and was receiving grant aid. Shortly afterwards the Wesleyan community opened another school at the Moss Street Wesleyan Chapel in Moss Bank.

In 1865 The Widnes Local Board was set up to handle responsibility for public sewage and other important aspects of urban development. Although in some respects the Local Board was progressive in their approach to urban improvement, unfortunately the education of local children was not a priority. In fact, in the years before the passing of *1870 Education Act*, the subject of education did not appear to be a consideration as it was felt that the existing arrangements were adequate. However, by 1871 the rapid increase in population brought an influx of young families into Widnes and this resulted in an acute shortage of educational accommodation. Despite this shortage, there was no initial effort locally to take up recommendations outlined in *The Education Act* which came into being in 1870. The *Act* attempted to provide education for all children and, to facilitate this, it endorsed the setting up of Local School Boards. The School Boards were empowered to build schools where voluntary school places were insufficient and they were also authorised to compel attendance[130]. Fees of a few pennies per week were to be charged, with exemption for the poorer parents. An additional component of *The Elementary Education Act* was that it placed a duty on parents to ensure that their children received elementary instruction in reading, writing and arithmetic.

One would have assumed that immediately after the passing of *The Education Act* Widnes ratepayers would have been keen to forge ahead

---

[130] In 1880 school attendance became compulsory for children aged 5 to 10 years.

Education

and form a Local School Board. However this was not the case. It seems that there was great reluctance to set the ball rolling and some did not want a School Board at all. In October 1871 a meeting was held in the Public Hall, under the provisions of the *Elementary Education Act,* to discuss the forming of a Widnes School Board. One of those present, the Rev. J.C. Holland, a Roman Catholic priest, said *"that it would be better to wait until we are compelled by the Education Department to select a School Board"* this resolution was carried and no action was taken.

A statement regarding the existing school accommodation was made at that meeting:

"That, in the first place, according to the census of this year, there were in the township, of children over five and under thirteen years of age 2,833. Of these only about 100 were attending schools of a better class, leaving 2,733 for whom the Education Act requires the provision of elementary school accommodation.

That next, according to the returns made by the managers of various elementary schools to the Education Department last December, there were in actual attendance at the:

Church of England Schools	657
Wesleyan Schools	233
Dame Schools[131]	186
Roman Catholic Schools	454
(Total in all)	1530

That these schools will accommodate under the Revised Code, at the outside 300 more, or 1830. There were therefore, last April in the township 903 children of school age who could not find room in any school; and by next April, computing a rate of increase in the population slower than that of the last ten years, there will be 200 more children of school age.

No new school could possibly be got to work before next April, so that the township ought at once to set to work to supply accommodation for 1,103 children, simply to fulfil the requirements of the Act. And indeed it seems most probable that even this amount will be insufficient to meet the demands

---

[131] Private Schools for working class children – usually run by elderly women in their own homes.

Into The Crucible

of the law, for it is understood that every single one of the so-called Dame Schools will be condemned by the Education Department as insufficient."

One speaker, Dr. O` Keeffe, went on to say *"I cannot believe that a town which has shown so much public spirit as regards to sanitary affairs, will consent to wait to be compelled by Government to provide for its future morality".*

The above dialogue, which shows that some people thought they should hold back until the Government forced them to act, may in part explain the reason why Widnes was comparatively late setting up a School Board. Liverpool had appointed its Board by November 1870 and even places with small populations, like Prescot, had resolved to form a School Board in March 1871. A Local School Board was eventually set up in Widnes in 1874. The first meeting was held on 17th November 1874 in the Local Board Room in Victoria Road. The members of that first School Board Committee were: Henry Deacon; Major Cross; C. Sutton Timmis; Richard Bradshaw; Martin Taylor; Robert Shaw and Father James Clarke. Mr. G.H. Danby was appointed clerk and held that position until 1903.

The newly formed School Board was a good mix because, as well as consisting of local employers, it was seen to represent both Anglican and Catholic interests. Some members had fairly similar business backgrounds whilst others had educational or pastoral experience. The Anglicans were represented by Henry Deacon and Martin Taylor who were manufacturers; James Cross, an engineer who held in an important position in the Hutchinson Company; Mr. T. Sutton Timmis, a soap manufacturer who later became a governor of Farnworth Grammar School; and Robert Shaw, an industrialist with earlier links to canvas manufacture. Joining these gentlemen were two representatives of the Roman Catholic communities; Richard Bradshaw, the owner and master of Appleton Academy and also the Manager of St. Bede`s School; and Father James Clarke, an Irish priest who had recently come to Widnes from a poor parish in a depressed area of Liverpool.

It might be interesting to add a little more information on Father James Clarke who was to serve on the School Board for the next 49 years. He was only 37years old when he first took his place on the Widnes School Board Committee in November 1874. He was to remain

Education

a member of the Board for its entirety, being a member till its dissolution in 1903. He also served for many years on the Prescot Board of Guardians. He was known as a kind and considerate man who devoted his life to the underprivileged in society. Among his many achievements was the fact that he was instrumental in urging the Local Board to form a Relief Committee during the terrible trade depression of 1879. After his death some ground fronting Lugsdale Road was turned into a garden which was named Clarke Gardens in his memory.

Special reference should also be made to Mr. George H. Danby who was appointed clerk to the newly formed School Board. Mr. Danby held that position for almost 30 years before becoming Director of Education. In fact, up until his retirement, Mr. Danby had been connected with the educational life of Widnes for over 38 years. Of course it is probably unfair to single out individuals as there were several people who gave truly outstanding service. Over the following years there were many long standing School Board members who diligently served the educational interests of the children in our communities. Several local employers were active members of The Board and became managers of schools, feeling it a duty to become involved in the provision of education for the children of their employees. It has been suggested that they were also interested in creating a better-educated workforce for the future.

At the inauguration of The School Board the town already had a number of schools. These included two National schools and three Roman Catholic schools, as well as the Grammar School and a number of Dame Schools. In April 1875 The School Board opened its first temporary school in the Wesleyan schoolroom in Oakland Street, offering accommodation for 200 infants. A month later a second temporary school was opened in Bank Street. This was a mixed school offering accommodation for 200 children. Mrs. Upton was appointed headmistress of the Oakland Street School at a salary of £75 per annum and Mrs. Ferguson was appointed to the Bank Street School at a similar salary.

Into The Crucible

Widnes School Board – May 1903

(Standing from left) D. Lewis; S. Quinn; G. Danby; Mr. Thomas; Mr. Dodd; Rev. Wright-Williams
(Seated from left) J.J. Williams; F. Neill; H. Wade Deacon; Dean Clarke; Dean Finnegan

Education

One of the priorities for the new School Board was finding suitable sites on which to build schools. In 1875 they bought the land on which Warrington Road School and West Bank School were built. These schools were ready for occupation in 1877. They also purchased a large plot of land at Simms Cross for the purpose of providing a school for children in that locality. In the interim period the Wesleyan School in Suttons Lane was rented from the owners, *The Sheffield and Midland Railway Company*, until Simms Cross School was ready for occupation. On completion of the new schools the School Board appointed Mr. J.S. Snoddy as the Head Teacher of the newly opened West Bank School, while Mr. G. Faulkner and Mr. T. Showan filled the corresponding posts at the Warrington Road and Simms Cross Schools.

WORRALL`S DIRECTORY (1876)
LIST OF WIDNES SCHOOLS

Private Schools

Richard Bradshaw – (Boarding) Appleton Academy
Margaret Haddock – Lune Hey, Farnworth
Jane Hulme – Bell House farm
Annie Kidd – Farnworth
Paulina & Caroline King – Mersey Road
Sarah Anne Moore – (Boarding) Hale
St. John O'Meara - Irwell Street
Annie Syred – Bradley Cottage, Appleton

Board Schools, National Schools and Church Schools

Bank Street Infants – Sarah Ferguson, mistress
Oakland Street Infants – Mary Upton, mistress
Grammar School Farnworth – James Raven, master
Farnworth – Enoch Brown, master; Ellen Crossley, mistress
Ditton – Thomas Holbrook, master
Hale – Martha Lomas, mistress
St. Mary's, Waterloo Road, - John Charles Crawford, master.
　　　Emily J. Hind, mistress; Alice Molyneux, infants` mistress

Into The Crucible

>St. Patrick's, Hutchinson Street – William Atherton, master
>   Mary Sinnott, mistress; Lucy McCartan, infants` mistress
>St. Bede's, Appleton – Ann McKenzie, mistress; Emma Gosford
>St. Mary's, Newtown - Amy Prout, mistress; Catherine Moran,
>St .Mary's, Hale Lane, Ditton – Ellen McGinty, mistress
>Wesleyan Methodist School, Suttons Lane – Edward Gleave, master
>   Bessie Arnold, mistress.

Most people assume that the *Elementary Education Act of 1870* provided "free" compulsory education for all children. Regrettably this was not the case. Education at this time was not free although under a bylaw of *The Act* The Board was obliged to help in cases of hardship. In response to difficulties in paying fees The Board stated: *"If parents are unable to pay school fees the School Board will pay the whole or part of the school fees, in the case of a school furnished by the Board or any other Public Elementary School. Payment is not to exceed 6 months or 4d per week for any one child".*

The fees charged at School Board schools between 1876 and 1878 were:

>*Senior boys and girls 4d per week*
>*Senior boys and girls (advanced classes) 6d per week*
>*Junior boys and girls 4d per week*
>*Infant boys and girls 4d per week*

Obviously the Widnes School Board was only directly concerned with the three Board schools. Voluntary and church Schools collected fees but they were unable to claim a share of the rates.   However there were far more children on roll in the voluntary and church schools than there were in the Board schools.   The non-Board schools were controlled by school managers and were completely separate and totally independent from the School Board. They did not receive any support from the ratepayers and did not send any attendance returns to the School Board.   This made it difficult for The Board to collect accurate information on the numbers of children attending school. In order to make an assessment each year School Board attendance officers made house-to-house visits taking a census. This annual survey was intended to provide a total number of all school-age children in the town. Despite this painstaking survey, the figures collected were not at all reliable. As education had become compulsory, many parents made

Education

false statements, especially those with a number of school-age children in the family. In these cases some would have found it difficult to pay the fees and many of those surveyed declined to give information or else gave incorrect numbers.

The School Board census of 1879 showed that of the 5858 children of school age in the town there were 1276 that did not attend any school. However, as we have seen, this survey was not an accurate source of information. In fact, The School Board was well aware of the flaws in this poll. There is mention in The School Board Records of May 1881 of a letter being sent to *The Lords Committee on Education* requesting them *"to take the necessary steps to obtain permission from The Registrar General, permission for Local Authorities to be supplied with information from the recent Census as to the ages and residence of all children of school age in the district"*.

The following is a list of schools in the town and numbers on roll in 1879 and 1889.

	1879	*1889*
West Bank School	829	1109
Warrington Road School	411	620
Simms Cross School	648	1421
Farnworth National School	441	353
St. Mary's National School	597	671
St. Patrick's R.C. School	769	630
St. Marie's R.C. School	362	910
St. Bede's R.C. School	308	466
Private Schools	218	126
Not attending any school	1276	1334

The first School Board Committee did not have an easy time. Within the first year they encountered personnel problems at the *Oakland Street School*. During the meeting of The Board in December 1875 it was recommended that the managers should inform Mrs Upton that her services were no longer required. The following April, the Board reported the suspension of Mrs. Upton. However the suspension of Mrs. Upton was not the end of the matter. The saga continued as two more teachers, Miss Brunsden and Mrs. Gill, resigned from their posts.

Into The Crucible

A short while afterwards the Board also accepted the resignation of another teacher, Mrs. E. Rogers. In the wake of these events, Miss Helen Swain was appointed Assistant Mistress at a salary of £40 per year. Nevertheless, despite staff changes, the trouble at *Oakland Street School* continued. In October 1876 the School Board received a further resignation, this time from one of the school managers, the Rev. Leathley. It is clear that there were some serious staff issues in this establishment. One cannot help but feel intrigued as to what could have caused these problems. Alas the School Board Records do not shed any further light on the subject.

Towards the end of December 1877 the Widnes School Board had agreed *"that the managers for the Board schools were to be chosen from the ratepayers or ratepayers` wives"*. The first group of managers for *Simms Cross School* were transferred from the temporary school in the Wesleyan Methodist Chapel in Suttons Lane. The members were:

> Mrs. Robinson, Moorside Terrace.
> Mrs. Joseph Robinson, 50 Irwell Street
> Mr. W.T. Husband, Victoria Road
> Mr. W. Berrington Jones, Deacon Road
> Mr. Thomas Sadler, Widnes Road
> Mr. Samuel B. Stringer, Victoria Road
> Mr. J.W. Wareing, Hall Nook, Penketh

In 1884 a report on *St. Marie's Boys` School* described the educational environment and standard of education thus:

"The discipline, though rather perhaps of too military rigidity is very creditable; the boys being well behaved, docile and industrious. The instruction though still uneven and not of sufficiently high quality has made much progress, and the work done at this examination is more successful and of much better quality than last year".

The following year the manager's report included the following observation: *"The boys are very orderly and well conducted but are dirtier in person and more untidy in dress than really well disciplined scholars should be. Their homes and surroundings present indeed difficulties but not so formidable as not to be overcome by perseverance and example on the part of the teachers"*.

Education

St. Marie's School in Lugsdale Road

The annual manager's report was an important procedure in all schools that received any form of grant aid. The report was important to both the pupil and the teacher as at that time teachers were paid by result. Children were tested in the three "R's" each year and if they passed the test the school would gain a grant which helped to maintain the school and pay teachers' wages. In 1884 the manager recommended that the grant to *St. Marie's Boys` School* should be at the lowest level. The following year the grant was again at the lowest level. The grant for *"Music by Note"* was recommended :*"..with hesitation on account of inaccuracy in the ear tests, and the harshness of voice in singing".*

In January 1873 the new *St. Patrick's School* reopened after the Christmas holiday under the charge of Sarah Byrne who had just completed 2 years at Liverpool Training College. The Assistant Teachers at that time were Miss Lucy McCartan, Miss Mary Scully and Miss Alice Flanagan. The School Manager was Rev. Father J.C. Holland. The School Log Book for that era tells us that *"the books and apparatus for carrying out our schoolwork consisted of: 4-dozen copies of*

Into The Crucible

Burns` Primers, 2-dozen slates and 2 boxes containing 200 slate pencils". Later in the month the school took delivery of *"2 blackboards, a large slate, and an easel"*.

Although *St. Patrick's School* could cater for over 600 pupils the number of children on roll in January 1873 was less than 100. From time to time throughout that first year attendance fell even lower. In August and October reasons for this were given as *"attendance very bad owing to a Circus being in the location."* In November the *"Gunpowder Plot"* affected attendance. However things picked up and from 1886 there was a steady increase in the number of new scholars being admitted. This was probably a result of new families moving into the town. Although the numbers on roll were stable the attendance figures fluctuated. One of the reasons given for absence included an alarming number of children suffering from *"sore eyes"*. This was also frequently given as a cause for absences at *St. Marie's School* during the same period. One *St. Patrick's* pupil, John Henry Rice, *"has suffered greatly from sore eyes for the greater part of the year and consequently cannot get on with his class work"*. [132] I do not know if the sore eyes were the result of noxious vapours from nearby factories or due to some vitamin deficiency because of poor diet.

Despite the efforts of the Government and local officials, it was apparent that education did not rate high in importance among the population. Most parents appeared to be reluctant to avail themselves of the newly provided facilities for the education of their children. In January 1876 The School Board arranged for 4000 handbills to be distributed to parents to make them aware of the services on offer. One wonders how useful this exercise could have been, in view of the fact that many of the targeted parents were unable to read. Two years later, a doorstep survey revealed that at least a thousand Widnes children of school age did not attend school.[133] Almost twenty years later attitudes had not greatly improved. One week in June 1896 thirteen fathers were fined 6d each for neglecting to send their children to school.

In addition to the inability to pay fees, children were kept away from school for a variety of reasons. An entry in *St. Marie's School* Log

---

[132] *Cheshire Record Office–* SL492/2/1 and SL429/2/4
[133] George E, Diggle - *"A History of Widnes"* 1961

Education

Book for February 1889 gave the following reason for low attendance: *"A heavy fall of snow and rough cold winds had prevented a number of poorly clad children from attending"*. Another entry from the same book said *"attendance had fallen off in consequence of many of the children going for firewood to some of the works"*. The poverty in these areas is brought to our attention once again, when a reason for absence at *St. Patrick's School* in 1895 is given: *"low attendance due to the discontinuance of tickets for food and clothing among the poorer children"*. Much later, in 1910 it was said that: *"a fair number of boys came to school without shoes or stockings and the partially asphalted school yard, of which the surface is broken in places, is hardly suitable for marching and drilling these scholars"*.

Some interesting pieces of information emerged from this research into school attendance figures. Evidence suggests that in the early days the poorest parents, mainly from the Newtown area, had the highest percentage of children attending school. It is believed that this trend ran contrary to the national average. Another point worthy of note was that the traditional craftsmen at Appleton and Cronton regularly failed to send their children to school. The artisans, mainly watchmakers, may have thought that school was a superfluous institute because their children were already guaranteed an apprenticeship through their fathers' occupations.

The Admission Registers for *St. Marie's School* and *St. Patrick's School* during the 1880s demonstrate the predominance of Irish names in both these schools. The movement of labour into the town from other parts of the country is demonstrated by the locations of previous schools attended by some of these children. Also, in numerous instances, in both the *St. Patrick's* and *St. Marie's* registers, *The Kirkdale Industrial School* is given as a "previous school". That particular "school" was located in Major Street, near the top of Scotland Road in Liverpool. *The Industrial Schools,* or *Ragged Schools,* were places where children of the poorest class of the population received an elementary instruction and were also taught the rudiments of some menial occupation. Often these schools were extensions of the workhouse, as in the case of the *Kirkdale Industrial School.* This school was opened in 1845 by the Liverpool Select Vestry as a school for the Liverpool Workhouse. In 1869 some of the children from the *Kirkdale Industrial School* were taken to Canada and placed with families in Ontario and Nova Scotia. This was the start of a questionable practice initiated by a Miss Maria Susan Rye. This

Into The Crucible

programme continued under her authority until 1895. She is known to have placed over 5,000 children, mostly girls, in many parts of Canada and America.

Apart from being resident in a workhouse, there were other reasons why a child might attend an Industrial School. *The Industrial Schools Act of January 1888* provided for Local Authorities to commit children to these schools for any of the following reasons:

1. *For habitually begging or receiving alms.*
2. *For not having any home or settled place of abode or proper guardianship.*
3. *For frequenting the company of thieves or common prostitutes.*

Under the provisions of this Bill a child could be detained in a certified Industrial School until he attained the age of 18years. The Bill contained several clauses and referred to *The Elementary Education Act of 1879.* In Widnes there were many cases of children being sent to these establishments. In 1881 there were thirty-three Widnes children in Industrial Schools. The School Board minutes for 15th January 1882 states that:

No child has for many years been sent to an Industrial School by the Magistrates of this division until thorough enquiry has been made by the School Board.

That by a Committee of the Board and the use of three Attendance Officers your Memorialists have excellent means of inquiring into the cases of neglected, vagrant and incorrigible children.

That Truant Schools are only of use where the home influences brought to bear on the children are brought to bear. Industrial Schools are impossible to greet in communities of scattered population.

In June 1903 the Widnes Education Authority made an application to commit a child to *St. Thomas' Home* at Talkeith Hall, Preston. In the same year application was also made for one boy to be sent to *The Boys' Refuge* which was located at 62 Ann Street, Liverpool. Another child was sent to *St. Nicholas' Industrial School,* at Manor Park, in Ilford, Essex. Two boys were also sent to the training Ships *"Wellesley"* and *"Clio".* In

Education

July 1903 the School Attendance Sub-Committee reported that a deputation had visited *St. Joseph's Industrial School* in Longsight, Manchester, and *The Barnes' Home* in Heaton Mersey.

The following descriptions of some of these establishments were given in the 1890s:

Kirkdale Industrial and Ragged School
This is the only one of the kind in England. It is both a refuge and a reformatory for beggar and vagrant children. The school is available for 750 children in conjunction with this school which has no less than 24 certified homes in which the most necessitous of the children are lodged.

Barnes' Homes – Heaton Mersey
School erected in 1871 for the education and training of neglected and destitute boys under the provision of the Industrial Schools Act of 1866.

Training Ships
From 1856 the hulls of obsolete wooden warships at permanent moorings in harbours and rivers around Britain, were used as training ships. They were originally established to provide further education and nautical training to boys who were not old enough to enlist in either the Royal Navy or the Merchant Navy. Many were run by charitable societies for the benefit of paupers and orphans.

Some of these institutions were also used as reformatories, especially the training ships, which were known as nautical schools. Often children were sent to them for truancy or general bad behaviour. In fact, there were four training ships moored in the Mersey. Two of these were specifically for training boys in poor circumstances to become merchant seamen. The other two were reformatory ships, *The Clarence* and *The Akbar*. *The Clarence* was used for the reform of Roman Catholic boys and *The Akbar* was for the reform of Protestant boys.

Punishments meted out to children appeared to be particularly harsh. Joan Rimmer, in her history of the *Liverpool Reformatory Association*, cites some early examples from the 1850s. "*A young Salford child was charged with stealing two biscuits and his sentence was 3 months hard labour and whipping.*" Thankfully by 1882 a more enlightened

Into The Crucible

attitude began to appear. The Local School Board meeting in November made the following ruling:

> *"That the Board disapproves of the use of corporal punishment except in extreme cases and views with especial disfavour its infliction on girls and infants."*

The Board also ruled that only Head Teachers should inflict corporal punishment and that any infringement of that ruling should be reported directly to the School Management Committee. Teachers were also advised that they must only use the cane and nothing else. Despite these guidelines, some teachers continued to flout the rules. In March 1895 the Head Teacher at *St. Marie's Boys` School* made the following entry in the school Log Book. *"In spite of repeated cautions, Mr. Clinch hit one of his boys (Kelly) a sharp blow across the side of his head with a small cane. I am ordered by the Rev. Manager to record this incident"*. The Manager at that time was the Rev. Fr. Clarke.[134]

A large number of children registered at *St. Patrick's* and *St. Marie's* schools had previously attended *Holy Cross School* in St. Helens. This indicates movement of chemical labourers from that town to Widnes during this period. Other previous school locations included Wales, Birmingham, Manchester, Isle of Man, Ireland and Scotland. It is also sad to note that even up to the first decade of the 20th century a number of children had previously resided in the workhouse.

The continued growth of the Irish community is evident in the *St. Marie's* registers. These records indicate a sustained movement of Irish labour into Widnes, not only directly from Ireland but also from other manufacturing areas in the northwest. In addition to the Irish, the appearance of Eastern European names, particularly in the West Bank area, became apparent in *St. Patrick's School* records during the years 1889 and 1890. It is possible that some of these surnames may have been anglicised at a later date.

---

[134] *Cheshire Record Office - SL565/4917/4*

Education

Extracts from St. Marie's Admissions – 1882

Name	D.o.b	Parent	Address
Joseph Carroll	25/11/69	Mary	34 Margaret St.
Patrick Derham	15/12/69	Patrick	Market St.
Peter Donoghue	15/12/69	Thomas	3 Suttons Lane
Thomas Dillon	24/12/68	Joseph	13 Suttons Lane
Patrick Mulloy	17/3/69	Thomas	15 Victoria St.
Thos. Hughes	19/3/70	Michael	11 Earle St.
John Ford	30/9/69	T.McLure	12 Elizabeth St.
Lawrence Glasheen	29/6/70	William	10 Caroline St
James Hogan	1/8/70	Thomas	93 Midwood St.
Denis Murphy	1/5/69	Denis	30 Lugsdale Rd
Charles Lavin	16/1/69	Barthol	6 Caroline St.
John Condron	10/2/70	Patrick	Mary Street
Francis Cummins	15/9/69	Timothy	6 Warrington Rd
Joshua Smith	16/2/70	John	21 Moss Bank Rd
Thos. Griffin	7/4/69	Peter	3 Elizabeth St.
James Plunkett	13/2/71	James	Mary St.
Thos. Boyle	15/9/70	Mary	10 Mary St.
M.J. Leonard	12/10/71	Martin	8 Margaret St.
Bart. Dunnigan	18/8/70	Bernard	3 Elizabeth St.
Chris. Mannion	1/1/71	James	2 Elizabeth St.
James Fox	11/1/71	Owen	21 Charlotte St.
Patk. Nicholson	17/4/70	John	23 Railway St.
Thos. Flanagan	28/8/70	Martin	40 Caroline St.
Henry Smith	9/6/68	John	13 Railway St.
Thos. Hynes	7/5/71	Edward	22 Catherine St.
John Woods	10/1/71	Peter	12 Pool St.
Jas. Matthews	24/12/70	James	36 Harris St.
Peter Cullen	8/9/68	Peter	Catherine St.
John King	14/1/72	Edward	26 Victoria St.
Michael Riley	1/6/71	Michael	Midwood St.

Into The Crucible

Extracts from St. Patrick's Admissions - 1886[*]

Name	D.o.b.	Address	Previous
Joseph Clarke	29/10/76	12 North St.	Runcorn
Thos. Clarke	13/10/78	12 North St.	Runcorn
Thos. Byrne	4/11/75	25 Dock St.	St. Bede's
Thos. Connolly	11/8/78	Dock St.	St. Mary's
Chas. Kelly	10/12/75	18 Peel St.	Ireland
Patrick Woods	17/3/76	8 Nelson St.	St. Helens
Thos. Day	12/4/75	5 Barn St.	Glasgow
Edward Allen	21/3/79	45 Dock St.	Wales
Joseph Ryan	22/8/79	Wellington St.	St. Helens
Edward Glover	4/1/79	-	St. Mary's
Wm. Halligan	14/7/79	James St.	-
Daniel Glynn	13/4/79	36 Water St.	Liverpool
Thos. Daley	13/9/76	15 Nelson St.	St. Mary`s
James Burns	27/3/78	17 Dock St.	Birmingham
Dan Redmond	19/12/77	Cromwell St.	Kirkdale
Thos. Flynn	4/6/79	44 Wright St.	St. Patrick's
Ptk. Sweeney	4/5/80	21 Pitt Street	-

Extracts from St. Marie's Admissions - 1889[*]

Name	D.o.b.	Address	Previous
Jas. Holland	19/12/79	Lee St.	St. Patrick's
John Byrne	6/1/81	Walmsley St.	St. Joseph`s, Bury.
Thos. Byrne	15/6/78	Walmsley St.	St. Joseph`s, Bury.
Wm. Riley	11/7/79	Victoria St.	St. Marie's
Edward McKay	23/4/76	Travis St.	Earlestown
Thos. Grayson	16/10/79	Charlotte St.	Warr. Road
John Grayson	21/11/80	Charlotte St.	Warr. Road
James Clayton	16/5/80	Pleasant St.	St. Patrick's
Wm. Clayton	17/9/81	Pleasant St.	St. Patrick's
Bernard Ryan	31/1/77	Walmsley St.	Ireland
Wm. Dogherty	3/5/80	Victoria St.	St. Patrick`s

[*] *Cheshire Record Office* (Microfilm)
[*] *Cheshire Record Office* (Microfilm)

Education

Thomas Boyle	*1/6/82*	*Lacey St.*	*Ireland*
John Flanagan	*8/10/77*	*Margaret St.*	*Kirkdale*
Nicholas Doyle	*5/8/80*	*Railway St.*	*Kirkdale*
Peter Keeffe	*10/5/81*	*Moss Bank Rd.*	*-*
Thos. Doyle	*10/5/77*	*Railway St.*	*Kirkdale*
John Gettings	*1/12/78*	*Ann St. West*	*St. Helens*
Patrick Welsh	*23/7/82*	*Grove St.*	*St. Bede`s*

Extracts from St. Patrick's Admissions - 1889/90

Name	**D.o.b.**	**Address**	**Previous**
Ant. Valinski	*3/10/82*	*Cromwell St.*	*-*
A. Boucauson	*23/1/82*	*61 Pitt St.*	*-*
F. Killinsky	*23/12/83*	*14 Water St.*	*-*
W. Adamavage	*9/3/84*	*56 Cromwell St.*	*-*
Theo.Wasaleski	*10/6/78*	*Cromwell St.*	*Poland*
L. Wasaleski	*5/6/81*	*Cromwell St.*	*Poland*
M. Dubicki	*8/6/81*	*Barn Street*	*Poland*
Adam Cubik	*-*	*Water St.*	*Austria*
Martin Dubitski *	*8/6/81*	*46 Cromwell St.*	*Scotland*
Joseph Yasitus	*-*	*48 Cromwell St.*	*Poland*

Whilst there was a preponderance of Irish names in both the *St. Marie's* and *St. Patrick's Schools,* the surnames of children attending *Simms Cross School* were mainly English in origin. It was also interesting to see the occupations of the children's fathers. Generally, in the *Simms Cross School*, the father was a skilled or semi-skilled worker, while at the other two schools the main recorded occupation was "Labourer". A selection of occupations recorded in the first *Simms Cross School* Admission Register include: Stonemason, Brass Moulder, Watchmaker, Blacksmith, Waggoner, Foreman, Joiner, Grocer, Plumber, Carter and Boilermaker. Of course there *were* Labourers but far fewer than in the other two schools.

Held at Cheshire Record Office (Microfilm)

Into The Crucible

Extracts from Simms Cross School Admissions – July 1877

Name	Parent	Occupation	Address
BOYS			
Thomas Sadler	Thomas	Builder	16 Frederick Street
Thomas Jones	Isabella	–	40 Major Cross St.
Thomas Hartley	Henry	Foreman	16 Pool Street
Joseph Forrest	Thomas	Labourer	27 Princes Street
John Wright	James	Labourer	26 Pool Street
George Whitfield	Thomas	Butcher	38 Ann Street
William Leather	Thomas	Blacksmith	3 Lugsdale Road
Arthur Hunt	Robert	Labourer	2 Charles Street
William Barrow	David	Watchmaker	29 Kent Street
Edward Bibby	Edward	Labourer	10 Ann Street
Arnold Charles	George	Labourer	23 Charlotte Street
Edward Bouldin	James	Boilermaker	19 Grenville Street
George Anderson	Joseph	Cooper	Carlton Terrace
GIRLS			
Elizabeth Roberts	William	Brickmaker	19 Railway Street
Emily Pennington	James	Labourer	25 Caroline Street
Anne Bevan	Mchl.	Labourer	41 Charlotte Street
Anne Lightfoot	Thomas	Labourer	37 Dog Lane
Jane Hulme	James	Coal Dealer	17 Railway Street
Ellen Davies	James	Foreman	Victoria Road
Annie Farrell	Thomas	Labourer	29 Kent Street
Jessie Poulson	Andrew	Moulder	Widnes Road
Mary Wiles	Thomas	Carter	3 Victoria Street
Margaret Leather	Thomas	Blacksmith	3 Lugsdale Road
Ellen Hunt	George	Engine Driver	29 Charlotte Street
Edith Whitfield	Thomas	Butcher	38 Ann Street
Mary Booth	Samuel	Furnaceman	6 Charles Street

Education

In 1898 The Local School Board introduced a 3 year sponsored scholarship scheme. On offer to the children of Widnes were *Science & Arts Scholarships* and *Continuation Scholarships*. These were the rules set out by the Board:

a) *The object of the fund shall be to remove some of the hindrances that arise in the way of continuous and higher education in the case of children in the Widnes Public Elementary Schools whose conduct is good, whose attendance at School is regular, and who show capacity for special and advanced work, but whose parents find a difficulty in continuing their education.*

b) *On a basis of Elementary Education, it is intended to super add a system of higher education that will train pupils for industrial, manufacturing and professional pursuits. This system of instruction will have its beginning in the Elementary School but will be practically carried out in a 3 year course or more beyond the Standards.*

c) *Each Scholarship may bear the name of the donor; and when donors express a wish that the Scholarship should be applied in assisting scholars to pursue the study of particular subjects, the Board shall be guided by such expressions of desire, so far as the same are consistent with the general interests of education.*

d) *An annual statement shall be published of the progress of the scholarship holders, the working of the scheme, and the expenditure of the fund, and shall be forwarded to each donor.*

In addition to the scholarships, which offered opportunities for continuing academic education or skill training, young men were also able to expand their knowledge by attending evening classes. *The Mechanics Institute* in Waterloo Road [135] held popular lectures and classes and provided the use of a reading room. In 1893 evening continuation

---

[135] H.S.L.C. Vol. 141 *Mechanics Institute* – In Dock area from 1853.
Afterwards, in some towns, Mechanics Institutes developed into Technical Colleges.

classes were also available at the Simms Cross, Warrington Road and West Bank schools. By the end of 1895 evening classes were being offered in St. Patrick's; St. Bede's; Farnworth National and St. Mary's National schools. With this enthusiastic interest in continuing education came the realisation that a dedicated Technical College was needed in the town. Construction commenced on a new building in Victoria Square in 1895 at an estimated cost of £12,000.

1892, the year the town received its Charter of Incorporation as a Borough, was also the year in which the last School Board elections were held. Unfortunately one of its stalwart members, Major Wareing, lost his place on the Board at that election. His shock defeat was due almost entirely to an unusual incident that occurred at one of the Polling Stations. The Presiding Officer at one of the booths accidentally set fire to the ballot box and a large number of voting papers were destroyed. It was generally accepted that this incident cost the Major his place on the Board. I do not know what the correct procedure would have been in this case; perhaps a re-run would have been in order? In any event, the remaining papers were counted and the Major was defeated.

In 1902 the Association of School Boards approved a new *Education Act* which subsequently came into operation on 1st June 1903. The last meeting of The Widnes School Board was in May 1903, when control was formally handed over to The Widnes Education Committee. The new committee took responsibility for the eight elementary schools in the town, which had between them in the region of 6700 scholars. The first Director of Education was Mr. George H. Danby who had previously held the position of clerk to the old School Board. Mr. Danby's tenure got off to a difficult start as controversy raged over the subsidised teaching of religious doctrine in church schools. The controversy was not a local issue but a national one, and many ratepayers refused to pay the educational rate. In Widnes a *Passive Resisters' League* was formed but in 1910 this was disbanded after having failed to achieve any change in the provisions.

By 1912 there was an acute shortage of qualified female teachers, not only in Widnes but in the country at large. In response to this, there were several national debates as to whether or not a married woman should be allowed to teach. An Education Inspector suggested a

Education

reversion to the regulation prevailing before 1910 *"...as since then married women have been turned out of jobs at considerable expense to themselves and to the taxpayer"*.

One local report into the lack of women in the teaching profession stated that The Widnes Education Committee was experiencing great difficulty in filling vacancies due to the prevailing shortage of teachers. The insufficient supply of suitably qualified female teachers was due to the fact that, at that time, women teachers were not allowed to continue their careers once they married. In relation to that prerequisite, it is interesting to read some of the terms and conditions written into the contracts of female teachers in Widnes during this period. The terms of appointment included the following stipulation:

"That from this date, the appointment of all female Teachers be immediately revoked upon marriage, and that such Teachers be required to undertake, as a condition of appointment, to give one month's notice prior to marriage.

Into The Crucible

West Bank School – 1890s

Crime

In relation to crime in Victorian Widnes, we are told by George E. Diggle in his *"History of Widnes"* that this town was no worse or better than any similar town during that period. Others have painted a different picture. One amateur historian gave an alarming account of riots and general public disorder attributable to the arrival of Irish and Eastern European immigrants. It was also said that *their* behaviour prompted the building of a new Police Court and Station in 1866. In fact, the Eastern Europeans did not arrive in Widnes in any significant numbers until the 1880s/1890s which was well after the building of the Police Station and Court. The suggestion that their presence, in particular, contributed to the need for new police premises is inconceivable. Furthermore, the problems and crimes associated with drunkenness and violent behaviour were widespread throughout the country. *The Warrington Guardian* gave numerous reports of drunkenness and fighting in the town of Warrington from the 1870s onwards. The same newspaper, reporting in 1873, said it was a *"very serious problem"*. Editions of *The Runcorn and Widnes Chronicle* from the 1880s and 1890s report numerous cases of drink related crime involving sailors and dockworkers in Runcorn. It should be emphasised that this widespread *"problem"* was not confined to any particular ethnic group but was prevalent amongst all sections of working society.

In 1842 William Cooke Taylor published a series of literary works on behalf of the Anti-Corn Law League. His book, *"Notes on a Tour in the Manufacturing Districts of Lancashire"*, gives a contemporaneous observation of life and conditions in these areas. When writing about crime in Manchester he wrote the following:

"The third document to which I shall direct your attention is an abstract of a paper read by Sir Charles Shaw to the Statistical Section of the British Association, entitled "A report of the cases brought before the Police of Manchester on Saturdays and Sundays", (which he described as the great days of crime in this part of the country), from 22nd January to 15th June,

Into The Crucible

> 1842. The number apprehended was 646, consisting of 440 males and 206 females. Of these 320 had been out of employment an average of 8 months and 25 days previous to their apprehension. He had been told, when he came to Manchester, that the whole of the crime was committed by the Irish but he was sceptical on the point, for the best and most orderly soldiers he had commanded were Irish. The table justified his doubts, for out of the 646 only 172 belonged to the sister Kingdom".[136]

The above extract reveals the willingness of the general population to lay the blame for crime entirely at the door of Irish immigrants. Possible reasons for this attitude are offered for consideration in an earlier chapter of this book which relates to *"The Irish"*. To reinforce this viewpoint we have only to look at documentary evidence. The Charge Book for the Prescot Division of the Lancashire Constabulary for the period 1849-52 shows that 131 people were arrested during that 3year period, which is quite a low figure. Of the 131 arrests only 25 of these were Irish – just 18%. Furthermore, to emphasise the point, at that period in time the Irish were by far the largest ethnic group in the population. Most of the crimes in The Charge Book were alcohol related; which was by no means a problem peculiar to a specific group but was widespread amongst the working population of Widnes and other industrial towns of that era. A random glance at the records of the *Widnes Petty Sessions* for October 1869[137] exhibits a preponderance of drunkenness and fighting crimes. These crimes were largely attributable to the celebration of *Farnworth Wakes* which began around 1714 and was notorious for violent and drunken behaviour. The lack of many Irish names and the complete absence of Eastern European names from these sessions would confirm that, certainly at this time, targeting them as the main source of crime was completely unjustified. Among those summoned in October 1869 were:

> *John Lightfoot, John Hayes, Joseph Hayes, John Abbott who were all charged with breach of the peace for fighting in the streets. Edward Himes, Frederick Brunt, Martin Santley, William Taylor, Robert Case, Thomas Cowley and John Cornes were all charged with drunkenness.*

---

[136] W. Cooke Taylor -" *A tour of the manufacturing districts of Lancashire*" London 1842

[137] *The Widnes and Runcorn Guardian* – October 1869

Whilst mentioning the large amount of drunken and disorderly behaviour attributable to the celebration of *"Farnworth Wakes"* perhaps it should be pointed out that this event attracted visitors from far and wide. Therefore it is clear that the indigenous population of Widnes was not solely responsible for the entire amount of disorderly behaviour. An advert from October 1858 shows that the event was popular throughout the neighbouring localities and drew people from these areas.

> **FARNWORTH WAKES AND FAIR,**
> **NEAR WARRINGTON.**
> The ANNUAL WAKES will be held on MONDAY, the 18th instant.
> The AUTUMN FAIR will be held on TUESDAY, the 19th instant.
> An ORDINARY will be provided at the George and Dragon Hotel each day during the week, by the Proprietor, JOHN J. HEYES.
> The Trains direct are old Garston. Passengers to start by the Omnibus, from North John street.
> Trains from Lime-street Station leave Rainhill.   d-oc 16

Reports on the administration of Lancashire for the period 1838-1889 tell us that a large building scheme was carried out throughout the whole county during this period. This included three new county asylums, new county offices at Preston, new assize courts, eight militia storehouses and one hundred and fifteen new police stations. Included in the programme were Widnes Police Station and a new Police Court in St. Helens.[138] In addition to carrying out this ambitious building scheme, during this period the County Constabulary was also expanded considerably. The number of police increased from 352 men in 1840 to 1,321 in 1888.[139]

In March 1870, four years after the building of the Police Station in Widnes, the Lancashire and Cheshire Prison Returns for the County and the Borough Prisons were published. The Returns show that religious instruction was available to prisoners of different denominations during their term of imprisonment. Regular reports

---
[138] St. Helens Courthouse was brought into service on 28th January 1876.
[139] S. Peter Bell - "Victorian Lancashire" (David & Co.) 1974

Into The Crucible

were published giving the number of prisoners in each prison and specifying what denomination they belonged to. The cost involved in providing religious support for each prisoner was also given. Extracts published in the *Widnes and Runcorn Guardian,* on 12th March 1870 cover Lancashire County Gaol and the Borough Gaol in Kirkdale. If one assumes that the majority, if not all, the Irish and Eastern European immigrants were Roman Catholic then these figures would indicate that they were by no means in the majority amongst the lawbreakers.

Lancashire County Gaol

Criminal Prisoners:

Church of England	54
Methodists	4
Presbyterians	1
Roman Catholics	30
Independents	2
No Religion	1
Total:	92

Debtors:

Church of England	77
Methodists	6
Presbyterians	4
Roman Catholics	10
Independents	2
Morovian	1
Total:	100

The cost of each Protestant Prisoner is £1.6s.4d. No appointed Minister other than Church of England.

Borough Gaol – Kirkdale

Criminal Prisoners:

Protestant	239
Roman Catholic	193
Dissenters	7
Total:	439

One Protestant Clergyman is appointed, at a salary of £300 per annum and one Roman Catholic at a salary of £150.

It is important to say that, despite the fact that the Widnes Law Courts and the new Police Station were not built as a direct result of criminal activity by any *specific ethnic group*, one must stress that they were not all entirely blameless. In later times there was a high level of drink related crime and other more serious crimes attributable to members of these communities. In press accounts of the Widnes Petty Sessions we will find numerous Irish and Lithuanian surnames alongside English ones. Newspaper reports of the Widnes Petty Sessions make for fascinating and revealing reading. These reports enable us to reconstruct in our imagination the scenes of Victorian Widnes and the lives of its inhabitants. Murder, theft, vagrancy, quarrels, breach of promise and bigamy, each charge a story in itself.

In 1872 some of the cases appearing before the Widnes Bench made their way into the pages of T*he Runcorn Guardian*. Among them was the case of James Morris, a 10year old child. He was charged with stealing four oranges from the shop of James Hoole in Ann Street. The Magistrate, Mr. Deacon, said *"the Bench hesitated very much whether or not to send the lad to prison and order him to be flogged"*. He decided instead to fine the child the enormous sum of 10 shillings, saying, that if the money was not paid the lad would be committed to prison. Superintendent Fowler said *"the practise of stealing from shops in the way the prisoner had done was very common in Widnes. The lads dodged about the shops, took off their shoes when they entered them, so as not to be heard, and the shopkeepers were robbed"*. Mr. Deacon said that if anymore such cases were brought before the Magistrates they would be severely dealt with.

A case called *Master and Apprentice* also came up before the Bench in the autumn of 1872. The following report appeared.

"Frederick Harper, aged 18 years, a very respectable looking young man, was charged with unlawfully leaving on the 14th October the service of Horatio Syred, a Widnes pawnbroker, to whom he was apprenticed. He pleaded not guilty. Horatio Syred said the defendant was his apprentice as shown by the articles produced. He had occasion to reprimand him, and in reply to his remonstrance's the defendant gave him so much insolence, that

Into The Crucible

he boxed his ears. He then left the house, and did not return until the next night. During the past week he had paid the sum of £1.2s. for the assistance of other persons who were not as efficient as the defendant was. Mr. Syred said he required the defendant to go to Church on the Sunday evening, and when he spoke to him about not being there, he said he would see about it, meaning he supposed that he would bring his big brother, as he did on a previous occasion to challenge him out to fight. He clothed and fed the defendant, allowing him a shilling a week for pocket money. This was the second time the defendant had left him, but it was the first time he had brought him before the magistrates. He did not wish the indentures to be cancelled as the defendant was now of great use to him, and but for his insolence to him and his wife, suited him well. In reply, the defendant said he would go back again but on different terms. His master had not behaved to him as he ought to have done, and at times cursed him. The Magistrate, Colonel Blackburne said: you cannot dictate your terms. You are bound apprentice to Mr. Syred, and if you do not promise to go back and do your best to do your duty, we shall have to send you to prison, which we are very unwilling to do. You must serve your master to the best of your ability, and if he does anything wrong to you, if you will, summon him to appear here we will see that you are properly dealt with, and that justice is done to you. The defendant then promised to return to his employment and the charge against him was withdrawn."

The pages of *The Widnes Weekly News* are liberally sprinkled with reports of crimes of drunkenness and brawling among the working communities in the south end of the town. There are also stories of murders, assaults and thefts, as well as the occasional light-hearted or amusing episodes. The following short extracts will give you a flavour of life in Victorian Widnes.[140]

In 1879: *Dennis McGanley was convicted of manslaughter for kicking to death Thomas Melia outside the Golden Bowl Hotel in Moss Bank.*

In March of that same year: *Michael Delaney of Pleasant Street, aged 38, was brutally murdered at his place of employment, The Phoenix Chemical Works. Delaney and 7 others had gone on strike against a reduction of 2d per ton in the rate paid to Salt-cake men. Delaney decided to return to work*

---

[140] Some of the more serious cases, such as the murders of Delaney and Treacy, are covered in greater detail in *"Yesterday's People"* – Jean. M. Morris (Springfield-Farrihy)

the following week and shortly afterwards, when working on the nightshift, two assailants beat him with an iron bar. Despite other workers being in the area, no one was able to give a description of the attackers or any useful information that would lead to an arrest. Dr. O` Keeffe organised a public meeting in the Drill Hall. He called on the citizens of Widnes to support a fund for the unfortunate widow and children. He said, "If something is not done there does not appear to be any means of support for them other than the workhouse". A reward of £500 was offered for information, but the murderers were never traced.

In October 1879: *Patrick Tracey of 60 Sankey`s Row, Oxford Street, a 36 year old Irishman and father of three young children, was found murdered in his bed.* Two lodgers, Patrick Kearns and Hugh Burns were convicted and hanged for his murder. This was a shocking and horrific crime and the population of the town were stunned as the events of that dreadful night unfolded. During the trial of the two men it transpired that his wife had plotted the crime and had taken part in the murder of her husband by holding a lighted candle to illuminate the bedroom while they committed the dreadful deed.

Patrick Tracey was employed as a chemical labourer at Muspratt`s Works. He and his family shared the house with a number of lodgers including the two convicted of his murder. Mrs. Tracey claimed that she had been woken by the sound of a pistol shot and found her husband dead in bed beside her. She then called the lodgers who went to get Dr. O` Keeffe and Fr. Clarke, the Parish Priest from St. Marie's.

The two lodgers were subsequently arrested. The funeral of Patrick Tracey caused something of a stir and Mrs. Tracey was unable to attend because of fear of trouble. The murdered man was buried in St. Bede`s Graveyard and his coffin was carried by members of Widnes Police force including Police Sergeants West, Vicars and Kelly and Police Constable Lucas.

The firearm, a small hand pistol, had been purchased along with a quantity of gunpowder, from Mr. Jervis, an Ironmonger in Victoria Road, at a cost of three shillings. The crime was cold-blooded and premeditated. The motive was £500 insurance money. Mrs. Tracey's involvement came to light during the trial when it emerged that she had been having an affair with one of the men. The two lodgers were subsequently hanged, although it was generally believed that one was totally innocent. Mrs Tracey was pregnant at the time so her sentence was commuted to life. Her child, a daughter, was born in Kirkdale Goal.

In July 1881: A man called Edward Foy, who had been on the run after the murder of his wife in St. Helens, was captured by Police Constable George Laing, in the factory of Messrs. Gaskell and Deacon at Widnes.

In October 1881: James Taylor of High Street, and Michael John Keegan and Simon Kilroy of Barn Street, were charged with stealing a quantity of iron hoops valued at 1s.8d. the property of Messrs. Gaskell & Deacon Works.

In October 1881: Thomas Coleman, a neglected child of some six summers, was brought up on remand charged with stealing a quantity of scrap iron from the yard of the Widnes Foundry Co., at Lugsdale. Superintendent Barker pointed out the neglected state of the child, and said that he had been confined since Saturday morning. It transpired that the boy had not been visited by any of his relatives nor were any of them now in court. The Bench agreed the charge should be withdrawn.

In October 1881: James Hynan was charged with neglecting to comply with a magistrates order made on the 30th of June 1880 to contribute 2s a week towards the support of his son, who had been sent to a reformatory school.

In October 1884: A report entitled *"A trio of Wife Deserters"*
At the Prescot Petty Sessions a plasterer, named James Starkey of Lugsdale Lane, Widnes, was charged with neglecting his wife and child, and allowing them to become chargeable to the common fund of the Prescot Union.

David Murray, a chemical works labourer, of Elizabeth Street, Widnes, was charged with deserting his wife and child on 26th August. Mr. Scannell, the Relieving Officer for Widnes, said that previous to going away the prisoner was employed at the Widnes Alkali Works. He got drunk and was fined by the magistrates, but sooner than pay the fine he left town. A witness visited his wife and child and found them in a very sad state of destitution. The woman was near her confinement, and was unable to do anything towards her support and she and the child were accordingly sent to the workhouse.

Crime

Michael Glynn, a labourer of Water Street, was charged with deserting his wife and three children, of the respective ages of seven years, five years and one year. The prisoner was lately employed by Mr. William Ince, contractor at Messrs. Goulding, Davis & Company's Chemical Works, but was very much addicted to drink, and frequently left his wife and children in a starving state. On the 15th September, a witness visited the family in Water Street, and found them dirty, naked and in a destitute condition. The wife told the witness that she had that morning pawned a quilt, the last article she possessed, for 9d. adding that for years she had been in a similar condition, as her husband drank all the money he could get. The Bench considered the case a very bad one and sentenced the prisoner to three months hard labour.

February 1886: Eliza Roberts, a married woman, of John Street, was brought up on remand, charged with stealing five eggs valued at 6d. from a shop in Mersey Road. The shopkeeper said that the prisoner came into her shop and asked for a pennyworth of potato pie. As there was none ready, Mrs. Roberts left her basin and went away. The shopkeeper then went back into her kitchen, leaving the shop unattended. A few minutes later, a policeman came into the shop and asked if anything had been stolen, but the shopkeeper did not appear to have missed anything. However, on closer inspection she realised that five eggs were missing. The constable returned with the woman and the eggs. Mrs. Roberts was distraught. She said, "I took the eggs, I am very sorry, I hope you will forgive me". Mr. Knowles, who spoke for the defendant, said that the prisoner "had had nothing to eat but bread and butter for the past week and, on seeing the eggs, let her hunger get the better of her". She was a married woman with two small children. Her husband had been out of work for over two months and their poverty was so great that they had pawned everything they possibly could. The prisoner was also suffering from a diseased leg and had recently been in hospital. From what the husband had told him unless her leg was taken off, she would very likely die. He remarked that the only money the family had was 5 shillings, and this would have to keep them for a week. The Magistrate, Mr. Holbrook Gaskell, said that poverty was no excuse for theft. The prisoner was fined 5 shillings or seven days in prison.

January 1888: The Sad and Mysterious Death of a Woman at Ditton. Elizabeth Taylor of Charlotte Street was found dead under suspicious circumstances in Ditton Brook.

March 31st 1888: *John Horabin – Grocer of Halton View was given a heavy penalty of £20 for selling adulterated milk.*

April 28th 1888: *Daniel Gilmore of Barn Street, said to have been one of the survivors of Rorke`s Drift in the Zulu Wars, was charged with grievous bodily harm with intent to kill and murder one Joseph Donovan.*

November 9th 1889: *Before the Court for Drunkenness - Martin Ford of Elizabeth Street; John Rigby who had charge of a shooting gallery on the market ground and abused his wife; John Hallwood, Dock Street; and Patrick Rafferty, no residence, were fined 5s and costs, for having been drunk early on Sunday morning and for a similar offence, William Burns of Ann Street West, was fined 7s.6d and costs.*

November 9th 1889: *Charged with Vagrancy. John Egan of no fixed abode, for begging in Lugsdale Road on Saturday, was sent to gaol for seven days on the evidence of Police Constable Thompson. The prisoner had 1s.8d. in his possession when apprehended.*

Some reports offered shocking headlines which were designed to incite or titillate the reader. If the case involved an Irish or Lithuanian (Pole) offender prominence was invariably given to their nationality.

Murderous Assault by a Pole (1885)
A young man named Joseph Kazlensky, a native of Poland who resides at 40, Barn Street, and is employed at one of the local chemical works, was brought up on remand charged with unlawfully wounding another Pole named John Butinsky, residing at 50 Cromwell Street.

As the prisoner in this case could not speak English, the whole of the evidence had to be interpreted by Mr. Frank Harper of Liverpool. It appeared that this skirmish started over a game of cards. The prisoner was sent for trial at the Quarter Sessions. In a previous incident, a prisoner by the name of Joseph Revinski of Water Street was accused of stabbing Matthew Levitch of Barn Street. As in the previous case, an interpreter was used during the proceedings.

Crime

Alleged wounding by Poles (1899)
William Mitchell and William Smith two Russian Poles were charged with striking one Harry Smith, also a Russian Pole.

Again, with the aid of an interpreter, it was established that they were all in the home of a Mr. Pitchilingi of Cromwell Street. Harry Smith was playing a clarinet. The prisoners took the instrument from him and struck him on the head with it! Obviously they were not music lovers – or maybe they were?

A Vixen:
Catherine O`Toole, who was brought up on warrant, was charged with damaging the shop windows of Mr. William Palin, provision dealer, Ann Street West. Mr. Palin said that on Friday last he was having tea in the parlour, when the prisoner came up the street and threw stones and bricks through his shop window. She said when doing it that if he would come into the shop she would throw the missiles at him, and that she would break all the windows in the place. Her reason for acting in this manner was that he had occasion to summon her in the County Court some time ago for not keeping up her payments. The Defendant was fined 1s. and costs of 4s. and was ordered to pay this amount or go to prison for seven days hard labour.

Alleged Ferocious Woman at Widnes (April 1888)
One Catherine Lawrinson of 11 Marsh Street, Widnes, was accused of unlawfully wounding George Jackson, by biting his finger.

An Unhappy Marriage (November 9th 1889)
John Tinkler, a middle-aged man living at 19 Wellington Street, had been apprehended on warrant for not having contributed to his wife's maintenance as ordered by the magistrates. Mr. Rideal, solicitor, stated that the prisoner had paid the money in arrears, therefore he would have to be discharged. Mr. Gossage asked Mr. Tinkler why he had given all this trouble, but he did not vouchsafe any reply, whereupon Mr. Lewin (deputy-magistrates` clerk) said that if he did not keep up the payments in future another warrant would be issued for his apprehension.

The pages of our local newspaper sometimes offered intriguing snippets of local scandal, such as an extra-marital affair at Farnworth. We note that generally, in reports of this type, the parties are usually anonymous although in most cases clues as to their identity are clearly given.

Elopement at Farnworth (September 28th 1878)
For some time past a fickle matron at Farnworth has been receiving the surreptitious attentions of an amorous lodger. The delinquent swain had his unlawful wooing pretty much his own way, from the fact, that the outraged husband is a signalman, and frequently compelled to work on the night turn. The lovemaking of the guilty pair advanced apace, and the treacherous porter, for such was he, made secret arrangements for a safe and speedy flight. He caused to be constructed a box, specially designed, of ingenious workmanship, and sufficient capacity, to hold his belongings and the apparel of his partner in flight. The faithless wife also made ample preparations. She got all the available coin together, and a gold watch, which had been given her by her spouse to mark some era of love, was placed ready for removal. On Saturday last, the plot being ripe, and the opportunity favourable, the elopers took their departure. The male villain was observed to remove the box referred to above, to the station and take tickets for Lime Street station. The heartless mother has left four children behind, whose ages range from 13 months to seven years.

During this same period Farnworth was in the news again, being the scene of further shocking activity.

Outrage Upon Ladies at Farnworth
Two boys, named Patrick Burns (13) and John McCabe (12) were charged with assaulting two ladies at Farnworth – one the wife of a medical man and the other the daughter of a clergyman – James Priestley, a boy, 14 years of age, residing with his parents at Widnes, said that on Monday last he was at Farnworth, when he saw Burns act indecently towards the ladies referred to by disarranging their clothes with a stick. McCabe used bad language to them and said if they did not give him a halfpenny he would knock their….eyes out. Edward Douglas, 11 years old, said he was in a lane behind Mrs. Deacon's house at Farnworth when he saw the prisoners assault the ladies, and heard them call the ladies bad names. The ladies told them to go away, but they would not do so. After one of the ladies had given corroboratory evidence, Mr. Holt said it was a very serious thing for boys to go about annoying ladies in the manner the prisoners had done. Superintendent Wood said McCabe had served seven days imprisonment for

Crime

wilful damage and he had also been birched. There was nothing against the other boy. The Prisoners were sent to Gaol for 21 days hard labour.

In the edition of 12th November 1892, an intriguing headline tells us *"Ditton Bigamist again in Trouble"*. Bigamy was not at all uncommon at this time. In 1912 the Liverpool Assizes tried three separate cases from this area. A Widnes woman cited her husband's *"disinterest and neglect"* as her reason for bigamously marrying another man. The two other cases were males, one a Widnes man the other a Runcorn man.

In June 1898 a disturbing caption *"Another child's body found in Ditton Book": Suspicious circumstances: an open verdict.* The headline leads us to believe that similar incidents had taken place previously, although the article gave no detail. However, cases of infanticide and the concealment of births occurred with alarming regularity in Widnes during this time. In fact, this crime was quite common throughout the entire country in this era. Sadly, it was not unusual to find the bodies of new-born babies dumped in ash pits or concealed in other places.

John Hankin, a blacksmith's labourer said he was standing on the railway bridge on Tuesday night when he saw the body of a small child in Ditton Brook. He told another man and went down to the water and got it out. It was wrapped up and only its feet were uncovered. The police were then sent for. Police Sergeant Twentyman said he received the body from James Cooke and James Lewis. It was the body of a fully developed male child, and was dressed in a flannelette nightdress, linen shirt, linen binder and linen napkin. There was also part of an old chemise wrapped around the body. It had been high tide at about half-past two that afternoon.

The newspaper gives an account of Dr. Hutchinson`s report on the post-mortem examination. He said that the child was about two months old and appeared to be well nourished. It was his opinion that the child was alive when thrown into the water and that the cause of death was drowning. The identity of the child was never established and an open verdict was recorded.

A drunken brawl one Saturday night in January 1903 resulted in the death of Patrick Cain, a young man from Catherine Street. Cain and his companion, Lawrence Bowles, of Edmund Street had spent the evening drinking in the Ship Inn in Victoria Street. The licensee, Mrs. Jones, said that both men had left the pub in good humour but once outside a disagreement developed. Another witness saw both men take their coats off and start to fight – they were both the worse for drink. After the fight Cain made his way home but the following day he lapsed into a coma and died. Lawrence Bowles was convicted of manslaughter and was beside himself with remorse as both young men were friends and in the past their two families had shared the same house.

In the same year, as was the pattern of all previous years, the local press reported with predictable regularity numerous cases of drunkenness and fighting. It continued to highlight the misdemeanours of "Poles" and make reference to their nationality in cases where they were involved. A headline in December 1903 ran: *"Brutal Scene in a Public House – Dangerous Poles"* In fact this headline exaggerated what seems to have been a minor disturbance where the assault charges had been dismissed by the Court. However, the headline emphasised the involvement of Poles – who were in fact Lithuanians.

Sadly, other distressing cases such as that of child neglect were not infrequent. The NSPCC brought cases against two sets of Widnes parents in 1912. One case told of a family in Margaret Street who lived in appalling conditions. Their sleeping arrangements consisted of two beds for eight persons, six adults and two children. They had no bedding as the mother had pawned it during a strike. The children were infested with vermin and needed delousing. The mother claimed the children had been infected at school. They were pupils of the Waterloo Road National School. Another case was that of a family from Timperley Street, where the parents and children slept on a dirty mattress on the floor. As in the previous case, these children, who went to Simms Cross School, were also infested.

In 1910 two middle aged men named Patrick Leonard and John Crawley, of Catherine Street, were taken into custody charged with producing illicit spirit. Mr. John Patterson, a supervisor from the Inland Revenue, described how he had searched the house and found an illicit still on the premises. The still had been made out of a milk-can and measured 2 ft. 6ins. high with a diameter of about 15ins. It was standing on bricks against a wall with a fireplace underneath complete

Crime

with a flue. In another area of the house he found a fermenting tub covered with sacks. The tub contained about 30 gallons of liquor. The tenants of the house, Mr. and Mrs. Leonard, claimed that the operation had been set up by a lodger who had left about a week ago. Both men pleaded not guilty and said they knew absolutely nothing about it. The Magistrate did not accept their story – he obviously thought it was just a load of moonshine!

The production of illicit booze may have been a fairly common occurrence and probably took place in most communities. In March 1911 at an inquest in Widnes into the death of a "Polish" woman it was established that she had died from the effect of drinking a homemade type of whiskey. It was said that she had died *"from inflammation of the stomach as she had been in the habit of drinking Polish whiskey, a mixture of methylated spirits, water, tea, sugar and pepper. Poles, it was said, made this drink themselves, and sixpennyworth would make four persons drunk".*

In 1912 the Widnes Police spent some considerable time observing a house in Sankey Street, West Bank. They noticed that large numbers of men visited the house on a regular basis. Their observations resulted in them producing evidence of *"frequent acts of immorality".* The female tenant of the house was charged with keeping a disorderly house and was fined £5. Her daughter and two other women, one a widow who had four children in the workhouse, were charged with aiding and abetting and were also fined.

The Widnes Weekly News continued to report a large number of drink related crimes but in February 1917 a surprising survey by the local Police Superintendent appeared thus:

LESS DRINKING CONVICTIONS AT WIDNES
Gradual Decrease over eight years
A survey, which extended over a period of eight years, was presented to the Widnes Licensing Sessions by Police Superintendent Foster. He outlined a gradual decrease in the number of drinking convictions in Widnes. One of the reasons cited by Superintendent Foster was a reduction in the strength of certain alcoholic liquors. However, the report said that there was still a considerable quantity of methylated spirit consumed in the Borough.

Into The Crucible

Much earlier, in 1901, The Chancellor of the Exchequer, when making his Budget Speech, said that revenues from beer duties had fallen drastically during the previous year. He was of the opinion that this was *"possibly due to a diminished spending power and to the absence of so many beer consumers in South Africa"*. One would assume that, in addition to the absence of men away at war, there were other factors that contributed to the reduction of drink-related crime. Licensing hours had been reduced, and other forms of entertainments and pastimes had evolved which offered working men an alternative to the pub.

In conclusion, when reviewing the subject of crime in Victorian Widnes, we should remember that although there is no doubt that the town was often a violent and lawless place, it was certainly no worse than any other industrial town of that period. If one were to examine any newspaper of that era, from any town of similar size and social composition, one would find comparable patterns of crime and disruptive behaviour.

Culture

The rich inheritance of culture and folklore among all the immigrant communities inevitably diminished, often with the first generation born here. The immigrants themselves might have continued their customs in their homes and amid their compatriots, but to the generations born here talk of the "old country" did not have the same emotional significance, even though they would have been aware and appreciative of their origins. For most first generation Widnesians, despite their probable feelings of affinity with their heritage, their knowledge of life outside Widnes would have been limited. It the therefore understandable why most would have been keen to conform to the attitudes and behaviour of their Widnes peer groups. This attitude accelerated the process of assimilation but also sounded the death knell for many age-old cultural customs.

In the early days the Polish and Lithuanian communities had numerous attributes that set them apart from other immigrants into Widnes. When they first arrived many women still wore an east-European style of dress. George Diggle, in his *History of Widnes*, tells us that their colourful costumes caused some curiosity among the populace. Eventually they adopted more conventional dress and their beautiful Lithuanian fashions were kept for weddings or specific events such as church walking days or even their own funerals. In a social context, there is no clear record of any identifiable Lithuanian or Polish groups or clubs where national dance or music was performed. One would suppose that this type of activity was perhaps carried out within the family circle or among close friends, or at weddings etc. However, as we have seen from the translation of *"Britain's Lithuanians 1947-1973"*, there was a short revival of Lithuanian cultural activities in the town in 1949. This resurgence was attributed to the arrival and influence of Father J. Steponaitis in St. Patrick's Parish. We can also see from the same translation that during that time a *Widnes Lithuanian Community Committee* had been formed. Interestingly, the names on the Committee represented surnames which also appeared in the town's Lithuanian records several decades earlier, *Karalius, Grazulis and Valinskas*. Unfortunately after this brief interest, and some mention of religious events, little more is known about Lithuanian activities in the area.

Traditional Lithuanian style female clothing

As many of the early immigrants into the town were unable to speak English, the Lithuanian language would have been widely spoken within their own communities. Indeed, it may have been the case, as it was in Bellshill, that the community was so insular that some Lithuanians really had no need to speak English. Although some of the older generation never completely mastered English, in most families the parents learned the English language from their children. The children who were usually bi-lingual, having been born and schooled here, were often interpreters for their parents when shopping or dealing with minor officialdom. Although the Polish and Lithuanian languages eventually disappeared from use within families, as the older generations died out, some remnants of the old life did remain longer. One example was the cooking of traditional food such as ausuki, kugalis, blinis and other potato based dishes that were still being served and enjoyed in some families of Lithuanian origin right up to the 1960s. The Black Rye bread, known as Duona, was available locally, courtesy of the Karalius/Vasilouskas bakery in West Bank. Another example was the feather quilts called Patalynes, filled with goose or duck down,

Culture

which took the place of the usual blankets used by the native English and Irish population. Of course, eventually we all caught on to that great idea, and started to use *"continental quilts"* (duvets) on our beds.

The Lithuanian rituals associated with death and funerals were also similar to the Irish traditions of waking, in that family and friends would keep watch by the side of their dead, by day and night, until the removal of the corpse to church prior to burial. Lithuanians always dressed their dead in their best clothes rather than the white shroud that was the usual death garb in Britain. Women particularly, often had outfits ready for this purpose; this was usually a traditional Lithuanian headdress with ribbons and a dress with an apron. The men wore their best suits and shoes. This tradition of sending the dead off to the afterlife was like sending them off to a festival, well dressed, with abundant decorations.

Unlike the Lithuanians, who for various reasons may have felt a need to conform and be accepted; the Irish preserved their culture much longer. This preservation of Irish traditions was helped in some ways by the Catholic Church that was still served by numerous Irish priests. Irish dance culture was popularised by the weekly ceilidh held in parish halls and the steps and movements of traditional dances like *The Siege of Ennis, The Walls of Limerick* and *The Waves of Tory* were handed down through generations of dancers. The oral history of music and Irish songs also continued, and was sustained into the 20th century by popular ballads sung by Count John McCormack, Delia Murphy and Josef Locke. This type of entertainment was a successor of the pseudo-Irish vaudeville or stage-Irish songs that were popular decades before. They were the kind of songs sung in the Music Halls and locally in places like *The Alex Theatre,* whose productions included shows like *The Lily of Killarney* and other Irish themed performances which catered to the large Irish community in the town.

The celebrating of St. Patrick's Day was a twofold event. It was primarily a Saints Day; a religious festival that was commemorated in most Roman Catholic Churches and Schools in England by the singing of the hymn *"Hail Glorious St. Patrick"*. Despite its obvious religious association, the day was also viewed as a traditional way of emigrants declaring their Irishness. The rituals associated with the day would have become all the more important the longer they were away from their homeland. It was a personal way of acknowledging their roots and remembering the people and places they had left behind. The wearing of shamrock and the wearing of green on this day was also an important tradition proudly upheld by generations of Irish immigrants. The shamrock, the trefoil used by St. Patrick to demonstrate the Holy Trinity, was a symbol of Ireland's conversion to Christianity. Along with this display of shamrock, wearing the colour green, even if only characterised by a small item of clothing, was customary. The significance of wearing green was in part an act of defiance against England. Although it may sound ludicrous today, in earlier times English laws had forbidden the native Irish population to wear this colour as it had become associated with anti-English sentiments. The same draconian laws had proscribed the singing of songs that mentioned the name of Ireland. To triumph over these laws the native Irish had devised secret words or names to describe their country in song. Countless well-known Irish love songs are about Ireland although their true meaning is well disguised. These usually refer to Ireland as a beautiful woman, i.e. *The Dark Rosaleen* or *Cathleen Na Houlahaun*.

The Irish "Wake", which has previously been mentioned, was a tradition that derived from ancient Celtic spiritual rites. As with the Lithuanians, the waking of a body was considered an important religious ritual and most people had their laying-out clothes, sheets and candles put away in readiness for their death. The washing of the body also had certain rules, for instance it was considered bad luck to be involved in the washing of the body of a member of ones` own family. The covering of mirrors, the closing of curtains, all of these actions were of significance during the time prior to the funeral.

Membership of Irish clubs and organisations appeared to flourish in the last decades of the 19th century and the early years of the 20th century. *The Irish National League,* which formed a local branch in Widnes in 1885, had a huge membership. This organisation had political influence with the Irish voters in Widnes and speakers regularly came to town to talk about Irish issues. *The Irish Foresters` Association* also had an active branch in Widnes. In Liverpool, *The Gaelic League*, which promoted the preservation of Gaelic culture through language, music and song, had a healthy membership. This

Culture

organisation was still active in Liverpool up until the 1960s. In the Widnes section of *Slater's Directory* of 1895 we see that there was an *Irish Social Club* at 90 Victoria Road. Daniel Lowry, an estate and insurance agent from Lugsdale Road, was named as Secretary of this Club. Mr. Lowry later moved to America where he became a famous impresario who owned several theatres in New York. Interestingly, television's *"Choir Master"*, Gareth Malone, is a descendant of this man.

The Welsh too were members of clubs and organisations. *The Welsh National Society* and the many Welsh orientated church organisations had large memberships. The Welsh language was still widely spoken and, as in the case of the Lithuanians, in their own designated area of the town their native language was the primary method of communication. Their much loved musical traditions were maintained by the establishment of the annual *Widnes Eisteddfod* which became a recognised event that attracted first-class performers from far and wide. The Welsh churches were also places of social gatherings and there are numerous reports of concerts and outings. The Welsh residents of the town did maintain a degree of their culture for some considerable time, and the Welsh were a notable ethnic presence well into the early decades of the 20th century. However, the fact that the Welsh were assimilated into the general population much earlier than other groups meant that their traditions probably became diluted sooner too.

On the face of it, one would not expect to find too many parallels between Irish, Eastern-European and Welsh immigrants. Nevertheless, when we scratch the surface we find numerous similarities. Comparisons and obvious affinities between the various immigrant communities probably derive from their shared rural backgrounds, also the like experiences which made it necessary for them to leave their native lands. The early Irish and Eastern-Europeans immigrants were similar in that they were refugees as well as economic migrants, and both were the targets of discrimination. In addition, the rural origins of all the groups meant that their experience of adapting to urban life was the same. Apart from the obvious shared experience of migration, there were also many other joint or comparable traditions. It should not be forgotten that the Welsh, as Celts, shared many of the Celtic traditions of the Irish, particularly those associated with seasonal or rural rituals. Furthermore, the Irish and Lithuanian groups also had many similar or

Into The Crucible

shared traditions. Arranged marriages, which involved the services of a *"matchmaker"*, were common practice in both cultures, although this would probably not have been in evidence once they arrived in this country. The waking of the dead, or the night watch, was also a shared ritual as was their religious affiliation. Therefore, when one looks beneath the veneer of ethnicity or religious division, we can see that these individual groups had more in common than they might have thought.

The War Years

The 1st Company of the 47th Lancashire Rifle Volunteers was formed in Widnes in 1871 and during the first few months their numbers grew to around 50. In 1872, due to the increasing membership, a second company was formed. In those early days, before they had the luxury of a proper venue, the Volunteers drilled in the "National School" in Waterloo Road and their commanding officers were Major James Cross and Captain Wareing.[141]

Speaking in 1872, at the Annual Dinner of *The Widnes Cricket Club*, of which he was a member, Major Cross said:

"As to the Widnes Volunteers, everyone would be glad to know that they were getting on in such a way that he hoped next summer to see them attending battalion drills with something not far short of 400 men. With their friend, Mr. Kershaw's* assistance they would soon have a new Drill Hall, 100 ft. long by 50 ft. wide, fitted with sergeant's residence, office, and every convenience"

As hoped, Mr. Kershaw, the builder, was able to meet expectations and the new Drill Hall[142] in Victoria Road was duly completed. As a finishing touch, and a lasting reminder, the crest of The Rifle Regiment was proudly displayed above the doorway. This building was to serve the Volunteers well for the next forty years or so, until it was replaced in 1912 by a new Barracks in Peelhouse Lane. The old Drill Hall was subsequently sold and many years later the building became known as The Black Cat Billiard Hall.

Just before Christmas in 1889, two men from Widnes enjoyed a pleasant evening at The Crosby Hotel in Withy Grove, Manchester.

---

[141] In 1880 the 47th Lancashire Rifle Volunteers became the 21st Lancashire Rifle Volunteers.
* *Mr. Kershaw was a local builder*
[142] Drill Hall built in 1873

Into The Crucible

They were attending the 6th Annual Dinner for the survivors of *"The Charge of the Light Brigade"*. There were just nine survivors of that infamous event present on that evening, including Sergeant MacGregor and Thomas Wright who both lived in Widnes. It was said that Sergeant MacGregor wore the Victoria Cross and other medals at the dinner, although I can find no mention of him in any list of VC recipients. Sergeant Macgregor had had an eventful military career. He served in the Punjab and Kaffir Wars and went all through the Crimea. He subsequently took part in the quelling of the Indian Mutiny and the Chinese War. He was discharged on full pension in 1862 after 20 years' service. However he was not content to finish with the military and when the American Civil War broke out he joined in the fray, losing his right arm in the process. He lived in Hutchinson Street where he traded as a herbalist. At this point in time Thomas Wright, (of whom more is written in this chapter), lived in Cholmondeley Street and was employed as a labourer at the Gaskell Deacon works.

At the outbreak of the Boer War the Widnes Volunteers made an offer to serve overseas. They joined with the 1st Battalion of the South Lancashire Regiment at Ladysmith in March 1900. Some historians have described the Boer War as the *"last of the little wars"*. To those taking part this was no "little war" but almost three years of tough battle before the defeat of the Boers, Afrikaners and other foreign volunteer forces. I am sorry to say that the British forces, apart from the obvious dangers of conflict, were also exposed to diseases and infections and many died as a direct result of these additional hazards.

The famous sieges of Ladysmith, Mafeking and Kimberley and the subsequent relieving of these places are well documented. While it is almost impossible to place ourselves into a mental image of those times, television documentaries and history books allow us to scratch the surface. Not surprisingly, the story of this conflict takes on a special poignancy when we realise that hundreds of local volunteers left Widnes to take part in this historic event. Included here are two letters written by Widnes men. The letters give us a personal and moving account of the experiences of ordinary soldiers in the Boer War. I think it is fair to say that no matter how many books and films we read and watch, nothing compares to first-hand descriptions penned by brave young men who came from our own town. Some of the content, though distressing, allow us to see these real events through the eyes of

The War Years

the participants rather than from the pens of historians. The fact that they were written by young Widnesians, who had volunteered to go, make them all the more interesting.

The first letter is from Private E. Donnelly who was writing in September 1900 to his friend Alexander Hillock, of 21 Harris Street, Halton View.

6th Brigade, South African Field Force, South Africa.
September 17th 1900.

"Dear Alexander.

I received your welcome letter safe, and was very glad to see that you are all well in Widnes. I am still in the best of health and have not got touched by the Boers as yet. I heard today that De Wet had been killed, but don't know whether it is a fact or not. It's a pity if he is killed, for we might have got him for schoolmaster to our generals when the war is over, but nevertheless I think it will cause a change in the course of events, as he caused more trouble out here than all the rest of the Boers combined. They have got a complete smashing up all round here lately, and I think it won't last very long now, but one doesn't know what may turn up. I assure you I won't be sorry when it's all over. I think if I get to bed again I'll never rise. All our sides are like shoe leather, - lying around on stones and lumps, but our health as a general rule is very good. I see some of the Brooksboro` chaps have arrived home. John Kenny, the policeman's son, was the first. They burned a tar barrel and stood a barrel of porter on his arrival, and had a general flare-up all round the city. I know if they stand a barrel when I arrive I will make a big hole in it myself. There are a great many chaps getting knocked over from time to time, and also a lot dying from disease. As a matter of fact a lot of them are completely done up, and no wonder considering the hardships they have endured. It has been very cold at night during the last few months, but it is getting nice and warm now, which will make it more pleasant for us. I think by the time you receive this letter the war will be about over, but the women are going to start when the men finish. A few days ago a woman shot a scout, and while he lay on the ground she actually riddled his body with bullets. It was the most brutal thing I have come across since the war started. Give my love to all my old friends about Widnes."

E. DONNELLY.

Into The Crucible

The second letter is from Private Jeremiah McDonald, writing in April 1900 to his wife, who resided at 44 Brown Street, Moss Bank.

Private Jeremiah McDonald 1st South Lancashire Regiment.

"Dear wife and family,

I now take the pleasure of writing these few lines to let you know that I am going on alright. It was a stiff do we had for the Boers did not like the idea of losing the position they were in – that was around Ladysmith. We lost our Colonel and about three hundred men. The last hill we took was the hill that relieved Ladysmith. We fell in on the morning of 28th February, and Sir Charles Warren* told us we must take the hill at all costs, so when we marched out we were just like one man, never losing a single man until we got to close quarters. Then the bullets were flying all around us. It did not matter – on we went, and instead of taking one hill we took three, so when Sir R. Buller saw what we had done he ordered the remainder of the troops to fall in, and told them that our regiment had taken the hills. They gave three cheers, and the cavalry marched into Ladysmith that night, and our division marched in next morning and relieved 20,000 people in addition to our troops. There was cheering! I thought they would have gone mad, after having been closed up for five months. I came across Duffy just as we started the battle, but how he has gone on I could not say. You might remember the young fellow I called back when we were in the dockyard for a drink. He was close by me when he got shot in the head, and died shortly after. I have been sick for a few days. The reason of it was that we had to lie where the Boers had to bury their dead. But I am all right again. I am very pleased that your mother is stopping with you. She should have come long ago. Tell her I will be able to tell many a good story about this lot. It is a splendid place out here. They got a sovereign a day out here in the gold fields, but everything is very dear. You must excuse me for not sending any money home, for I have not received any pay since I left Preston. I hear that we are leaving Natal, going round by Capetown and through the Orange Free State. That is what we are told. We will have three days sailing from Durban, so it might be a few weeks before I can write again. If you write to Jimmy Colber tell him that Farmer got killed, and Tom Pickering got his leg blown off with shot from Long Tom. Tell your Jim to keep the old jug until I have a good drink when I land home again. The latest game out here is

---

* Sir Charles Warren was previously the Chief Commissioner of the Metropolitan Police during the period of the "Whitechapel Murders"

The War Years

"Duck down boys, there's Long Tom again". Tell your Tommy and Billy that I have got the Queen's chocolate for them as soon as I get some money to send it with, and another thing don't forget the bell-bottoms. Many a time I laugh when I think of it. So I have no more to say this time. Give my best regards to your sister and her husband, and your Jim, and tell them I am doing very well. There is a nobleman's wife asking me if I had anyone depending on me at home, so I told her I had a wife and two children. She took my address and said she would send you some money. If she does, write a nice letter and thank her for it. They are going mad about the relief of Ladysmith, that is the reason they are sending it, so let me know in the next letter whether she wrote or not.

*With loving regards,
from your husband".*

The experiences related by Private McDonald where he talks of two friends being killed and another having his leg blown off are indeed shocking. No doubt, for those at home, the knowledge that their friends and loved ones were facing such dangers was hard to endure. When Private Donnelly had written to his friend in September 1900 he expressed an opinion that the War would soon be over. Unfortunately it continued for a further twenty months. On Sunday morning, 2nd June 1902, the piercing sound of Bolton's Factory buzzer[*] gave the first indications to most Widnesians that peace had been declared in South Africa. Many were in their churches at morning services when the welcome news arrived. Those who were gathered in the Milton Congregational Church at Simms Cross were about to leave when on opening the doors they heard young boys outside shouting *"Peace declared"*. The congregation returned to their seats and at this point, led by the organ, sang *"Praise God from whom all blessings flow"*. It was observed that *"some hearts were too full to sing and their gratitude found expression in tears of joy"*. In St. Mary's Parish Church in West Bank there were similar emotional scenes as worshippers gave thanks to God for peace.[*]

---

[*] This buzzer is reputed to have once belonged to Isambard Kingdom Brunel's famous Ship *"The Great Eastern"*
[*] *Widnes Weekly News* – June 1902

Into The Crucible

In Newtown, St. Mary's (Marie's) Band quickly assembled for parade and marched down past the Town Hall, through Victoria Road, Waterloo Road, and Mersey Road to the delight of people who had gathered to celebrate the long-awaited news. Churches throughout the town rang their bells to spread the good news to those further afield. The exuberance was no less on Monday morning as public buildings hoisted their flags. In no time at all flags and bunting festooned most of the streets throughout the town. Shops in district thoroughfares quickly decorated their windows with patriotic emblems and flags.

In September, the Lord Mayor of Liverpool gave soldiers from the 3rd and 4th battalions of the *King's (Liverpool) Regiment*, who had been on active service in South Africa, a splendid welcome home. Among the returning men were a number of Local Reservists from Widnes and Runcorn. The Widnes men were:

Private T. Burke	*Gossage Street*
Private R.M. Jones	*Kent Street*
Private P.Cain	*Edmund Street*
Private A. Fitzharris	*Oxford Street*
Private P.Hooligan	*Suttons Lane*
Private M. Livingston	*Pear Street*
Private J. McCormick	*Water Street*
Private J. Murphy	*George Street*
Private M.Mullen	*Chatham Street*
Private M.Mulloy	*Fisher Street*
Private W. Mitchell	*Rose Street*
Private M.Mannion	*Elizabeth Street*
Private H. Peake	*Warrington Road*
Private W. Peake	*Dixon Street*

The following year, 1903, the exuberance experienced when our soldiers returned from war was dampened by the death of one of our well-respected citizens. The town was in mourning for 71year old Thomas Wright who had died at his home in Major Cross Street. Although Thomas Wright was actually born in Warrington he had spent a large part of his life in Widnes and was a *"local hero"*. In the early 1850s he enlisted into the 17th Lancers *"Death or Glory Boys"* and served in the Indian Mutiny and all through the Crimean War. He also rode at Balaclava in the famous *"Charge of the Light Brigade"*. *The Widnes*

Weekly News voiced the opinion that he should be afforded a full military funeral, but this did not happen. In April 1903 a memorial stone was placed over his grave at Widnes Cemetery, paid for entirely by public subscription. After a public ceremony, the grave and memorial were officially handed over to Widnes Town Council, as the representatives of the townspeople. Also donated to the town, to be hung in the Widnes Public Library, was a *"large carbon portrait, handsomely framed, of the great hero"*. This portrait, also purchased by public subscription, was given to the town on the explicit understanding that it would be placed on permanent display in the Public Library in Victoria Square.

An additional point of interest regarding the survivors of The Charge of the Light Brigade is that, subsequently, many of them lived in abject poverty. Furthermore they were unable to gain any form of assistance from the British Government. George McGregor, the other Widnes survivor of that calamitous event, wrote numerous letters to the press regarding the callous behaviour of the British Government towards the veterans who had taken part in that blood-soaked battle. One of his letters included the following text:

> *"The old accusation still remains that a man may fight for his country, may lose a limb, be crippled for life, be reduced to the lowest edge of poverty, and the country won't acknowledge him. I am not speaking for myself just now. Providence has placed me above the cringing posture of begging bread from my countrymen. But I am writing on behalf of many a poor fellow, survivor of those inglorious days, who would be glad of a little help from the War Office. Surely, the time is gone by when the bravest nation under the sun will hesitate to perform such a noble act, and thus wipe away one terrible blot which bids fair to eternally besmear her escutcheon."*

I think that most people reading this today will share George McGregor's sense of outrage that these gallant men were treated in such a cavalier and shoddy manner. The fact is that those who survived were lucky to have escaped with their lives because of an appalling mistake by their commanding officers. One can only hope that Mr. McGregor's campaign to get reparation for his fellow veterans had a successful outcome.[143]

---

[143] *"Across The Gap"* – Jean M. Morris (Springfield Farrihy 2016)

Into The Crucible

The jubilation that marked the end of the Boer War was relatively short-lived. Barely twelve years later, in 1914, the country was at war once again; this time with Germany. As in previous conflicts, a large number of the male population of Widnes were away fighting for their country. Nearly every home in the town had someone serving or knew someone who was serving at the front.

The War was never far from the minds of the public and constant reminders of it were on view everywhere. The following notice appeared in all local places.

Recruiting Notice
WARNING TO EMPLOYERS
***Extract from Amendments of Defence of Realm Regulations
dated 22nd December 1916***

Every person who employs any man or men between 18 and 41 years of age is required by Regulation 41a made under the Defence of the Realm Acts to make and keep constantly posted up in some conspicuous place on the premises where such men are employed or on his own premises or, then on said premises, a list of such men in the form provided for the purpose and obtainable at any Post Office.

*It shall be the duty of every person who under this Regulation is required to make such a list aforesaid, or who keeps such record as aforesaid to **deliver forthwith** to the Recruiting Officer for the locality in the first week in each calendar month.*

There were also numerous regulations in force that were considered necessary to national security. The issuing of permits to gain entry to controlled factories was considered to be extremely important. The following case was the first of its kind in the area. The site referred to was the Pilkington Sullivan works.

The War Years

ILLEGALLY ENTERING CONTROLLED WORKS
Workmen sent to prison for exchanging permits
The first case in Widnes under the regulations for safeguarding munitions works and preventing wrongful entry thereto was heard at the Widnes Petty Sessions on Thursday. James Foy of Waterloo Road, was charged with unlawfully having in his possession on February 12th 1917 a permit issued to Thomas Killgallon to enter a certain place in which work was carried on by the Ministry of Munitions, as being a place in the public safety necessary to be safeguarded. Thomas Killgallon also of Waterloo Road was charged, being a person to whom a permit was issued for his own use to enter the works, handed it over and allowed James Foy to use it. Major B. Lewis and Captain Roberts of the R.D.C. were present on behalf of the military.

A number of local men of foreign origin were interned at the outbreak of war. Among these was Mr. Meuller who was the chief glassblower at Towers Glassworks. It was also a bad time for the Lithuanian and Polish communities of the town. The hostility they had faced when they had first arrived in Britain in the 1880s began to resurface.

Lithuanians and Poles living and working in England, although classed as aliens, were also deemed to be subjects of an allied power, Russia. Because of this, they were excluded from *compulsory* service in the British forces. Unfortunately, as a result of their exclusion from military conscription, a great deal of resentment developed. In Lanarkshire there is oral and written history telling of windows of Lithuanian homes being smashed, graffiti on walls and general harassment. There is also an oral history of similar happenings here, although only on a very small scale. Some foreign owned shops in West Bank had their windows smashed. Although a great many of the Widnes Lithuanians and Poles *did* enlist voluntarily, some did not feel any commitment to do so. This was not surprising in view of the fact that they had absolutely *"no rights"* as aliens. They were not British citizens and could not vote or enjoy any of the benefits afforded to British citizens. Therefore perhaps it is understandable why they would be reluctant to put their lives on the line for a country that did not allow them any constitutional liberties.

The increasing resentment regarding the non-conscription of foreigners resulted in the *Anglo-Russian Military Agreement.* This

Into The Crucible

agreement provided for a reciprocal liability to military service. Aliens were given the option of returning to "Russia" or enlisting in the British Services. However, it appears that Scotland was the only place in Britain where the full implementation of the convention took place. Around 1200 Lithuanians from Scotland elected to return to Russia to fight[144]. However, we should not suppose that Lithuanian and Polish residents in Widnes did not make any firm commitments to the war effort. Coal and iron industries, under wartime requirements, were being urged by the Government to give their utmost efforts in the production of vital materials to feed the wartime industrial machine. A significant number of Poles and Lithuanians from this area took up employment in the coalmines at Sutton Manor and Bold during this time, making their own valuable contributions to the war effort in this way.

The Irish were technically British and had been settled here longer. Most had Widnes born sons old enough to enlist. Of course the Irish had a long history of joining the British Army and did so in large numbers both here and over in Ireland. In the small town of Carrick-on-Suir, taken as our example in another chapter, it was said that around a thousand men left the town in British uniform and headed off to France, many never to return[*]. Nearby in Waterford, in just one small street there were numerous men listed as *"killed in action"* or *"missing"*. In Doyle Street, also in the city of Waterford, one family lost four sons. A monument to the memory of the Waterford men who died in that war has recently been erected in the city. Particular mention is made of a young 14year old Waterford boy, John Condon, who was the youngest Irish soldier to die.[*]

The Irish of Widnes also enlisted in large numbers. In Newtown almost every house had a husband or son in the war. Some time ago Harry Jones produced a very moving book *"I Don't Want To Be A Sunbeam"* in which he lists the WW1 dead on the Widnes War Memorial. This poignant and very worthwhile book has proved a valuable resource to the local historian. More importantly, it tells a

---

[144] In Scotland, after men had returned to Russia their wives and families experienced great hardship. Many were evicted from their homes as most houses were tied to employment.

[*] Dr. Patrick C. Power *"Carrick-on-Suir and her people"*

[*] Information supplied by Bernard Flanagan of Waterford.

The War Years

story of human sacrifice and paints a graphic picture of the terrible suffering and loss felt by countless families in this town.

I list below the names of the Irish born men whose names appear on the Widnes War Memorial.[145]

Name	*Born*	*Resided*
Peter Bennett	Cork	Widnes
William Burns	Wicklow	Ireland
Martin Connor	Wicklow	Wicklow
Brien Devaney	Mayo	Widnes
Patrick Gallagher	Bundoran	Widnes
Edward Halpine	Meath	Farrant Street
John Holligan	Wexford	Widnes
John Lane	Longford	Oakland Street
Pte. P. Melia	Mayo	Mayo
John Sutherland	Enniscorthy	Unknown
Andrew Tighe	Galway	Galway
Michael Treacey	Limerick	Brown Street
Thomas Tunney	Mayo	Timperley Street

In addition to these names there were in the region of fifty other men who were Widnes born of Irish parents.

A soldier listed as Frank Kennedy was in fact a young Lithuanian called Pitchilingi who enlisted under another name. It is quite probable that there were many others from the Lithuanian or Polish communities who had anglicised their names or taken another name when they enlisted. Obviously these were in addition to the many from that community who enlisted under their own names.

The Welsh community also suffered numerous losses. Listed below are the names of Welsh born men whose names appear on our local Cenotaph. In addition, like the Irish, there were also numerous other men who were Widnes born of Welsh parentage.

---

[145] Harry Jones *"I Don't Want To Be a Sunbeam"* - (Cenotaph Publishing, Widnes) 1999

Into The Crucible

Name	Born	Resided
John Richard Brown	Wrexham	Widnes
Thomas Dean	Flint	Widnes
Lewis Griffiths	Flint	Widnes
Conway Griffiths	Holywell	Widnes
Thomas Harding	Cardiff	Widnes
Albert Roberts	Ruthin	Widnes
William Roberts	Festiniog	Widnes
Harold Thompson	Pontypridd	Widnes
George F. Powell	Ruthin	Widnes
Ernest Williams	Denbigh	Widnes

Recruitment continued throughout the War and by 1917 the army was recruiting for the so called *"Bantam Regiments"*. The requirements for age, height and chest measurements for the *"Bantams"* were obviously less than for other regiments. The rising casualty lists and the insatiable demand for reinforcements caused the army to relax standards and accept younger men of small stature. Those who earlier in the War would have been rejected for lack of physical stature were now able to enlist. This new lower standard encouraged young boys to lie about their age in order to join up. Many of them did so, often using another person's birth certificate.

In his book *"A History of Widnes"* George Diggle makes reference to the recruitment of *"Bantam Regiments"* in Widnes. He says: *"Men born and bred in Waterloo Road, Newtown, Lugsdale or Moss Bank might hope to qualify by such meagre standards."*[146] In view of the large number of men from these districts who had been to the fore in enlisting from the very beginning of the War, some making the ultimate sacrifice, this statement is both misinformed and curious. Did he imagine that the main inhabitants of these areas were in some way physically substandard?

The Widnes Weekly News of those years makes depressing reading as the weekly lists of local dead appear to grow longer. The local population were kept up to date with happenings at *"The Front"* by watching the newsreels at the local picture houses. A new picture house in Albert Road, *"The Premier"*, opened its doors to the public for

---

[146] George E Diggle – *"A History of Widnes"* page 136

The War Years

the first time on 14th June 1915. In November of that year, directly across the road, the old *"Albert Hall"* was refurbished and re-opened as *"The Bozzadrome"*. Sadly, the new wonder of cinematography also brought the horrors of war home to this first generation of picture-goers

The Co-operative Hall, in Lugsdale Road, endeavoured to lighten their programmes with live entertainment after the films. On the 26th February 1917 the following advert appeared:

> *THE BATTLE OF THE ANCRE*
> *and*
> *THE ADVANCE OF THE TANKS*
> *Supported by*
> *DNIG SEN BROTHERS*
> *(The Great Chinese Hair Gymnasts)*

In Widnes, life appeared to proceed with some degree of normality. We read about horticultural shows, church events and the all-important hints and tips for allotment holders who were instructed in the merits of growing potatoes, leeks, and haricot beans. The allotments had become very important in providing an additional source of food in those times of shortage. Various portions of land had been provided in the town for this purpose. By 1918 there were almost 400 allotments providing valuable crops of vegetables to supplement the meagre and expensive food supply. The shortage of basic food items like tea and meat had caused prices to rise and long queues outside grocery and butchers shops were a common sight.

Some of the local cinemas and theatres placed a large advert saying that they would not be increasing their admission prices in spite of a new tax on amusements. The newest picture house, *"The Premier"* was among those who did not propose a price increase. The other premises keeping prices at the same level were *The Alexandra Theatre; The Co-operative Hall; The Picturedrome* and *The Bozzadrome.*

Into The Crucible

The Co-operative Hall continued to offer popular and novel entertainment. On May 11th 1917 a lady called Madame Ali made an appearance:

> ### MADAME ALI – the Wonder Woman
> ### Special Matinee for Ladies
> *All persons desiring information of friends and relatives are requested to bring photographs of persons they inquire about.*

One would assume that Madame Ali was a medium or fortune-teller. This appears at odds with an article that appeared a short while earlier, in the January 19th edition of *The Widnes Weekly News*. The article seems to suggest that fortune-telling was illegal at that time. The report concerns a West Bank fortune-teller who was brought before the Court on a charge of deception. Unfortunately one of her clients was the daughter of a senior policeman.

WIDNES FORTUNE TELLER HEAVILY FINED
Strange tales told to Police Inspector's daughter

Hannah Proffitt of Beaumont Street was charged with unlawfully deceiving his Majesty's subjects by professing to tell fortunes. Superintendent Foster said one of those who visited the defendant was the daughter of Detective Inspector Davidson. The defendant told her among other things that her father would die shortly.

There was a sharp fall in drink related crimes in Widnes during the war years. The Government had introduced legislation to reduce the opening hours of pubs in an attempt to curb and control the drinking habits of the workforce, particularly those who were involved in munitions or engineering occupations. These new licensing laws greatly contributed to the reduction in the crime rate.

As had happened at the end of The Boer War, Bolton's buzzer was again the first of the works sirens to herald the end of the war This time however, Bolton's siren was accompanied by a cacophony of buzzers

The War Years

and hooters from other works, as well as maroons and fog signals. The Mayor, Alderman Davies, announced the good news from the steps of the Town Hall where a large crowd had gathered in anticipation of the event. As with the end of the previous war, there was great jubilation throughout the town as mothers, fathers, wives, sisters, brothers, sons and daughters looked forward to welcoming their loved ones home. Of course for some unfortunate families their loved ones would never return.

In the immediate aftermath of the War many of the returning soldiers faced unemployment and homelessness. By 1920 there were almost 3,000 unemployed in the town. The General Election in 1919 saw the election of Widnes' first Labour MP, Arthur Henderson. Widnes now had its own Constituency Labour Party, affiliated to the National Labour Party. During the War years all municipal elections had been suspended, but as soon as elections resumed Labour councillors started being elected onto the Town Council. Labour stalwarts like Daniel Garghan, John Millar and John Travers were among the first elected.

Into The Crucible

Church Street, Farnworth (now known as Farnworth Street)

Epilogue

Into the Crucible, the title of this book, describes what happened in Widnes in the nineteenth century when concentrated industry reached our area and Widnes became the *"Crucible"* that held a multitude of people from diverse backgrounds and ethnicities. Widnes had once been a pleasant place, a destination for day-trippers retreating from the bustle of Liverpool. Before the end of the 19th century that rural idyll was just a memory as the area was transformed from a collection of small pastoral hamlets into a place of dense industrialisation. The once bucolic landscape was replaced by a forest of smoking chimneys and large scale atmospheric contamination. As well as the environmental transformation, there was a marked shift in the fabric of local society as the area became a magnet for a flood of new workers.

The sweeping changes brought about through rapid industrialisation were drastic, both environmentally and in human terms. The indigenous population, as well as the majority of newcomers, were mainly farm workers or rural artisans with little or no experience of heavy industry. They were unused to organised work patterns or the unique problems of concentrated urbanisation. The incomparable alteration in their lifestyles, and the massive volume of people from diverse backgrounds who had been thrown together, meant that the composition of society and its behaviour had been completely transformed. The traditional and accepted social order had been swiftly converted from a rural society into an industrial one – in fact our first truly industrial society.

One of the aims of this book was to record the history of the ordinary working people who populated our town, and also to examine the process involved in the creation of our first industrial society. As I have explained, this new society was a difficult complex mix of people from different backgrounds and cultures, who were all dealing with the exceptional problems of an unfamiliar urban routine. I have endeavoured to describe the ordinary experiences of their lives and the work they did; the conditions they worked under; and the environments they lived in. I have also examined the building up of *"minority"* communities; and the continuance of previous cultural customs, as well as the problems associated with racial tensions and discrimination.

When exploring the creation of our nineteenth century industrial society, and its relevance to present-day people, it is important to recognise the extreme diversity of the population at that time. Therefore it should be acknowledged that immigration is a very important part of our local story because of the varied collection of people and traditions that helped to shape our local identity. Most Widnes families descend from immigrant origins, be their roots in other parts of the British mainland, or on the island of Ireland or from the shores of the Baltic. What is certain is that very few of us can claim to be descended from the original indigenous populations of the villages and hamlets in and around Widnes. Indeed, our present society is the product of immigration and integration. From the inception of the chemical industry in the mid-1840s and onwards, the rapid influx of people from outside the area is clearly defined in census returns. The original population prior to that time was little more than 3000 people, with the population figure reaching over 30,000 by 1891, followed by a steady rise afterwards. Although these figures include a natural population growth amongst the established populace, nevertheless, from 1850 until the early years of the 20th century the population was swelled by a flood of people from elsewhere. Therefore it is safe to assume that very few of us have local origins.

With that fact in mind, it was important to look at the configuration of our early industrial population. Who were they, where did they come from and why did they come here? It was clear that many were internal migrants from mainland Britain, from the north the south, the east and the west of the country, as well as from Scotland and Wales. However, it was also evident that there were huge numbers from Ireland who made up a large portion of our population. In later times there was a new wave of migration that involved people from the Baltic region who also had a significant impact upon the structure of our society. The mix of people was astounding and more astonishing was the fact that the society they created was something of a phenomenon. It was a new type of social order with no natural blueprint or points of

Epilogue

reference to guide it. It was a collection of mainly rural folk, thrust into an unknown environment of urban housing and factory work. Studies have shown that the subsequent behaviour of the new society that emerged after The Industrial Revolution was shaped by their new surroundings, rather than by their previous way of life. Of course the effects of The Industrial Revolution were fairly late in reaching our area. Nevertheless, when it did happen the impact was intense both environmentally and in human terms. As we see in this book, the rapid development of industry and the employment opportunities this presented made our area a magnet for people from near and far.

It was my intention to present to this reader an explanation as to why foreign migrants came here, and to highlight the contributions they made to our town. Of course the answer to the first part is that they came here simply because they needed to, and because there was an opportunity to work. The historical backgrounds to their migration are in some cases complicated and involve the complex histories of their native countries. In many cases there are tales of hardship and political and religious oppression and, in the case of the early Irish migrants, starvation and the tyranny of landlords were major factors. Although all of the "external" immigrants, without exception, came here in the hope of finding a better life, most were unwelcome and faced a huge amount of hostility. They were looked upon as a threat to the labour market and were treated with resentment and aggression in the workplace. Local inhabitants in all the areas they populated behaved in a similar manner, treating them with contempt and antipathy. Because of this attitude many were forced to live a transient lifestyle, moving from place to place in the hope of finding somewhere better, where settlement seemed possible. How and why did they put up with this? The answer is obvious, whatever the conditions, however hard the work, or whatever hostility faced them, it was, they believed, infinitely better than what they had left behind.

Throughout this book I have tried to show how hard it was for these early incomers who, in many cases, were as much refugees as economic migrants. In all honesty I have struggled not to show bias, or to be unduly generous towards them. However, when one reads actual documentation and newspaper reports of those times, it is very hard not to feel an overwhelming sympathy and sadness for their plight. It is also difficult not to feel a degree of anger and shame at the way some of these poor unfortunate people were treated when they arrived here. One assumes that most believed that once they reached our shores their lives and the lives of their families would improve. Unfortunately the "hoped for" improvement rarely materialised.

Once on these shores the immigrants found work only in the lowest and worst paid occupations. They came in right at the bottom of the labour market, doing work which even the poorest English worker would not do if they could help it. They lived in the slum environment of poor housing although their rural backgrounds made them especially ill-fitted for the ordeal of slum life. For many of the immigrants this new urbanisation and factory life had detrimental effects on family life. The family unit often had difficulty adapting to their changing circumstances. The proliferation of public houses on their doorstep was a great temptation after an arduous day working under unpleasant and often dangerous conditions. The fact that living space was often shared with others (to economise on the rent) also made the public house a more attractive proposition. The warm hospitality of the pub was probably a marked contrast to the bleak squalor of their homes. This meant that the obvious benefit derived from a regular income was often negated by the amount spent on drink. However, it should be stressed that not all immigrants were drinkers. Many of the Irish and Lithuanians were teetotal, although contemporary newspapers and journals of the time would lead us to believe that they were all brawling drunkards. The vast majority were decent law abiding citizens who came here simply to find a better life for themselves and their families.

Of course, when we review the above paragraph, it should be stressed that the living and working conditions of the native English workers were identical. Many of them were originally rural workers who were ill-suited to the trials of slum living and dense overcrowding. They too were unused to the routines of factory work, having previously only worked to the rhythm of seasonal or climatic requirements. In the same way, the problems associated with alcohol abuse and crime was also replicated among the native English population. In fact, in many ways their work and life experiences in Widnes were identical and equally gruelling. However, they did not face hostility, nor did they have the added difficulties of language and cultural discrimination to overcome. More importantly, they were not

Epilogue

compelled to come here because of a background of civil and religious oppression or certain death from starvation.

By the second decade of the 20th century most of the second generation Irish, Lithuanian, Polish and Welsh, an increasing number of who were born in Widnes, had begun to lose their ethnic characteristics. These people now behaved more like the population in general and had become more recognisable as part of mainstream working-class life, although most of them retained a residual awareness of their ethnic heritage. In the case of some ethnicities assimilation into other ethnic groups was a slow process; nevertheless, this did eventually happen. As a consequence, integration between communities by inter-marriage with both the indigenous population and those of other ethnicities brought forth a new breed of citizen - *The Widnesian.* This integration may also be responsible for what was once a unique accent, having been remarked upon as being dissimilar to other dialects in the area. It was generally believed that its uniqueness was attributable to the various influences of differing tongues. However, in modern times this accent has given way to a new mainstream version which is influenced more by the media and youth trends.

In conclusion, it is obvious that in the Widnes of today, even though our town is mainly populated by descendants of this first industrial society, whatever impact or influences the early immigrant communities had is gone. There is no longer evidence of strong ethnic characteristics in our local society. In fact, many of these succeeding generations may be only dimly conscious that their great-great grandparents came from across the Irish Sea or from somewhere on the Baltic. Alas, surnames are all that remain to remind us of our rich multi-cultural heritage and the people who came here in search of a better life.

Jean M Morris
2005

(Revised edition 2018)

Appendix

POPULATION RETURN FOR THE DIVISION OF PRESCOT, FOR 1811.

	Males.	Females.	Total.	Total in 1801.
Allerton	134	124	258	178
Bold	372	401	773	713
Bootle & Linacre	324	286	610	537
Cronton	166	168	334	311
Cuerdley	112	136	248	251
Childwall	88	74	162	152
Ditton	219	203	422	401
Everton	328	585	913	499
Eccleston	803	781	1584	1362
Formby	555	546	1101	1045
Fazakerley	160	169	329	272
Great Sankey	219	247	466	431
Garston	299	298	597	458
Huyton and Roby	485	470	955	862
Hale	254	273	527	537
Halewood	464	439	903	777
Kirkdale	284	381	665	593
Knowsley	449	464	913	739
Kirkby	474	438	912	883
Liverpool	41296	53080	94376	77708
Little Woolton	249	279	528	419
Much Woolton	293	308	601	439
Penketh	690	715	1405	1181
Parr	170	171	341	326
Prescot	1747	1931	3678	3465
Rainhill	278	267	545	402
Rainford	643	672	1315	1185
Simonswood	194	170	364	274
Speke	223	186	409	374
Sutton	1065	1049	2114	1776
Torbock	276	258	534	412
Toxteth Park	2643	3221	5864	2069
West Derby	1639	2079	3718	2636
Widnes	611	593	1204	1063
Whiston	500	514	1015	1031
Walton	354	440	794	681
Windle	2114	2180	4294	3252
Wavertree	626	772	1398	860
Total	61800	75369	137169	110304

POPULATION FIGURES FOR 1811

Appendix

Changes in Occupation Structure 1851-1861
(Sources – Census Returns)

Occupation	1851	1861
Watchmakers	60	24
Canvas Weavers	49	41
File-makers	15	23
Agricultural Labourers	73	50
Chemical Labourers	70	233
Watermen	43	48
Dock Workers	18	8

Into The Crucible

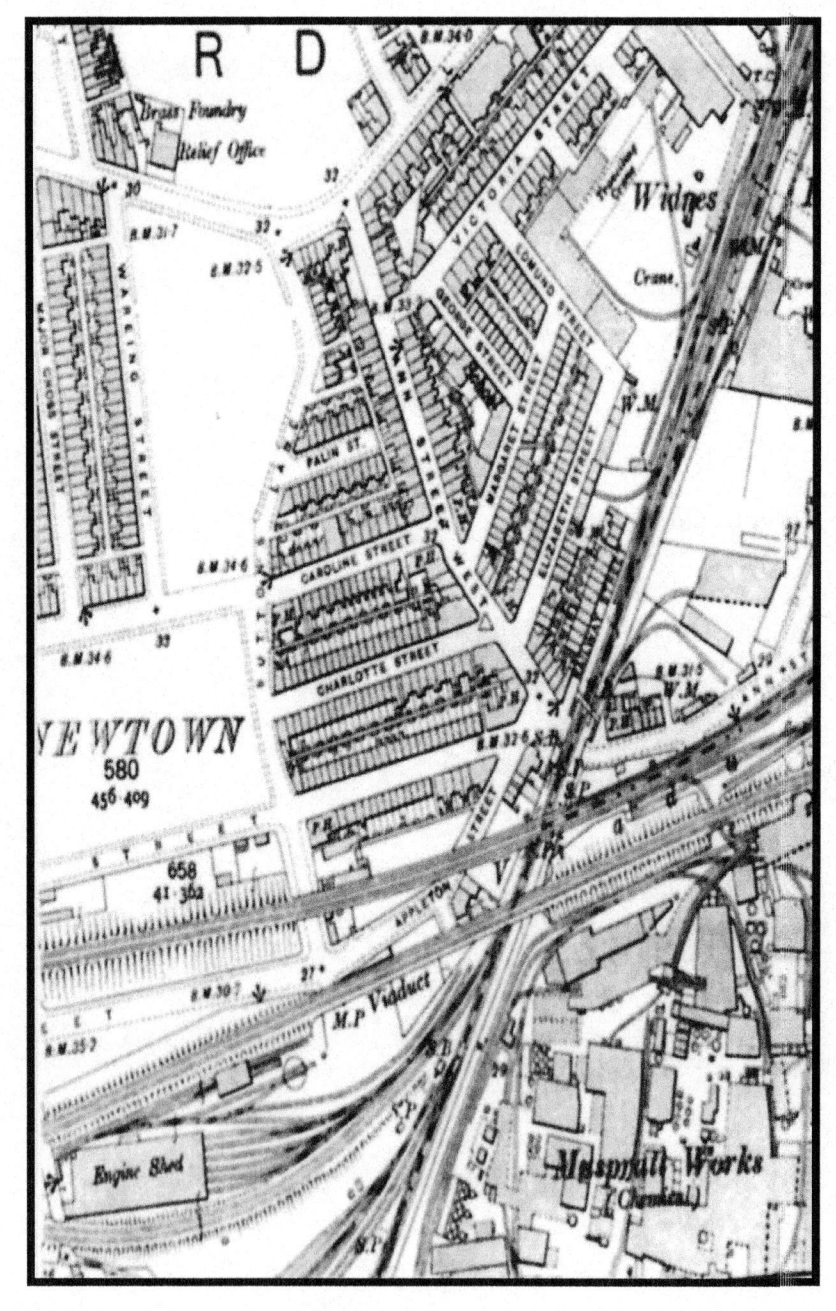

Newtown Area – 1907

Appendix

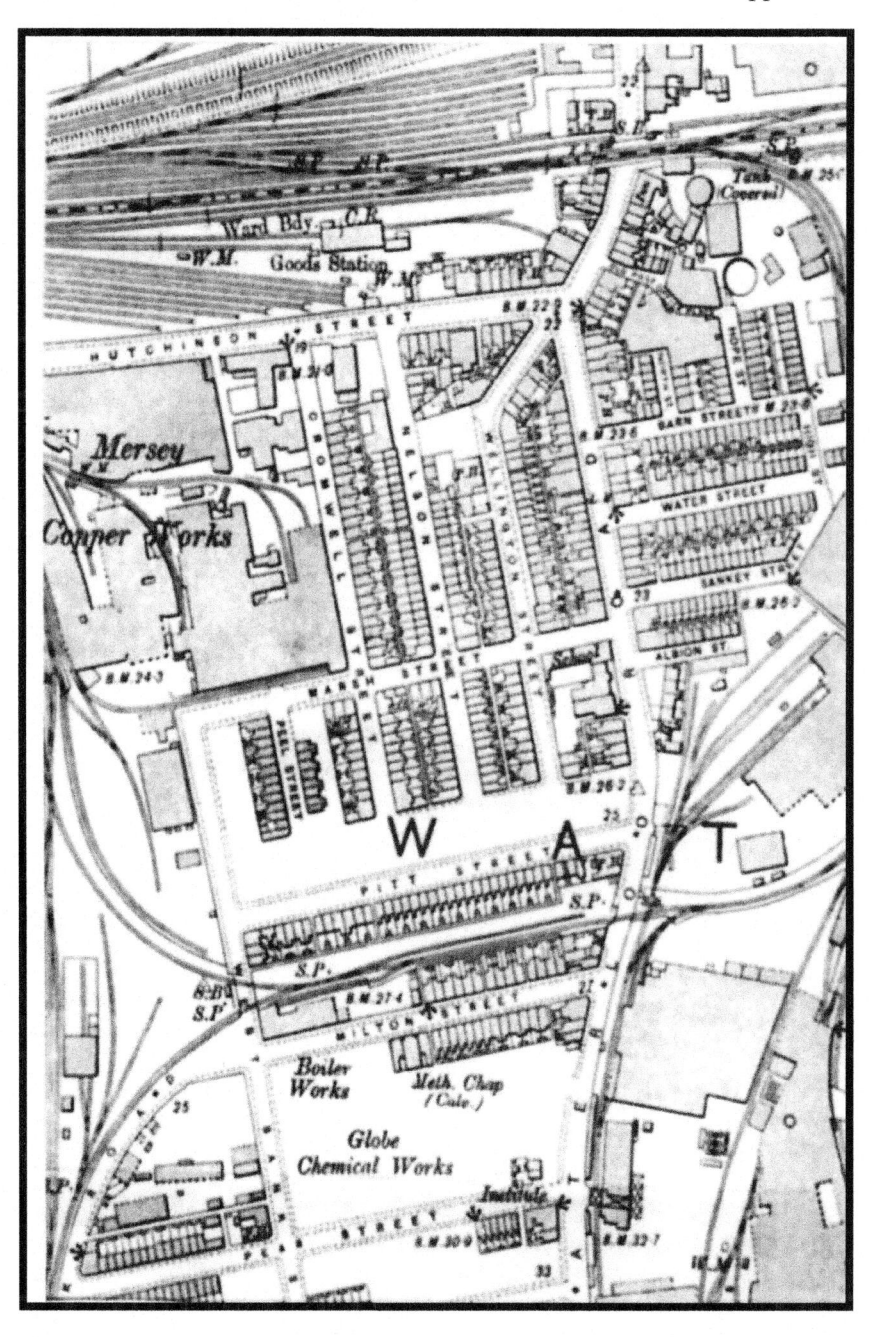

Waterloo Area - 1907

405

Into The Crucible

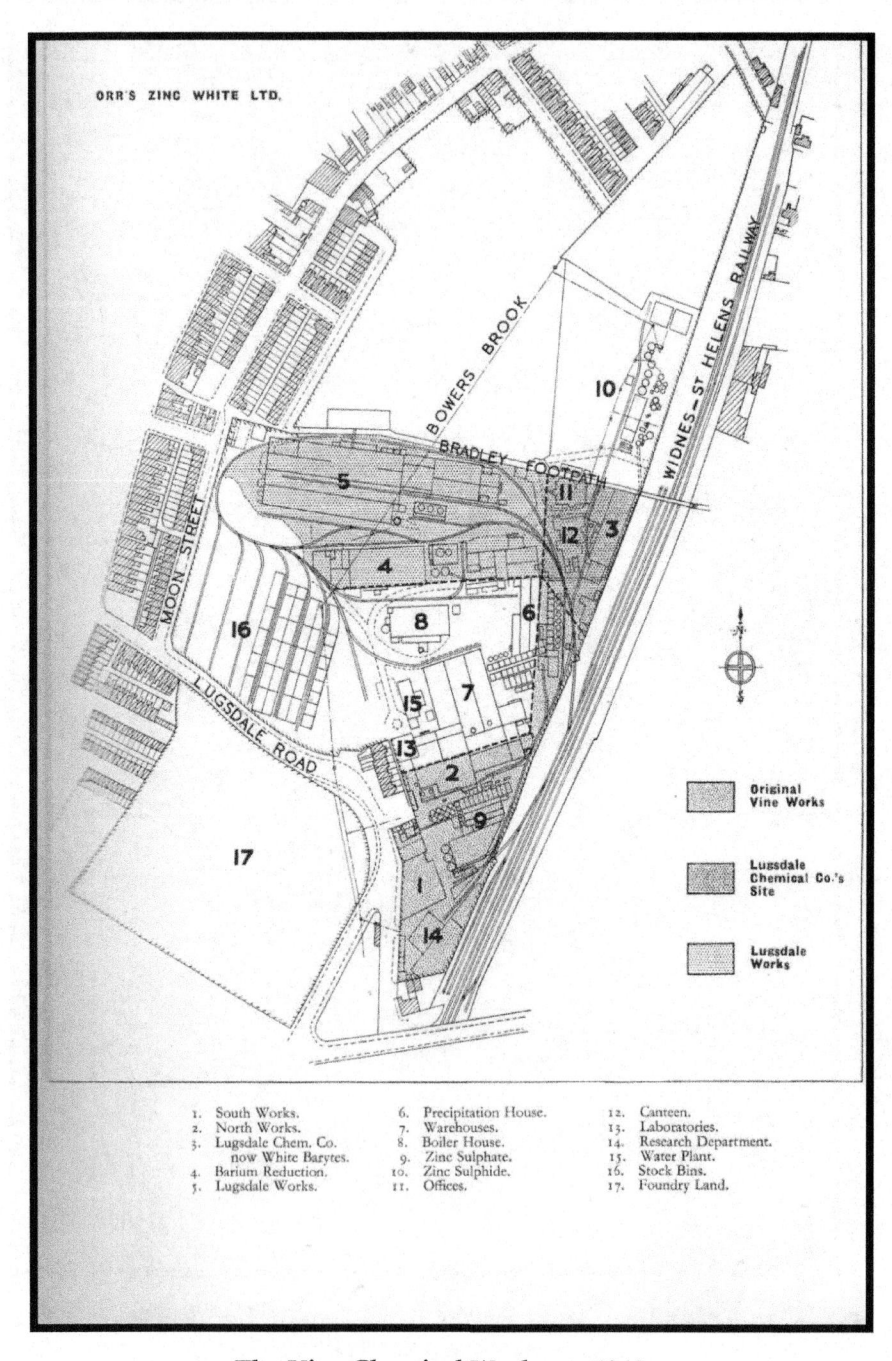

1. South Works.	6. Precipitation House.	12. Canteen.
2. North Works.	7. Warehouses.	13. Laboratories.
3. Lugsdale Chem. Co. now White Barytes.	8. Boiler House.	14. Research Department.
	9. Zinc Sulphate.	15. Water Plant.
4. Barium Reduction.	10. Zinc Sulphide.	16. Stock Bins.
5. Lugsdale Works.	11. Offices.	17. Foundry Land.

The Vine Chemical Works – c.1948

Bibliography

The following books, publications and documents have been consulted for research purposes during the writing of this book. Quotes and extracts used have been formally acknowledged in the body of the text or in the footnotes.

The History of Widnes: George E. Diggle
(Corporation of Widnes) 1961

The History of the Chemical Industry in Widnes: D.W. Hardie
(I.C.I.) 1950

Widnes– a review and Forecast: Councillor David Lewis, J.P.
(T.S. Swale, Widnes) 1911

The Victorian Economy: Francois Crouzet
(Methuen & Co.) 1982

Miners, Quarrymen and Saltworkers: Raphael Samuel
(Routledge) 1977

Dangerous Trades: T.Oliver
(London) 1902

St. Helens, a Lancashire town in the Industrial Revolution :
T.C. Barker & J.R. Harris (Frank Cass & Co. Ltd) 1992

Industrial Activity and Economic Geography :
R.C.Estall & R.O. Buchanan
(Hutchinson University Library) 1961

The First Industrial Society: Chris Aspin
(Carnegie Publishing) 1995

Into The Crucible

The Irish Working Classes: Peter Beresford Ellis
(London) 1972

The Irish Empire : Patrick Bishop
(St. Martin`s Press) 1999

Ireland since the Famine : F.S.Lyons
(Fontana) 1972

Black `47: Britain and the Famine Irish: Frank Neal
(Palgrave MacMillan) 1997

The Honey Meadow and Beyond : Jean M. Morris
(Greengage Press) 2002

Across The Gap: Jean M. Morris
(Springfield-Farrihy) 2016

Carrick-on-Suir and her people: Dr. Patrick C. Power
(Blackwater Press) Dublin 1976

Carrick-on Suir Town and District 1800-2000: Dr. Patrick C. Power
(Carrick Books) 2003

Cobbett`s Writing on the Irish Question: Molly Townsend
(London) 1993

Cobbett with Hazlitt`s Essay: A.M.D. Hughes
(Clarendon Press) 1923

Men, Machines and History: S. Lilley
(Cobbett Press) 1948

England in the Nineteenth Century : David Thomson
(Penguin Books) 1950

Sectarian Violence – The Liverpool Experience : Frank Neal
(Newsham Press) 2003

Modern Britain : T .K. Derry & T .L. Jarman
(John Murray, London) 1979

Polish Immigrants into Britain: J.Zubrzycki
(Liverpool University) 1956

The Lithuanians in Scotland: John Millar
(House of Lochar) 1998

The Chemical Industry : W.A. Campbell
(Longman) 1971

John Brunner, Radical Plutocrat : Stephen Koss
(Cambridge University Press) 1970

The Changing Morphology of Widnes 1841-1871 –
David F. Swann. Dissertation – Padgate College of Education, 1975
(Lodged in Widnes Library)

Made in Lancashire : Geoffrey Timmins
(Manchester University Press) 1998

A Scientific Survey of Merseyside: W.A.Smith
(Liverpool) 1953

Irish Migrants in Modern Britain 1750-1922: Donald MacRaild
(Macmillan 1999)

Yesterday`s Naughty Children: A History of Liverpool Reformatory Association : Joan Rimmer

Class and Ethnicity: Steven Fielding
(Open University Press) 1993

The Economic History of England 1760-1860: Arthur Redford
(Longmans) 1960

Newspapers:
The Runcorn and Widnes Guardian
The Widnes Weekly News
The St. Helens Standard
The Liverpool Mercury
The Liverpool Daily Post
The Liverpool Mail
The Chester Chronicle
The Manchester Guardian
The Clonmel Nationalist
The Munster Express
The Bellshill Speaker
The North-East Lanarkshire Gazette
The Glasgow Herald
The Leeds Mercury
The Halifax Guardian
The Times

Journals:

Historical Society of Lancashire and Cheshire
Vols. 110; 134; 141; 147.
Society of Chemical Industry – Journals (misc.)

Documents: (locations)
(Details are indicated in footnote throughout the book)

National Archives, Kew
Cheshire Record Office, Chester
Lancashire Record Office, Preston
Liverpool Record Office, Liverpool.
Public Record Office of Ireland, Dublin
National Library of Ireland, Dublin
The National Archives, Dublin
Local History Library, Bellshill, Lanarkshire.
The Lithuanian Society

Further acknowledgments:

I wish to thank **Imperial Chemical Industries Ltd***. for giving me permission to use the "Le Blanc Widnes Map" and other material.*

Also Chris Walker, of **Trinity Mirror North West & Wales***, for allowing me to reproduce material from their archives*

Author`s Note:
Unfortunately, due to their age, the print quality of some old original newspapers and photographs mean that they do not reproduce very well and are not always easy to read. Despite that fact, I have included them whenever possible in order to give readers an authentic historic record.

INDEX

A

accident · 67, 68, 70, 71, 247, 256, 259, 279, 329
Alexandra Theatre · 262, 320, 393
Aliens Restriction Act · 174
Alkali Manufacturers Association · 63, 65
All England Air Race · 326
Appleton Academy · 333, 341
Atlas Foundry & Engineering Works · 33

B

bare-knuckle fight · 299
Barkla · 330
Billiards · 307
Black Cat Billiard Hall · 308, 381
Boat House Inn · 42, 225
Boer War · 382, 388
Bolton & Sons · 53, 259, 335
boxing · 299, 304
Brennan · 296, 297, 298, 299
Bridgewater Canal · 21
British society · 223
Brunner · 32, 51, 65, 73, 74, 85, 86, 87, 88, 111, 112, 130, 249, 263, 264, 409
Buffalo Bill · 306, 325
Burns · 117, 120, 300, 301, 302, 304, 346, 352, 365, 368, 370, 391

C

Carey · 59, 86, 118, 179, 180, 182, 183, 185, 186
Carrick-on-Suir · 209
Cemetery · 278, 310
Chemical Labourers Union · 62
Conservative Club · 265, 270
copper industry · 195

D

Dame Schools · 332, 337, 338
Davitt · 104
Deacon · 23, 24, 25, 65, 66, 67, 69, 70, 85, 86, 225, 338, 344, 363, 366, 370, 382
Delaney · 124, 211, 275, 364
Diggle · 25, 36, 83, 160, 240, 324, 346, 359, 375, 392, 407
Ditton Junction · 327, 329
Drill Hall · 108, 109, 248, 292, 308, 365, 381

E

Earle · 29, 351
Eisteddfod · 202, 205, 379
Engels · 105
Everton · 48, 254, 278

F

famine · 91, 119
Faraday · 24
Fardon · 25
Farnworth and Appleton Football Club · 295
Farnworth Free Grammar School · 331
Father Fisher · 268, 335
Fenians · 104, 105, 108
Ferry · 244
Ferry Road · 244
Fidler`s Ferry · 20

413

G

Garghan · 314, 315, 316, 395
General Election · 108, 110, 313, 395
Germany · 87, 88, 138, 141, 156, 220, 221, 273, 388
Gladstone · 27, 110, 126, 131, 132, 308, 320, 323, 329
Gossage · 23, 24, 25, 26, 34, 42, 53, 76, 193, 225, 275, 291, 313, 369, 386
Gossage's Prize Band · 234
Gossage's Works · 244

H

Handley & Beck · 55
Hardie · 45, 49, 66, 83, 149, 240, 407
Hazelhurst · 20, 22
Hemingway · 278, 308, 324
Home Rule · 107, 108, 109, 111, 112, 131, 132, 205, 308
Home Secretary · 233
Hurst · 42, 43, 227
Hutchinson · 22, 23, 24, 25, 28, 29, 31, 32, 41, 54, 55, 62, 70, 71, 83, 240, 241, 268, 274, 277, 335, 342, 371, 382, 407
Hutchinson & Earle · 29, 244

I

Independent Labour Party · 313, 314, 324
Industrial Revolution · 15, 19, 23, 25, 46, 62, 98, 407
Irish immigrants · 89, 99, 102, 103, 115, 208, 360
Irish National League · 108, 109, 111, 112, 124, 126, 127, 128, 213, 275, 378

K

Keir Hardie · 149
Kennedy · 22, 299, 391
Kent · 225, 228, 386
King · 28, 60, 62, 63, 64, 65, 110, 194, 246, 314, 341, 351, 386
Kirkdale Industrial School · 347

L

Labour Party · 65, 149, 308, 313, 314, 315, 316, 317, 318, 324
Lambert Works · 244
Lanarkshire · 13, 139, 141, 150, 151, 153, 158, 161, 188, 189, 389, 410
Lancashire · 244, 263
Lancashire and Cheshire · 263
Lancashire Rifle Volunteers · 381
Lancaster Buildings · 29, 32
Letters Patent under the Great Seal of the United Kingdom · 275
Lewis · 197, 199, 201, 265, 270, 310, 313, 320, 371, 389, 407
Library · 13, 115, 123, 130, 248, 249, 271, 276, 278, 387, 407, 409, 410
Lithuanian · 13, 35, 136, 137, 139, 141, 144, 146, 147, 150, 153, 157, 158, 159, 162, 163, 165, 167, 170, 172, 177, 187, 188, 189, 190, 216, 217, 218, 219, 221, 267, 375, 376, 377, 379, 391, 401, 410
Liverpool · 21
Local Board of Health · 226
Local School Board · 338, 350, 355
Lugsdale · 28, 113, 114, 119, 120, 232, 239, 259, 267, 279, 288, 329, 351, 366, 368, 379, 392, 393
Lugsdale Road · 244

M

Maguire · 22
Manchester · 21
Mann · 63, 65, 73, 314

Mathieson & Sons · 71
Mayo · 99, 100, 212, 391
McClellan · 23, 28, 225, 334
McKechnie Brothers · 54
Methodists · 196, 233, 235, 336, 362
Milton Congregational Church · 385
Moss · 111
Moss Street Wesleyan School · 336
murder · 107, 247, 365, 366, 368
Muspratt · 20, 23, 24, 26, 27, 28, 48, 62, 68, 85, 109, 110, 111, 114, 160, 183, 194, 228, 365

N

National School · 334, 336
Newtown · 34, 104, 107, 113, 114, 116, 125, 161, 171, 227, 232, 259, 297, 300, 335, 342, 386, 390, 392
North British Chemical Company · 28

O

O`Keeffe · 68, 75, 107, 108, 109, 123, 124, 126, 129, 130, 248, 249, 251, 252, 255, 365
Oakland Street School · 343
oil works · 47
Orange · 106, 107, 112, 113, 114, 268, 269, 384
Orange Lodges · 106, 114

P

Pankhurst · 314, 318
Parliament · 245
Parys Mountain · 195
Pawnshops · 229
Pearson`s Magazine · 36
pitch and toss · 307
Poles · 33, 36, 135, 136, 137, 138, 139, 149, 159, 160, 165, 166, 168, 170, 174, 177, 179, 187, 188, 196, 369, 372, 389, 390
Police Station · 244
police stations · 361
poverty · 100, 102, 103, 132, 138, 189, 216, 224, 229, 282, 283, 347, 367
pre-industrial times · 42
Prescot Union · 121, 122, 166, 167, 252, 366
Prisons · 361
Public Houses · 239, 240, 400

R

Robinson · 32, 33, 54, 344
Rocksavage · 22
Roman Catholics · 119, 132, 269, 271, 362
Runcorn Gap · 47
Runcorn-Latchford Canal · 21
Russia · 83, 136, 137, 159, 185, 187, 188, 217, 219, 220, 273, 317, 389

S

sailcloth · 43, 50, 193
Salvation Army · 269, 272, 314, 318, 319, 320, 321, 322, 323, 324
sandhookers · 78, 79, 80
Sankey Navigational Canal · 20
School Board · 130, 168, 201, 334, 337, 338, 339, 342, 343, 344, 348
Scotland · 33, 35, 55, 85, 109, 122, 139, 140, 141, 144, 147, 153, 156, 158, 161, 189, 193, 265, 347, 350, 353, 409
Seaforth Hall · 27
Sherard · 36, 56, 73, 75, 76
Simms Cross · 111, 113, 114, 253, 255, 264, 269, 273, 291, 297, 330, 344, 372
Snig Pie House · 42, 244
Spike Island · 20, 22, 23
Spring Heel Jack · 254, 255

415

Into The Crucible

St. Ambrose · 242
St. Ambrose Church · 233
St. Bede's · 119, 268, 333, 342, 353, 365
St. Helens · 44, 48
St. Helens Canal and Railway Company · 20, 22
St. Helens to Runcorn Gap Railway · 34, 49
St. Marie's · 120, 171, 172, 298, 329, 344, 347, 350, 351, 352, 365
St. Patrick's · 119, 159, 162, 335, 347, 350, 352, 353
St. Paul's · 60, 308
St.Mary's · 119, 296, 334, 335, 341, 342, 352
Stoke Prior · 25, 34, 193
storm · 279
Superintendent Strickland · 319
Sutton's Lane · 235
Szabo, · 32

T

Temperance Bands · 246
The Charge of the Light Brigade · 382
The Londonderry · 91
Toll Bar · 244
Tontine Clubs · 230
Town Hall · 108, 276, 280, 308, 310, 324, 386
Transporter Bridge · 263, 264
Treacey · 247, 365, 391

U

unfit for human habitation · 259

V

Victoria Park · 281

Victoria Road chapel · 236
Victoria Square · 234, 315, 316, 317, 320, 323
Vilkovishk · 219, 220, 221
Vineyard Public House · 244

W

War Memorial · 391
Warrington · 21
watchmakers · 44
Waterloo Road · 244
Welsh Calvanistic Methodists · 194
Welsh Congregationalist Church · 197
Welsh National Society · 199, 379
Welsh Wesleyans · 202
Wesleyan Chapel · 244
Wesleyan Methodists Chapel · 336
West Bank · 31, 42, 71, 77, 80, 111, 119, 156, 157, 165, 195, 225, 227, 232, 233, 240, 247, 274, 278, 279, 280, 307, 326, 334, 335, 350, 373, 385
West Bank House · 244
Widnes Cricket Club · 291, 381
Widnes Foundry · 32, 33, 54, 68, 84, 279, 366
Widnes Free Church Council · 320, 321
Widnes Improvement Act · 245
Widnes Local Board · 82, 226, 248, 266
Widnes Marsh · 23, 42, 240
Widnes Methodism · 234
Widnes Queen's Nurses Association · 313
Widnes Temperance Hall · 242
Wiredrawing · 45
Woodend Cricket Club · 291

Printed in Great Britain
by Amazon